OUTCOMES

ADVANCED
STUDENT'S BOOK

HUGH DELLAR
ANDREW WALKLEY

IN THIS UNIT YOU LEARN HOW TO:

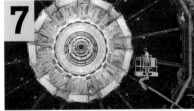

Contents   **3**

Contents   5

1

Housing developments in West Palm Beach, Florida

IN THIS UNIT YOU LEARN HOW TO:

- describe different aspects of cities and city life
- add interest to stories by emphasising and exaggerating
- reinforce and exemplify points you've made
- talk about urban problems and how to tackle them
- talk about changes in urban areas
- tell stories and urban myths

SPEAKING

1 Work in groups. Look at the photo. Make a list of as many advantages and drawbacks of living in this place as you can think of.

2 Work in pairs. Discuss to what degree you think each adjective would apply to West Palm Beach. Explain your ideas.

dull	well-run	congested	spotless
chaotic	run-down	sprawling	hot and humid
compact	affluent	vibrant	safe and secure
polluted			

3 Would you like to live in a place like this? Why? / Why not?

CITIES

A REAL BUZZ ABOUT THE PLACE

VOCABULARY City life

1   Check you understand the words and phrases in bold in the sentences below. Then put these words into the correct place in the sentences. The first one is done for you.

~~springing up~~	showing off	choke	condemned
muggings	smoothly	crawl	dropping

springing up
1   There are new businesses all over the place. There's a real **buzz** about the place.

2   The **crime rate** is pretty high. There are a lot of and **shootings**.

3   There's a big **network of buses and trams** and it all runs very.

4   The **smog** is awful – you have to wear a mask or you'd on the **fumes**.

5   The cars just along most of the time – you **might as well** walk.

6   There's a lot of **conspicuous consumption** with people their wealth.

7   There's not a **trace** of litter anywhere. Apparently, you can **get fined heavily** for it.

8   The area is a **slum**. A lot of buildings should just be and rebuilt.

2   Work in pairs. Answer the questions.

1   Which adjectives from Exercise 2 on page 7 would you use to describe the places in Exercise 1? How would you say the opposites?

2   What other things might give a place a buzz?

3   What else might you choke on?

4   What are examples of conspicuous consumption?

LISTENING

3   ▶ 1 Listen to two conversations about cities. List the good and bad things you hear about each place.

4   Work in pairs. Compare your ideas. What cities do you think the speakers could be describing? Why? Which place would you rather live in? Why?

5   ▶ 1 Listen again and complete the sentences.
Conversation 1

1   It's really wild. It _____, actually.

2   We went out with these people and _____ at about four in the morning.

3   Actually, that was _____, the congestion.

4   Honestly, you walk out of your hotel and _____ this thick wall of heat.

5   It does _____ but, as I say, it just has a real buzz.

Conversation 2

6　It is, if you like _____.

7　It's more lively. There's _____, you know.

8　So you wouldn't _____ to live there?

9　Don't _____, it is a good place to live if you're bringing up kids.

10　So if I _____, I might move back. It's just not what I want right now.

6　Work in groups. Discuss the questions.

- What places, people, etc. have taken you by surprise?
- Have you ever been out till four? Where? When?
- What drawbacks are there to the place you live in?
- What 'scenes' are there where you live?
- Where's a good place to settle down in your country / region? Why?

UNDERSTANDING VOCABULARY

Emphasising and exaggerating

We often use particular vocabulary and patterns to emphasise how we feel or to make an experience sound more interesting. For example, we use:

- repetition: **really, really** vibrant / **loads and loads** of people / see for **miles and miles**
- intensifying adverbs: **unbearably** humid / **incredibly** lively
- 'extreme' words that include the meaning of 'very': packed / spotless / crawl / stink
- expressions with like: it's like hitting this thick wall of heat

7　Work in pairs. Do the following:

1　List four other intensifying adverbs.

2　List six other 'extreme' adjectives or verbs.

3　Decide in what situations people might say the following like expressions.
  - It was like being at a rock concert.
  - It was like living in a war zone.
  - It's like Buckingham Palace.
  - It was like the Arctic in there.
  - It's like talking to a brick wall.

8　With your partner, rewrite these sentences to make them more interesting. Try to use all the different patterns in the box above.

1　*It's an absolutely enormous city.*

1　It's a big city.

2　They're doing a lot of building work.

3　The city's a bit run-down.

4　It's not very expensive there.

5　Some parts of the city are quite dangerous.

6　It's quite interesting.

DEVELOPING CONVERSATIONS

Reinforcing and exemplifying a point

When we emphasise or exaggerate, the listener may question us using *Really?*, *Yeah?*, etc. We often respond by giving an example. Notice the adverbs we often use to reinforce the truth of what we're saying.

B:　*... the nightlife is **totally insane**.*

A:　***Really?***

B:　***Honestly**. We went out with these people and ended up in a place at about four in the morning and it was **absolutely packed**.*

A:　***Yeah?***

B:　***Seriously**. You **literally couldn't move**.*

9　Match the sentences (1–5) to the examples (a–e).

1　The place is like a war zone.

2　The place is absolutely spotless.

3　The way people drive is insane.

4　We were staying in a really, really posh area.

5　There's a real buzz about the place.

a　They race along the main roads at about 100 miles an hour.

b　There isn't a trace of litter or chewing gum on the pavements.

c　It was like Beverly Hills. I felt a bit conspicuous walking around there.

d　There's a huge music scene. There are loads of venues springing up.

e　There's so much crime and hundreds of places have been condemned.

10　Use the sentences and examples in Exercise 9 to have conversations. Add words like *honestly*, *seriously* and *literally* where appropriate.

A: *The place was like a war zone.*

B: *Really?*

A: *Honestly. There's so much crime and literally hundreds of places have been condemned.*

CONVERSATION PRACTICE

11　Write the names of two cities you have been to. Make notes about aspects of the cities and think of at least one thing that happened to you in each city. Use as much language from this lesson as you can.

12　Work in pairs. Have conversations about your chosen cities. Start with *Have you been to ...?* Keep the conversation going by asking questions to get more details or by using comments like *Really?* or *Yeah?*

 1 To watch the video and do the activities, see the DVD ROM.

URBAN RENEWAL

READING

1 **Work in groups. Discuss the questions.**

- What effects do you think the following can have on a city? How serious are they?
- Which three things are of greatest concern where you live and which is of least concern? Why?

an economic downturn	a hurricane	an armed conflict
an earthquake	flooding	a high crime rate
severe pollution	terrorism	a huge fire

2 **Work with the same group. You are going to read about a city and how it was affected by one or more of the problems in Exercise 1. Find out what happened.**

Group A: read the text in File 1 on page 185.

Group B: read the text in File 2 on page 186.

Group C: read the text in File 3 on page 197.

3 **With a person from your group, do the following:**

1 Compare what you understood and what you think of the story.
2 Discuss what you learnt about the city.
3 Check you understand the phrases in bold – and try to remember them.

4 **Make new groups: a Student A, B and C. Close your books. Tell each other about the cities you read about, using some of the words in bold that you learnt. Decide what similarities there are between the three cities.**

5 **With your group, decide which city each sentence refers to: Bilbao, Bogota or Manchester. Look back at the texts if you need to.**

1 Some other cities have unsuccessfully tried to copy what it did.
2 The government forced people to sell something.
3 Sport has played a role in the city's redevelopment.
4 Some of the changes were paid for by motorists.
5 It has a more diverse economy than it did in the past.
6 It has aimed to create a child-friendly environment.
7 The changes made it better able to survive a second downturn.
8 A bad event turned out to be fortunate.

6 **With your group, discuss the questions.**

- Which of the cities you read about has the most interesting story? Why?
- Are there comparable cities in your country? In what ways are they similar / different?
- How child-friendly is your city?
- What cities in your country have new iconic buildings?
- Why do you think some redevelopment projects fail?
- Do you think hosting sports events is good for a city?

Bilbao

Bogota

VOCABULARY Recovery and change

7 Replace the words in italics with the correct form of these verbs. Then decide which of the synonyms are more common in academic / written English.

undergo	flourish	pour	be neglected
impose	demolish	soar	initiate

1 The city has *gone through* huge changes in recent years – not entirely for the better.

2 The government will have *invested* £3 billion into the transport system by the end of this parliament.

3 The slums were *knocked down* to make way for a golf course and the inhabitants were re-housed nearby.

4 The previous mayor *set out* an ambitious plan to develop the city centre, but it's run into financial difficulties and the new mayor has cancelled the project.

5 The whole area has *become run-down* and the council has managed to secure EU funding to halt the decline.

6 The city has managed to attract a lot of inward investment and businesses are springing up and *doing very well.*

7 Crime had *gone up a lot* in the 1980s and the mayor's zero-tolerance policy was credited with reversing the trend.

8 In order to ease congestion, the government *brought in* restrictions on car use.

8 Work in pairs. Give one example of each of the following:

1 a place or institution that has undergone big changes

2 a place or section of society that has been neglected

3 a plan or strategy the government has initiated

4 someone or something that is flourishing

5 something the government has poured money into

GRAMMAR

Perfect forms

Perfect forms use a form of *have* + past participle. Passive perfect forms use a form of *have* + *been* + past participle. Primarily, perfect forms emphasise that something happened or started before another event or point in time.

9 Work in pairs. Complete the sentences from the texts with the correct perfect form of the verbs. Decide what time or event each one happened before.

1 Since its completion in 1997, the Guggenheim Museum in Bilbao, the capital of the Basque region of northern Spain, _____ one of the most famous buildings in the world. (become)

2 There _____ some voices of opposition that suggest the process did not benefit the working-class people ... (be)

3 The slum _____ effectively _____ a barrier between the affluent north and the more deprived south of the city. (create)

4 Up until the early 80s, Bilbao _____ by steel plants and shipbuilding. (dominate)

5 If other mayors _____ the city's finances before him ... the changes wouldn't have been so successful. (not / secure)

6 If we ever achieve a successful city for children, we _____ the perfect city for all citizens. (build)

7 Other cities trying to replicate the so-called 'Guggenheim effect' _____ because they didn't take up the other strands of Bilbao's regeneration project. (fail)

8 _____ one space, Peñalosa's administration then expropriated the land of a private country club. (clear)

 Check your ideas on page 166 and do Exercise 1.

10 Work in pairs. Discuss the questions.

- How has your city changed in the last few years?
- How do you think your city or country will have changed in ten years' time? Why?
- What are the two most important events in your city's / country's history? Why?
- Can you think of any places that have suffered any of the situations or events in Exercise 1? What happened?

 For further practice, see Exercise 2 on page 166.

SPEAKING

11 Work in groups. You are going to decide how to spend some funding on a town called Oldbury. First read the information and the ideas on how to spend the money in File 4 on page 186. Then put the ideas in order of priority and decide how much should be spent on each idea and an approximate timescale for change.

12 Write a short pitch for your proposal to present to the class. Explain the reasons for your choices, the timescale for the different strands and what the outcomes will be.

Manchester

URBAN TALES

SPEAKING

1 **Work in groups. Look at the comments below, then discuss the questions.**

- Have you heard about any of these stories before?
- Which stories would you find most / least interesting to talk about? Why?
- What connection might there be between the six comments?

> Did you see that thing about Google Street View capturing a murder in Edinburgh?

> In any big city, you're never more than two metres from a rat.

> I read somewhere that we only use 10% of our brain capacity.

> Did you know that Walt Disney had his body frozen after he died?

> I heard somewhere that they think lemon peel can cure cancer.

> I heard they've spotted these huge alligators in the sewers under New York.

READING

2 **Read this article about a similar story. Find out:**

1 what the story is and what impact it had in New Orleans.

2 what's known about the roots of the story and how it spread.

3 what connects this story to the six comments in Exercise 1.

BUYING INTO THE MYTH

In early 1997, as the city of New Orleans was busy getting ready for its annual Mardi Gras carnival, an email entitled 'Travellers beware' went viral, **sparking** hundreds of calls to the local police department, who felt **compelled** to issue an official statement designed to **calm** public fears.

The email claimed that an organised gang was planning to **drug** visitors to the city, surgically remove their kidneys and sell them on the black market. Now, you may well be thinking this story sounds familiar. If so, that's because versions of it have been around for over three decades now. Back in the 1980s, Guatemala was **gripped** by stories of Americans kidnapping local children and harvesting their organs. By the early 1990s, there were stories in the States about Latino women tempting American men to a similar fate, and before long the idea appeared in TV dramas and movies – and variations started to appear all over the world.

One thing that **unites** all these stories – and others like them – is that no hard evidence exists of them ever having occurred. These urban myths apparently **emerge** from nowhere and take on a life of their own. This **raises** interesting questions about why we continue to share them and, on occasion, even fall for them!

Festivities in the streets of New Orleans

3 Work in pairs. Discuss what you think the words in bold in the article mean. Then use the words in bold to complete each group of phrases below.

1 ~ the issue at the meeting / ~ fears / ~ doubts about ...

2 be ~ to appear as a witness / feel ~ to resign / feel ~ to respond

3 ~ and rob tourists / ~ someone's drink / ~ his victims

4 ~ as a global power / ~ from recession / the ideas ~ from ...

5 ~ the markets / ~ my nerves / ~ the angry crowd

6 ~ a wave of protests / ~ criticism / ~ fears

7 ~ the whole community / what ~ them is ... / ~ the (political) party

8 the country is ~ by recession / the trial has ~ the nation / ~ by fear

4 Work in groups. Make a list of reasons why people both tell urban myths and believe them. Then compare your list with another group. Which do you think is the most likely reason?

LISTENING

5 ▶2 Listen to three people telling urban myths. You won't hear the end of each story yet. Answer the questions about each story.

1 Who did it (supposedly) happen to?

2 Where did it happen?

3 Who else appears in the story?

4 What was the key thing that happened?

6 ▶2 Work in pairs. Retell the stories in as much detail as you can using these words. Then listen again and check your ideas.

1 stolen – reported – driveway – note – ill – concert – fantastic time

2 collapsed – rushed – diagnosed – poisoned – incident – the case

3 elderly – desperately sad – a loaf – freaked out – run out of – cashier – trolley – the spitting image – favour – good deed

7 ▶3 With your partner, discuss how you think each story will end. Then listen and see if you guessed correctly.

8 Work in groups. Discuss the questions.

• Which story do you like best? Why?

• What do you think of the main characters in the three stories? Why?

• What do you think the moral message of each story is?

• Do you agree with the messages?

UNDERSTANDING VOCABULARY

Binomials

Binomials are pairs of words usually linked together by *and*. The words are always used in the same order. The two main words in a binomial may: start with the same letter or contain similar sounds; be near synonyms; be connected in meaning or be opposites.

*He went to a supermarket to buy a few **bits and pieces**.*

*He was walking **up and down** the aisles.*

9 Complete the binomials in the sentences with these words.

foremost	miss	order	regulations	there
hard	off	quiet	then	tired

1 I've been studying Russian for about six years now **on and** _____.

2 There's a huge number of places to eat in the city, but the quality is a bit **hit and** _____.

3 I still like to party **every now and** _____, but I've calmed down a lot.

4 It's quite hard to find **peace and** _____ in the city.

5 I **thought long and** _____ about it before deciding.

6 It's a fairly affluent area, but there are still little pockets of poverty **here and** _____.

7 I can't take it anymore. I'm **sick and** _____ **of** the constant noise.

8 After the hurricane struck, there was a complete breakdown of **law and** _____ in the city.

9 The city's being ruined by the ever-growing number of stupid **rules and** _____.

10 Cities should be **first and** _____ places for kids.

10 Work in groups. Think of examples of the following:

1 three places where people who live in cities can go to get a bit of peace and quiet

2 three big decisions people usually have to think long and hard about

3 three things people that live in cities may get sick and tired of

4 two reasons why law and order might break down

5 two examples of stupid rules and regulations

SPEAKING

11 Work in pairs. Choose one of these tasks.

a Student A: read the urban myth in File 5 on page 187.

   Student B: read the urban myth in File 6 on page 185.

   Try to remember the details. Then tell your partner your story.

b Search the Internet for an urban myth that you find interesting and want to share with other students. Try to remember the details. Then tell your partner your story.

2

DUCKIE
YOUNG
SMITH

(VERGED
TAMPA

HER RAREIS
AS SUENG AS
HER NOSE?

A husband and wife who met at high school attend their school reunion

IN THIS UNIT YOU LEARN HOW TO:

- talk about people you know
- give your impression of people you don't know well
- talk about romance and science
- talk about different kinds of relationships
- express opinions in more tentative ways
- share and talk through problems

SPEAKING

1   **Work in groups. Look at the photo and discuss the questions.**

- Do you think you'd want to attend a school reunion now or at some point in the future? Why? / Why not?

- Can you think of anyone who turned out to be successful after doing badly at school – or vice versa? What happened?

- Can you think of anyone whose character has changed in other ways? In what ways? Why?

- Have you ever been to any other kinds of reunion?

- In what ways have your friendships changed over time? Why?

RELATIONSHIPS

GET THE IMPRESSION

VOCABULARY Describing people

1 Choose the correct option.

1 He's a complete *snobbish / snob*. He only talks to people who went to the 'right' school.

2 He's so *cynical / cynic*. He thinks everyone's got an agenda.

3 She has strong *principled / principles*. I completely trust her.

4 He's ever so *charming / charm*. He makes everyone feel special.

5 She's *a real / really* bitchy. She can be quite nasty about people.

6 She's a bit of *painful / a pain*. She really makes life difficult.

7 It's his sheer *arrogant / arrogance* that I hate. He thinks he knows it all.

8 She's completely *incompetent / incompetence*. She's really messed things up.

9 He's got a real *stubborn / stubbornness* streak. You won't get him to change his mind.

10 She's incredibly *intense / intensity*. We always seem to end up having quite heavy conversations.

11 She's very *willing / wilful* to listen. I'm sure you'll get a good response if you tell her what the problem is.

12 He's a right *laid-back / slacker*. He just seems to lie around all day.

2 Work in pairs. Think of typical things the people in Exercise 1 might say.

a snob: I couldn't possibly stay in a cheap hotel like that.

3 Complete the sentences below with these pairs of words. Underline the whole phrase each word forms part of. The first one is done for you.

back + undermine	~~mind + back down~~
bothered + notice	panics + stride
easiest + lighten up	remind + prone
boss + get ahead	shy + centre
exaggerating + seriously	stands up for + principles

1 Once he's <u>made up his *mind*</u>, he <u>won't *back down*</u> even if he's in the wrong.

2 She's constantly going behind my _____ and saying things to _____ me.

3 He never seems that _____ by criticism or bitchy comments. He just takes no _____ of it all.

4 She _____ what she believes in and she sticks to her _____. She's not easily bullied.

5 He's one of those people who never _____. He just takes everything in his _____.

6 She's not exactly _____ and retiring. She loves to be the _____ of attention.

7 He's not the _____ person to talk to. I wish he'd _____ a little.

8 You'll need to _____ her about it. She is _____ to forgetting things like that.

9 He's a bit prone to _____, so I wouldn't take what he said too _____.

10 She's the kind of person who's constantly sucking up to the _____ in order to _____.

4 Work in pairs. Think of adjectives or nouns you could use to describe each of the people in Exercise 3.

16

5 Work in pairs, Student A and B. Student A: say the sentences in Exercise 3. Student B: close your books. Respond to Student A using the adjectives you thought of in Exercise 4.

A: *Once he's made up his mind, he won't back down even if he's in the wrong.*

B: *I know, he's so stubborn. It drives me crazy sometimes!*

DEVELOPING CONVERSATIONS

Giving your impression

If we want to give our impression of people in the public eye or people we haven't met many times, we often use these structures.

He seems *fairly laid-back.*

She strikes me as *someone you can trust.*

He comes across as *a real gentleman.*

I get the impression / **feeling** *she's very principled.*

6 Work in pairs. Together, think of five people currently in the public eye. Then spend a few minutes thinking about your individual impressions of them and why you feel like this.

7 Share your impressions of each person using the structures in the box. Use the questions below in your conversation.

So what do you think of …?

What do you make of …?

What's your impression of …?

LISTENING

8 ▶ 4 Listen to three conversations about different people. Answer the questions for each conversation.

1 Who is the person they mainly talk about?

2 What is the person like?

9 ▶ 4 Work in pairs. Try to remember the missing words from the sentences. Then listen again and check your answers.

1 a He's _____ with him.

b He always just gets really defensive and _____ big barrier.

c Maybe you need to _____ and talk to his line manager about it?

2 a I've always thought he _____ a really decent guy.

b I just think you've got him wrong. He's _____ of various different causes.

3 a She's really nice and very bright and chatty. We _____ .

b The only problem is she kind of _____ every morning.

c The guy on the other side seems pleasant enough, but he _____ a bit of a slacker.

10 Work in groups. Discuss the questions.

• What would you do in the first speaker's situation?

• Do you know anyone who has a difficult relationship with their boss? Why?

• Can you think of any celebrities who try to raise awareness of a cause? What's the cause? What do you think about it?

• How common is it for people to share accommodation in your country?

• Have you ever shared accommodation with anyone? If yes, how was it? If not, how would you feel about it?

• Have you ever hit it off with someone straight away? Who with?

CONVERSATION PRACTICE

11 Write a name for each of the five kinds of people below. Think about: the words and phrases from this lesson you could use to describe them; examples of their behaviour or habits; the kinds of things they say or do; how you feel about them and why.

Someone:

1 in your family

2 that can be described with one or more words from Exercise 1

3 you get on really well with

4 quite unusual, eccentric or annoying

5 you admire

12 Work in pairs. Swap names. Ask and tell each other about the people on the lists. Find out as much as you can.

 2 To watch the video and do the activities, see the DVD ROM.

GETTING TOGETHER

SPEAKING

1 **Work in groups. Discuss the questions.**

- What do you think are the pros and cons of the following ways of meeting a partner?
  - having an arranged marriage
  - going on a blind date
  - meeting through work or university
  - meeting via an Internet dating site
- How do you think the photo relates to meeting a partner? What do you think of this method?
- Which other ways of meeting partners can you think of? What's good / bad about each one?

READING

2 **Read the article opposite about love and relationships. Answer the questions.**

1 How are the three strands of science – social science, neuroscience and computer science – possibly helping to improve relationships?

2 How convinced is the author that science will actually provide benefits in this field?

3 **Work in pairs. Discuss why the following were mentioned.**

1 doing your own thing	5 kids
2 changing partners	6 thousands of online profiles
3 patience and perseverance	7 collaborative filtering
4 artists, poets and playwrights	8 arranged marriage

4 **Complete the sentences with some of the phrases in bold from the article.**

1 We constantly update the website and have special offers to _____.

2 As a company, we _____ building long-term relationships with our clients.

3 The important thing is _____ past failures.

4 There is now _____ to support the idea of banning laptop use in the classroom.

5 No single test would _____ the product is safe for human consumption.

6 I'm speaking at a conference for _____ biometrics.

7 The discovery _____ the key to developing a cure for dementia.

8 *The Guardian* spoke to Tim Watson about his clash with the press and how he _____.

5 **Choose two of the topics below to talk about. Spend a few minutes preparing what you want to say about each one. Then work in groups and share your ideas.**

- why divorce rates are rising
- how to have a long and happy relationship
- the pros and cons of having kids
- what you should look for in a partner

UNDERSTANDING VOCABULARY

Phrasal verbs

A phrasal verb is a verb with one or two linked particles. These particles are words we use as prepositions or adverbs in other contexts. Often the meaning of a phrasal verb is not obviously connected to either the verb or the particle.

*We've always **got on** very well.* (= We've always liked each other and been friendly.)

*You're expected to **come up with** clear ideas about who you're looking for.* (= suggest or think of)

As with normal verbs, you need to notice the collocations that phrasal verbs are used with. Some phrasal verbs may also:

- form part of commonly used phrases.
- be usually used in the passive.
- have more than one meaning.
- require object pronouns (*me, you, he, she, it, us, them*) to be placed between the verb and the particle.

6 **Use these phrasal verbs from the article to complete each group of phrases below.**

sound out	sort out	narrow down
be subjected to	end up	move into

1 ~ a place to stay / ~ a visa / ~ our differences / ~ the dispute

2 ~ a thorough examination / ~ terrible verbal abuse / ~ torture / ~ regular safety checks

3 ~ new premises / ~ publishing / ~ the Latin American market / ~ my new apartment

4 ~ voters / ~ your views / ~ the members of the board / ~ staff about the changes

5 ~ the list of suspects / ~ your options / ~ the focus of the essay / ~ your topic

6 ~ in trouble / ~ homeless / ~ getting to bed at four in the morning / ~ spending over £200

7 Look at these phrases containing two-word phrasal verbs which have already featured in this book. Which phrasal verbs usually use object pronouns between the verb and the particle? Which have the pronoun after the particle?

1 bring in new restrictions
2 drag down the rest of the team
3 embark on a strategy
4 give away his millions
5 go through huge changes
6 knock down the slums
7 set out an ambitious plan
8 set up a recycling centre
9 stick to your principles
10 take over the bathroom

8 ▶ **5** Listen and check your answers.

9 Work in groups. Answer the questions.

1 How important do you think it is to stick to your principles? Can you think of times when maybe it's better to abandon them?

2 Do you know anyone who's ever quit their job and embarked on a whole new career?

3 Which people you know have been through the biggest changes since you've known them?

4 Can you remember a time you ended up spending more money than you'd planned to?

5 Do you know anyone who's ever set up a company?

FROM CUPID TO COMPUTER

Rose McLoughlin explores the brave new relationship between romance and science

Fred and Doreen Wilson are not your average husband and wife. In fact, having just **celebrated their 75th wedding anniversary**, they may well enjoy the nation's longest-lasting marriage. 'There's no great secret to our success,' muses Fred. 'We've always got on very well and we've always respected each other, but neither of us has ever expected the other to be the only source of happiness in life. We've been off and done our own things, but we've always come back to each other afterwards and that's helped **keep things fresh**. When things go badly, people often think changing partners will help, but hardly anyone ever ends up better off as a result.'

Given that in many European countries over six out of ten **marriages** now **end in divorce** and even in more culturally conservative places rates of 20% are no longer uncommon, such patience and perseverance may seem like **a thing of the past**. In fact, though, researchers are convinced that we can all learn how to be happier by **drawing lessons from** couples like the Wilsons.

Over recent years, social science has increasingly moved into what was traditionally the domain of artists, poets and playwrights, and one result has been **a wealth of studies** exploring love and marriage and the experiences of those who've been through it all already – and **lived to tell the tale**. This research reveals that we have more chance of staying together if we **contribute equally to** the household, don't attempt to sort out problems by text message, get plenty of sleep … and avoid having kids!

While social scientists analyse the wisdom of life-long partners, **researchers working in the field of** neuroscience believe they can now **detect the signs of** true romance in those embarking on new relationships by observing which parts of their brain light up – and to what degree they do so – during scans. Distinctive patterns of electrical activity are noticeable in volunteers who claim to have recently fallen in love and an informed viewing of neuron activity could **be sufficient to determine whether** their feelings are strong enough for their relationships to last.

However, it is in the field of online dating that the appliance of science **may well prove to be** most lucrative. Where early sites simply promised access to thousands upon thousands of profiles, an excess of choice that did not result in **a huge increase in the number of** couples finding love, their modern counterparts are increasingly narrowing down our choices by using sophisticated mathematical formulas to try to ensure subscribers are matched to those they are supposedly most compatible with.

Subscribe to a site today and you're expected to not only come up with clear ideas about who you're looking for but to also answer upwards of 200 extra questions designed to sound out your morals, values and beliefs. These details are then subjected to an analysis called collaborative filtering, whereby the preferences of large numbers of people are collected and divided into groups of similar users.

There is, of course, a deep irony in all of this. In the West, we tend to regard arranged marriage as an outdated relic from a distant era and we **pride ourselves on** our freedom and individuality. Yet it could easily be claimed that we've simply replaced one kind of (human) matchmaker with another technological one. **The degree to which this will** ensure marital success **remains highly contested**. Perhaps, in the end, we may have to accept that chemistry will never be completely understood by scientists!

MIXED MESSAGES

Chicago Sky coach Pokey Chatman talks with students during a charity event

SPEAKING

1 Choose which relationships from the box below you have had. Put them in order from the biggest influence on your life to the smallest influence. Then work in groups. Compare and explain your choices.

siblings	grandparent – grandchild
life partners	parent – child
colleagues	teacher – pupil
business partners	coach – athlete
neighbours	doctor – patient

LISTENING

2 ▶ 6 Listen to five people talking about a young man called Toby and an incident he's been involved in. Decide:

1 who each speaker is and what their relationship to Toby is.

2 what you think the incident they refer to was.

3 ▶ 6 Work in pairs. Check you understand the phrases in bold, then discuss the questions. Listen again and check your ideas.

1 What were the **mixed messages** Toby received?

2 What will help him **get back on the straight and narrow**, according to his grandmother?

3 How did the **ridiculous confrontation** come about?

4 Why do you think Toby was **unwilling to back down**?

5 Why has the incident **come as a shock** to his coach?

6 What did Toby **confide to** his coach?

7 Why did the doctor say the man **was in remarkably good health**?

8 Who **came to his aid**?

9 Why did they split up, **when it came down to it**?

10 Where was there **a scene** and what do you think caused it?

GRAMMAR

Would

Would has many different uses, including talking about past habits, giving advice, talking about the future in the past, and explaining hypothetical consequences in conditional sentences.

4 Match each sentence from the listening (1–6) to a sentence (a–f) that has the same meaning of *would*.

1 I probably would've stayed with him if he'd apologised.

2 When he was a toddler, I'd do the childcare most days.

3 I knew it would come to no good, but you can't really interfere, can you?

4 I remember once I asked him to change desks and he just wouldn't – just refused point blank.

5 He should obviously be punished, but after that I'd still give him another chance.

6 I would say he has a stubborn streak and he's been prone to outbursts and answering back.

a I'd consider talking it through with a therapist. You shouldn't bottle these things up.

b For some reason, the car wouldn't start this morning so I'm waiting for the breakdown people.

c They said it would be miserable today, but it's actually turned out quite nice.

d If they'd intervened, the situation would be a lot worse now.

e Before the anger management classes, he'd often get into unnecessary confrontations.

f I wouldn't say it's a disaster – just a slight setback.

 Check your ideas on page 167 and do Exercise 1.

5 Use structures and phrases with *would* to write sentences about the story of Toby. Think about:

- what you'd say his childhood was like – what he and his parents would do and how they got on.

- why you'd say different people have the opinions they do.

- why you think he was arrested and how it would've been different in other circumstances.

- what you'd imagine / hope would happen to Toby now.

- what you would advise him and the people he knows to do.

I'd say he had a difficult childhood because his parents would argue a lot and they wouldn't spend a lot of time with him.

I would've thought Toby still likes his ex-girlfriend.

6 Work in groups. Share your ideas and see if you agree.

 For further practice, see Exercise 2 on page 168.

VOCABULARY Relationships

7 Work in pairs. For each sentence below, decide:

a what relationship in Exercise 1 you think is being talked about.

b if you think the relationship is good or bad – and why.

c if you could say this about any relationships you know.

1 They're **going through a bit of a rough patch** and have talked about splitting up.

2 I **keep an eye on her** as she's quite frail and has no relatives nearby.

3 As a teenager, she really **sparked my interest in** science.

4 I've **collaborated with him on** a number of projects and he's taught me a lot.

5 They're **not on speaking terms** at the moment, which can **make it awkward** at meetings.

6 We're **on first-name terms** as I have to go and see him so often.

7 They **maintain a professional relationship**, but they **don't see eye to eye** on many issues.

8 They **get on each other's nerves** all the time and they're constantly **competing for** my **attention**.

9 She **puts people at their ease** and reassures them about the whole process.

10 He **pushes** his kids **incredibly hard**.

11 I don't really know any of them as we tend to **keep ourselves to ourselves**.

12 He **doesn't** tend to **pull his weight**, which causes some **friction** in the office.

SPEAKING

8 Work in groups of three. You are going to roleplay some conversations.

Student A: look at File 7 on page 187.

Student B: look at File 8 on page 185.

Student C: look at File 9 on page 189.

Read your three problems and choose the one that you think is most interesting. Plan how to describe the problem as if it was really happening to you. Think about some details to add.

9 Now roleplay a conversation about each problem. You can start the conversations like this:

A: *What's up?*

B: *Oh, it's …* (explain the problem)

Continue the conversations by sympathising, sharing experiences, giving advice, offering reassurance, etc. Use some of the language below.

- Oh dear!
- That must be difficult.
- How awful!
- I know exactly what you're going through!
- Something similar happened to a friend of mine.
- I'd talk it over with them (if I were you).
- Have you been in touch with the police?
- I'd have thought they could help.
- I'd imagine it'll all blow over.
- I wouldn't worry about it.
- What an idiot!

10 When you have discussed one problem each, choose another one or invent your own relationship issue. Have further conversations.

VIDEO 1

BIG CITY CONSTRUCTION

1 Work in pairs. Check you understand the phrases below. Discuss what you think could go wrong with each of these aspects of building a skyscraper, what the consequences of the errors might be, and how they might be resolved.

- get planning permission
- employ a building crew
- blast a hole for the foundations
- bring in and remove materials from the site
- erect and operate cranes
- deal with suppliers
- ensure site safety
- protect adjacent buildings

2 Work in groups. Rank the topics in Exercise 1 in order of how difficult you think they will be when developing a site like the one in the photo (1= the most difficult, 8= the least difficult).

3 ▶3 Watch the video and decide what you think the three main challenges are. How do they resolve them?

4 ▶3 Work in pairs. Do you remember any of the numbers missing from the sentences? Watch again and complete the sentences.

1 There are nearly _____ skyscrapers in New York City.

2 When preparing the foundations, it took a year to remove _____ cubic metres of earth.

3 About _____ pounds of building material comes in on each truck every day and they do around _____ lifts each day.

4 The building crew are working about _____ metres above ground level.

5 The average weight of a load of steel beams is about _____ tons.

6 The trucks sometimes have to cut across _____ lanes in order to turn.

7 The five water tanks will eventually contain _____ litres of water.

8 The spire is assembled from _____ pieces at a height of _____ metres above ground.

9 Once complete, the building will stand at _____ metres high.

5 Work in groups. Discuss the questions.

- What do you think of the building design in the video? What do you think the building is for?
- What buildings that you know would you describe with each of the adjectives below? Why?
  amazing   hideous   unusual   controversial
- What buildings are being erected in your town at the moment?
- What are they for? Do you think they're a good idea? Why? / Why not?
- Have you ever had to put up with building work? Where? What happened?

UNDERSTANDING FAST SPEECH

6 ▶4 Listen to an extract from the video said at natural pace. Try to write down what you hear. Then compare your ideas with a partner.

7 ▶5 Try again. This time you will hear a slower version of the extract.

8 Check your ideas in File 10 on page 189. Groups of words are marked with / and pauses are marked //. Stressed sounds are in CAPITALS. Practise saying the extract.

REVIEW 1

GRAMMAR AND UNDERSTANDING

VOCABULARY

1 Complete the text with one word in each space.

Many people [1]_____ now consider New York to be among the safest major cities in the world, but it has [2]_____ to overcome huge problems to reach this situation. Back in 1990, the place was [3]_____ a war zone, with the murder rate [4]_____ risen to almost 2,500 a year and thousands of shootings taking place too. Fewer and [5]_____ tourists [6]_____ venture beyond a small central area of the city. So how did New York manage to restore law and [7]_____ and become what it is today? First and [8]_____, its citizens got to the point where they were [9]_____ and tired of the situation and demanded political change. The government brought [10]_____ tougher and more efficient policing. However, this probably would not [11]_____ been enough on its own without an economic recovery and huge investment in the poorest areas of the city. Successive governments stuck [12]_____ these policies to ensure success.

2 Complete the second sentence so that it has a similar meaning to the first sentence using the word given. Do not change the word given. You must use between three and five words, including the word given.

1 We generally used to play in the street when we were kids.
By _____ in the street when were kids. **WOULD**

2 If you ask me, he's too demanding of the kids.
I would _____ the kids too hard. **SAID**

3 The city is completely different to what it was like when I lived there.
The city _____ some huge changes since I lived here. **THROUGH**

4 I know the coach was bad, but it's terrible that people abused him that way.
The coach should _____ abuse like that, however bad he was. **SUBJECTED**

5 From what I heard, they have reduced the list of candidates to five.
They seem _____ list to five candidates. **NARROWED**

6 Things still need to improve, but at least they demolished the slums.
The city would be a lot worse if they _____ the slums. **DOWN**

3 Choose the correct option.

1 I doubt you will *hear / have heard* of the place I come from.

2 We got approval for a loan to start a restaurant so we're hoping to *set it up / set up it* next year.

3 The mayor introduced sweeping changes *being elected / having been elected* by a huge majority.

4 I wish we *would do / had done* something about the litter before it got so bad.

5 I knew the whole venture *would fail / will fail* as soon as we *embarked on it / embarked it on*.

VOCABULARY

4 Match the verbs (1–8) with the collocates (a–h).

1	undergo	a	me / my authority
2	demolish	b	huge changes / an operation
3	undermine	c	the decline / traffic
4	set out	d	restrictions / a heavy fine
5	impose	e	on the fumes / on a bone
6	spark	f	a building / all his arguments
7	choke	g	my interest / waves of protest
8	halt	h	an ambitious plan / the options

5 What do the adjectives describe? Put them into two groups.

condemned	vibrant	stubborn	sprawling
prone	principled	congested	laid-back
willing	affluent		

6 Complete the idioms with a preposition in each space. Then think of a real example for each one.

1 She takes everything _____ her stride.

2 They don't see eye _____ eye on many issues.

3 He often goes _____ my back.

4 We're not _____ speaking terms.

5 He has to be the centre _____ attention.

6 There's a real buzz _____ the place.

7 She really puts people _____ their ease.

8 It really gets _____ my nerves.

7 Complete the sentences. Use the word in brackets to form a word that fits in the space.

1 He can be very _____ about food. Only the most expensive will do. (snob)

2 I think you need a bit of _____ to be successful. (arrogant)

3 We stayed in this _____ little village. (charm)

4 People are quite _____ about politicians, but I think we can change things. (cynic)

5 The city became run-down because of the sheer _____ of city council. (competent)

6 It's quite a rough area. I've heard about several _____ round there. (mug)

7 He can be very aggressive and he gets involved in stupid _____ about nothing. (confront)

8 The doctor said I was in _____ good health. (remark)

8 Complete the text with one word in each space. The first letters are given.

I shared a flat with a friend at university, Miguel. We were fine most of the time but [1]n_____ and again we'd [2]e_____ u_____ having an argument. Cleaning caused the most [3]fr_____. Miguel is quite intense and fussy. He can't stand seeing even a [4]tr_____ of dirt in the house, whereas I'm a bit more [5]l_____-b_____. He'd sometimes accuse me of not pulling my [6]we_____, which would annoy me because I often cooked for him, so I'd tell him to [7]li_____ u_____ and that the place didn't have to be absolutely [8]sp_____ all the time.

3

CULTURE AND IDENTITY

The centuries-old village tradition of *galena*, Ribnovo

IN THIS UNIT YOU LEARN HOW TO:

- discuss different aspects of culture and society
- politely disagree with people's opinions
- express feelings and opinions more emphatically
- describe useful objects and household jobs
- discuss your own personal and national identities

SPEAKING

1 Work in pairs. Look at the photo and discuss the questions.
- Who do you think the people are?
- In what country do you think the photo was taken?
- What do you think is happening in the photo?
- What do you think it might say about the culture of the place and people?
- How important do you think it is to maintain traditions? Why?

VOCABULARY Society and culture

2 Check you understand the words and phrases in bold. Then discuss to what degree the sentences apply to your country.

1 The people are incredibly welcoming because **hospitality** is central to the culture.

2 It's quite **male-dominated**. Women are looked down on and there's still a lot of discrimination.

3 It's quite conservative, so if you don't **conform**, life can be quite difficult.

4 Religion **plays a powerful role** in society.

5 Everything's very **bureaucratic**. You need a permit or ID card for everything.

6 I think it's a very family-centred culture. Most people's social life **revolves around** their extended family.

7 It's basically a very **secular society** and people have **lost touch with** their traditions.

8 Socially, it's a very liberal society. People don't like to **interfere** – it's very much **live and let live**.

9 Life is **tough**, but people generally have a very **positive outlook**.

10 **Class** is a big thing. People are very aware of your background and there's not much **social mobility**.

11 Humour is a key part of how people **relate to** each other. People often **take the mickey** out of each other.

12 People are very **reserved** – you can only relate to them **on a superficial level**.

3 Do you think the descriptions in Exercise 2 are good for a country? Why? / Why not? In each case, try to think of one flip side.

THINGS ARE DIFFERENT THERE

DEVELOPING CONVERSATIONS

Challenging overgeneralisations

When people use stereotypes or overgeneralise, we often want to challenge what they say – or moderate it. We can use various phrases to do this.

Come on!

That's a bit harsh / of an overstatement / a stereotype, **isn't it?!**

I wouldn't go that far.

What? Everyone? / **All** women?

It's not as though we're all like that.

That can't be true! It's like saying all Dutch people are tall!

Just because you're Brazilian, it **doesn't mean** you like football.

There must be loads of British people who don't drink tea!

1 Work in pairs. Take turns to say and respond to the overgeneralisations below. Use the phrases in the box.

1 Men are no good at listening.

2 Women are terrible drivers.

3 Young people these days have no respect.

4 The people from the South are more friendly.

5 The rich are only interested in themselves.

6 People who are on benefits are just lazy – they don't want to work.

7 The British are such hypocrites!

8 How come you speak my language? You're British!

2 Work in groups. Discuss the questions.

- What stereotypes are there of your country?

- Are there stereotypes of people from particular cities or areas in your country?

- Are any of these stereotypes positive? How fair do you think they are?

- Do you think you've ever been stereotyped? How?

LISTENING

3 ▶ **7** Listen to three conversations about society and culture in different countries. Answer the questions for each conversation.

1 What aspect/s of culture do they talk about?

2 Are the speakers talking about their own culture?

3 What feelings are expressed about the culture?

4 ▶ **7** Are the sentences true (T), false (F) or not mentioned (N)? Listen again and check your answers.

1 a Zoe's partner is from a different country.

  b The people Mehdi works with are making fun of him.

  c Mehdi wants to change jobs.

2 a They don't have enough admin people.

  b People are happy to queue.

3 a The speaker stayed with friends who live there.

  b Most women don't work.

  c The government is encouraging changes in attitudes to women.

5 Work in groups. Discuss the questions.

- Do you know any couples who are from different cultures? Where are they from?
- Do you think different countries have a different sense of humour? Why? In what way?
- Have you ever misinterpreted something or been misinterpreted? What happened?
- What is your best / worst experience of bureaucracy?
- Do you think the government can change aspects of culture?
- What effect can each of the following have on society and culture?
  TV & film education money travel & immigration

GRAMMAR

Cleft sentences

The sentences below, based on the listening, use the common structure of subject–verb–object:

He seems to be struggling with the people.

He hates all the bitchy comments and gossip.

They only stared at their computer screens or filed papers.

They only ever seem to have one person serving you. It really frustrates me.

However, we sometimes use different sentence structures to highlight particular aspects – the subject or object, the feelings people have, the actions people do, etc.

6 Work in pairs. Look at audio script 7 on page 199 to see the actual sentences that the examples in the box are based on. Answer the questions.

1 How does the sentence structure change?

2 What words / phrases begin the sentence?

3 What extra words (if any) are added to the sentence?

4 Why did the speaker want to add this emphasis?

G Check your ideas on page 168 and do Exercise 1.

7 Complete the dialogue by making cleft sentences using the words in italics. You will need to add words and you may need to change the form of the verbs.

A: I think it's a shame we don't keep up traditions here anymore.

B: Yeah, but ¹*thing / like about our way of life / fact / be yourself.*

A: Yeah, but ²*what / concern / people lose touch with their roots.*

B: Come on. It's not as though we've become a classless society. In fact, ³*one / frustrate / lack / social mobility.*

A: Maybe – but the government could do something about that.

B: ⁴*it / not the government / do something; / people's attitudes / need to change.*

A: I wouldn't go that far. I'm not sure it's that bad.

B: Well, I guess. ⁵*one / give / hope / fact / young people / don't seem all that interested in people's backgrounds.*

A: Only because they aren't interested in anything! ⁶*all / want / go shopping.*

B: That's a bit harsh. There are loads of young people who take an interest in politics.

8 Work in pairs. Practise reading out the dialogue.

9 Complete the sentences so they are true for you. Use the ideas in brackets.

1 The thing I find most _____ about my _____ (person) is _____ .

2 The main thing I *love / hate* about my _____ (person) is _____ .

3 All I tend to do most _____ (day / time) is _____ and _____ .

4 The place I'd most like to visit is _____ .

5 One _____ I have absolutely no interest in *visiting / trying* is _____ .

6 The main reason that I _____ (activity) is _____ .

10 Work in pairs. Compare your sentences and explain your ideas.

G For further practice, see Exercises 2 and 3 on page 169.

CONVERSATION PRACTICE

11 You are going to have a conversation about the place where you live now. Make a list of things that you like about the place and another list of things that annoy you.

12 Work in groups. Explain your ideas. Agree or disagree with your partners. Use as much language from this lesson as you can.

 6 To watch the video and do the activities, see the DVD ROM.

IT'S A CULTURAL THING

SPEAKING

1 **Work in groups. Discuss the questions.**

- Do you think the place you live in is typical of homes in your country? Why? / Why not?
- Think of the objects in your house. Which do you think are very common in homes in your country? Do you have any objects that are less typical? Why?
- Have you ever been in any homes in other countries? If yes, was there anything about them that you thought was strange or unusual?
- In what ways do you think homes / rooms / household objects can reflect a person's nationality or personal cultural identity?

VOCABULARY Household objects

2 **Match the actions on the left with the objects on the right they usually go with. More than one verb may be possible with some objects.**

climb	load		bucket	oven
cover	run		carpet	pan
cut	spread		cloth	pin
fill	stick in		dishwasher	sink
flush	thread		glue	string
heat	unblock		ladder	tap
lay	wring out		needle	toilet

3 **Work in pairs. Discuss the difference between the following:**

rope and **string**   a **mop** and a **brush**

wire and **cable**   a **nail** and a **screw**

a **cloth** and a **sponge**   a **ladder** and **stairs**

a **bucket** and a **bowl**   a **knee pad** and a **bandage**

a **drill** and a **hammer**   **soap** and **washing-up liquid**

4 **Decide which five actions below are problems. Discuss with your partner what would need to be done after each of them. Which five are solutions? To what kind of problems?**

spill some water	flood the kitchen
rip your trousers	sweep the floor
soak your jeans	drop a glass
stain your top	rinse a glass
mend your shirt	wipe the table

5 **With your partner, take turns to choose objects or actions from Exercises 2, 3 and 4. Either draw, act or explain them without using the actual words on this page. Your partner should say the name of the object / action.**

READING

6 **Read the introduction to an article about differences people noticed when living in other countries. Decide which sentence below best summarises the point the writer is making.**

1 The way we feel when we're abroad is similar to how foreigners feel in our countries.
2 It can be really shocking to discover how different homes in other countries are.
3 Definitions of normality vary across time and across different countries.
4 Globalisation means more people around the world have the same kinds of things in their homes.
5 Travel helps to broaden our minds and shows how we're similar to – and different from – others.

7 **Work in pairs. Discuss the questions.**

- How far do you agree with the basic point of the introduction?
- Can you think of anything that:
  - you sometimes take for granted?
  - you've reacted to with confusion or disgust?
  - your culture has adopted from abroad?

8 **Read the rest of the article. Then discuss the questions with your partner.**

- Are any of the things mentioned usual in homes in your country?
- Would you like to have any of the things mentioned in your house? If so, why?
- Which of the things mentioned do you find the strangest? Why?
- Did any of the things mentioned help you understand these countries better?

9 **Read the article again. Match each of the following to the people in the article.**

Which person:

1 gets a puzzled reaction when they explain where they lived before?
2 initially felt slightly restricted in the kitchen?
3 is deprived of a luxury they used to enjoy?
4 has adapted to cold winds blowing into rooms?
5 mentions an object that helps people relax together?
6 was surprised how well people cope without a particular object?
7 found the space where a common household chore gets done a bit odd?
8 expresses considerable frustration?

10 **Think about your own answers to the questions below. Then work in groups and compare your ideas.**

- Which household objects do you think most reflect your national culture? In what way?
- Can you think of three objects that you strongly associate with other countries?
- Which household objects would you find it hardest to live without? Why?

FOREIGN OBJECTS

In our globalised world, we often take it for granted that the things that surround us are universal, sensible and normal. So when we travel or live abroad and discover new objects – or the absence of ones we expected to find – it can be surprising. We may react with confusion or disgust, but it's always good to bear in mind the fact that visitors travelling to our own countries must doubtless have similar experiences. It's also worth remembering that what we see as extraordinary or ridiculous today, we may end up adopting as our own in the future. Take an English aristocrat's comment on seeing a bizarre instrument in 17th century Italy: 'Why should a person need a fork when God had given him hands?'

IN-HA, SOUTH KOREA

I've more or less got used to most of the odd things I've encountered in Britain – the houses that are old and draughty; the fitted carpets on the stairs and even in the bathrooms; the presence of kettles and toasters in every single kitchen. One thing I still struggle to understand, though, is why so many places still have separate hot and cold taps at the sink rather than a mixer tap. You have to fill the sink in order to get the water at the right temperature, but then you can't rinse your face properly because the soap stays in the water. It's much better with a mixer tap because you can wash with running water. In fact, what drives you really mad is if there's no plug. Then you end up either getting freezing hands or burning them – or trying to move between the two. Useless!

JIM, NORTHERN IRELAND

There are loads of things I've noticed here in Spain that are different to back home. For example, in Belfast I used to live in a basement flat, which people here find really weird as basements are mainly used for storing things! Then there's all the kitchen equipment: we've got a *jamonero*, which is a kind of clamp that holds meat in place while you slice it; and a *paellera*, which is this flat, round, shallow pan with two handles for cooking paella in. A lot of the time, folk cook on gas burners to ensure the heat is evenly distributed, so of course we have one of those as well. Best of all, though, is the *brasero* – a kind of electric heater that you place under a table covered with a long cloth going right down to the floor. All the heat gets kept in and it's lovely and cosy when everyone's sitting round the table.

KASIA, POLAND

I'm Polish, my husband is Brazilian and we met in Sweden! We've been living in his hometown of Belo Horizonte for the last four years now and life is different here. For example, back in Lublin, I used to love soaking in a nice hot bath, but here we don't even have a tub! It's much more of a shower culture here – usually both before and after work as it's so hot and humid. Another weird thing for me is the fact that the place we're renting has a large, deep separate sink next to the washing machine in this kind of little utility area, where your clothes can be soaked and scrubbed and more delicate items can be washed. Oh, and I mustn't forget that staple of Brazilian kitchens: the pressure cooker. We use ours all the time, especially when cooking black beans – *feijão*.

ED, CANADA

I spent two years living and working in Qingdao, on the east coast of China, and found the homes there quite fascinating. Most people I knew there live in apartments in high-rise blocks and though they do have some modern appliances, dryers were unusual and you'd often see washing hung out to dry on the balconies. Some places lack fridges too, which didn't seem to bother people as much as you'd expect as all the food is bought fresh in the market every day. My place didn't have an oven either, which somewhat reduced the scope of my cooking, though I got pretty good at using a wok – a big, round Chinese frying pan – on just a single gas ring. One other weird thing I remember is that when you enter a Chinese home, you'll usually find a shoe shelf that you place your shoes on while visiting.

A UNITED KINGDOM?

SPEAKING

1 Work in groups. Discuss the questions.

- Look at the photos. What aspects of UK culture do you think each one shows?

- How do you think each of the things in the box below is connected to UK culture?

Bonfire Night	God Save the Queen
car boot sales	Islam
Carnival	the NHS
curry	the public school system
fish and chips	regional autonomy
football	St George's Day
Glastonbury	the trade union movement

- What else do you know about UK culture? Think about: literature, theatre, music, broadcasting, visual arts, fashion, religion, cuisine, sport, buildings, monuments.

- How important is UK culture in the world? In your country? For you personally?

LISTENING

2 ▶ 8 Listen to three people from the UK talking about their own cultural identities. Which three things from the box in Exercise 1 does each person mention and why?

3 ▶ 8 Listen again. Are the sentences true (T) or false (F)? How do you know?

1 a Savannah's parents were from different ethnic backgrounds.

   b The place she lives in is very racially diverse.

   c Her friends in the city often laugh at her.

2 a Callum gets annoyed by a common false assumption.

   b He complains about how tight government control of Scotland still is.

   c His outlook is fairly narrow and provincial.

3 a Amir acknowledges he doesn't conform to a certain stereotype.

   b He gets quite upset about the things people sometimes say to him.

   c He retains a sense of his family roots.

4 Work in pairs. Discuss the questions.

- What was the most interesting thing you heard? What was the most surprising? Why?

- How racially diverse is your country? How common is it to see mixed-race couples?

- Are there strong regional differences in your country?

- Do you think it's good for regions to have a lot of autonomy from central government?

UNDERSTANDING VOCABULARY

Words and phrases

In the listening, you heard the phrases *it's no big thing* and *a whole new thing*. Many words like *thing* are used as part of fixed phrases. These phrases sometimes have meanings that aren't obviously connected to the meaning of the single words in them. At Advanced level, it's not enough to just know single words. You need to learn as many phrases as you can.

5   Make phrases with *thing* by putting the words in brackets in the correct order.

1   Don't make such a fuss. _____. (really / is / thing / big / no / it)

2   It's rude. _____ (just / thing / the / is / not / done / it) in our society.

3   I'd love to do it, but _____ (fine / be / a / thing / chance / would)!

4   _____ (the / mind / is / from / it / my / thing / furthest) at the moment.

5   I always do it _____ (morning / in / the / thing / first).

6   _____ (makes / you / sort / it / that / the / thing / is / of) glad to be alive.

7   It's difficult, _____ (with / another / one / thing / what / and).

8   I didn't plan it. _____ (thing / to / one / another / led / just).

6   Work in pairs. Discuss what *it* could be in each of the sentences in Exercise 5.

7   ▶ 9 Listen to the phrases from Exercise 5 and notice which sounds are stressed. Then listen again and repeat the phrases.

8   Work in groups. In the listening in Exercise 2, you also heard the phrase *die laughing*. Think of five more phrases using either the word *die* or the word *laugh*. Write example sentences to show how they're used. Use a dictionary to help you if you need to.

LISTENING

9   ▶ 10 Listen to part of a lecture about identity. Summarise the main message in a sentence.

10   Work in pairs. Compare your ideas and discuss how far you agree with this message.

11   ▶ 10 Listen again. Why was each of the following mentioned?

1   global uncertainty

2   commerce

3   a French TV show and a German car

4   a ballet lover and a marketing manager

5   terrible tensions

6   the ruling elite

12   Work in pairs. Which sentences below do you think the lecturer would agree with? Explain your ideas by referring to things the lecturer said.

1   Globalisation has led to an increase in nationalism.

2   We should all buy more locally-made products in order to boost the economy.

3   You could easily have more in common with someone in a different country than with your neighbour.

4   Every single person living in a society contributes equally to the nation's identity.

5   Schools play a key role in developing critical thinking about culture and identity.

6   More and more people are going to suffer identity crises in the future.

SPEAKING

13   Work in groups. Choose one of these tasks. Then spend a few minutes preparing for the task on your own.

a   Make a list of eight people or things from your country that you think are culturally important. Think about: people, cultural / youth movements, kinds of food / drink, special days, places, sports, etc.

b   Make a list of eight people or things from anywhere in the world that are an important part of your own cultural identity. Think about: people, historical events, books, films, music, kinds of food / drink, places, sports and sporting events, etc.

14   Now take turns to present your lists to your group and to explain them. Your partners should comment or ask questions to find out more.

4

POLITICS

IN THIS UNIT YOU LEARN HOW TO:

- describe politicians and their qualities
- give opinions about politics
- talk about consequences of political proposals
- tell jokes
- talk about voting and elections

SPEAKING

1 **Work in pairs. Look at the photo and discuss the questions.**

- Do you know which country the parliament building in the photo is in?
- What do you think the building says about the way the country wants to portray itself?
- How similar / different is the parliament building in your country?
- Have you ever been to the parliament building in your country?

2 **Choose the five qualities below that you think politicians most need. Then explain your ideas to your partner.**

honesty	compassion
ruthlessness	flexibility
passion	bravery
charisma	excellent communication skills
self-confidence	the ability to compromise

The National Congress building designed by Oscar Niemeyer

I DON'T KNOW WHERE I STAND

DEVELOPING CONVERSATIONS
Giving opinions

1   Find six pairs of sentences with a similar meaning.

1   I'm a huge fan of the idea.

2   I don't really know where I stand.

3   I'm totally against it.

4   I think the negatives far outweigh the positives.

5   I can't pass judgement. I don't know enough about it.

6   It's a good idea in theory, just not in practice.

7   I am in favour. I just have some slight reservations.

8   I have some major doubts about it.

9   It's OK in principle. I just think it's unworkable.

10   I'm completely opposed to it.

11   It's not without problems, but on the whole I like it.

12   I'm totally in favour of it.

2   Work in groups. Use sentences from Exercise 1 to explain how you feel about the following:

*   nuclear energy
*   globalisation
*   free health care
*   putting up taxes
*   increasing military spending
*   raising the age of retirement to 70
*   introducing a maximum wage
*   your country hosting a major international event
*   limiting the working week to a maximum of 35 hours
*   banning cars from city centres

LISTENING

3   ▶ 11 Listen to two conversations about topics from Exercise 2. Answer the questions for each conversation.

1   What is the topic of the conversation?

2   Where does each person stand on the issue?

4   ▶ 11 Work in pairs. Look at these sentences from the conversations. Decide which are incorrect and then correct them. Listen again and check your answers.

Conversation 1

1   Some of these salaries are obscene.

2   It all just puts up prices.

3   They'd just detail it as part of their income.

4   They'd be able to find ways through it.

5   I'm just playing devil's advocate.

Conversation 2

6   Did you hear about this proposal to bid to hold the Olympics here?

7   Won't the Games earn a lot of money?

8   They always talk about them leaving a good facility.

9   We don't have a hope in hell.

10   It'd be a receipt for disaster.

5   With your partner, discuss the questions.

*   Which of the opinions expressed do you have most / least sympathy with? Why?
*   What are the advantages of playing devil's advocate? Are there any downsides?
*   In what other ways might cities run up huge debts?
*   Have you ever heard any stories about cities going bankrupt? Where? What happened?

GRAMMAR

Conditionals 1

Conditionals can be used to talk about general truths as well as both probable and imagined events now or in the future. They usually – but not always – introduce conditions with the word *if*.

6 Match 1–5 to a–e to make extracts from the conversations.

1 And what would you include in pay?
2 Even if they do manage to introduce this new law,
3 Imagine if we actually won it.
4 If they're earning that much,
5 As long as there's the official desire to make it work,

a it encourages other people to ask for more.
b It'd be a recipe for disaster.
c Supposing they were given a boat, or whatever, instead of money?
d then it'll work.
e it's basically going to be unworkable.

7 Work in pairs. Look at the extracts in Exercise 6 and answer the questions.

1 Which sentence describes something generally true?
2 Which sentences describe probable events in the future?
3 Which sentences describe imagined events now / in the future?
4 What tenses are used in the conditional parts of each sentence?
5 What structures are used in the result clauses?
6 Which other words apart from *if* are used to introduce conditions?

G Check your ideas on page 169 and do Exercise 1.

8 Work in pairs. Use different conditional structures to think of at least two responses to each sentence. Then compare your ideas with another pair. Who has the best ideas?

1 I'm not going to vote. What's the point? It's not like it makes any difference, does it?
2 They say they're going to make it much harder for people to get into the country.
3 I read somewhere that they're going to start privatising more of the health service.
4 He's been accused of lying about his expenses and claiming more than he should've done.
5 He can't go on holiday now, not with a crisis like this developing.
6 Smoking kills thousands every year. It should just be completely banned.

G For further practice, see Exercise 2 on page 170.

VOCABULARY Consequences

9 Complete the sentences with these verbs.

bankrupt	boost	devastate	lead
trigger	benefit	compound	discourage
reduce	undermine		

1 It might _____ people from working.
2 It might _____ the rich, but it'll harm the poor.
3 It'll _____ the economy and result in the creation of new jobs.
4 It could _____ the whole area and leave thousands unemployed.
5 It'd put an enormous strain on finances. It could _____ the city.
6 It's a bad idea. If anything, it'll _____ the existing social problems.
7 It might _____ an election earlier than they wanted.
8 It's bad. It'll _____ relations between the two countries.
9 It might help to _____ drug abuse.
10 It'll create divisions and _____ to tension.

10 Work in pairs. Think of one event that could make each of the things in Exercise 9 happen.

If they put up taxes, it might discourage people from working.

11 Use these verbs to rewrite four sentences from Exercise 9 so they mean the opposite. You may need to change more than just the verbs.

damage	encourage	resolve	strengthen

CONVERSATION PRACTICE

12 Work in pairs. Think of two proposals in areas such as those in the box below: one that you would both like to see happen, and one – either good or bad – that you have heard is happening. Discuss the possible consequences of each proposal.

education	foreign policy	finance	health
housing	the economy	culture	transport

13 Work with a new partner. Take turns to start conversations about the proposals. You can use the phrases below to start your conversations.

I don't know about you, but I'm personally in favour of ...

Did you hear about this proposal to ...?

7 To watch the video and do the activities, see the DVD ROM.

NO LAUGHING MATTER

READING

1 **Work in groups. Discuss the questions.**

- Where do think the photo opposite was taken? What do you think is happening in the photo?
- Is film of politicians inside parliament shown on TV in your country? If yes, do you ever watch it?
- How do most politicians behave in parliament? What do you think of the way they behave?

2 **Read the article about Prime Minister's Questions in the UK Parliament. Then work in pairs and answer the questions.**

1 What happens in Prime Minister's Questions?
2 What does the author think of it?
3 What did you find most surprising / interesting in the article?
4 How far do you agree with the author's opinions?

3 **Based on what the author says, are the sentences true (T), false (F) or not mentioned (N)?**

1 The prime minister only attends parliament on a Wednesday.
2 MPs may exaggerate how funny they find the jokes during PMQs.
3 Satire was invented in the eighteenth century.
4 The main political parties share a similar approach to certain policies.
5 Satirical shows on TV encourage activism.
6 The author believes in the value of politics.
7 The Yes Men leak information that big companies would rather the media didn't see.
8 The author wants to abolish PMQs.

4 **Complete the sentences with the correct form of the words in bold in the article. The first one is done for you.**

1 There's still insufficient *representation* of women in our parliament. Only 15% of MPs are women.
2 The Black Power movement that _____ in the 1960s grew out of the civil rights struggle in America.
3 A lot of young people are very _____ with politics but just not with the traditional parties.
4 They're not trying to undermine the whole system. They're _____ pointing out where there is corruption.
5 He has a very _____ following so he always attracts big crowds when he speaks.
6 They're very concerned with ensuring the security of _____ systems such as passports.
7 It's an old book but still funny and relevant today. It's a _____ of war and life in the army.
8 They _____ lowering the tax because they said it would only benefit the rich.

5 **Work in groups. Discuss the questions.**

- Is there anything similar to PMQs in your country?
- Do British politicians sound similar or different to politicians in your country? In what way?
- Are there any satirical programmes or satirists on TV in your country? If yes, do you watch them?
- What funny videos, images or short texts are doing the rounds on the Internet at the moment?
- Do you ever tell or make jokes? If yes, who with?

LISTENING

6 ▶ **12** **Listen to a joke about politicians. Decide:**

1 how funny you think it is on a scale of 1–5.
2 what aspect of politics it's joking about.
3 if you think there is an element of truth about it.

UNDERSTANDING VOCABULARY

'Ways of' verb groups

The person telling the joke used some descriptive verbs that show the way something was done.

*He arrives at the gates of heaven **clutching** his bags.* = hold (tightly)

*He **strolls** along the beach.* = go / move (on foot with leisure)

*He **gazes** at the beautiful sunset.* = look (with wonder)

*He **gasps**, 'But what are you doing ...'* = say (in shock)

*His old friends are ... **chattering** to each other.* = talk (continuously)

*The devil **chuckles** ...* = laugh (quietly)

These descriptive verbs are usually used with the same prepositions and with the same grammatical patterns as the more basic verbs such as *hold, move, look*, etc. Sometimes recognising these patterns can help you to guess unknown words.

7 **Work in pairs. Look at audio script 12 on page 201 and put the words in bold into groups according to their basic meaning.**

8 **Add these words to the groups you made.**

grab	glare	creep	race	mumble
giggle	mutter	stare	stagger	scream

9 **Work in pairs. You are going to tell each other a joke.**

Student A: read the joke in File 11 on page 187.

Student B: read the joke in File 12 on page 188.

Replace the words in italics with more descriptive words. Then tell the joke to your partner. Decide how you would rate each one on a scale of 1–5.

Symbol of democracy is a joke

There are some who say that Prime Minister's Questions (PMQs) is a great symbol of democracy. Every Wednesday the head of our government is forced to attend parliament and answer questions from MPs. As MPs are **representatives** of the people, PMQs offers a direct line of access to the top where we, the public, can hold the government to account for their actions. That's the theory. However, the reality is somewhat different and actually symbolises much that is wrong with politics here.

What usually happens is this: the leader of the main **opposition** party stands up and asks a question about a new policy or about some recently released figures that show the government is failing. I say asks a question, but half the time it's just a joke at the prime minister's expense. The prime minister then essentially ignores the question and pokes fun at the leader of the opposition, who then has to ask another question or say something funny. All of this is accompanied by MPs on both sides shouting or laughing like hyenas as they compete to demonstrate **loyalty** to their leader.

> **❝ What has this got to do with politics or democracy? ❞**

Defenders of the ritual note that this type of humour has a long history in British politics. Records of politicians insulting each other in this manner date back to the eighteenth century. They also claim it engages voters in issues and represents the values of free speech. They even argue that such satirical humour prevents the **emergence** of dictators by using mockery and ridicule to reduce fear and build confidence.

While there may well be elements of truth in the historical claim, the bottom line is that what we are really seeing here is politics being turned into **mere** entertainment. The politicians actually *pay* professional comedy writers to write jokes for them, and the rest of the media love it because it fits neatly into

a five-minute slot on the TV news. This is not satire championing truth and exposing the corruption of power. It's more like kids in a playground throwing insults. The kids don't really mean it – it's just a game – and the same goes for the politicians. As 'opposing' parties have more or less adopted the same economic outlook, the only way to mark a difference is through this mock abuse.

And those comedy writers for PMQs are probably the same kind that write for the TV satirists, who the academic Russell Peterson says are undermining the value of politics. He argues that real satire adopts a moral stance – it has an agenda and seeks change – whereas most **satirical** TV programmes only seek balance. They aim to take the mickey equally out of *all* politicians based on character more than policy. As a result, *all* politicians are seen as bad and political **engagement** is discouraged.

But elsewhere it seems humour *can* engage voters. For example, a popular blog by the satirist Bepe Grillo in Italy led to the formation of a movement that gained 25% of the vote in the 2013 elections. And as can be seen from the exploits of the activist duo Jacques Servin and Igor Vamos – better known as the Yes Men – laughter can still pose a serious challenge to the rich and powerful. The pair have developed a technique they call '**identity** correction'. Posing as representatives of entities they dislike – the World Trade Organization, for instance, or the ExxonMobil oil and gas company – they issue shocking, ridiculous press releases that exaggerate official positions in order to force back into the news stories that corporations would rather bury. Whatever your politics, surely such tactics serve as a braver, better symbol of democracy than a couple of comfortable middle-aged white blokes exchanging empty insults once a week.

Comments 146 | Add a comment | Share

CAST YOUR VOTE

READING

1 Work in groups. Discuss what you know about Switzerland. Think about the following:

- its geography
- its history
- famous Swiss people – living or dead
- its famous products, brands and services
- its political system

2 Read an article about the Swiss electoral system. Find:

1 three ways in which Swiss MPs are quite unusual.

2 three examples of how Swiss people participate in politics.

3 how members of the National Council and the Senate are selected.

4 one reason that may explain why not many Swiss people vote.

3 Read the article again. Tick (✓) what you think are positive aspects of the Swiss system. Cross (✗) what you think is negative.

4 Work in pairs. Compare and explain your ideas. Discuss what is similar to / different from the system in your country.

5 With your partner, discuss what you think the words and phrases in bold in the article mean.

VOCABULARY Elections and politics

6 Use these nouns to complete each group of phrases below. There are two nouns you do not need.

| consensus | figure | party | scandal | victory |
| election | MP | poll | strike | vote |

1 a prominent ~ in the anti-war movement / a hate ~ / be seen as a ~ of fun / a very influential ~

2 the ~ takes place in May / call an ~ / rig an ~ / in the run-up to the ~

3 carry out a ~ / conduct a ~ among students / in the latest ~ / go to the ~s

4 reach a ~ / establish a ~ / an emerging ~ / a broad ~

5 expose a bribery ~ / a sex ~ / be mixed up in a ~ / cover up a ~

6 stand as an ~ / lobby ~s / a right-wing ~ / an outspoken ~

7 a unanimous ~ / cast your ~ / a protest ~ / alleged ~-rigging

8 a narrow ~ / a landslide ~ / a hollow ~ / claim ~

7 Underline any phrases in Exercise 6 that are new for you. Write example sentences for each.

8 Work in pairs. Compare your sentences. Then think of one more verb or adjective that can be used with each of the ten nouns in the box in Exercise 6.

 THE ELECTORAL SYSTEM SWISS STYLE

Consisting of 26 cantons, or member states, the country of Switzerland has a long tradition of democracy – some claim it dates back to the 13th century. It is also perhaps unique in the amount of power it **allocates** to regional and local institutions. Parliament only sits 12 weeks a year and MPs are paid modest salaries compared to **counterparts** abroad. Most have second jobs in the community.

In fact, this devolution of power extends to individual citizens. Even when the national parliament decides to change **federal** law, individuals can challenge the decision by collecting 50,000 signatures on a **petition**. This triggers an automatic **referendum**. Furthermore, anyone can propose laws by getting 100,000 signatures. Similar processes exist at a local level. People may vote on these single issues 15 times a year or more. The vast majority of votes are cast by post.

The Swiss have a federal parliament with two bodies – the National Council and the Senate – which choose the government. The Senate is formed by the individual cantons electing two representatives each, irrespective of population size. The 200 MPs in the National Council are elected via a complex form of **proportional representation**. Each canton is allocated a number of seats according to population, ranging from 34 (Zurich) to one (Uri). The political parties provide lists of candidates for each canton, which are sent to the electorate. Voters can vote not only for the party but also for specific candidates. They can even make their own list.

The number of seats each party gains in any canton is determined by the percentage of party **ballot papers** returned. The specific people who are then chosen for each party depends on the individual votes cast for each candidate. Because of this system, individual representatives maintain a direct relationship with their voters, often rejecting **the party line**. Special interest groups often **lobby** voters to support MPs favouring their cause.

Coalitions are the norm in Switzerland as parties don't gain an absolute majority, with the result that a tradition of **consensus** has become established. This may partly explain why voter turnout is often less than 50% of the electorate.

LISTENING

9 Work in groups. Answer the questions below about these events.

an election for a student council	a referendum
a general election	a strike ballot
a local election	a talent show vote
an opinion poll	a vote in parliament

1 In which of the above do you vote for a person or party? In which for a law or action?

2 Who votes in each case?

3 Which ones have you voted in and why? What was the outcome?

4 Which one of the above is the only event you don't directly vote in? How is it sometimes connected to voting?

5 Can you think of any other times you might vote?

6 Have you ever stood for election or campaigned in a vote? When? What happened?

10 ▶ **13** Listen to five people talking about events from Exercise 9. Match each speaker (1–5) to one of the events.

11 ▶ **13** Listen again. Match each speaker to one of the following. There is one that you do not need.

Which person:

a mentions a broken promise?

b talks about vote-rigging?

c talks about voter turnout?

d talks about standing for parliament?

e expresses surprise at something?

f is defending an unpopular decision?

People in Glarus, Switzerland continue their 700-year tradition of open-air voting

GRAMMAR

Conditionals 2

Conditionals can be used to talk about:

1 general past truths.

2 imagined events in the past.

3 imagined events in both the past and the present.

12 Match the sentences from the listening (a–e) to the functions (1–3) in the box. Then work in pairs and compare your ideas.

a It **helped** the programme's ratings if they **had** a kind of hate figure.

b I **might not have minded** so much if the calls **were** free, but they're making a fortune on them.

c If they **hadn't been** so reluctant to negotiate, we **would not be taking** this action now.

d If they**'d called** on another day, I **wouldn't have taken part**.

e It's unlikely we **would've abolished** uniforms if we **didn't have** a body like this.

G Check your ideas on page 170 and do Exercise 1.

13 With your partner, decide which option is *not* possible. Then discuss the difference in meaning between the two possible options.

1 If the parliamentary vote goes against the government next week, *it could trigger / it'll trigger / it triggered* an election.

2 The government should've done more for the middle classes if they *want / wanted / would've wanted* to win the election.

3 If they complain, *tell / I wouldn't tell / I told* the boss.

4 If I'd heard something, *I'd told / I would tell / I would've told* you.

5 If it hadn't been for him, *I wouldn't be working / wouldn't have been working / would never have got* a job here.

14 Think about the past and present results of the following things. Write two conditional sentences about each. Then work with your partner and compare your ideas.

- the result of the last election
- the impact a famous figure has had in your country
- an important moment in your life

G For further practice, see Exercise 2 on page 171.

SPEAKING

15 Work in groups. Discuss the questions.

- What's voter turnout like in your country? Why?
- How do you think democracy could be improved?
- Which elections were significant for you personally / your country / the world? Why?
- Have you heard of any scandals? What happened?
- What would be your proposals if you stood for a school body / a local election / parliament?

VIDEO 2

SONGLINES
OF THE ABORIGINES

1 **Work in groups. Discuss these questions.**

- What do you think of the painting in the photo?
- Do you think the painting represents anything – or is it just abstract?
- What do you know about the Aborigines in Australia?

2 **▣ 8 Watch the video. Are the sentences true (T), false (F) or not mentioned (N)?**

1 Aborigines were one of the first groups to move from Africa.

2 Traditional Aboriginal culture still exists today.

3 Aborigines used to have innovative farming techniques.

4 By the mid-20th century, the Aborigine population had halved in size.

5 The decision to settle in towns had a negative impact on Aboriginal culture.

6 Songlines serve both a practical and symbolic function.

7 You can purchase maps of the routes that the Songlines take across Australia.

8 The Dreaming allows Aborigines to maintain contact with their ancestors.

3 **▣ 8 Work in pairs. Try to complete the sentences about the video with a noun in each space, then watch again and check your answers.**

1 Aboriginal culture survives today in remote _____ of the outback.

2 In a sense, Arnhem Land is the _____ of Aboriginal culture.

3 European _____ to 'civilise' the Aborigines had tragic _____.

4 There have always been strong spiritual _____ to the landscape in Aboriginal culture.

5 Aboriginal beliefs are founded on a deep _____ for and _____ to the land.

6 Walking the Songlines is a way of tracing the _____ of their ancestors.

7 Songlines mark _____ between different _____.

8 They also represent a spiritual _____.

4 **Work in pairs. Discuss the questions.**

- Did the video give you any further thoughts about the painting above?
- What did you find surprising / unsurprising / interesting / depressing? Why?
- Do you know of any other indigenous groups? How strong is their culture today?
- How important do you think rituals are in everyday life? Give some examples.

UNDERSTANDING FAST SPEECH

5 **▣ 9 Listen to an extract from the video said at natural pace. Try to write down what you hear. Then compare your ideas with a partner.**

6 **▣ 10 Try again. This time you will hear a slower version of the extract.**

7 **Check your ideas in File 10 on page 189. Groups of words are marked with / and pauses are marked //. Stressed sounds are in CAPITALS. Practise saying the extract.**

REVIEW 2

VOCABULARY

1 Complete the email with one word in each space. Contractions count as one word.

Dear Claude,

Thanks for the wedding invitation. I ¹_____ have replied ²_____ thing, but I wasn't sure I could get time off and what ³_____ one thing and another it's taken longer than I thought to sort out. Anyway, I'd love to come. The only thing ⁴_____ is still uncertain ⁵_____ whether Maddie can come too. I know you said the wedding was ⁶_____ big thing, but we would really like to buy you something special. The main ⁷_____ Maddie and I got together ⁸_____ that you introduced us. It wouldn't feel right if we ⁹_____ get you anything – and it's not as ¹⁰_____ we can't afford it.

James

2 Complete the second sentence so that it has a similar meaning to the first sentence using the word given. Do not change the word given. You must use between four and five words, including the word given.

1 There's not much to see there except maybe the ruined castle.
The only _____ the ruined castle. **WORTH**

2 If it wasn't seen as inappropriate here, I would've gone with you.
I would've gone with you, but it _____ here. **DONE**

3 It's just been a series of unfortunate events that's caused this mess.
I wouldn't be in this mess if one thing _____. **ANOTHER**

4 He just looks endlessly at the screen and pretends to work.
All _____ the screen and pretend to work. **STARE**

5 I'm glad it wasn't me because I always laugh uncontrollably in those situations.
I wouldn't have been able to _____ been me. **GIGGLING**

6 He always speaks very unclearly, which is very annoying.
What annoys me _____ all the time. **MUMBLES**

3 Choose the correct option.

1 Me? Have a holiday? Chance would be a *fine / good* thing.

2 I *staggered / glared* home at about six in the morning.

3 He *muttered / screamed* something under his breath.

4 I could've helped if you had ever *ask / asked*.

5 I saw something *scamper / grab* across the kitchen floor.

6 What concerns me is the *number / amount* of crime in the area.

VOCABULARY

4 Decide if these adjectives refer to society, politicians or both.

hypocritical	family-centred	outspoken
secular	conservative	male-dominated
right-wing	liberal	powerful
welcoming	diverse	ruthless

5 Match the verbs (1–10) with the collocates (a–j).

1	flush	a	a carpet / the foundations
2	load	b	my jeans / up the contract
3	lay	c	the table / your feet
4	rip	d	the toilet / the pipes out
5	wipe	e	my shirt / his reputation
6	sweep	f	the result / the election
7	stain	g	the floor / to power
8	unblock	h	the top shelf / a broad consensus
9	rig	i	the sink / the drain
10	reach	j	the dishwasher / the rifle

6 Complete the sentences. Use the word in brackets to form a word that fits in the space.

1 If you ask me, our society is far too _____. (bureaucracy)

2 I'm against laws to restrict the Internet. I think they are _____. (work)

3 There continues to be a lack of social _____ in our country. (mobile)

4 The _____ for the economy is not very bright. (look)

5 The _____ of Internet start-ups is threatening traditional businesses. (emerge)

6 I haven't read the book so I can't pass _____ on it. (judge)

7 She was a very _____ figure in the feminist movement. (influence)

8 We should _____ the power of the police. (strong)

7 Complete the text with one word in each space. The first letters are given.

We are going to have a general election here soon. The election was ¹tr_____ by a huge bribery scandal that was ²ex_____ in the press. Several ministers were ³m_____ u_____ in it, but the government had tried to ⁴c_____ it u_____. In the last election, the governing party won a ⁵la_____ victory, but all the latest ⁶p_____ suggest they've lost a lot of support. The main opposition party also has a new leader who has been a ⁷pr_____ figure in the fight against corruption and is seen as having a lot of ⁸ch_____, which is attracting many new voters. The only thing in the government's ⁹fa_____ is that they have succeeded in ¹⁰bo_____ the economy after it was devastated by a banking crisis. That's obviously ¹¹be_____ a lot of people so they could still win. I don't know where I ¹²st_____ yet. I might not vote at all!

5

GOING OUT, STAYING IN

IN THIS UNIT YOU LEARN HOW TO:

- talk about nights out
- comment on what people say
- change the subject
- talk about tourism and tourist sites
- describe and review books

SPEAKING

1 Which sentence below best describes your feelings about the night out shown in the photo?

  1 It looks like my idea of hell. Nothing in the world would induce me to go there!

  2 It's not really my kind of thing, but I'd probably give it a go if the opportunity arose.

  3 It looks like a laugh. It could be fun.

  4 It looks like a brilliant night out – tailor-made for someone like me!

2 Work in pairs. Compare your ideas and explain your choices. Then discuss:

- whether you've ever been to any similar kinds of events.
- what the best / worst thing about a night like this would be.
- other occasions you can think of when people go out in costumes.

A foam party in the Amnesia Club, Ibiza

I BET THAT WAS FUN

VOCABULARY Nights out

1 Complete the sentences below with these pairs of words. You may need to change the order of the words.

awkward + scene	disappointment + hype
bits + floods	do + rough
bored + yawning	hilarious + stitches
burst + courses	mortified + swallow
crawl + exhausted	overwhelmed + tears

1 It was awful. I just couldn't stop _____. I was _____ out of my mind!

2 I'm _____! I didn't _____ into bed until after four.

3 She was so _____ by it all that she actually burst into _____.

4 There must've been at least ten _____. Honestly, I thought I was going to _____!

5 We were all on the floor in _____. It was _____!

6 Honestly! I was absolutely _____. I just wanted the ground to open up and _____ me!

7 It was such a _____. It really didn't live up to the _____.

8 I feel a bit _____ today. I had a big work _____ last night and didn't get home till two.

9 It was awful. He was in _____ when he heard – just in _____ of tears.

10 It caused a bit of a _____, actually. It was really quite _____, to be honest.

2 Choose the four words / phrases from Exercise 1 that you think you will use most often. Then decide if there are any words or phrases you don't think you will ever use. Think about why.

3 Work in pairs. Compare the words and phrases you chose for Exercise 2 and explain your ideas.

4 With your partner, think of a situation in which you might:

1 find yourself bored out of your mind.
2 be so overwhelmed that you burst into tears.
3 end up on the floor in stitches.
4 be absolutely mortified.
5 find that something doesn't live up to the hype.
6 go to a do.
7 end up in floods of tears.
8 witness a bit of a scene.

LISTENING

5 ▶ 14 Listen to two conversations. Answer the questions about each conversation.

1 What kind of night out do they talk about?
2 What other main topic do they discuss?

44

6 ▶ **14** Listen again. Which words and phrases from Exercise 1 are used in each conversation?

7 Complete the sentences from the conversations with the correct prepositions or adverbs. Then look at audio script 14 on page 201 and check your answers.

Conversation 1

1 She's been _____ a lot recently.

2 She soon got _____ it.

3 They went _____ really, really well.

4 He's so full _____ himself, that guy.

5 Hey, talking _____ dancing, are you still going to those tango classes?

6 I'm still a bit prone _____ treading on toes.

Conversation 2

7 It's all _____ hand.

8 It's just that I could do _____ it at the moment.

9 I've got far too much _____.

10 Thanks for being so _____ top of things.

11 Oh, _____ the way, how was your meal the other night?

12 This guy at a table in the corner just suddenly burst _____ screaming at one of the waiters.

8 Work in groups. Discuss the questions.

- Have you ever been to a surprise party? How was it?
- When was the last time you had a very late night? Why?
- How do you usually celebrate your birthday?
- Do you like dancing? What do you usually dance to?
- When was the last time you went out for a meal? Where did you go? What was it like?
- Have you ever complained in a restaurant? If so, why?

DEVELOPING CONVERSATIONS

Commenting on what is said

We use *I bet / imagine*, *must / must've* and *can't / can't have* to comment on what is said.

I bet she was pleased. (= I'm fairly sure she was.)

*You **must be getting** quite good, then.* (= I'm fairly sure you are getting good.)

*That **must've been** quite filling!*

*That **can't have been** much fun.*

We usually respond to comments like these by showing whether we think the comments are accurate or not and then adding follow-up comments of our own.

B: *You must be getting quite good, then.*

A: *I wouldn't go that far. I'm still a bit prone to treading on toes.*

C: *That must've been quite filling!*

D: *It was. I was ready to burst by the end of it all.*

9 Use *must / can't* to rewrite the comments below without changing the basic meaning.

1 I bet that was pretty dull, wasn't it?

2 I bet you're not feeling your best at the moment, are you?

3 I don't imagine he was very pleased when he found out.

4 I imagine you're glad you didn't go now.

5 That must've cost a fortune.

6 She can't have been feeling very well.

7 Judging from his accent, he must be foreign.

8 You can't be serious!

10 ▶ **15** Listen and check your ideas. Which comments in Exercise 9 were accurate, according to the way the other person responded?

11 Work in pairs. Choose four rewritten comments from Exercise 9. Decide what you think was said before each one and how the comments could be responded to if they are accurate – and if they're not.

A: *The guy sitting next to me spent the whole evening talking about golf.*

B: *Wow! That must've been pretty dull.*

A: *Yeah, it was. I had to stop myself from yawning. / You'd think so, wouldn't you, but he was actually pretty funny about it all.*

CONVERSATION PRACTICE

12 Choose one of these tasks.

a Think of a memorable night out you have had. Think about where you went, who with, what it was like, what happened, how you felt, what time you got home, etc.

b Invent a night out. You can imagine it was an amazing night or an awful one. Decide where you went, who with, what it was like, what happened, etc.

13 Now work in pairs. Tell each other about your nights out. Try to use as much language from this lesson as you can. Your partner should ask questions and add comments while listening.

🎥 **11 To watch the video and do the activities, see the DVD ROM.**

OFF THE BEATEN TRACK

READING

1 Work in pairs. List as many famous sites and things to do in London as you can. Then share your ideas with the class. Which places / things to do sound best? Why?

2 Read the introduction to an article about visiting London and explain:

1 the title of the article.

2 what kind of impression of London the writer thinks tourists are getting.

3 Read the rest of the article. Match the headings (a–h) to the parts of the article (1–6). There are two headings you do not need.

a Festive food
b Free view
c Far out night out
d Leisurely stroll
e True insights
f East End playhouse
g Not just chippies
h Quiet night out

4 Work in pairs. Try to remember how the words and phrases in italics were expressed in the article. Then read the article again and check your answers.

1 had never *risked going outside of* Zone 1

2 *people go swimming throughout the year*

3 if you're *a bit hungry*

4 it also *keeps and displays* a collection of household objects

5 *Charlie Chaplin once performed at the theatre*

6 *a typical kind of show in Britain*

7 we've *happily accepted a large variety* of international food

8 it's *almost impossible to logically choose* where to go

9 was *known for being socially deprived*

10 after the usual family visitors *have gone to* bed

5 Work in pairs. Discuss the questions.

• Which two recommendations most appeal to you? Why?

• Which places don't interest you? Why?

• What's the best museum you've been to? What's the most unusual one?

UNDERSTANDING VOCABULARY

Noun + of

In the article, you saw several nouns with *of*. They may describe:

• a group (*herd of cows*).

• number / amount (*all manner of*).

• a part (*the rear of the building*).

• the content (*photographs of domestic life*).

• the thing that was done (*performances of everything from stand-up comedy to opera*).

• the feeling something gives (*the weirdness of a silent disco*).

6 Match the nouns + *of* (1–8) to their endings (a–h) to make noun phrases.

1 sign of
2 tip of
3 floods of
4 bunch of
5 swarm of
6 pleasure of
7 supply of
8 creation of

a goods / blood / labour
b reading / eating / their company
c mosquitoes / flies / wasps
d the EU / jobs / a new art form
e life / things to come / weakness
f my tongue / the iceberg / the pen
g flowers / mates / stuff to do
h complaints / tears / enquiries

7 Work in pairs. Choose a noun phrase from each of the groups in Exercise 6 and make sentences that are true.

GRAMMAR

Noun phrases

We can add a lot of information before and after a main noun in different ways.

A walk will lead to a panorama.

*A **ten-minute** walk **up a steep path** will lead to an **amazing** panorama **of London**.*

8 Work in pairs. Look at the underlined noun phrases in the article. Match each noun phrase (1–9) to one of the ways information is added (a–i).

a adding a name of something to the kind of thing it is

b adding a noun before the main noun to describe it

c adding several adjectives

d using a number + noun compound adjective

e adding a prepositional phrase to show a feature

f a relative clause

g a reduced relative clause using a present (-*ing*) participle

h a reduced relative clause using a past participle

i a reduced relative clause using an adjectival phrase

G Check your ideas on page 171 and do Exercises 1 and 2.

9 Work in pairs. Add information to the subjects and objects in these sentences. Which pair in the class can write the longest correct noun phrases in each case?

1 The museum houses a collection.

2 Man seeks woman.

3 A man has won a prize.

10 With your partner, decide two places to contribute to 'A hidden guide to …' about a city / town you both know. Write two short paragraphs in a similar style to the article. Use extended noun phrases.

G For further practice, see Exercises 3 and 4 on page 172.

A hidden guide to London

DON'T BE A SHEEP! Seeing tourists being guided around London like herds of sheep, you do wonder what impression of London they're getting. They queue for hours outside Madame Tussauds to see a waxwork of Cristiano Ronaldo, eat in the Hard Rock Café, race round the British Museum looking at mummies from Egypt, then buy a postcard of the Queen and London is done. Paris, here we come! I met a foreign businessman recently who'd been coming to London every year for 20 years but had never ventured beyond Zone 1 on the underground or the classic sites. Come on, people! London has so much more to offer! So let's tempt you off the beaten track and leave the hordes of tourists behind.

Hampstead Heath

1   Forget spending a small fortune climbing The Shard in central London – hop on a C2 bus and go to Parliament Hill. A ten-minute walk up a steep path will lead to an amazing panorama of London – on a clear day, anyway. And if it's not clear, you can still stroll round [1]Hampstead Heath with its natural ponds, where some go for a dip all year round. Alternatively, visit [2]the 18th-century stately home, Kenwood House, with its fine collection of art. And if you're feeling peckish, they serve classic English [3]cream teas.

2   Yeah, the British Museum is great, but as more than one person has pointed out, it's not very British. So if you really want to see how we've lived through the ages, you should check out the [4]Geffrye Museum, which contains eleven living rooms from different periods of history. It also houses a collection of household objects and photographs of English domestic life. At the rear of the building, there are four period [5]gardens showing changing trends in that most British of pastimes, gardening.

3   There are all manner of performance spaces outside the West End, but we've chosen The Hackney Empire, a theatre that once hosted Charlie Chaplin. Today, you can see performances of everything from stand-up comedy to opera, but it's perhaps best known for its award-winning Christmas pantomimes. The pantomime is a peculiarly British show loosely based around a fairy tale, with audience participation and satirical jokes, and where the leading man is a woman and the main comic woman character is a man!

4   They say British cuisine is dreadful, which is why we've embraced a huge array of international food. That said, even supposedly typical British dishes like fish and chips originally came from Europe, so perhaps things have always been this way. We'd say it's a toss-up where to go for [6]our best multicultural cheap eats. Go north to Harringay for the best Turkish kebabs. Another option would be to head west to Southall for top South Indian food. While you're there, you could even do [7]a six-hour course with Monisha, where you'll tour the local shops for produce and learn to cook the best curry. And if you really want fish and chips? Toffs of Muswell Hill is a classic [8]'chippie' run by second-generation Greek immigrants!

5   There was a time that Dalston was synonymous with social deprivation, drugs and crime. These days, it's known as one of the hippest [9]places in town, full of trendy bars and restaurants, underground clubs and cool young things hanging out. The only problem is, there's no tube station so it takes a while to get there.

6   So it's not exactly off the beaten track – it's London Zoo – but it sneaks into our list for its great Zoo Late evenings, held throughout the summer after the usual family visitors are tucked up in bed. As well as seeing the animals under the stars, you can enjoy live stand-up and the cool weirdness of a silent disco in which everyone wears headphones (silent apart from some tuneless singing along!).

The Hackney Empire

Cooking curries in London

IT CAME HIGHLY RECOMMENDED

SPEAKING

1 Work in groups. Discuss the questions.

- Look at the photo of a book club meeting. What do you think it involves?
- Do you know anyone who belongs to either a real-world book club or an online one?
- Can you think of three reasons why people might join book clubs?
- What was the last thing you read? Would you recommend it? Why? / Why not?
- How do you usually decide what to read next?

LISTENING

2 ▶ 16 Listen to a radio feature about the explosive growth of book clubs. Find what evidence is given of:

1 Mark Zuckerberg's eccentric resolutions.
2 the difference that the page *A Year of Books* makes to sales.
3 how *A Year of Books* is in keeping with cultural trends.
4 how face-to-face reading groups have thrived.
5 how book clubs can result in increased sales.
6 opposition to the boom in book club membership.
7 the seemingly universal appeal of book clubs.

3 ▶ 16 Match the verbs (1–8) to the words they were used with in the radio feature (a–h). Then listen again and check your answers.

1	vow	a	a marked influence on reading choices
2	get through	b	these trends in a positive light
3	make	c	the power of Facebook
4	have	d	a book every fortnight
5	pick	e	to learn Mandarin Chinese
6	factor in	f	the spread of communal reading
7	see	g	six books a year
8	halt	h	a huge difference to sales

4 Work in groups. Discuss the questions.

- What do you think about Mark Zuckerberg and his resolutions?
- Is reading a big thing in your country? How does it manifest itself?
- Who do you think has the most influence on popular taste in your country? Why?
- Is the influence they have more positive or negative? In what way?
- Have you ever bought anything because of an online recommendation? If so, what?

VOCABULARY Describing books

5 Choose the correct option to complete the book reviews below.

6 Underline any phrases in the book reviews that are new for you. Then compare what you chose with a partner and discuss what they mean.

7 With your partner, discuss the questions.

- Have you read any of the five books? If you have, do you agree with the review?
- If not, which of the books would you most / least like to read? Why?
- Have you ever read anything similar to any of the books described?

SPEAKING

8 Imagine your class has started a book club. Think of the book you would most like other students to read. Who is it by and what is it called? Decide how to describe it. Use some of the language from Exercise 5.

9 Work in groups. Take turns to explain why your book is so good and try to persuade your partners to read your choice first. Then vote to decide which book to read first.

---

1 The Son *Jo Nesbo*

This crime thriller [1]*centres / revolves* on a young man in prison for confessing to crimes he didn't commit. The novel starts slowly, but the pace picks up as the [2]*argument / plot* develops. With a [3]*star / protagonist* who remains thoroughly likeable despite his flaws and its crisp, credible [4]*dialogue / speech*, there's much to enjoy here.

2 Lies My Mother Never Told Me
Kaylie Jones

In this moving [1]*memoir / memory*, Jones confronts her childhood and her troubled relationship with her abusive mother, whose [2]*conflict / struggle* to overcome her alcoholism is explored in heart-wrenching detail. The book [3]*treats / deals* with the themes of acceptance and transcendence and is a real page-turner from start to finish. I can't [4]*suggest / recommend* it highly enough.

3 The Hunger Games *Suzanne Collins*

[1]*Sorting out / Tackling* such issues as poverty and oppression and [2]*basing / revolving* around a televised survival game in which kids fight to the death, this may seem an unlikely best-seller. However, as it [3]*traces / discovers* the influence that society has on the young, it manages to function as a gripping read while also [4]*exploring / finding* teenage identity.

4 Katherine *Anya Seaton*

This vivid portrayal of love and politics in medieval England is [1]*rooted / based* on a true story and manages to [2]*bring / carry* its characters and era to life through its rich, vibrant language. If you believe that love conquers all and enjoy stories [3]*held / set* in the past, then this uplifting [4]*history / tale* may well be for you.

BOOK OF THE WEEK

"CONSTANT SUSPENSE . . . I COULDN'T STOP READING"

THE HUNGER GAMES

SUZANNE COLLINS

5 Things My Girlfriend and I Have Argued About *Mil Millington*

This comic novel is so frequently laugh-out-loud funny that you might not want to read it in public! Told in the [1]*main / first* person, the book explores the many arguments between the [2]*narrator / commentator* and his German girlfriend – to hysterical effect! By [3]*turns / episodes* absurd, dark and full of [4]*insight / judgment*, it's a must-read for anyone who's ever been in a relationship!

6

CONFLICT AND RESOLUTION

IN THIS UNIT YOU LEARN HOW TO:

- handle arguments in a constructive manner
- defend and excuse positions and behaviour
- talk about how you'd like things to be different
- discuss conflict and resolution
- understand and use extended metaphors

SPEAKING

1   Work in pairs. Discuss the questions.

- What do you think the relationship is between the people in the photo? Why?

- What do you think they might be arguing about? What might they be saying?

- Which sentences about arguing below do you agree with? Why?
  - It's healthy to let off steam every once in a while.
  - As soon as you lose your temper, you lose the argument.
  - Sometimes people need a good row to clear the air.
  - Arguing can become addictive and can have a terrible impact on relationships.
  - Raising your voice is a form of aggression.
  - An argument may be unpleasant, but it's often the first step towards a solution.

2   Work with a new partner. Look at the things people often argue about below. Discuss how each might lead to an argument and the kinds of things that might be said during each argument.

careers	politics	silly annoyances
exes	religion	household chores
homework	sport	stress and tiredness
in-laws	kids	time spent together
money	work	

3   Which three things above do you think generally cause the worst arguments? Why?

Accusations and recriminations

CLEAR THE AIR

VOCABULARY
Arguments and discussions

1 Make phrases people may use in arguments by putting the words in brackets in the correct order.

1 I hear what you're saying, but _____ (my / point / view / see / it / try / from / to / of).

2 That's not what I meant at all. _____. (words / my / you're / twisting)

3 _____. (our / crossed / I / we've / got / think / wires) That wasn't my intention at all.

4 Hey, chill! _____. (there's / voice / no / to / raise / need / your) I can hear you perfectly well.

5 I've obviously done something to upset you, so _____ (I / clear / we / think / air / should / the).

6 OK. You've made your point and I heard you. _____? (just / now / on / can / we / move)

7 _____. (wrong / sorry / out / came / all / that) Just pretend I didn't say that.

8 Alright! Calm down! _____! (world / it's / not / end / of / the / the)

9 It's done. Just forget about it. _____. (milk / no / there's / crying / spilt / over / point)

10 We're getting nowhere here. _____. (circles / going / just / round / we're / in) Can we just agree to disagree?

2 Work in pairs. For each phrase, decide:

1 whether it could be translated directly into your language.

2 whether you think saying this would calm an argument or make things worse – and why.

3 Look at these other phrases used in discussions. What word can complete all of them?

1 What's the _____ you're trying to make?

2 Doesn't that prove my _____?

3 I think you're missing the _____.

4 OK. Fair enough. I take your _____.

5 I wish you'd just get to the _____.

4 Work in pairs. Close your books. How many of the fifteen phrases from Exercises 1 and 3 can you remember?

5 Work in groups. Think of a time you might have said one of the following. Then tell each other what happened.

1 There's no point crying over spilt milk.

2 I think we've got our wires crossed.

3 Just pretend I didn't say that.

4 We're going round in circles.

5 I take your point.

LISTENING

6 ▶ 17 Listen to two conversations in which arguments occur. What is the main problem between the two people in each conversation?

7 ▶ 17 Decide if the following refer to Conversation 1, Conversation 2 or neither. Then listen again and check your answers.

Someone:

a has tripped over.

b has lost business.

c says they're very busy.

d says something sarcastic.

e has failed to pass on a message.

f takes offence.

g has spent money they didn't have.

h deliberately broke something.

i has had a series of difficulties over the day.

j was annoyed about a previous conversation.

8 Work in pairs. Discuss the questions.

• How are the two arguments resolved?

• Do you think the underlying problems have actually been resolved? Why? / Why not?

• Do you know anyone who is untidy, sarcastic, a control freak or easily offended? Does it bother you? Why? / Why not?

• Have you ever had any recurrent arguments with anyone? What about? Did you resolve them eventually?

DEVELOPING CONVERSATIONS

Defending and excusing

We often use the patterns *It's not as though / if ...* and *It's just that ...* to defend and excuse our position and / or behaviour.

A: *I almost broke my neck!*

B: *OK. Sorry.* **It's not as though** *I did it deliberately.* (= I didn't do it deliberately.)

It came out wrong. I'm sorry. **It's just that** *it's been a long day and this was the last straw.*

9 Work in pairs. Complete these exchanges with your own ideas.

1 A: There's no need to shout!

 B: I know. I'm sorry. It's just that ...

2 A: Why did you buy that?

 B: What's the problem? It's not as if ...

 A: I know. It's just that ...

3 A: Why can't someone else do it? It's not as though ...

 B: I know. It's just that ...

4 A: I didn't want to ask you.

 B: Why not? It's not as though ...

 A: I guess. It's just that ...

5 A: I can't believe you did that.

 B: It's not as though ...

10 Work with a new partner. Practise reading out the exchanges in Exercise 9. You may need to give different responses depending on what your partner says.

GRAMMAR

Wish and *if only*

We often use *wish* or *if only* to talk about things we want to be different. As these are hypothetical ideas, we use past forms (as we do in some conditional sentences). In conversation, *wish* may be followed by only a modal / auxiliary verb.

11 Work in pairs. Complete the sentences from the conversations with one word in each space. Then explain the function of each of the gapped sentences.

1 A: If only you ¹_____ put things away properly! ...

 B: I was going to take it to my room ...

 A: Well, I wish you ²_____.

2 D: What? You're joking?

 C: I wish I ³_____.

3 C: I wish you ⁴_____ said something sooner.

 D: I ⁵_____ have, but you hardly come out of that office.

Check your ideas on page 172 and do Exercise 1.

12 Choose three of the comments below. Write three-line dialogues based around them.

A: *I can't believe you left the keys at home!*

B: *I know, but I wish you would drop it!*

A: *I would if I hadn't reminded you three times to get them!*

1 I wish you would drop it!

2 I wish I had. The whole thing's a nightmare!

3 To be perfectly honest, I wish I didn't have to.

4 If only you'd mentioned that an hour ago!

5 I wish I could!

6 We wouldn't have if you hadn't been so keen!

13 Work in groups. Use different patterns with *wish* to tell your partners something:

1 you regret (not) doing.

2 you regret not being able to do.

3 you'd like to be different about your life.

4 you'd like to be able to do.

5 you'd like to be different in the world.

6 you'd like to be different about someone you know.

For further practice, see Exercise 2 on page 172.

CONVERSATION PRACTICE

14 Work in pairs. You are going to roleplay two conversations.

Student A: read File 13 on page 187.

Student B: read File 14 on page 188.

Spend a few minutes planning what you are going to say and what language from this lesson you will use.

15 Now roleplay the conversations.

🎥 12 To watch the video and do the activities, see the DVD ROM.

WAR AND PEACE

READING

1 You are going to read an article about the growth of the academic subject Peace Studies. Look at the photo opposite and discuss the questions.

- What do you think these Peace Studies students are doing – and why?
- Have you ever heard of this subject before? What do you think it involves?
- What kind of work do you imagine it would help graduates get?
- Do you think it would be a good degree to do? Why? / Why not?

2 Read the article and answer the questions in your own words.

1 What is the Tolstoy Cup and how did it get its name?
2 What does Stephen Pinker claim has led to a reduction in the levels of violence?
3 How and why has the image of Peace Studies changed?
4 What kinds of topics does the subject cover?
5 What are the main goals of peacebuilding?

3 Work in pairs. Discuss why the writer:

1 begins by talking about the Tolstoy Cup.
2 mentions the results of previous matches.
3 tells us about Stephen Pinker's book.
4 quotes George Orwell.
5 mentions hippies, John Lennon and nuclear weapons.
6 talks about the content of Peace Studies courses and peacebuilding.
7 finishes by talking about the Peace Studies footballers.

4 Find the nouns or noun phrases that go with these adjectives in the article. Then work with your partner and think of true examples for five of these collocations.

annual	dramatic	aggressive	legitimate
notable	associated	former	lasting
historical	diverse		

5 Work in pairs. Discuss the questions.

- Can you think of any other notable peace campaigners? What were their main achievements?
- Do you believe Stephen Pinker's claim that we are less violent? Why? / Why not?
- How do you think the five factors he mentioned may have helped to reduce violence?
- Which factor do you think has had the biggest effect? Why?
- Which of the peacebuilding goals do you think is hardest to implement? Why?

VOCABULARY Conflict and resolution

6 Put each group of words into the most likely order they happen, starting with the words in bold.

1 **be invaded** / defend yourself / join forces / defeat the enemy / gain ground / lose ground
2 **tension rises** / negotiate a ceasefire / the conflict escalates / fighting breaks out / war rages
3 **be surrounded** / be under siege for weeks / run out of food / become a prisoner of war / surrender
4 **plant a bomb** / put on trial / arrest / cause casualties and fatalities / track down / claim responsibility
5 **plot to overthrow the president** / return to democracy / seize control of the country / suffer sanctions / stage a coup / undermine economic stability
6 **receive reports of human rights violations** / seek a UN resolution / withdraw troops / send in international troops / re-establish security
7 **declare a ceasefire** / restart negotiations / sign a peace agreement / begin negotiations / talks break down / achieve a resolution

7 Work in groups. Think of examples of the following and talk about them in as much detail as you can using some of the new vocabulary from Exercise 6.

- an invasion
- a civil war
- a terrorist attack
- a coup
- an international intervention
- a peace process

PEACE TO DEFEAT WAR
YET AGAIN?

This weekend sees the renewal of one of the great college sports rivalries. No, not the Oxford-Cambridge boat race down the River Thames but rather the return of the Tolstoy Cup. Established as an annual event back in 2007, the Cup is a football match between students from the Department of Peace Studies at the University of Bradford and the Department of War Studies at King's College, London, and takes its name from the Russian author of the 1869 novel *War and Peace*.

Over the years, the Peace Studies teams have featured a suitably international range of players, including several women, and wear the names of notable peace campaigners such as M. L. King and Gandhi on the backs of their light blue shirts. In what could be seen as an ironic inversion of the world off the pitch, Peace has defeated War every single year except one.

In fact, though, as Stephen Pinker observed in his book *The Better Angels of Our Nature*, despite appearances to the contrary, violence is actually in decline in many domains, including military conflict, murder, torture, and the treatment of children, animals and minority groups. Pinker credits five main historical forces with having brought about this dramatic reduction: the growth of nation states and legal systems; the increasingly global nature of commercial transactions; an increased respect for the interests and values of women; the spread of mass media and greater human mobility; and the increased importance of reason, which he claims helps us to see violence as a problem that can be solved rather than as a battle that has to have a winner.

While football remains, as George Orwell once noted, 'the continuation of war by other means', the increasing desire to solve conflict by means other than war can be seen in the huge growth of Peace Studies and the changing attitudes towards it as an academic subject. When Bradford University opened the UK's first school of Peace Studies in 1973, the subject was seen as a fringe area of study and Peace Studies students were stereotyped as hippies prone to lazing around, hugging one another and listening to John Lennon while dreaming of how nice the world would be if only everyone could just get on. However, the 1970s and 1980s saw a huge increase in the number of nuclear weapons – brought about by the ongoing Cold War freeze in US-Soviet relations – and the associated threat of mass destruction served to accelerate the expansion of the subject. Now in the 21st century, there are study institutes all over the world and courses exploring an incredibly diverse range of topics.

So what do Peace Studies programmes cover? Well, everything from terrorism, poverty and social inequality to group dynamics and aggressive tendencies in human nature. Courses today stress the complexity of conflict and the way such global crises as hunger, climate change, resource shortages and so on all feed in. At the very heart of the subject lies peacebuilding, a notion which contains lessons for all of us as we seek to ensure the world our children inherit continues to be less violent than the one we were born into. Peacebuilding works to ensure the surrender of weapons and reintegration of former soldiers into society. At the same time, it encourages the creation of better infrastructure and of legitimate state institutions. Finally, it attempts to stimulate community dialogue, bridge building, broader economic development, and so on.

Having seen previous Peace Studies players striving to win the battle on the football field, I can only hope they bring the same desire to the fight for long-term, lasting peace once they graduate.

A WAR OF WORDS

UNDERSTANDING VOCABULARY

Extended metaphors

We create metaphors by exploiting basic word meanings in order to refer to something else – because we think these things share qualities. So we *spend money*, but then we also *spend time*. The idea that time is equivalent to money is extended to many other verbs (*waste, use, lose*, etc.).

1 **Work in pairs. Read the short article about another extended metaphor. Answer the questions.**

   1 In what areas of life do we use words connected with war?

   2 Do these metaphors exist in your language?

   3 Do you agree they could impact on attitudes and behaviour? If yes, how? If not, why not?

For most of us, war and conflict is not something we have experienced directly, yet they have become a major part of how we describe many aspects of our world.

Perhaps unsurprisingly, in sport we talk about *attacking* and *defending*. A team may even *lay siege to* the goal, while their opponents refuse to *surrender* their lead. However, similar language is also found in health and medicine, where people talk about *battling* cancer, and business, where a firm might *launch* an *aggressive* marketing *campaign*. It's used in court, where *hostile witnesses* and lawyers try to *destroy* each other's arguments, and in politics, where governments may try to *combat* poverty by *targeting* their efforts on certain groups, and protesters (like soldiers) may *march* to defend rights that are *under attack*.

Most of the time, we are probably unaware of these metaphors, but some argue they have an impact on attitudes and the way we behave in areas such as relationships, medicine and politics – and that we should seek to express our ideas in more constructive ways.

2 **Put these words into the correct place in the sentences below. The first one is done for you.**

army	challenging	defences	target
guns	~~war~~	bombarding	invasion
capture	battle		

1 They've been <u>engaged in a fierce price</u> ⟨*war* which has <u>hit profits</u>.

2 The party has recruited a huge of volunteers for the campaign.

3 They are desperately trying to attract female voters and have been them with messages seeking support.

4 They're gaining ground in the polls and hope to 20 new seats.

5 They have a huge sales force compared to ours so we have to really our efforts.

6 She has won her fight to stop the photos being published, which she said was an of privacy.

7 All the big are through to the semi-finals of the competition so it's going to be a tight battle to get through.

8 The fifth set became a of wills as both players tired and it was Murray who finally surrendered.

9 They've had to join forces to fight off new businesses that are their position in the market.

10 Tiredness can often reduce our against viruses that attack our bodies.

The New Zealand national men's rugby union team, known as the All Blacks, perform a *haka* (a Māori challenge) before each international match.

3 Work in pairs. Compare your answers. Decide which area of life is being discussed in each sentence.

4 Underline the words in each sentence that are part of the same metaphor. The first one is done for you.

5 With your partner, answer the questions.

1 What else can reduce your defences against a virus?

2 How can we combat poverty / disease / addiction?

3 Who are the big guns in sport in your country?

4 Have you ever had to battle for something? What? Did you win or give in?

5 What companies, political parties or ideas are gaining ground at the moment? Why?

LISTENING

6 Work in groups. You are going to hear four news stories based on the headlines below. Discuss what you think has happened. Try to use vocabulary from Exercises 1 and 2.

SOFT DRINK SPY TRIAL STARTS

TV presenter defends himself against harassment allegations

Government policy hit by victory for liberty groups

PEACE BREAKS OUT OVER PIG STATUE

7 ▶ **18** Listen to the four news stories and find out what actually happened. Then work in pairs and rank the stories from 1 (= least serious) to 4 (= most serious).

8 ▶ **18** Listen again. Which sentences are true?

1 a Dan Craddock has been found guilty of spying.

  b Mr Craddock was a manager for Pit-Pots.

  c Jazz Drinks has a bigger market share now.

2 a Jonas Bakeman is in danger of losing his job.

  b Bakeman spoke to the press and fully apologised.

  c Ms Campbell claims she didn't initiate the affair.

3 a A court decided people didn't have to submit to body scans at airports.

  b One lobby group funded the woman's defence.

  c The government has accepted the ruling.

4 a Pig farming is an important industry in Paulston.

  b Both sides in the dispute inflicted some kind of damage.

  c The sides agreed a settlement between themselves.

9 ▶ **19** Work in pairs. Try to complete the full noun phrases from the news stories. Then listen and check your answers.

1 The two companies have been engaged in a _____ battle _____.

2 ... to pass on information _____ and _____ for _____ year.

3 He released a statement _____.

4 She had been bombarded with emails and _____ messages _____.

5 Campaigners have claimed victory in their battle _____ in _____.

6 The scanners play a _____ role _____ the _____ terrorism.

7 ... a statue of St John of Bidshire, the _____ local farmer Tim Langford.

8 It stood as a _____ symbol of the _____ Paulston is famous.

10 Work in groups. Discuss in as much detail as you can any stories you've heard about the following:

- spying
- celebrity affairs
- court cases and appeals
- community disputes

SPEAKING

11 As a class, choose two of the following statements to debate. Then divide into groups – half the class will agree with the two statements and the other half will disagree.

- You should never negotiate with terrorists.
- There should never be international intervention in a country's internal affairs.
- Wars are a necessary evil.
- You can't win the war on drugs.
- Peaceful protests are the only ones that work.
- Companies are too concerned with market share and growth.
- There should be more restrictions on advertising.

12 In your group, prepare your ideas and think how you might knock down your opponent's arguments. Choose a spokesperson for your group.

13 Now have the debate about the first statement. The spokesperson for the 'for' group should speak for two minutes. Then the 'against' spokesperson should speak. When they have finished, anyone can comment or ask questions.

14 Repeat Exercise 13 with the other statement.

VIDEO 3

THE BRAILLE HUBBLE

1 Work in pairs. Discuss the questions.

- How do you feel when you look at photos like the one above? Why?
- Have you ever used a telescope? What did you look at?
- How much do you know about space?
- Do you ever watch TV programmes / films or read books about space?
- What do you think we can learn from the exploration of space?

2 📹 13 Watch the video about a book of photographs of space. Find out:

1 who the book is aimed at.

2 how it works.

3 how the students have influenced the creation of the book.

3 📹 13 Work in pairs. Discuss your answers to the questions, then watch again and check your answers.

1 Are all the students completely blind?

2 Why did the photo showing different gases cause problems?

3 What does author Noreen Grice believe the book can achieve?

4 How did the students' attitude to the images change? Why?

5 What was the biggest problem with the early images?

4 Complete the sentences about the video with these nouns.

| feel | prototype | room | way |
| place | ridges | sheet | window |

1 The photos have found their _____ into a classroom for visually impaired students.

2 Each photo is overlaid with a transparent plastic _____.

3 The plastic overlay is covered with raised dots and _____.

4 The images help people with vision loss get a _____ for the far reaches of space.

5 The images may help people to better grasp their _____ in the universe.

6 Feedback from the students helped to shape the _____ of the book.

7 Later versions of the images left more _____ to manoeuvre.

8 The Hubble Telescope images provide a _____ on the wonders of space.

5 Work in groups. Discuss the questions.

- Do you know of any special schools for people with disabilities?
- What are the pros and cons of educating people with disabilities in special schools?
- How easy do you think it is for people with disabilities to get work in your country?
- What facilities are there for people with disabilities in your town / city? How could they be improved?
- Can you think of any well-known deaf or blind people? How did they become famous?

UNDERSTANDING FAST SPEECH

6 📹 14 Listen to an extract from the video said at natural pace. Try to write down what you hear. Then compare your ideas with a partner.

7 📹 15 Try again. This time you will hear a slower version of the extract.

8 Check your ideas in File 10 on page 189. Groups of words are marked with / and pauses are marked //. Stressed sounds are in CAPITALS. Practise saying the extract.

REVIEW 3

GRAMMAR AND UNDERSTANDING
VOCABULARY

1 Complete the text with one word in each space.

I've always wished I [1]_____ get a book published and last month I finally [2]_____. The book is a novel [3]_____ an old woman [4]_____ fights a six-year [5]_____ to stop her home being destroyed by developers. The sales have been good, so let's hope that's a sign of things to [6]_____ as I'd love to write full time. Unfortunately, [7]_____ is fierce among authors and the publishers are also engaged in a price [8]_____, so it's only really the [9]_____ guns of fiction who make any money. If [10]_____ I was one of them!

2 Complete the second sentence so that it has a similar meaning to the first sentence using the word given. Do not change the word given. You must use between three and five words, including the word given.

1 Many people emailed us complaining about the service.
We _____ about the service. **FLOODS**

2 When the Euro was created, prices rose in some countries.
Prices rose in some countries _____ Euro. **OF**

3 I don't think we have seen anything like the whole story.
Sadly, I think this is only _____. **TIP**

4 I hate how they're constantly sending me all these emails.
I wish they _____ all these emails. **BOMBARD**

5 It was a mistake not to work together earlier.
I wish we _____ earlier. **FORCES**

6 The course lasts two weeks and all the tutors are experts.
It's a _____ experts. **BY**

3 Choose the correct option.

1 I agreed to do it, but now I wish I *haven't / didn't / hadn't*.

2 The opposition are gaining *territory / ground / share* in the polls.

3 A huge *army / herd / swarm* of volunteers helped out during the Olympics.

4 The exhibition contains Chinese artifacts *date / dated / dating* back 3,000 years.

5 We took a guided tour *Jones Travel / from the hotel / featured actors*.

4 Change the information around the nouns in bold to create a new sentence.

The Oscar-winning director **Joel Riley**, whose latest documentary *Sick Life* is currently on release, **gives a talk** at the Barbican tonight, explaining his take on the current state of the film industry in the UK.

VOCABULARY

5 What is the connection between each set of words? Think of a verb or adjective collocation for each noun.

1 flaw / plot / protagonist / insight / memoir

2 siege / talks / sanction / casualties / ceasefire

6 Match the verbs (1–10) with the collocates (a–j).

1	explore	a	a bomb / the idea
2	plant	b	troops / the accusation
3	seek	c	the hype / my expectations
4	withdraw	d	the theme / English identity
5	raise	e	into bed / along the floor
6	clear	f	a scene / fatalities
7	twist	g	the air / the stage
8	crawl	h	my words / the top off
9	live up to	i	support / to solve the conflict
10	cause	j	your voice / your hand

7 Complete the sentences with a preposition in each space.

1 I was bored _____ _____ my mind.

2 Try and see it _____ my point of view.

3 Listen, there's no point crying _____ spilt milk.

4 I think we're just going round _____ circles here.

5 The story revolves _____ life in one London street.

6 He just burst _____ tears when I told him.

8 Complete the sentences. Use the word in brackets to form a word that fits in the space.

1 It's just silly _____ which set off most arguments. (annoy)

2 The whole region wants to seek a _____ to the conflict. (resolve)

3 No-one has claimed _____ for the bombing. (responsible)

4 Hopefully, the agreement will bring _____ peace. (last)

5 The experience was quite _____ – I couldn't speak. (overwhelm)

6 The president scored a _____ success in the negotiations. (note)

9 Complete the text with one word in each space. The first letters are given.

The other day I watched the 1964 film *Seven Days in May*. It [1]tr_____ the plot by some US generals to [2]ov_____ the President after he [3]s_____ an agreement with the Soviet Union to disarm. As debate [4]ra_____ over the treaty, some generals see it as [5]su_____ to the communists and un[6]_____ the security of the country, so they plan to [7]st_____ a coup and [8]se_____ control of the communication systems in order to stop the treaty's implementation. The film follows the race to [9]t_____ d_____ all the plotters and [10]de_____ them. I thought it was quite [11]gr_____ but my son was [12]ya_____ most of the way through it!

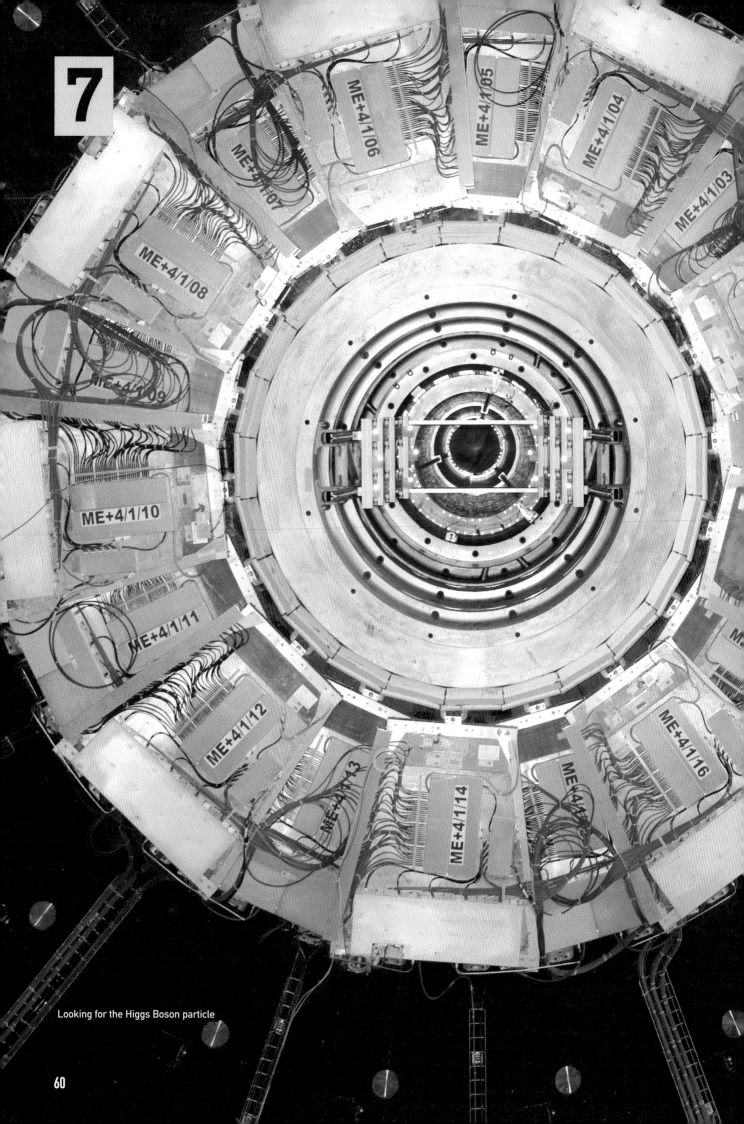

7

Looking for the Higgs Boson particle

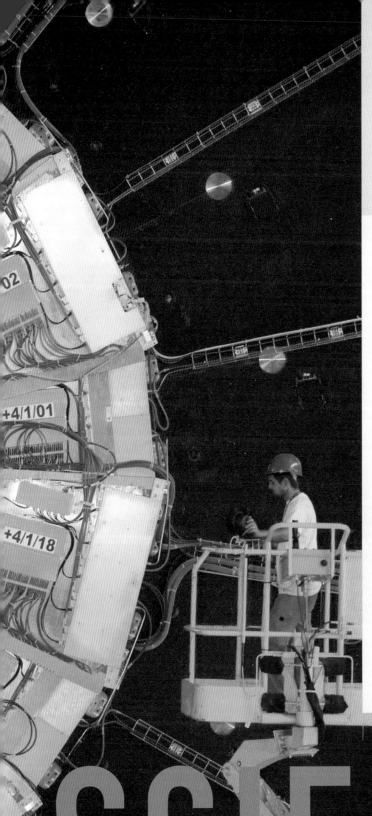

IN THIS UNIT YOU LEARN HOW TO:

- discuss different areas of work in the field of science
- explain and discuss news stories about science
- express surprise and disbelief
- talk about science-fiction films
- form nouns and adjectives
- discuss the uses and abuses of statistics

SPEAKING

1   Work in pairs. Discuss the questions.

- The photo shows the Hadron Collider in Geneva. What do you know about its history, its size, what it is, how it works and what it's being used to research?

- Would you like to work in an environment like this? Why? / Why not?

- Do you know of any other major research projects going on anywhere in the world?

- To what degree do you see science as a force for good?

- What do you think are the most important scientific discoveries of recent times? Why?

2   Work with a new partner. Discuss the questions.

- Who are the most famous scientists you can think of? What are they famous for?

- What do you know about each of the different kinds of scientist below?

agricultural scientist	hydrologist
anthropologist	immunologist
astronomer	marine biologist
neurologist	military scientist
geologist	educational psychologist

- What's the main point of each job?

- Do you know anyone who works in the field of science? What do they do?

SCIENCE AND RESEARCH

IT'S A SLIPPERY SLOPE

VOCABULARY Talking about science

1   Replace the words and phrases in italics with the correct form of these synonyms.

adverse	insert	carry out	remove
devise	reproduce	disorder	root
due	a slippery slope	lead to	step forward

1   It's a major *breakthrough* in the fight against AIDS.

2   They basically need to address the *underlying* cause of the phenomenon.

3   For his homework the other day, my son had to *extract* DNA from a banana.

4   They *stuck* probes into the brains of rats.

5   To me, this experiment represents *the thin end of the wedge*.

6   Researchers *undertook* the survey to establish a link between attitudes and health.

7   The findings could *pave the way for* new techniques.

8   Other scientists are yet to successfully *duplicate* the results under laboratory conditions.

9   The lack of funding was *down* to the radical nature of the theory.

10 There are concerns about *negative* side effects of the procedure.

11 The study found that the genetic *condition* was more prevalent than first thought.

12 Scientists have *created* a way to detect seismic waves before earthquakes hit.

2   **Work in pairs. Test each other.**

Student A: say the words and phrases in italics in Exercise 1.

Student B: close your books. Say the synonyms.

LISTENING

3 Work in pairs. Look at the newspaper headlines below. Discuss what you think each of these true stories is about. What research / experiments do you think may have been carried out in each case? What purposes might the results serve?

1 Hormone inhaler may help autism

2 Cat owners are more intelligent

3 Backing for space sun shield

4 Gay penguins adopt chick

5 DNA fragrance with the smell of Elvis Presley

6 Scientists breed see-through frogs and fish

7 Scientist gets funding for time-reversal experiment

8 Scientists successfully transplant mosquito nose

4 ▶ 20 Listen to two conversations about news stories related to the headlines in Exercise 3. Take notes on the stories.

5 Work in pairs. Compare your notes and check what you understood about each news story.

6 ▶ 20 Try to complete the sentences from the conversations with phrases. Then listen and check your answers.

Conversation 1

1 _____ do they do that?

2 They extract the DNA from the receptors, or something, and then insert it into the eggs. It's _____, really.

3 It sounds a bit peculiar, _____. I mean, what's the point?

4 A: They could use those smells to manufacture traps ...

   B: OK. I suppose _____. I have to say, though, I still find all that gene manipulation a bit worrying.

5 B: One moment it's mosquito noses, the next they'll be engineering babies.

   A: _____! It's hardly the same thing!

Conversation 2

6 How on earth are they going to build something that big, _____ get it up there?

7 C: It'd take ten years to make.

   D: _____, then!

8 _____! What a waste of money!

9 C: They wouldn't have just made it up.

   D: Pah! _____ whether the whole climate change thing isn't all just a scam.

10 C: The evidence is pretty conclusive.

    D: _____?

7 Work in pairs. Discuss the questions.

• Which of the two stories you heard about is more important? Why?

• Do you have any concerns about genetic research?

• Is there any other kind of scientific research that you think is unethical?

• How far do you believe in climate change?

• Why do you think some people refuse to believe in things like climate change, despite fairly conclusive evidence?

• Are there any scientific theories that you – or people you know – are sceptical about? If so, why?

DEVELOPING CONVERSATIONS

Expressing surprise and disbelief

When we talk to people we know well, we can show surprise or disbelief by adding *on earth* to questions.

How on earth do they do that?

How on earth are they going to build something that big?

8 ▶ 21 Listen and repeat the questions. Pay attention to the stress and intonation.

9 Write questions using *on earth* in response to these comments.

1 We're developing a Nanobridge.

2 They've managed to grow a human ear on a rat's back.

3 Their head office is in Flitwick.

4 They're planning to send farm animals into space.

5 I've decided to take part in a drugs trial.

6 Apparently, they've bred see-through frogs to sell.

10 Work in pairs. Take turns to say the comments in Exercise 9. Your partner should respond with their question. Continue each conversation for as long as you can.

CONVERSATION PRACTICE

11 Work in groups of three. You are each going to read two true science news stories related to the headlines in Exercise 3.

Student A: look at File 15 on page 187.

Student B: look at File 16 on page 190.

Student C: look at File 17 on page 195.

Read your stories and make sure you understand them.

12 Now close your books. Take turns to start conversations by saying *Did you read that thing about ...?* Your partners should ask questions and make comments to find out more. Discuss your opinions about each of the stories.

🎥 16 To watch the video and do the activities, see the DVD ROM.

THE TEST OF TIME

SPEAKING

1 Work in groups. Discuss the questions.

- Do you like science fiction? Why? / Why not?

- Have you seen or read any of these sci-fi films or books? If yes, what did you think of them?
  - *The Time Machine*   - *Avatar*
  - *Star Wars*   - *Godzilla*
  - *The Stepford Wives* - *Interstellar*

- Are there any famous sci-fi books or films in your language? What are they about?

- Do you think any predictions in sci-fi films have – or could – come true?

READING

2 Read the article about science-fiction films. Decide:

1 what mark out of five you think the reviewer would give for each film – and why.

2 if you agree with the reviewer's idea of what makes science fiction great.

3 According to the article, are the sentences true (T), false (F) or not mentioned (N)?

1 *Gojira* was a commercial failure.

2 The new *Godzilla* has better special effects than the first movie.

3 Countries were competing to get more nuclear weapons in the 50s.

4 People don't worry as much about nuclear weapons as they used to.

5 The Stepford wives do whatever their husbands want.

6 Joanna is killed at the end of *The Stepford Wives*.

7 There have been real stories of misuse of personal online information.

8 The writer of the article is against government control of the Internet.

4 Work in pairs. Discuss the questions.

- If you have seen any of the films mentioned, do you agree with the interpretations of them?

- Do you agree nuclear war is not a big worry these days?

- Do you agree that the stereotypes of the Stepford wives have disappeared?

- Does the Web really connect and liberate people? Is there no role for external control?

5 Complete the sentences with words from the article. The first letter of each word is given.

1 The film p_____ us to speculate about the role and limits of science.

2 The series r_____ people's attitudes towards women at the time.

3 The film a_____ the issue of old age.

4 As the plot u_____, the computer begins to take increasing control.

5 When it c_____ _____, the film created a storm.

6 Although it's around 40 years old, the film has s_____ the test of time.

7 The story r_____ with many people at the time.

8 The plot has distinct p_____ with the story of *Macbeth*.

9 The story can be seen as a m_____ for the struggle for freedom.

10 The ending leaves a number of plot strands h_____.

6 Work in groups. Discuss films, books or TV series that fit the descriptions in Exercise 5.

UNDERSTANDING VOCABULARY

Forming nouns and adjectives

There are regular ways of changing the endings of basic words when we want to change word class (noun, verb, adjective, etc.). For example, *colonial exploitation* is based on *colony* and *exploit*. However, remember that often no changes are needed.

remake the film / the **remake** wasn't very good.

7 Complete the rules with the words *nouns*, *adjectives* or *verbs*.

1 _____ based on _____ often have the following endings: *-al, -ial, -y, -ic, -ical, -less, -ful*.

2 _____ based on _____ often have the following endings: *-ive, -ative, -ed, -ing, -able, -ant*.

3 _____ based on _____ often have the following endings: *-ity, -ness, -ance, -ence*.

4 _____ based on _____ often have the following endings: *-ment, -ion, -ation, -ance*.

8 Correct the words with the wrong form in the sentences below. Don't remove or add any extra words.

1 I don't get the point of films about time travel when it's a complete impossible.

2 I hate the utter stupid of action films. They're just meaningless.

3 The technology advances made over the last 50 years are incredibly impressing.

4 The level of ignorant of science among the public is a big concern.

5 Invest in space exploring is a total waste of money!

6 There's great reluctant to take prevention measures against global warming.

7 Scientists are not sufficiently reflect about the implying of their research.

8 I'm a bit cynic about drug companies' involve in medicine research.

9 Work in groups. Discuss how far you agree with each of the statements in Exercise 8.

GODZILLA
All roar and no bite

Godzilla is high on action but fails to speak to us as great sci-fi should, says Malcolm French

Perhaps the only good thing about watching Gareth Edwards' remake of *Godzilla* is it prompted me to speculate about what really makes sci-fi great. No doubt some ambitious movie executive, hearing of the original *Godzilla*'s box office success, saw the 1950s film, with its laughably unrealistic monster knocking down a model of Tokyo, and thought, 'We could do this better, make it more real, more impressive.' Of course, in terms of special effects they have, but with its super CGI and explosions that blast your senses for 90 minutes this new *Godzilla* entirely misses the point.

The original Japanese film, *Gojira*, was made in 1954 at the time of an accelerating arms race and America testing nuclear weapons over the Pacific Ocean. In the film, Godzilla was a product of these tests – a sea creature mutated by radiation and roused from the deep to attack Japan. Less than ten years after the devastation wreaked by atomic bombs over Hiroshima and Nagasaki, the film reflected the real, deep fears in Japan at the time. Edwards' *Godzilla* refers back to these origins, but the film's message simply doesn't carry the same weight. Few people these days would place nuclear war high on their list of worries for the world so it all becomes rather meaningless and merely addresses teenagers' apparently infinite desire for noise and violence.

Great sci-fi speaks to the society of the day and for that reason some films are resistant to updates. *The Stepford Wives* is another case in point. The story tells of a vibrant young professional woman, Joanna, who moves to the small suburban town of Stepford with her husband. The place is full of 'perfect-looking' women who do housework and shopping and submit to their husbands' wills. Joanna rebels against this and, with two other recently-arrived friends, sets up a women's liberation group. As the plot unfolds, we discover that the Stepford wives are in fact robots controlled by the leader of a men's social club, who threatens to kill Joanna and her feminist friends. When the film came out in the mid-70s, these tensions between the traditional image of a wife, a growing feminist movement and an oppressive male society were very real. Almost 40 years later when it was remade, these stereotypes had all but disappeared and so a chilling thriller became a lame comedy.

Still, one story that has stood the test of time is James Cameron's *Avatar*. On its release, the film's incredible 3D world created much hype, but more importantly it also resonated with the political situation of the day. The depiction of humans invading a planet to exploit its natural resources had obvious parallels with colonial exploitation and came in the midst of the Iraq War, which many saw as being motivated by a Western desire to control oil supplies.

However, *Avatar* can also be seen as a metaphor for the ongoing struggles for control of the Internet, especially in the light of recent revelations about companies exploiting private data and governments spying. The planet in *Avatar* is a living network that the natives plug into through what appear to be fibre-optic cables. In this metaphor, the violent invaders are the government, intent on disrupting the freedom of Internet users. Cameron clearly presents an unfettered world-wide Web as the ideal: the invaders are sent packing and the main human protagonist fully integrates himself with the Web by *becoming* his avatar. However, like all the best sci-fi, the film also leaves some questions hanging. How real is the online world? Does the Web really connect and liberate people? Is there no role for external control?

Unfortunately, the only question *Godzilla* left me with was: 'Has anyone got any paracetamol?'

VITAL STATISTICS

SPEAKING

1 **Work in groups. Discuss the questions.**

- Do you think you're good at using and understanding maths, data and statistics?
- What do you think are the most important uses of data and statistics?
- Do you have to use data or statistics in your work / studies? If so, to do what?
- Can you think of times in your daily life when you're exposed to statistics?

VOCABULARY Statistics

2 **Complete the sentences with these nouns.**

anomaly	ends	link
belief	evidence	research
correlation	interest	scrutiny

1 **Contrary to popular** _____, the latest statistics show crime has been falling and not getting worse, as some newspapers suggest.

2 The _____ they carried out is **fundamentally flawed**. The sample group wasn't chosen at **random** – they were **self-selected**.

3 Because **a number of variables** weren't covered by the data, it's difficult to **establish a causal** _____ **between** gaming and bad behaviour.

4 There is **conflicting** _____. Some data shows a correlation, some doesn't.

5 The data showed **a negative** _____ **between** income **and** birth rate: the richer the country, the lower the birth rate.

6 The research didn't come up with the 'right' result so the company **twisted the figures to suit its own** _____.

7 As it's the run-up to the election, the government **has a vested** _____ **in** removing people from the unemployment figures.

8 The figures **don't stand up to** _____ when you look at them closely. They're full of holes.

9 It's too early to say if these two figures are part of a new **upward trend** or whether they are **a statistical** _____.

3 **Work in pairs. Use some of the language in bold in Exercise 2 to discuss why it might be important to ask these questions about research.**

1 Who was the research commissioned by?

2 How was the data collected?

3 How big was the sample?

4 Has the research been peer reviewed?

5 Are the figures presented in their full context?

6 Does the data explain the conclusions?

LISTENING

4 ▶ 22 **Listen to an extract from a radio programme about statistics. Why is each question in Exercise 3 important to consider when talking about statistics?**

5 ▶ 22 **Work in pairs. Why were the groups of numbers and statistics below mentioned? Listen again and check your ideas.**

1 60%, 2, 50% and 25%

2 50 and 5,000

3 10,000, 12,000 and 20%

4 1,000, 1,400 and 40%

5 twice and 1,600

6 50%

6 **Work in pairs. Discuss the questions.**

- Which do you think is the most important question to ask about research? Why?
- What organisations commission research? What about? Is it all equally trustworthy?
- What other correlations about what makes people healthy or ill have you heard of? Has a causal link been proved yet? Why? / Why not?
- Have you heard of any politicians using statistics that don't stand up to scrutiny?
- Have you heard of any other stories about statistics or conclusions being twisted? What happened?
- What downward and upward trends have you heard of recently? Do you know what caused them?

GRAMMAR

Passives

We use passives to focus attention on who or what an action affects. Passive verb forms use the verb *be* + past participle. However, other passive constructions are also commonly used.

7 Work in pairs. Look at the sentences from the listening and do the following:

1 Underline the passive constructions.
2 Decide who / what the doer of each action is.
3 See if you can write each sentence without using passives.

a *Far from doing 100% better than a rival, Company B's actually being hugely outperformed.*

b *Statistics can be used to manipulate, but they also inform policy development.*

c *Researchers may get pressured into finding positive results.*

d *A food company is having some research done to see if its product has health benefits.*

e *So next, statistics – often thought to be the worst kind of lying there is!*

f *They may worry about not being employed again, which may affect their conclusions.*

g *Obviously, research in a respected journal, reviewed by other experts, will be better than something published anonymously online.*

G Check your ideas on page 173 and do Exercise 1.

DO YOU AGREE THAT NATIONAL POLLS ARE FAIR AND UNBIASED, OR ARE YOU SOME KIND OF MORON?

©Glenn and Gary McCoy/Distributed by Universal Uclick via CartoonStock.com

8 Complete the stories with the correct form (active or passive) of the verbs.

1 Whenever heavy snow [1]_____ (fall), a journalist would call the headquarters of the traffic police and ask how many car crashes [2]_____ (report). The news would then [3]_____ (lead) with a story like: 'Two feet of snow [4]_____ (dump) on the South today, causing huge traffic jams and 28 accidents.' One day, the journalist asked how many crashes were typical for clear sunny days. The answer? 48!

2 A study [5]_____ (publish) in a child education journal [6]_____ (find) that toddlers in pre-school were more aggressive than kids who [7]_____ (keep) at home with Mum. The kids were observed over six months from their third birthday and 'aggression' [8]_____ (define) as stealing toys, pushing other children and starting fights.

3 A small study conducted after motorcyclists [9]_____ (force) by law to wear helmets discovered that the actual number of injuries [10]_____ (treat) in hospital leapt suddenly.

4 Last year, an online magazine on ecological topics conducted a poll that [11]_____ (reveal) that 85% of people felt that rules around experiments [12]_____ (conduct) on live animals ought [13]_____ (tighten).

5 The government claimed that, as a result of their policies, the murder rate in the city [14]_____ (reduce) by 30% in just eight years, falling from 130 a year at the beginning of the period to just 91 last year.

9 Work in groups. Discuss what problems there might be with the statistics above. Think about the questions in Exercise 3.

10  **23** Listen and see if you were right about the problems. What lessons can be learned from each story?

G For further practice, see Exercise 2 on page 173.

SPEAKING

11 Work in groups. Discuss what you think each quotation about statistics means. How far do you agree with each one? Explain why.

'There are three kinds of lies: lies, damned lies and statistics.'

'Statistics are no substitute for judgement.'

'Statistics go in one ear and out the other. We respond more to stories than numbers.'

'Statistics show that of those who contract the habit of eating, very few survive.'

'Smoking is one of the leading causes of all statistics.'

'We are all just statistics, born to consume resources.'

8

IN THIS UNIT YOU LEARN HOW TO:

- describe scenery and natural landscapes
- emphasise your opinions
- tell the stories behind photos
- talk about communication
- discuss stereotypes
- describe animals, their habitats and their habits

SPEAKING

1 Work in pairs. Student A: you are the photographer who took this photo. Student B: interview Student A to find out the story behind the photo and how they came to take it.

2 Change roles. The person being interviewed should now think of a different story.

3 Work in groups. Tell each other about a time when you saw an animal in the wild. Then choose the best story to tell the rest of the class.

NATURE AND NURTURE

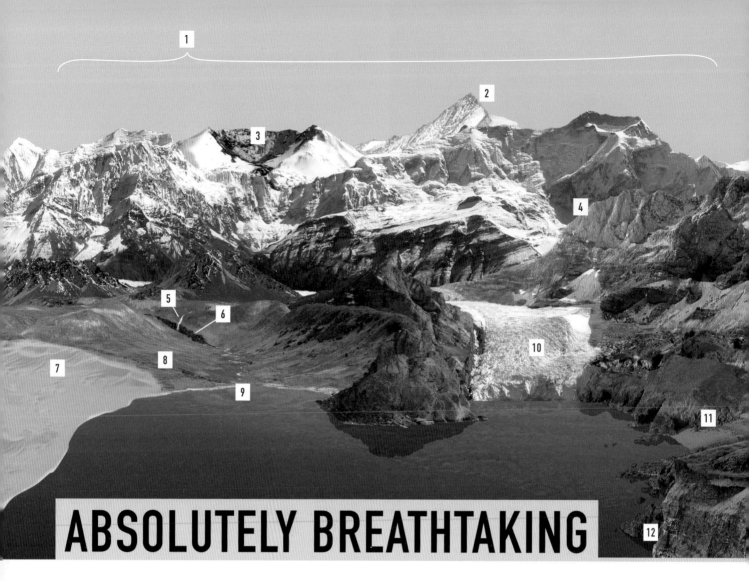

ABSOLUTELY BREATHTAKING

VOCABULARY Describing scenery

1 Label the picture with these words.

range	plains	crater	river mouth
cliff	dunes	cove	glacier
peak	ridge	gorge	waterfall

2 Work in pairs. Decide if both or only one of the words in italics is possible.

1 It's very popular with birdwatchers because it's at the mouth of *a river* / *some dunes* and there's a lot of *wetland* / *craters* that attract birds.

2 There's a very *narrow* / *steep* ridge leading up to the main peak and the views are *breathtaking* / *stunning* – if you're not too scared to look down!

3 We sometimes gather mushrooms in the woodland near us, but you have to be careful not to *stray from* / *stick to* the paths as it's so *thick* / *dense* you can easily get lost.

4 It's miles from civilisation, really. You just drive along dirt *roads* / *tracks* across these huge *flat* / *rolling* plains. And it's all pretty *lush* / *barren* – just brown grassland.

5 It's a mecca for climbers because there are these amazing *sheer* / *jagged* cliffs on either side of the *valley* / *gorge*. I saw quite a few people climbing without ropes. They must be nuts.

6 The road winds along the coastal cliffs and there are these little coves where you can scramble down to *sandy* / *rocky* beaches and have a dip. The water's amazing – *crystal clear* / *very murky*.

3 With your partner, discuss the questions.

- Which of the features in Exercises 1 and 2 do you have in your country? Whereabouts?

- Which parts of your country do you think are the most beautiful? Which are the worst? Why? Have you been to these areas? When? Why?

- Are any parts of your country popular with these people? Why?
  birdwatchers   climbers   hunters
  cyclists   divers   campers

LISTENING

4 ▶ 24 Listen to two conversations where people are talking about photos. Answer the questions about each conversation.

1 Where were they?

2 What were they doing there?

3 What was the scenery like?

5 ▶ 24 Work in pairs. Try to remember what the speakers said about the following. Then listen again and check your ideas.

Conversation 1	Conversation 2
1 a cable car	6 a family reunion
2 a bit of a scramble	7 some creepy-crawly
3 rusty cables	8 paradise
4 a head for heights	9 jellyfish
5 a death wish	10 debt

70

6 With your partner, discuss the questions.

- Which of the two places sounds better to you? Why?
- Do you have any photos of your friends and family – or of recent holidays – on your phone? If you do, show them to your partner and talk about them.
- Would you ever do any extreme sport like base jumping? Do you know anyone who has?
- Are there any things you think you would appreciate more now than you did in the past?

DEVELOPING CONVERSATIONS

Emphatic tags

We often add tags to emphasise our opinions. We usually begin with a pronoun + *really* and we then either repeat the auxiliary if there is one or add *do / does / did* if there isn't.

A: *Wow! The view from up there must've been pretty breathtaking!*

B: *Yeah, it was stunning, **it really was**.*

7 Add emphatic tags to the sentences.

1 I wouldn't drive it if I were you.
2 The views were just stunning.
3 The scenery takes your breath away.
4 I just love it there.
5 It made no difference whatsoever.
6 He'll never change.
7 I've never been anywhere like it.
8 That sounds amazing.

8 ▶ 25 Listen and check your ideas. Then practise saying the sentences with the added tag. In the tag, stress *really*.

9 Work in pairs. How many different replies using emphatic tags can you think of for each sentence below?

1 *Oh, it was just perfect, it really was.*

   Put it this way: I wouldn't recommend it, I really wouldn't.

   Wonderful! I could've quite happily stayed for another week, I really could.

1 What was your hotel like? Was it OK?
2 So, was it worth climbing to the top?
3 What was your tour guide like?
4 You cycled there, didn't you?
5 It must've been nice being away from civilisation for a few days.
6 What did you think of the place?

CONVERSATION PRACTICE

10 Choose one of these tasks.

a Think of a place you have visited that had interesting scenery. Think about what you were doing there, how you travelled around and what the place was like.

b Choose two or three photos from File 18 on page 196. Imagine you took them and be ready to explain where they are, what was happening, what you were doing there and what the places were like.

11 Now work in pairs. Tell each other about your places. Try to use as much language from this lesson as you can. Your partner should ask questions and add comments while listening.

🎥 ► 17 To watch the video and do the activities, see the DVD ROM.

NURTURE NOT NATURE

SPEAKING

1 **Work in groups. Read the introduction to an article. Then discuss the questions below.**

You've probably heard of the idea that men and women are so different they could be from different planets. The theory was actually popularised over 20 years ago by Dr John Gray, author of the book *Men are from Mars and Women are from Venus*, which has now sold over 50 million copies worldwide. The book suggests that relationships fail because we don't take account of the fundamentally different ways men and women communicate. His book's been followed by numerous other self-help guides over the years, many by Gray himself. There have also been other best-sellers such as Steve Harvey's *Act Like a Lady, Think Like a Man* and Sheryl Sanberg's *Lean In*, which suggests that women need to overcome their natural tendencies and be more pushy – more like men – in order to get ahead in business. But how far are these behaviours natural – hard-wired in our brains through evolution – and what role does nurture and culture have to play?

- Have you heard of any of the books mentioned? Are they the kind of thing you like to read?
- Why do you think such books are so popular?
- Which of these ideas from Gray's book do you think are true?
  - Women talk more than men.
  - Women know and use more words than men.
  - Women talk about their feelings more.
  - Men interrupt more than women.
  - Men are more competitive than women.
  - Men are more direct than women when speaking.
- Do you think these behaviours are 'hard-wired' or the result of nurture and culture? Why?

LISTENING

2 ▶ **26** **Listen to a lecture about language and gender by a lecturer in linguistics. Take notes on what you hear.**

3 **Work in pairs. Compare your notes and check what you understood.**

4 ▶ **26** **With your partner, use your notes to answer the questions. Then listen again and check your answers.**

1 How are the figures 20,000, 7,000, 16,000 and 45,000 connected?
2 Which of these figures are more reliable? Why?
3 What are the findings of the studies by Hyde and Chambers?
4 Why does the lecturer cite the study in Gapun?
5 What do Deborah Cameron and Simon Baron-Cohen disagree about?
6 What's the lecturer's conclusion?

5 **Work in groups. Talk about note-taking. Discuss:**

- whether you think you're good at taking notes or not.
- what system you use when taking notes – and why.
- when you need to take notes in your daily life.
- whether you take notes in the same way in your own language and in English.
- what you normally do with your notes after your English class / a meeting / a lecture.
- how you think you could improve your note-taking skills.

6 **Look at audio script 26 on page 205. Find all the verbs and adjectives that collocate with these nouns.**

research	evidence	study
myth	stereotype	claim

7 **Work in groups. Discuss the questions.**

- Is there anything you didn't fully understand in the lecture?
- Is there anything in the lecture that surprised you?
- Is there anything you agree or disagree with? What? To what extent?
- Do you agree that nurture is more important than nature in determining how people act? Why? / Why not?

GRAMMAR

Auxiliaries

Auxiliaries are words like *be*, *have*, *do*, *will*, *must*, etc. that we use to make negatives and questions. We also use them to avoid repetition and to add emphasis.

8 **Work in pairs. Complete the sentences from the listening with the correct auxiliary verbs in the correct form. Explain why each auxiliary is being used.**

1 After all, women are better communicators, _____ they?
2 Baron-Cohen's choice is simply based on the fact jobs in such fields have traditionally been occupied by women. And why _____ they?
3 When talking to a boss, we won't butt in, but they _____.
4 Research in the journal *Science* has shown both sexes talk equally as much, and in _____ so use on average 16,000 words per day.
5 The neutrality of the situation is important. Some men _____ speak over others more, but this is not to do with gender.

G Check your ideas on page 174 and do Exercise 1.

9 Write responses to these sentences in different ways using auxiliaries.

1 *Have you? What did you think of it?*

Yeah. It's rubbish, isn't it?

1 I've actually read *Men are from Mars*.

2 I don't think you can just totally dismiss stereotypes.

3 I'd love to live on a tropical island.

4 I wasn't allowed to play with dolls when I was a kid.

5 I don't have much of a head for heights.

6 I find baking quite fascinating, as weird as that may sound.

10 Work in pairs. Take turns to say the sentences from Exercise 9. Your partner should reply. Continue each conversation for as long as possible.

11 Work with a new partner. Find six things you have in common and four you don't. Then report back your results to the class. How many different auxiliaries can you use?

My partner would like to do a Master's degree sometime, and I would too. She's thinking of going to Australia to study, though, whereas I'm not. I'd rather stay here. She's really into movies, and so am I, but she likes weird arty stuff. I don't. I'm more of a big Hollywood-blockbuster-type person.

G For further practice, see Exercises 2 and 3 on page 174.

VOCABULARY Communicating

12 Complete the sentences with these pairs of words.

articulate + struggle	bush + point
manners + butting into	mince + blunt
gossip + rumours	twisting + words
listener + shoulder	shuts up + word

1 He's a terrible _____ – he's always spreading _____ about everyone in the office.

2 She's never less than 100% honest. She certainly doesn't _____ her words. She can be very _____ sometimes.

3 Once he starts talking, he never _____. No-one else can get a _____ in edgeways!

4 She's always _____ what I say and trying to put _____ into my mouth.

5 He's got no _____! He's always _____ other people's conversations.

6 She's a great _____ – always good to go to if you need a _____ to cry on.

7 He's not very _____. I mean, he seems to find it quite a _____ to express himself.

8 I wish she'd stop beating about the _____ and get to the _____. This is taking forever!

13 Work in groups. Discuss the questions.

• Do any of the sentences in Exercise 12 remind you of people you know? In what way?

• Which do you think describe you?

SPEAKING

14 Work in groups. Discuss the questions.

• Do you know any men / women who completely defy traditional gender stereotypes?

• Do you know any men / women who completely conform to gender stereotypes? In what way?

• Do you know people who are very different to the stereotype that exists of them (age, gender, nationality, etc.)?

• What stereotypes do you think other people might think you fit in with? To what degree do you think you conform to these stereotypes?

• Why do you think people stereotype others? Do you think it's useful in any way? What harm might it cause?

THE ANIMAL KINGDOM

VOCABULARY Animals

1   Work in pairs. Look at the photos and for each animal discuss:

   - where you think it lives – in what kind of landscape and in what part of the world. Explain why.
   - why it might have adapted as it has and what special features it might have developed.
   - what you think it might eat. Explain why.

2   Find examples in the photos of these things.

hoof	legs	nostrils	horn	toe
scales	fur	claw	teeth	hump
tail	feelers	beak	wing	breast

3   Match the two parts of the sentences.

1	It builds	a	through tree bark.
2	It can sense	b	a high-pitched squeal.
3	It tunnels	c	reserves of fat.
4	It can blend	d	its chest.
5	It can withstand	e	a nest.
6	It gnaws	f	into the background.
7	It puffs up	g	the slightest movement.
8	It leaps out	h	and snatches its prey.
9	It stores	i	freezing temperatures.
10	It lets out	j	down into the earth.

4   Work in pairs. Think of an animal for each of the sentences in Exercise 3. Discuss why each action might be done.

5   ▶ 27 Listen to two short descriptions of animals. Find out:

   1   which animals in the photos are being described.
   2   what parts of the body are mentioned and what they are used for.

UNDERSTANDING VOCABULARY

Compound adjectives

Compound adjectives are made up of two or more words. We put a hyphen between these words. Compound adjectives are often formed using noun + adjective (*water-resistant*); adjective + noun (*last-minute*); adjective, adverb or noun + present / past participle (*good-looking, densely-populated, long-lasting*) or number + noun (*a ten-minute walk*).

6   Work in pairs. Think of one noun that each of these adjectives could describe.

water-resistant	star-shaped	award-winning
long-term	child-friendly	self-help
high-powered	six-lane	life-threatening
tailor-made		

7 Work in pairs. You have five minutes to come up with as many different compound adjective + noun collocations as you can, using the adjectives from Exercise 6. You can change either word of the compound adjectives to make new ones.

an Oscar-winning film   *an award-worthy innovation*

READING

8 Work in groups of four: two As and two Bs. You are going to read about another animal in the photos.

Student As: read the text on this page.

Student Bs: read the text in File 19 on page 190.

Find out about:

1 the animal's habitat.

2 its behaviour.

3 its unique physical features.

4 any threats it's facing.

5 conservation efforts being made to protect it.

9 With the person who read the same text, do the following:

1 Compare what you understood about the animal – its habitat and habits and the threats it faces.

2 Decide what you feel is the most interesting fact about the animal.

3 Check you understand the phrases in bold and try to remember them.

10 Now work in new pairs: one Student A and one Student B. Close your books. Tell each other as much as you can about the animal you read about using some of the phrases in bold from the text, then do the following:

1 Discuss which animal you feel is the most interesting – and why.

2 Discuss which animal you think has the bleaker future – and why.

3 Learn at least two new useful phrases from your partner.

11 With the same partner, decide if the sentences refer to one or other of the animals – or both. Then look back at the texts and check your answers.

1 The area it traditionally lives in is shrinking.

2 It travels extensively in order to find food.

3 It may have to cope with severe food shortages.

4 It's sometimes the victim of superstitious fears.

5 It's sometimes killed for the benefit of other animals.

6 The way it performs some of its unique abilities remains a mystery.

7 It's developed an extremely unusual way of finding food.

8 Efforts are being made to increase the population.

9 It's a relatively communal creature.

10 Its mating habits can have life-threatening consequences.

SHIPS OF THE GOBI DESERT

The wild Bactrian camel is found in the Gobi desert of Mongolia and China, which ranges from boiling sand dunes to frozen hills and mountains. It has evolved to withstand the extremes of heat and cold as well as the arid landscape. It has thick eyelashes that close to **form a protective barrier** against sandstorms and it can also completely close its thin, slit-like nostrils to prevent dust entering. It eats snow in the winter months and, unlike any other camel, can also drink salt water. It is still unknown how it processes the salt water.

Excess water is stored not in its humps but in the bloodstream. The humps are largely made up of fat. The camel **draws upon these fat reserves** in times of drought and famine. Like other camels, it reduces water loss by hardly sweating or urinating. It also has a remarkably tough tongue, capable of eating **the sharp thorns of desert shrubs**. These camels are incredibly resistant to disease, which may surprise people considering their numbers are dwindling.

The wild Bactrian camels **roam widely in small herds** of two to fifteen members and will travel vast distances in search of food and water. However, they are **threatened from a number of angles**. They were heavily hunted in previous years and continue to be so where there is competition for water sources from domestic herds. They have also suffered poisoning as a result of the use of dangerous chemicals in **illegal mining activities**. Finally, they often interbreed with domestic Bactrians, which leads them to lose the capability to drink salt water.

Despite efforts to **crack down** on illegal mining and hunting, the wild Bactrian camel has become one of the rarest mammals in the world. There are now **captive breeding programmes** aimed at restoring populations.

SPEAKING

12 Choose two of the topics below to talk about. Spend a few minutes researching and preparing what you want to say about each one. Then work in groups and share your ideas.

- how much (or how little!) we should spend on animal welfare – and why
- a remarkable animal
- an animal that's a national symbol or that's culturally important
- what I remember about the animals I studied at school
- two endangered animals – and what can be done to protect them

VIDEO 4

BABY MATH

1 **Work in groups. Look at the photo and discuss the questions.**

- What is happening?
- Do you think it's a good idea to do this in this way? Why? / Why not?
- Discuss whether you think each of the following is good for babies. Explain your ideas.
  - being allowed to eat whenever they want
  - having classical music played to them
  - sleeping away from their parents
  - being made to sit up as soon as they can
  - not talking to them until they're ready to talk

2 📹 18 **Watch the first part of a video about what knowledge babies are born with (0.00–1.44). How are the words below connected to babies' instincts and abilities – and how are some of these instincts related to other animals?**

   1 submerge
   2 suck
   3 grasp
   4 startle
   5 steps

3 **Work in pairs. Discuss the questions.**

- How do you think babies' mathematical ability might be tested?
- What problems might there be when researching this ability?
- What results do you think have been found?

4 📹 18 **Watch the second part of the video (1.45–4.15) and answer the questions in Exercise 3.**

5 **Work in pairs. Check you understand the words and phrases in bold. Then discuss what the words in italics refer to.**

   1 *It* arrives with a set of **reflexes** to help it survive.

   2 *It* will **intuitively** hold its breath.

   3 Perhaps *this* may be the **trace** of an **ancestral** instinct for holding onto a mother's back.

   4 One popular notion is that *it* starts out in the world with a completely **blank slate** mind.

   5 *It* has no expectations and finds the world this incredibly confusing, chaotic **barrage** of impressions and sensations.

   6 *It* seems surprised and stares at *this* **outcome** much longer.

   7 *They* are **pretty consistent** and suggest that babies as young as four months can add up.

   8 *They* can judge *this* with just a simple **glance**.

6 **Work in groups. Discuss how far you agree with each of the statements below. Explain your ideas.**

   1 The research methods used in the video don't prove anything.

   2 Kids could achieve so much more if only we pushed them a bit harder.

   3 We are basically no different to most other animals.

   4 Using babies in experiments is just totally unacceptable.

   5 Mathematical ability is at the heart of human intelligence.

UNDERSTANDING FAST SPEECH

7 📹 19 **Listen to an extract from the video said at natural pace. Try to write down what you hear. Then compare your ideas with a partner.**

8 📹 20 **Try again. This time you will hear a slower version of the extract.**

9 **Check your ideas in File 10 on page 189. Groups of words are marked with / and pauses are marked //. Stressed sounds are in CAPITALS. Practise saying the extract.**

REVIEW 4

GRAMMAR AND UNDERSTANDING
VOCABULARY

1 Complete the text with one word in each space.

Stuck in my dull office job, I often used to dream of ¹_____ transported to a tropical island. It's not an uncommon thought, ²_____ it? But then I was actually ³_____ the opportunity to fulfil that dream when I took part in an award-⁴_____ TV programme where a group of people ⁵_____ abandoned on a remote Pacific island to see how well they can survive. The island was beautiful, it really ⁶_____, but we quickly discovered its downsides. Only an hour after ⁷_____ dropped off, we had all ⁸_____ bitten by various insects, seen snakes and ⁹_____ lost in the dense jungle. I also suffered from severe dehydration, which can be ¹⁰_____-threatening if left untreated. But I ¹¹_____ survive for the full four weeks of the programme and in ¹²_____ so changed my outlook on life dramatically. I am so much more appreciative of what I have now than I used to ¹³_____ before the programme, I really ¹⁴_____.

2 Complete the second sentence so that it has a similar meaning to the first sentence using the word given. Do not change the word given. You must use between four and five words, including the word given.

1 I can't believe how stupid the government has been.
It's difficult to believe _____ the government's actions. **SHEER**

2 They are conducting the research for a cancer charity.
The research _____ on behalf of a cancer charity. **CARRIED**

3 I can understand why they're reluctant to help.
I think their _____. **IS**

4 We've won several prizes for the site because it's easy for children to use.
Our _____ several prizes. **AWARDED**

5 We know that the drug can help patients with heart disease.
The drug _____ in treating heart disease. **BE**

3 Complete the sentences. Use the word in brackets to form a word that fits in the space. Sometimes you need to make a compound adjective.

1 In updating the site we have created greater _____. (interact)

2 We will only find out in the _____ of time. (full)

3 The _____ nose enables the mole to find its way in the dark. (star)

4 We should be very concerned about the ongoing _____ of species. (appear)

5 It's easy to get downhearted at the _____ of the situation. (hope)

6 The animals are now bred in _____ because they are nearing _____ in the wild. (captive, extinct)

7 The breakthrough should lead to the production of more _____ _____ fabrics. (breathe, water)

VOCABULARY

4 Decide which of these nouns are parts of animals and which are connected to landscape.

claw	crater	cliff	scales	horn
hoof	cove	range	beak	jungle
fur	peak	hump	ridge	gorge

5 Match the verbs (1–10) with the collocates (a–j).

1 devise   a us to speculate / fears
2 insert   b my hand / its prey
3 reflect   c a way / a mechanism
4 prompt   d attitudes / the times
5 store   e a probe / the USB
6 snatch   f tiny movements / danger
7 sense   g the procedure / the analysis
8 address   h reserves / information
9 withstand   i the extreme cold / pressure
10 undertake   j underlying causes / the issue

6 Complete the sentences with a preposition in each space.

1 Contrary _____ popular belief, high-fat diets may not lead to heart disease.

2 The sample group was chosen _____ random.

3 Because of the small sample, several variables weren't covered _____ the data.

4 We all have a vested interest _____ the project being a success.

5 Attitudes _____ women have changed a lot since the 60s.

6 Honestly, I can never get a word _____ edgeways with him.

7 Remember, I'm always a shoulder to cry _____ if you need it.

8 Stop beating _____ the bush and get _____ the point.

9 I'm happy to take a back seat and blend _____ the background.

7 Complete the text with one word in each space. The first letters are given.

There has been an ¹up_____ trend in levels of obesity and the blame has generally been placed on saturated fat. Despite ²co_____ evidence over the years, the most ³pr_____ medical advice has been to reduce fats in our diet. However, a recent paper by Zoe Harcombe and James DiNicolantonio, which analysed the ⁴fi_____ of hundreds of other studies in the ⁵fi_____, has suggested this advice is ⁶fl_____ and that there is no ⁷co_____ between fat and heart disease. The researchers have themselves been criticised by some who suggest their figures don't ⁸s_____ u_____ to scrutiny and the results are ⁹d_____ to a failure to take into account all the ¹⁰va_____ involved. While debate on fat is unlikely to end with Harcome and DiNocolantonio's study, many health experts have discovered sugars are strongly ¹¹li_____ to obesity, which is ¹²pa_____ the way for new taxes being imposed on sugar in some countries.

9

Recharging the batteries

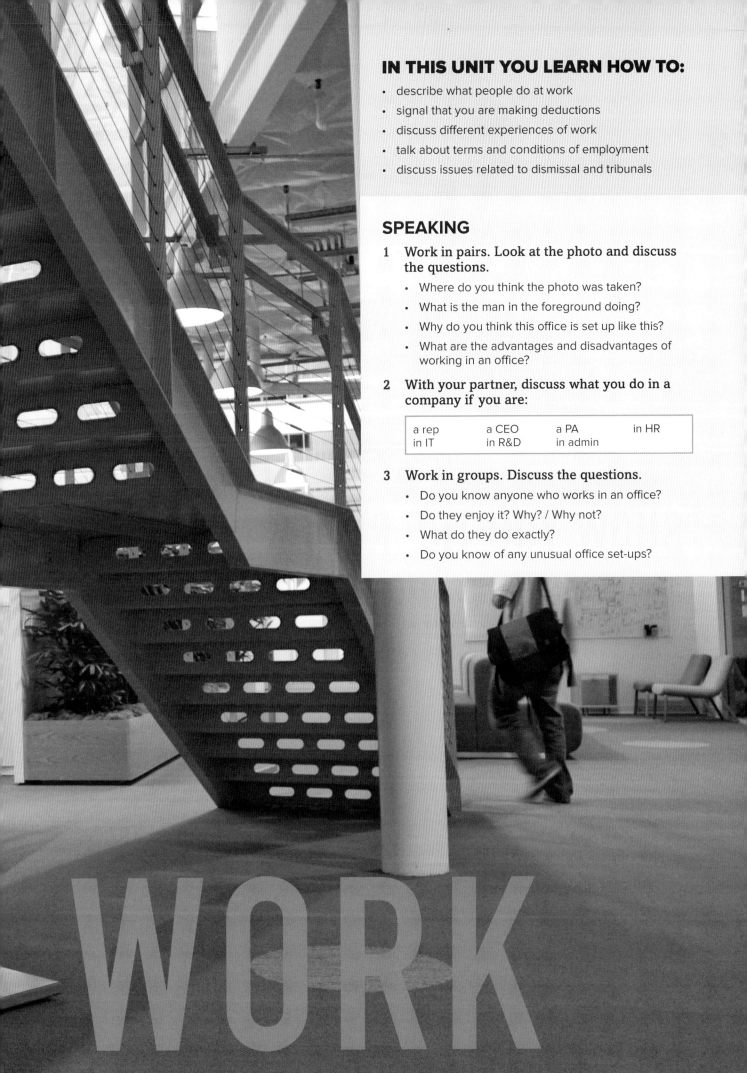

IN THIS UNIT YOU LEARN HOW TO:

- describe what people do at work
- signal that you are making deductions
- discuss different experiences of work
- talk about terms and conditions of employment
- discuss issues related to dismissal and tribunals

SPEAKING

1 **Work in pairs. Look at the photo and discuss the questions.**

- Where do you think the photo was taken?
- What is the man in the foreground doing?
- Why do you think this office is set up like this?
- What are the advantages and disadvantages of working in an office?

2 **With your partner, discuss what you do in a company if you are:**

a rep	a CEO	a PA	in HR
in IT	in R&D	in admin	

3 **Work in groups. Discuss the questions.**

- Do you know anyone who works in an office?
- Do they enjoy it? Why? / Why not?
- What do they do exactly?
- Do you know of any unusual office set-ups?

WORK

SHOW YOU THE ROPES

VOCABULARY Roles and tasks

1 **Complete the sentences with these words and phrases.**

troubleshoot	draw up	place	schedule
oversee	come up with	process	input
network	liaise		

1 I have to _____ information into the database.

2 We maintain the computers and network and we _____ any problems.

3 I have to _____ and **entertain a lot** to attract new business.

4 People **pass on their expense claims** and **invoices** to me and I _____ them.

5 I _____ everything, making sure everyone **meets their deadlines** and **stays on budget**.

6 I _____ the strategy and **provide leadership** and then **delegate** the work to others.

7 I _____ closely with designers to **implement our strategy**.

8 I have a budget to _____ ads in magazines and **put on events** like product launches.

9 Shall we _____ a meeting for tomorrow?

10 I _____ all the contracts and **deal with any contractual issues**.

2 **Work in pairs. Discuss the questions.**

1 Which tasks from Exercise 1 have you done?

2 Which tasks would you be good / bad at? Why?

LISTENING

3 ▶ 28 **Listen to someone being shown around on their first day in a new job. Take notes on what you find out about the following:**

Tasneem   Harry   Bianca

the photocopier   Mary   the company

4 **Work in pairs. Compare your notes.**

5 ▶ 28 **Listen again and write down four words or phrases that are new for you. Compare what you wrote with your partner. Then look at audio script 28 on page 205 and check your phrases.**

6 **With your partner, discuss the questions.**

- Do you like the way Tasneem shows Harry around? Why? / Why not?

- Do you think it's OK to jokingly make negative comments about colleagues? Do you ever do it? What about?

- What was your first day at work / school like?

- Can you remember what you did?

DEVELOPING CONVERSATIONS

Making deductions

To indicate we are making a deduction based on what someone has said, we often add *then* at the end. The intonation often sounds like we're asking a question and need a reply.

▶ 29 *You were eager to get here, **then**.*

*I'm not the only one who's being taken on now, **then**.*

*She's not in the office that much, **then**.*

7 Look at audio script 28 on page 205. Find the three examples in the box above and underline:

1 what prompted the comments / deductions.

2 the replies to these deductions.

8 Write a deduction based on each of these sentences.

1 *You travel a lot, then.*

You've been working late a lot, then.

Oh, you're married, then.

1 I've hardly seen my wife in the last few weeks.

2 I'm really sorry. I'm falling asleep.

3 You don't want to get on the wrong side of him.

4 I'm going to have to cover for him again.

5 Our reps in Russia are a really lovely bunch.

6 My boyfriend says I should slow down.

9 Work in pairs. Take turns to say the sentences in Exercise 8 and use your deductions to continue each conversation.

GRAMMAR

Continuous forms

Continuous forms use the verb *be* and the *-ing* form. They can combine with perfect forms (*have + been doing*), passives (*be + being done*), *is supposed to* and modals (*will / must*, etc. + *be doing / have been doing*). Continuous forms:

• show an activity or event is / was unfinished at a particular point in time or at the time of another action.

• emphasise that we see an activity or situation as temporary rather than permanent.

• focus on the activity happening over a period of time – as opposed to the result.

• talk about arrangements and activities based on a previous decision.

10 Complete the sentences from the listening with the correct continuous form of the verbs.

1 I _____ actually _____ in the coffee bar over the road for the last hour. (hang around)

2 I should've said – we _____ alongside each other. (work)

3 I _____ just _____ one of them to schedule a time for us all to meet when you arrived. (email)

4 I'm not the only one who _____ now, then. (take on)

5 Three or four more _____ in the next couple of weeks. (join)

6 She _____ probably _____ all kind and helpful now, but wait till you get started. (be)

7 To be honest, you _____ that much to do with them in your day-to-day dealings. (not / have)

8 I _____ about moving out there for a while and I happened to get the house just before I got this job. (think)

11 Work in pairs. Discuss why you think the continuous form is used in each sentence above.

 Check your ideas on page 175 and do Exercise 1.

12 With your partner, discuss the difference in meaning, if any, between the pairs of sentences.

1 a The company went bankrupt last year.

   b The company was going bankrupt last year.

2 a She's a pain.

   b She's being a pain.

3 a You must have been struggling.

   b You must be struggling.

4 a They should sort it out.

   b They should be sorting it out.

5 a Things are improving a lot.

   b Things have been improving a lot.

13 Make five short dialogues by writing sentences before and after 1b, 2b, 3b, 4b and 5b from Exercise 12.

 For further practice, see Exercise 2 on page 176.

CONVERSATION PRACTICE

14 Draw a rough plan of the place where you work / study. Then work in pairs and have similar conversations to the one in the listening. Explain about the following:

• who works where and what they do

• what the people are like

• any rules or things workers need to have

• any machines they might need to operate

• anything odd or temperamental

🎥 21 To watch the video and do the activities, see the DVD ROM.

OUT OF THE OFFICE

READING

1   You are going to read a true story from a book on management called *The Living Dead* by David Bolchover. Before you read, work in pairs and discuss what you think the theme of the book might be given the title.

2   Read Part 1 of the story. Then answer the questions with your partner.

1   What has happened to David (the author)?

2   How does his friend feel about it?

3   Why do you think David feels the system (of work) is cheating itself?

4   How do you think the situation came about?

3   Read Part 2 of the story and find out:

1   how the situation came about.

2   how it ended.

3   who 'the living dead' are.

4   Match 1–10 to a–j to make phrases from the story.

1   my vitality   a   new skills
2   acquire   b   the question
3   sponsor   c   to someone else
4   sparked   d   out of its investment
5   get the most   e   my interest
6   his mind   f   was drifting off
7   set   g   me
8   passed this on   h   a redundancy payment
9   which begs   i   drained away
10 get   j   the wheels in motion

5   Work in pairs. Retell the story using the phrases from Exercise 4 and your own words.

6   With your partner, discuss the questions.

1   Do you think what happened was a freak occurrence?

2   Who was most to blame for the situation? Why?

3   What lessons can you take from the story?

LISTENING

7   ▶ 30 Listen to a brief summary of the lessons David Bolchover takes from his experience. Answer the questions in Exercise 6.

8   ▶ 30 Listen again. Then work in pairs and answer the questions.

1   What statistics are connected to the numbers below and what point is Bolchover making with them?
- one in three
- 8.3 hours a week
- 24%

2   What is the 'conspiracy of silence'?

3   Why does it happen mainly in big companies?

4   How can breaking up large companies help?

9   Work in groups. Discuss the questions.

- Do you agree with David Bolchover's ideas? Why? / Why not?

- What would you have done in his situation?

- Have you heard of any instances of incompetence in the workplace? What happened?

- How do people get to the top at work? Does it depend on the industry? In what way?

- Which person you know has the best work-life balance?

UNDERSTANDING VOCABULARY

Adverb-adjective collocations

Adverbs that go before adjectives usually modify the strength of the adjective (*highly efficient*), but occasionally they may modify the meaning of the adjective (*The job was financially rewarding.*). Some adverbs collocate strongly with only one or two adjectives (*mind-numbingly boring*).

10 All the adverbs in italics in the sentences below are possible. In each sentence, choose the one you think is most true for you.

1   Most jobs are *mind-numbingly / largely / pretty* boring.

2   Gardening is *technically / physically / not terribly* demanding.

3   Nursing is *financially / immensely / fairly* rewarding.

4   Teaching kids is *emotionally / utterly / quite* draining.

5   You have to be *fiercely / very / quite* competitive to get ahead in business.

6   IT is *mildly / inherently / not even remotely* interesting.

7   The public sector is *highly / reasonably / not particularly* efficient.

8   I'm *blissfully / relatively / not entirely* happy with what I'm doing now.

11 Work in pairs and compare your choices. Discuss any differences.

12 Use each of the eight adjectives from Exercise 10 plus a connected adverb of your choice to tell a partner about things you have done – or something you believe to be true.

I find golf mind-numbingly boring. Why do people watch it?

I like climbing, but I don't do anything which is too technically demanding.

Banking is obviously very rewarding financially, but I wouldn't want to do it.

PART 1

I'm sitting in a café with my friend Paul. He lives in the States now and I haven't had the chance to chat with him for months.

'Now let me get this straight,' he leans forward on the edge of his seat. 'Your company has forgotten about you? You're on the payroll, but you've got nothing to do. And how long did you say this has been going on?'

'Six months.'

Paul leans further forward. It's clear he's not going to drop the subject.

'They pay you a full salary for sitting on your backside at home, apart from the times when you're not at home, but out and about with your mates or travelling round Europe to watch Man United play in the Champions League?'

'No, you've missed a bit; you've forgotten the rugby and the …'

'You jammy beggar!'

All the conversations I've had about this period of my life contain those words or similar. There is a depressing inevitability about it, although I always enjoy the sneaking respect I sense I get from people for having cheated the system. Except that I wasn't cheating the system. The system was cheating itself.

PART 2

I'd joined Giant – a big multinational insurance company – in June of 1997. The job was financially rewarding, but I quickly started to feel restless as some days I did nothing apart from make the occasional call. The Internet still hadn't taken off so I spent hours staring at the wall, drifting off into my own little world, while all my vitality slowly drained away. Every morning, I'd get up full of life, and every evening, I'd return with my shoulders slumped, my head bent and my mind numb. I was joining the terrible world of the living dead.

I decided that if I was going to get ahead, I needed to acquire new skills. It was clear that in my current post I wasn't exactly going to race to the top of the insurance world so I decided to persuade Giant to sponsor me to take a year off to do an MBA in return for me committing to the company afterwards. I presented the idea to my boss. He was about to retire and was looking for an easy life so he quickly agreed and, with his backing, the process was a formality.

The MBA filled me with renewed energy and optimism. After six months, I went back to the office to see my boss in readiness for my return on October 4th. I explained how the course had sparked my interest in management and business strategy. I suggested it was pointless me going back to what I had been doing and that instead Giant might think about a suitable post that would get the most out of its investment. It was a good speech full of common sense, but from the dull look in my boss's eyes I could've been talking to an Italian about cricket. You could tell his mind was drifting off to another place rather than focusing on a job which could benefit both me and the company. As a result, I consulted human resources. The woman I spoke to nodded and sounded interested and said she'd set the wheels in motion.

However, months past and I heard nothing. I was beginning to worry, not to say get angry, at the lack of communication so I arranged an appointment with someone higher up in HR. It didn't go well and on reflection I can imagine what he was thinking. 'I've got this guy who's a pain in the neck. We owe him a job, but he doesn't want to go back to his old post and there's no point in him going there on a temporary basis. It'd be better if I just passed this on to someone else to sort out before he makes me look like a fool.'

The 4th of October came. Nothing. A few days later, the guy from HR put me in contact with a guy in Finance, for whom I worked on a project at home but which he quickly dropped. A few weeks went by. Nothing. Well, nothing apart from October 26th when a nice big juicy pay cheque dropped through my letterbox.

In mid-November, the finance guy rang and told me to see this guy Nick, who was brilliant at assessing people and placing them in the post which would enthuse them most. It sounded impressive but the results weren't. After scheduling some meetings that didn't go anywhere, he came to the conclusion that basically people with MBAs didn't fit into the insurance sector, which rather begs the question: why on earth did Giant – an insurance company – agree to fund me?!

The months passed and I decided I should find a job elsewhere. Ironically, I was just about to phone my department to let them know I was leaving when HR called, inviting me to a meeting with the big boss. They were going to make me redundant! Of course! It's only fair that after being with the company for over two years and having done nothing for the previous ten months, I should get a redundancy payment and one-month's notice to leave. As I left the meeting, the big boss accompanied me to the lift. He uncomfortably tried to start some small talk. 'So … er … what have you been doing for the last few months?'

All I could think of was a variety of football matches, sunny days walking round London Zoo, afternoons in the cinema. However, instead I heard myself saying, 'Obviously, it's been a difficult time for me and my family.'

WORKING CONDITIONS

SPEAKING

1 Read the fact file. Then work in pairs and discuss the questions.

- Which facts surprise you? Why?
- Is there anything you don't find surprising?
- How do you think your country compares in terms of all the facts and figures?

VOCABULARY The world of work

2 Complete the sentences below with these pairs of words and phrases. You may need to change the order of the words.

crèche + childcare	compassionate leave + grateful
opposition + raise	voluntary redundancy + cuts
perk + subsidised	early retirement + pension
tribunal + dismissal	unions + casualisation
quit + notice	crackdown + absenteeism

1 If I want to _____, I basically just have to give my boss a week's _____.

2 We all get _____ travel, which is a nice _____ of the job.

3 When my father died, I was granted two month's _____, which I'm eternally _____ for.

4 We have a _____ at work where I can leave my daughter, which makes _____ much easier.

5 My dad was planning to take _____, but he basically can't afford to live on the state _____.

6 We're losing so much money because of _____ that we've decided to launch a bit of a _____ and start demanding sick notes.

7 He was sacked last year, but he took his employers to a _____ and was awarded compensation on the grounds of unfair _____.

8 The government promised to _____ the statutory minimum wage, but they're facing a lot of _____ from business leaders.

9 We were facing swingeing _____ across the department and in the end I just decided to take _____ instead.

10 There are fewer and fewer secure jobs, but the _____ have done nothing to prevent this _____ of the workforce.

3 Work in pairs. Cover the sentences in Exercise 2. See if you can remember the verbs that were used with these nouns and noun phrases.

a week's notice	a tribunal
compassionate leave	compensation
early retirement	the minimum wage
the state pension	a lot of opposition
a crackdown	voluntary redundancy

4 Look at Exercise 2 and check your ideas. Underline any other phrases that are new for you.

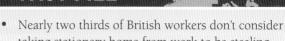

FACT FILE

- Nearly two thirds of British workers don't consider taking stationery home from work to be stealing.

- German women get 14 weeks' maternity leave at full pay, 6 weeks of which can be taken before birth. Both parents can take 12 months at around 67% of pay and have their jobs protected for 3 years.

- Japanese companies spend approximately $23.5 billion a year entertaining clients, which according to the IMF is the equivalent of the GDP of Estonia!

- The average monthly income in Guinea Bissau, West Africa, is around $20.

- Approximately 21 million people around the world are victims of forced labour and slavery.

- On average over a whole year, Mexicans (43 hrs/wk) and Greeks (42 hrs/wk) work the longest hours, and the Dutch work the least (27 hrs/wk).

- Nepal now has the lowest retirement age in the world at 58, while Australia has the highest at 70.

5 Work in groups. Answer the questions.

1 What other perks can you think of for different kinds of jobs?

2 Under what circumstances do you think it's OK to grant workers compassionate leave?

3 On what grounds is it OK to sack someone?

4 Are crèches common in workplaces in your country? Do you think they're a good idea?

5 What's the state pension like in your country?

6 Why do you think there is so much absenteeism? What's the best way to tackle the problem?

7 How does the workforce become casualised?

LISTENING

6 ▶ 31 Listen to five news stories related to work. Match each story (1–5) to one of the sentences below. There is one sentence that you do not need.

a The employer did something illegal.

b The employee did something illegal.

c The employer proved to be right in a dispute.

d The union are accusing the employer of breaking an agreement.

e The employer reduced staff to cut costs.

f The union want employment laws changed.

7 Work in pairs. Retell the stories in as much detail as you can using these words.

1 call centre – biscuit tin – CCTV footage – £150 – retraining

2 strike – raise – concerns – guarantee – assuring – prompted

3 £10,000 – mourn – tribunal – 137 days – injuries – step

4 concerns – insecure – subsidise – reluctant to – calling for

5 failed – refused – final straw – relieved – requirements – pass on

8 ▶ 31 Listen again and check your ideas. Which four stories do you think are true and which is not? Why?

9 Work in groups. Discuss the questions.

• Who would you side with in each case? Why?

• Have there been any industrial disputes in your country in recent years? What about?

• How strict are employment laws in your country? Do you think that's good or bad?

SPEAKING

10 Read about three cases that came before employment tribunals in File 20 on page 191. Decide what you think should be done in each case.

11 Work in groups. Discuss what you think should be done in each case. Try to reach a unanimous decision.

12 Have you heard of any other stories involving employment tribunals? When? What happened?

10

The administrative office of the Tekle Haimanot Higher Clinic

IN THIS UNIT YOU LEARN HOW TO:

- describe different medical and surgical procedures
- use vague language
- discuss different approaches to medicine
- describe things the mind and body do
- discuss issues doctors face

SPEAKING

1 **Work in groups. Discuss the questions.**

- In what country do you think this photo was taken?
- Compared to the doctor's surgeries you know, what's similar and what's different?
- What do you think the biggest problems facing a set-up like this might be?
- How easy is it to make appointments where you live? Is it different if you want to see a doctor or a dentist?
- What do you think the main reasons for visiting the doctor are?
- What are the waiting times for operations usually like?
- What do you think are the most common operations people have?

HEALTH AND ILLNESS

UNDER THE KNIFE

VOCABULARY Operations

1 Put each group of words into the most likely order they happen, starting with the words in bold.

1 **damaged her knee quite badly** / had it operated on / underwent extensive physiotherapy / the knee joint swelled up / had to have a scan

2 **broke his leg in three places** / was given an anaesthetic / had an operation to insert metal rods / had to fast for twelve hours / eventually had them removed

3 **the pain became excruciating** / had to have a few stitches / it somehow got infected / had a filling / had to have the whole tooth out

4 **was diagnosed with kidney disease** / had a transplant / was put on a waiting list / took part in a rehabilitation programme / finally found a donor

5 **suffered severe burns** / had to wait for the scarring to heal / was rushed to hospital / had a skin graft / was put on a drip

6 **found a lump** / suffered a relapse / it went into remission / had an operation to have it removed / it was diagnosed as cancer / underwent chemotherapy

2 Work in pairs. Answer the questions.

1 When else might someone have a scan?

2 What kind of thing might extensive physiotherapy involve?

3 Can you think of any other reasons why people sometimes fast?

4 What other kinds of transplants can you have?

5 When else might you have to take part in a rehabilitation programme?

6 Why are people usually put on a drip?

7 What are the possible side effects of chemotherapy?

8 What other kinds of relapses can people suffer?

LISTENING

3 ▶ 32 Listen to two conversations about surgical procedures. Answer the questions about each conversation.

1 What kind of procedure do they discuss?

2 What did the procedure involve?

3 Is any further treatment required?

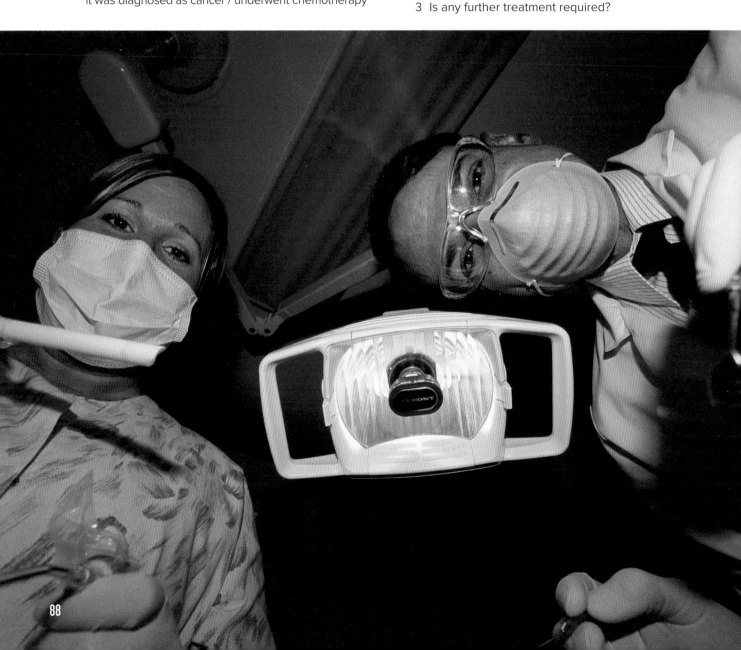

4 ▶ **32** Listen again. Are the sentences true (T) or false (F)? How do you know?

Conversation 1

1 Part of his eye had to be cut open.

2 He was given an injection to anaesthetise him.

3 He took further medication to ease the pain.

4 His eyes feel completely fine now.

5 She is not tempted to have the operation herself.

Conversation 2

6 The pain in her jaw a week ago was very severe.

7 She's sure her daughter damaged her tooth.

8 Measures were taken to ensure the tooth doesn't get infected.

9 She was unconscious during the whole procedure.

10 It's going to cost her over £500.

5 Work in groups. Discuss the questions.

- Do you know anyone who's had procedures like either of the ones described?
- Do you know anyone who has poor eyesight? How do they deal with it?
- What do you think the best way of dealing with poor eyesight is – wearing glasses, wearing contact lenses or having corrective surgery? Why?
- How expensive is it in your country to visit the dentist? What are average prices for a check-up, fillings and having a tooth out?
- How often do you go to the dentist's?

DEVELOPING CONVERSATIONS
Vague language

6 Work in pairs. Try to complete the sentences from the conversations with vague expressions. Then look at audio script 32 on page 207 and check your ideas.

1 They _____ clamp them open.

2 How did they give you the anaesthetic? Was it an injection _____?

3 They just poured in _____ these eye drops.

4 I have to go back a few times for the aftercare _____.

5 About a week ago _____, I got this excruciating pain in my upper jaw.

6 He told me that one of my teeth had died _____.

7 He said I must've taken _____ knock.

8 He stuck _____ temporary filling in to prevent bacteria _____ getting in.

7 With your partner, discuss how and why each of the vague expressions in Exercise 6 is used. Then read the box and check your ideas.

- We use *kind of* / *sort of* before verbs and nouns to show we can't find the exact word – or to avoid using a more complicated word.
- We can also use *some kind of* / *sort of* before nouns to show we're not sure what kind exactly.
- We add *or something* (*like that*) after a noun to suggest a non-specific alternative to the thing already mentioned. To suggest an absence of things, we use *or anything* (*like that*) and *or whatever*.
- We use many different quantifiers such as *a load of, loads of, a ton of* and *a whole bunch of* before nouns to talk about large, unspecified amounts.
- We add *and everything, and all that* (*sort of thing*), *and stuff like that* and *and so on* after a noun to refer vaguely to other associated things.
- We use *about ... or so* with numbers / periods of time to show we're not being exact.
- We use *somehow* with verbs to show we do not really know how something happened.

8 Make the sentences less exact and more vague using words and phrases from the box.

1 I asked for a second opinion, but they just ignored me.

2 He used bleach solution on my teeth.

3 If you want a check-up, it should cost about €100.

4 They told me that a build-up was damaging blood vessels in my brain.

5 They use this tiny little knife to make the incision.

6 It was quite a traumatic birth, but they managed to deliver her after about an hour.

7 They just glued the skin back together again using clear plastic tape.

8 Mercifully, there were no needles involved – just massage and traditional medicine.

9 Work in pairs. Use vague language to describe how you think the following work.

- surgery to relieve lower back pain
- hip replacement
- liposuction
- tooth whitening

CONVERSATION PRACTICE

10 Work in groups of three. You are going to have conversations about medical experiences. Choose one of these tasks.

a Think of some medical or surgical experiences that you – or people you know – have had. Spend a few minutes planning what you want to say about them. Then discuss your experiences.

b Read your roleplay card. Spend a few minutes planning what to say. Then have conversations about the experiences you read about.

Student A: read File 21 on page 191.

Student B: read File 22 on page 186.

Student C: read File 23 on page 197.

🎥 22 To watch the video and do the activities, see the DVD ROM.

KEEP IT IN MIND

SPEAKING

1 **Work in pairs. Take turns to ask the questions. Choose one of the answers given or think of your own. Your partner should ask extra questions to find out more.**

1 How does diet affect your mood?

  a A lot. I take dietary supplements so my body's always in balance.

  b I don't think about it. I eat whatever I like.

2 How well do you deal with pain and illness?

  a I tend to get quite grumpy and moan a lot.

  b By and large, I just get on with things and don't complain.

3 How would you describe your general outlook on life?

  a I'd say I'm pretty cheerful most of the time.

  b I'm prone to mood swings. I tend to be quite up and down.

4 How well do you deal with stress?

  a To be frank, not so well. I have a tendency to blow up.

  b Generally speaking, I'm pretty cool under pressure.

5 What do you do if you have negative feelings?

  a I'll often dwell on things and that sometimes makes me feel a bit down.

  b I'm usually able to shrug them off quite quickly.

READING

2 **Work in pairs. Discuss what – if anything – you know about the following topics.**

1 mindfulness and meditation

2 depression

3 life expectancy and well-being in the developed world

4 patients that doctors refer to as 'the worried well'

5 Traditional Chinese Medicine

3 **You are going to read an article about mindfulness and Eastern and Western medicine. With your partner, discuss which phrases you think are connected to each of the five topics in Exercise 2.**

> date back over 2,000 years
> low-level complaints
> a downward spiral
> be met with scepticism
> eradicate infectious diseases
> relieve minor conditions
> excruciating pain
> spark neural connections
> improve mortality
> trigger symptoms

4 **Now read the article and take notes on what is said about each of the topics in Exercise 2. Compare your notes with your partner.**

5 **With your partner, use the phrases from Exercise 3 and your own words to retell parts of the article.**

Mindfulness originates in Buddhist practices that date back over two thousand years.

6 **Use as many of the following sentence starters as you can to write sentences about the article that are true for you. Then discuss your ideas with your partner.**

- I already knew the bit about …
- I was interested in the fact that …
- I was surprised that …
- I find it hard to believe that …
- It's very true that …
- If this was in my country, …
- I didn't really understand this bit about …

VOCABULARY Mind and body

7 **Work in pairs. Discuss why the following actions might happen / be done.**

1 your mind drifts or wanders

2 your mind starts to race

3 your heart beats fast

4 your belly rises and falls

5 your body shudders

6 wipe your forehead

7 raise your eyebrows

8 raise your hand

9 clutch your chest

10 click your fingers

11 drop your head

12 shrug your shoulders

13 clench your fist

14 support your back

15 stretch your legs

16 flutter your eyelashes

8 **Which part of the body do you use for these actions?**

sniff	stroke	crouch	pat
scratch	blink	hug	spit
glare	frown	grin	punch

9 **Work in pairs. Test each other. Take turns to act out different actions in Exercises 7 and 8. Your partner should say the word(s).**

EAST MEETS WEST

The mindfulness boom gives Kasia Kowalski pause for thought

The spread of mindfulness has been little short of remarkable. Originating in Buddhist practices that date back over 2,000 years, it was relatively unknown in the West until just a few years ago and practised only by a handful of enthusiasts such as the late Apple CEO Steve Jobs. Recently, however, it has emerged as a multi-billion-dollar industry and has been embraced by everyone from celebrities and business leaders to doctors and parents. It has even been adopted by the US military, who use it to prepare troops for combat! So what exactly is mindfulness and how is it supposed to work?

Well, in essence, it's a meditation therapy designed to train people to focus fully on inner processes occurring in the here and now. Evidence is slowly mounting of its potential to combat a range of health problems. For instance, it's been claimed that it can break the cycle of recurrent bouts of depression and anxiety.

People suffering from depression often find their negative moods are accompanied by negative thoughts. While these thoughts usually disappear once the episode has passed or once medication has been prescribed, an association between the various symptoms has nevertheless been established in the brain. As a result, a mood swing caused by something trivial such as foul weather can trigger the symptoms, leading to a recurrence of depression. The more this happens, the more likely it is to recur, making the problem more resistant to drug treatment.

Mindfulness-based therapies encourage sufferers to break this downward spiral by noticing these patterns of thought and then focusing their minds on the present instead of the past or future. This can also bring about physical benefits too: the heart beats slower, muscles loosen and even brain structure may possibly be altered. Mindfulness is believed to spark new neural connections and studies have shown that the areas of the brain associated with the regulation of emotions are bigger in those who regularly practise meditation.

The spread of mindfulness exemplifies the interest many Western health professionals take in Eastern practices. Western medicine has been incredibly successful in improving mortality. During the 20th century, life expectancy doubled in developed countries and many infectious diseases were eradicated. However, while death may have been delayed, many are now living longer not in health but in sickness. Western medical practice is often less effective at dealing with long-term illness and general well-being. Unless you are in excruciating pain or have something life threatening, Western doctors often have little to offer. Indeed, many dismiss patients with low-level complaints as 'the worried well'. Eastern medicine such as Traditional Chinese Medicine (TCM), on the other hand, is more focused on maintaining good health, and through acupuncture, herbal remedies and massage is apparently more successful in relieving more minor conditions such as eczema, back pain and migraines.

TCM is underpinned by a philosophy that stresses harmony between mind, body and the environment. It aims to 'rebalance' patients and unblock natural energy flows called 'chi'. Unsurprisingly, such quasi-religious descriptions are met with scepticism from a science-based medical profession that wants evidence from randomised trials. However, for various reasons it has proved difficult to scientifically confirm the effectiveness of TCM. Medical research is always costly and as TCM does not require the use of many drugs, there's little financial incentive for pharmaceutical companies to invest in studies that may well prove it works. In addition, results can be difficult to quantify or randomise and even when positive results are gained, they can still be met with resistance and even ridicule.

None of this seems to be halting the march of mindfulness, though, and the millions around the world who claim to benefit from it seem unconcerned by the fact it has spawned more apps than conclusive critical studies.

BEDSIDE MANNER

SPEAKING

1 Work in groups. Discuss the questions.

- What's good / bad about being a doctor in your country? Would you like to be one?
- Do you know anyone who's a doctor? What do they think of their work and the health service?
- When was the last time you saw a doctor? How was the service? What were they like?

LISTENING

2 ▶ 33 Listen to five doctors talking about their jobs and issues connected to their work. Take notes on what they say. Which four speakers have something in common and which speaker is the odd one out? (There is more than one possible answer.)

3 ▶ 33 Work in pairs. Compare your notes. Then listen again and add to your notes.

4 Compare your notes again and discuss:

- whether you still agree who is the odd one out.
- which speaker you think is the most interesting.
- which speaker you would most like as a doctor.

5 With your partner, discuss the questions.

- What medical dramas do you know? How realistic do you think they are?
- How is the Internet good / bad in helping people deal with health? What do you think of the doctor's attitude towards Google?
- How can doctors best avoid communication breakdowns with patients?
- What do you imagine the man with Addison's disease went through?
- Have you heard of any unusual conditions? What do you know about the causes and effects?

UNDERSTANDING VOCABULARY

Nouns based on phrasal verbs

We sometimes make nouns based on phrasal verbs or other combinations of prepositions and verbs. Usually the verb comes first but not always as you can see in these sentences from the listening.

*When I see the mass of **printouts** in their hand, my heart sinks.*

*I had to stop because of the Ebola **outbreak**.*

There can also be other changes:

*A **passerby** stopped and called an ambulance.*

*There's been **a stepping up** in the pace of reform of the health service.*

*We're having **a get-together** after work.*

Hugh Laurie, star of the hit US medical drama *House*

6 Complete the sentences with nouns based on these phrasal verbs.

break out	break through	work out	drop out
bring up	crack down	run up	shake up

1 Our health system needs a serious _____ to cope with an aging population.
2 Good health in later life depends on your _____.
3 A vigorous _____ for 30 minutes each week is enough to stay fit.
4 I worry we might have an _____ of a disease we can't control.
5 There should be a _____ on the advertising of junk food to protect young people's health.
6 They have made some important _____ in tackling dementia.
7 Health will be a big issue in the _____ to the next election.
8 The _____ rate at medical school is quite high.

7 Work in pairs. Discuss how far you agree with the statements in Exercise 6. Explain why.

8 With your partner, discuss what you think the nouns in bold mean and who or what the words in italics refer to.

1 There was a big **cover-up** to stop the public finding out about *it*.

2 No-one was injured, luckily, but *it* was a complete **write-off** so I'll have to buy a new *one*.

3 We had a **break-in**, but luckily *they* didn't take anything too valuable.

4 *They* want to build a **bypass** to reduce traffic coming through the centre.

5 *They* have a **turnover** of billions of dollars because they are so dominant in the market.

6 *They* staged a **walkout** in protest at the cutbacks.

7 *We* had a bit of a **falling-out** over something stupid, but we're back on speaking terms.

8 *They* told me *it* had come back positive, but it turned out there had been a **mix-up** and I was actually fine, which was a relief.

9 Tell your partner about true examples for three of the words in bold in Exercise 8.

GRAMMAR

Modal auxiliaries

Modal auxiliaries (*will, should, must,* etc.) add meaning to the verb that follows them. For example, they can show ability, certainty or hypotheticality. The verb that follows is an infinitive without *to*. The infinitive can show a different time or aspect, such as perfect or continuous.

10 Work in pairs. Look at the sentences based on the listening. Discuss how the meaning or time changes with each possible ending.

1 I just know ...
   a they'll have been searching the Internet.
   b they can't have searched the Internet.

2 Norwegian doctors had reported into work with illnesses ...
   a that they would have issued a sick note to others for.
   b they could issue a sick note to others for.

3 Imagine what that patient ...
   a must've gone through.
   b might be going through.

4 If we come across a disease we don't immediately recognise, ...
   a we can feel lost.
   b we will often feel a bit lost.

5 They give poor treatment because ...
   a they won't admit to not knowing what the problem is.
   b they mustn't admit to not knowing what the problem is.

6 Nowadays, ...
   a most TV dramas will have more flawed characters.
   b most TV dramas should have more flawed characters.

7 We use it as a springboard for a discussion on the processes that ...
   a should've taken place.
   b may take place.

8 I later won a scholarship to study here in France and ...
   a I should qualify next year.
   b I shall qualify next year.

G Check your ideas on page 176 and do Exercise 1.

11 Work in pairs. For each of the situations below, discuss:
   • what caused / is causing the situation.
   • what you might say if you were in the situation.
   • what you think will (or should) happen next.

1 *It might be because it's winter and so more people get ill.*

   It wouldn't be happening if so many good doctors weren't leaving for the private sector.

   It'll only get worse in the months to come.

1 Waiting times for emergency treatment at the local hospital have shot up over the last six months.

2 On a bus, an unshaven man in dirty clothes is lying on the floor.

3 A large number of people at the hotel you run are off work with stomach problems and there's a conference starting, which means the hotel's going to be full.

4 A patient is suffering from severe headaches. The doctor has done a number of tests which came back negative.

5 A friend hasn't been in touch recently. You see them one day in a café but don't immediately recognise them. They leave before you can speak.

12 Work with a new partner. You are going to do a roleplay based on one of the situations in Exercise 11. First choose a situation and decide who will take which role below. Then spend a few minutes preparing your role.

1 the hospital manager with a journalist

2 two passengers who get on the bus

3 two managers of the hotel

4 the patient and doctor

5 you and another friend talking about the friend

13 Now roleplay the conversation.

G For further practice, see Exercise 2 on page 177.

VIDEO 5

THE CAT WHO ATE NEEDLES

1 Work in groups. Discuss the questions.

- Do you have any pets? Have you had pets in the past? If so, what kind?
- What benefits do you think there are to having pets? And what downsides might there be?
- Do you think being a vet is a good job to have in your country? Why? / Why not?
- What do you think the rewards of the profession might be?

2 ▶ 23 Watch the first part of a video about a pet in need of a vet (0.00–2.32). Find out:

1 what the problems are.
2 how the injury occurred.
3 what the vet did first.
4 what the vet fears could happen next.

3 Work in pairs. Compare your answers and discuss how you think Maxine the cat will be treated and whether she will survive.

4 ▶ 23 Watch the second part of the video (2.33–4.31). Are the sentences true (T) or false (F)? How do you know?

1 The thread was longer than they'd expected.
2 The main focus of the operation shifted as it progressed.
3 An instrument was attached to the needle.
4 The operation itself was remarkably swift.
5 Maxine's owner had to make sacrifices in order to provide her with all the aftercare she needed.
6 Maxine will never fully recover from the accident and the surgery.
7 Maxine's owner resents the time and effort this required of her.
8 The vet believes it was possible for things to have been much worse.

5 ▶ 23 Work in pairs. Check you understand the words and phrases in bold. Then put the sentences in the order you think you heard them. Watch the whole video again and check your answers.

a She needs **around-the-clock care** over the next few days.
b Catherine's dedication **pays off**.
c It felt like forever – just that not knowing what was going to happen.
d Doctor Yessenow was very helpful but also very **frank**.
e Doctor Yessenow immediately **puts** Maxine **under anaesthesia**.
f The **combs** point backwards.
g In two weeks' time, Maxine is **back to her old self**.
h I almost wanted to **take her place**.

6 Work in groups. Discuss the questions.

- Do you think it's good to dedicate so much time and money to a pet?
- Do you know anyone whose pet has had an operation? What happened?
- What do you think of the video? Would you watch a reality TV show like this?
- Do you ever watch other TV shows that feature animals in some way? If so, what?

UNDERSTANDING FAST SPEECH

7 ▶ 24 Listen to an extract from the video said at natural pace. Try to write down what you hear. Then compare your ideas with a partner.

8 ▶ 25 Try again. This time you will hear a slower version of the extract.

9 Check your ideas in File 10 on page 189. Groups of words are marked with / and pauses are marked //. Stressed sounds are in CAPITALS. Practise saying the extract.

REVIEW 5

VOCABULARY

1 Complete the text with one word in each space.

We're a growing company. Last year we had a ¹_____ of around five million dollars, mostly achieved because of a major ²_____ we made in the field of biotechnology. Things are still in their early stages, but potentially it ³_____ save thousands of lives. I've ⁴_____ working on the project since I started here – I ⁵_____ have been here three years next month – and none of the rapid progress ⁶_____ have been possible without the government funding we ⁷_____ been receiving during that time. People assume a discovery like this ⁸_____ have taken years of research, but actually it all happened very quickly.

2 Complete the second sentence so that it has a similar meaning to the first sentence using the word given. Do not change the word given. You must use between three and five words, including the word given.

1 He was texting while driving, so he's only got himself to blame.
It's his own fault. He _____ attention while he was driving. **MORE**

2 Things can't be easy for them now they're both unemployed.
_____ if neither of them is working. **STRUGGLING**

3 It's so annoying that he refuses to say when he doesn't understand things.
The fact that he _____ understanding things drives me mad! **ADMIT**

4 Things aren't as bad as they used to be, but there's still a long way to go.
Things _____ last few years, but we still have plenty to do. **OVER**

5 I'm only alive today because they managed to find a donor.
I _____ you today if a donor hadn't come forward when she did. **TALKING**

6 They're a nightmare to work with. They're so unreliable.
They're impossible! They _____ deadlines and breaking promises. **CONSTANTLY**

3 Choose the correct option.

1 The job's well paid, but it's mind-numbingly *demanding / boring / draining*.

2 I've just found your glasses. You can't *be looking / look / have been looking* very hard!

3 We're operating in *a blissfully / a fiercely / an utterly* competitive business environment.

4 There's a chance I *should / must / will* be talking at a conference on the 20th.

5 Students decided to stage *a dropout / an outbreak / a walkout* in protest.

6 The meeting *can / might / should* always be rescheduled if the date's not convenient.

VOCABULARY

4 Decide which of these verbs are more usually connected to the body and which are more usually connected to work. Think of a noun collocation for each verb.

clench	flutter	oversee	shrug
click	implement	stretch	place
come up with	input	schedule	wipe

5 Match the verbs (1–10) with the collocates (a–j).

1 undergo   a   your eyebrows / the minimum wage
2 suffer   b   a contract / guidelines
3 raise   c   a month's notice / advice
4 draw up   d   early retirement / no notice
5 maintain   e   chemotherapy / surgery
6 give   f   expense claims / my application
7 take   g   a crackdown / a new product
8 process   h   severe burns / a relapse
9 launch   i   a lot of opposition / swingeing cuts
10 face   j   a computer network / standards

6 Complete the sentences. Use the word in brackets to form a word that fits in the space.

1 I was granted a month's _____ leave when my partner died. (compassion)

2 I provide _____ and ensure projects get completed. (lead)

3 The unions have done little to halt the _____ of the workforce. (casual)

4 In the end, I just decided I couldn't stand any more and took voluntary _____. (redundant)

5 After the operation, I underwent _____ physiotherapy for a few months. (extend)

6 We lose millions of pounds each year because of chronic _____. (absent)

7 She'll be dealing with any _____ issues that may arise. (contract)

8 They've halved the infant _____ rate in a decade. (mortal)

7 Complete the text with one word in each space. The first letters are given.

In my last job, I had to go to lots of official events and parties and ¹ne_____ quite a bit. I enjoyed it because I've always been a sociable person. I liked taking clients out and ²en_____ them and it helped to ³at_____ new business. Also, getting to eat in fancy restaurants was very much a ⁴p_____ of the job. After one meal, though, I slipped while I was leaving and broke my leg in three ⁵p_____. It was horrible. The pain was ⁶ex_____! I was ⁷r_____ to hospital and they decided I needed an operation. The break was so bad they needed to ⁸in_____ metal rods! Apparently, they can be ⁹re_____ at some point if everything heals OK. Anyway, I was given an ¹⁰an_____ and can't remember much else about what happened. Two days later, though, I got an email saying I'd been fired! I couldn't believe it! I'm taking my old employers to a ¹¹tr_____ and hopefully I'll win some ¹²co_____.

11

PLAY

IN THIS UNIT YOU LEARN HOW TO:

- talk about sports you watch or do
- recognise and use irony
- discuss issues around gaming
- link ideas within and across sentences
- discuss and use playful language

SPEAKING

1   **Work in pairs. Look at the photo and discuss the questions.**

- What do you think is happening in the photo?
- Which of the phrases below could be used to describe the crowd or individual spectators in the photo? Why might people do these things?

go wild	abuse the referee or a player
boo	hold your head in your hands
chant a name	be on the edge of your seat
get upset	laugh at other people in the crowd

- Have you ever done any of these things when watching sport – or watching something else? If so, when and why?

2   **Work with a new partner. Discuss which of the options below you would rather do – and why.**

- watch sport or play sport
- do yoga or do a martial art
- go to the gym or play a video game
- run a marathon or do a triathlon
- go on a cruise or go on a walking holiday
- watch basketball or watch tennis on TV
- support the favourite in a match or support the underdog
- go to the final of the Football World Cup or the Olympic athletics finals

THEY BLEW IT

VOCABULARY Sports and events

1 Work in groups. Answer the questions.

1 What's the difference between **getting knocked out in** the second round and **going through to** the second round? And what happens if you just **scrape through**?

2 If a player **challenges a decision** or **a call**, do they hope the decision will be **upheld** or **overturned**?

3 How might someone be **caught doping**? What would happen after that?

4 What happens if a player or team **gets thrashed**? How might the crowd react?

5 Why might a referee **send** someone **off** or **sin-bin** them? Which is worse?

6 What's the difference between being **suspended**, being **substituted** and being **dropped**?

7 Why might you begin to **fade** in a race, game or competition?

8 What happens if you **blow it** in a game or season?

9 How can people **fix** a match, race or fight? Why do they do it?

10 What happens in a **close** game, a **one-sided** game and a **dirty** game?

11 What happens when someone **gets cramp**? And what's the difference with **feeling stiff**?

12 Why might you **sponsor** someone to do a marathon or some other physical challenge?

2 Choose five of the words or phrases in bold in Exercise 1 and say something true that happened to you or a team / player you know. It could be a non-sporting situation.

Liverpool had a great chance to win the league a few years ago, but they blew it when they lost to Chelsea.

When I played rugby at school, we always used to get thrashed. We lost sixty-nil one time.

I just about managed to scrape through my French exam at school. I got 51%.

LISTENING

3 ▶ 34 Listen to three conversations about sport. Decide in which conversation (1–3) a speaker says something about:

a a person overcoming a muscle problem.

b a person / team struggling to begin with.

c a person / team being the favourite.

d a person / team being exhausted.

e the result of a match being very close.

f a person / team having lessons.

g a change that helped a person / team.

h a famous player from the past.

i raising money.

DEVELOPING CONVERSATIONS

Irony and humour

Irony is quite commonly used in conversation. If we are being ironic, we say the opposite of what we think or we exaggerate the difference between the example we use and the reality.

I'm not exactly Picasso when it comes to painting.

We often use *manage to* ironically when we 'succeed' in doing something stupid.

Manu managed to kick the ball over the bar from about a metre out.

6 Work in pairs. Look at the underlined expressions in audio script 34 on page 207. Some show irony and humour, while some are just neutral. Discuss the questions for each expression.

  1 Is the speaker being ironic or not?

  2 Where they are being ironic, what's the reality?

  3 Could you make a similar ironic comment in your language?

7 Match 1–5 to the ironic comments a–e. Then practise saying the exchanges with your partner.

  1 So you're starting at high school next week?

  2 What did you think of the poems he wrote?

  3 He's a bit absent-minded, then?

  4 I'm not exactly the world's best tennis player.

  5 Did you see that goal he scored? It was amazing!

  a You could say that! He's managed to lose his passport three times.

  b It wasn't bad. I didn't exactly go wild, though.

  c Yeah. I can't wait – all that lovely homework!

  d Well, it's not exactly Shakespeare.

  e Come on! You only made about 20 double faults!

8 Complete each of the sentences below in two ironic ways that are true for you.

  1 I once managed to ...

  2 I'm not exactly ...

9 Work in groups. Compare and discuss your ideas.

CONVERSATION PRACTICE

10 Work in pairs. Choose one of these tasks. Use as much language from this lesson as you can.

  a Think of sporty things you have seen or done. Think of one 'success' and one 'failure' and make some notes about what happened. Then tell your partner about what happened. Your partner should comment and ask questions to help you.

  b Student A: read your rolecard in File 24 on page 191. Student B: read your rolecard in File 25 on page 192. Spend a few minutes planning what to say and then roleplay the conversations.

▶ 26 To watch the video and do the activities, see the DVD ROM.

4 ▶ 34 Work in pairs. Try to complete the sentences from the conversations using your knowledge of vocabulary and grammar and what you heard. Then listen again and check your answers.

  1 Shame _____ serving _____ end.

  2 Let's _____ there's _____ improvement.

  3 I've had that playing football _____ clutching _____ leg _____.

  4 Hey, I wouldn't _____ managed _____ beach.

  5 There's no _____ 60 million, _____ much he cost us.

  6 He _____ goal, _____ team going.

5 With your partner, discuss the questions.

  • Have you ever had any coaching? What for? Did it make much difference?

  • What things do you think show your age?

  • Would you like to do something like the swim to the island? Why? / Why not?

  • Are there any big physical challenge events in your country? Are they easy to enter? Do you know anyone who's done any of them?

  • Have you – or a player / team you know – ever won or lost when you shouldn't have? What happened?

  • What things / people do you think are overrated?

GAME THEORY

VOCABULARY Talking about gaming

1 Work in groups. How many different kinds of electronic games can you think of?

first-person shooter games

2 Complete the sentences with the correct form of these verbs.

collaborate	expose	let	provide
defy	foster	modify	stimulate

1 Gaming _____ an escape from the stresses and strains of everyday life.

2 You often have to work together and _____ to achieve success.

3 The fact you can _____ your environment to suit your own taste makes things very creative.

4 Gaming can actually help _____ family relationships if everyone plays together.

5 You _____ to a huge amount of English in most games, so they're a great way of practising.

6 A lot of the new multi-player online roleplaying games really _____ the imagination.

7 The graphics on some modern games are so incredible they _____ description.

8 First-person shooter games are a great way of _____ off steam.

3 Underline any phrases in Exercise 2 that are new for you. Then work in pairs and compare your choices.

4 With your partner, discuss how far you agree with each opinion in Exercise 2. Explain why. Can you think of any other benefits of gaming? What are the downsides?

READING

5 Read the blog post by a teacher. Answer the questions.

1 What kinds of gaming are mentioned – and why?

2 What benefits of gaming are mentioned? And what downsides?

3 How would you describe the blogger's attitude towards gaming? Why?

Just another secret teacher blogspot
PAY TO PLAY!

Like many of you, I suspect, I've lost the odd evening to online chess or snooker, and after particularly traumatic staff meetings I've even been known to get disturbingly engrossed in first-person shooters! I mean, it's not hard to grasp the appeal of most computer games, is it? All the same, surely only the most evangelical would claim that gaming comes with no strings attached.

It's the effect it seems to be having on the lives of half my students that worries me most – and frankly, I mean the male half! Now, it seems to be a fairly universal truth that girls do better than boys at school. Partly this is **down to** the fact that girls read more and, on top of that, they spend more time doing homework. **Meanwhile,** boys are busy playing games.

Of course, I've heard the arguments in support of collaborative gaming. I've read research claiming linguistic and social skills develop **on account of** the hours spent online – and that's all fine **so long as** it's done in moderation. Trust me, though, it rarely is! Many of the lads I teach are addicts, pure and simple. The roleplay games they're into are a chronic suck on their time – whether or not they start out with the intention of studying, before too long their evenings are lost to the virtual realm. Time flies by and they game till they drop – and **subsequently** drag themselves into class in the morning half-asleep at best.

Whichever way you look at it, the effects aren't great. Despite the friendships they may be cementing during these late-night sessions, during the day they're letting themselves down. They're less attentive than I'd like them to be, **not to mention** less verbal. That is, when they're not actually just nodding off! **Moreover,** in spite of all that time online, they're not ending up any more informed about the world around them. Just this morning I was confronted by a student who not only failed to recognise a photo of the president but also didn't even understand what an election was! Quite incredible!

To be fair, these are issues that senior management are aware of. The best solution they've come up with so far, though? Gamification of the syllabus! I despair sometimes, I really do.

6 Work in pairs. Discuss which of the following opinions you think the blogger gives. Underline the parts of the blog you believe support your ideas. Then decide which one is the main argument.

1 Gaming can be a great way to unwind.

2 Most gaming enthusiasts have a fairly balanced view of its benefits.

3 Teenage girls mature earlier than teenage boys do.

4 Gaming can have social and educational benefits.

5 Obsessive gaming is the main reason boys are falling behind at school.

6 It's easy to lose track of time when you're gaming.

7 Computers make you stupid.

8 The school bosses have a good grasp of the problems teachers face.

7 Read the comments on the blog post and decide how far you agree with them. Then write one more comment for yourself.

8 Work in groups. Discuss the comments on the post and the ones you wrote.

Comments

AliJenkins1992 27 November 14:42

Point taken about gaming addiction and its effect on student attentiveness. **That notwithstanding**, you're wrong about gamification. Thanks to the introduction of basic coding classes in schools, we're seeing some of the most exciting developments in education for decades.

BingBev 28 November 05:43

AliJenkins1992 Couldn't agree more. We really have to start getting boys more involved in learning. **Otherwise**, we'll lose a whole generation. Gamification talks to them on their level.

Bikinikill 27 November 14:23

Girls work harder **so as to** achieve more at school? No wonder given what we have to deal with afterwards!

Gelion 27 November 15:43

I played the first Tomb Raider way back in 1997, or thereabouts, and loved it. The problem-solving, finding stuff, the soundtrack, the sounds … amazing game. I also realised how addictive it was. Nights of good intentions went bad: 'I'll just get to the next level and then I'll turn it off' turned into early hours sessions and **consequently** I began to understand why many of my school students arrived at school bleary-eyed. **Whilst** I absolutely loved it, I realised what a major time suck getting into computer games can be and as such made the conscious decision to walk away.

GRAMMAR

Linking words and phrases

We use many different words and phrases to link two parts of sentences or to show the relationship between two separate sentences. We use linkers to show: (1) contrast, (2) condition, (3) time / order, (4) purpose / result, (5) addition, (6) cause. Linkers which serve the same function often take different grammatical patterns.

9 Match two linkers in bold in the blog post and comments to each of the functions in the box.

10 Decide which linkers in bold in the blog post could be replaced with these phrases.

all the same	as such	despite the fact that
on top of that	a result of	as well as
if we don't	provided	as a result of
in the meantime	in order to	then

 Check your ideas on page 177 and do Exercise 1.

11 Complete the descriptions of different games with these linkers.

as such	although	even though	owing to
whereas	as well as	down to	in spite of
similarly	whether		

1 It's the kind of thing you'd enjoy _____ you're an expert or completely new to the game.

2 It runs on both PCs and Macs, _____ you'll probably need to install some kind of web player.

3 It's a business simulation game and, _____, it's perfect training for the world of work.

4 I think a large part of its appeal is _____ how easy it is to modify and adapt.

5 It's a kind of sci-fi strategy game, but _____ space battles you can also fight battles on land.

6 _____ a few technical issues that sometimes affect it, it's still an incredible game.

7 _____ the graphics have quite an old-fashioned look, there's still something lovely about it.

8 _____ a lot of games are just down to luck, this one involves a considerable degree of skill.

9 It's really clever because the main character is this guy who's being treated for mental illness _____ his habit of playing violent video games endlessly!

10 I think it's basically quite nicely designed, but some of the graphics are quite limited. _____, some of the textures on the buildings could still be improved.

12 Work in groups. Think of two electronic games you like – preferably ones your partners don't know. If you don't play electronic games, think of board or card games you like. Spend a few minutes deciding how to describe them and how you could use linkers. Then work together and take turns to describe your games.

 For further practice, see Exercise 2 on page 178.

WORD PLAY

LISTENING

1 Work in pairs. Look at the photo and discuss the questions.

- Do you know the game that is being played in the photo?
- How does it work?
- What skills do you think you need?
- Are you / Would you be any good at it? Why? / Why not?

2 ▶ 35 Listen to the introduction to a podcast called *The Wright Word*. Find out why the game in the photo is mentioned and what the topic of the podcast is.

3 Work in pairs. Discuss the questions.

1 What do you think of the project? Do you think it will work? Why? / Why not?

2 What other examples of word games and wordplay can you think of?

3 In what ways might games and wordplay be good / not so good for learning a language?

4 ▶ 36 Listen to the rest of the podcast. What do the speakers say in relation to the questions in Exercise 3?

5 ▶ 36 Work in pairs. Answer the questions. Then listen again and check your ideas.

1 Why are hybrid cattle mentioned?

2 What point is made about the Carrier language having an oral tradition?

3 How does a Chinese crossword differ from a Western one? Why do you think Scrabble wouldn't work in Chinese?

4 What example is given of a pun?

5 What is described as a bit sexist?

6 What example is given of alliteration? How is alliteration linked to tongue twisters?

7 Why is the chat feature of an app mentioned?

8 Why does Christine call it a day?

6 Work in groups. Discuss the questions.

- It's claimed that 50% of the world's 6,500 languages will become extinct by the end of the century. Why do you think that is? Does it matter? Why? / Why not?

- Why do you think playing with language is universal?

- Which of the word games and kinds of wordplay mentioned had you heard of before? Which have you played? Do you like them?

- How can language be sexist? Do you have the idea of political correctness in your language (changing language to avoid sexism, etc.)? Do you think it's a good idea? Why? / Why not?

- How much do you make jokes about and banter with family / friends / colleagues? What about?

UNDERSTANDING VOCABULARY

Alliteration

As mentioned in the listening, many tongue twisters and idioms make use of alliteration, where several words in the phrase start with the same letter or sound.

*A **big black bug bit** a **big black bear**.*

*We need to make sure everything's **ship-shape** before the inspection.*

Alliteration may mean we favour the choice of some words in normal speech and collocation.

*The whole argument is **fundamentally flawed**.* (instead of *basically flawed*)

*They're **seeking sanctuary** from the war.* (instead of *looking for sanctuary*)

Some phrases repeat a vowel sound for a kind of rhyme that has a similar affect to alliteration.

*We shouldn't **play safe**.*

7 ▶ **37** **Listen to these tongue twisters. Then work in pairs and see who can say each one the fastest. Which of them do you find most difficult? Why?**

1 Three free throws.

2 A really weird rear wheel.

3 She sells seashells on the seashore.

4 Peter Piper picked a pickled pepper.

5 How can a clam cram in a clean cream can?

6 How much ground would a groundhog hog if a groundhog could hog ground?

8 **Complete the sentences with these phrases. Underline other alliterative phrases in seven of the sentences.**

give as good as she gets	peer pressure
on the tip of my tongue	reserve the right
the lap of luxury	love lost
bite the bullet	jump the gun
doom and gloom	stop the rot

1 It was another deeply disappointing result, but hopefully we can _____ in the next game.

2 There's little _____ between the two sides and unfortunately there was no meeting of minds.

3 It's expensive, but I think we just have to _____ and buy a new one. It's not going to break the bank.

4 It's not all _____, far from it. I still have my house and a family that loves me!

5 Oh, it's _____. It'll come back to me in a minute.

6 Don't give in to _____. Have the courage of your convictions.

7 It's the same old story. While they live in _____, the majority are struggling to make ends meet.

8 The organiser normally announces changes in the programme, but, strictly speaking, they always _____ to make amendments without prior notice.

9 He was making a few jokes at her expense, but then she can _____.

10 I don't want to _____, but preparations for the World Cup seem to be right on track and the stadiums are simply superb.

9 **Work in pairs. Choose six of the phrases from Exercise 8 that you would like to remember most. Write down the first letter of each word in the phrase, as below. Then close your books and say the phrases.**

It's o. t. t. o. my t. (It's on the tip of my tongue.)

She can g. a. g. a. she g.

10 **With your partner, think of true examples for the phrases you chose in Exercise 9.**

SPEAKING

11 **Work in pairs. Choose one of the following word games to play.**

Student A: use the words in File 26 on page 190.

Student B: use the words in File 27 on page 193.

Coffeepot
Say phrases and sentences using a word / phrase from the list but replace the word with 'coffeepot'. Your partner should guess the word. How many can they guess in one minute? For example:

'He's a coffeepot.' 'He always coffeepots at cards.' 'Stop coffeepotting!' 'We won, but then we were declared the loser because they said we'd coffeepotted.'

Act or draw
Act out or draw a word / phrase from the list *without speaking*. How many can your partner guess in one minute?

Taboo
Explain a word / phrase from the list *without using the words in brackets*. How many can your partner guess in one minute?

12

HISTORY

On top of the world

IN THIS UNIT YOU LEARN HOW TO:

- describe some of the key events in people's lives
- use similes to make descriptions more interesting
- give better presentations
- ask contextualised questions after presentations
- discuss important historical events
- present and debate arguments and theories

SPEAKING

1   **Work in pairs. Discuss the questions.**

- This photo shows a historically significant event. Do you know where and when it was taken?
- How much do you know about the event and the causes and results of it?
- Why do you think it's important to have an understanding of history?

2   **Imagine you are the man in the photo. Think about these questions.**

- Why did you decide to climb the Wall that day?
- How did you get up there?
- How did you feel?
- What was going on around you?
- What happened next?
- When did you first realise you'd been captured on film – and that the photo had become iconic?
- How has your life changed since then?

3   **Work with a new partner. Tell your story. Your partner should comment and ask extra questions. Then change roles.**

A REMARKABLE LIFE

War veteran Bernard Jordan enjoys his 90th birthday

VOCABULARY Personal histories

1 Work in pairs. Check you understand the words and phrases in bold in the sentences. Then discuss the positive / negative effects that each situation might have on someone's life.

1 He had a very **sheltered upbringing**.

2 She's from quite a **deprived** background.

3 They had to **flee** the country after the military **coup**.

4 He was very involved in **radical** politics in his youth.

5 She was **evacuated** during the war.

6 He saw **active service** during the war.

7 She built up a business **from scratch**.

8 He comes from a **broken home**.

9 He grew up in a very **close-knit** community.

10 She's from a very **privileged** background.

11 She won a **scholarship** to study in the States.

12 He was **orphaned** when both his parents died in a plane crash.

2 Tell your partner which sentences in Exercise 1 describe people you know or famous people you can think of. Add as many details as you can.

LISTENING

3 Work in pairs. You are going to hear someone describe his girlfriend's father. Discuss how these words and phrases could be connected to the father's life.

first generation	ice cream	outboard motors
poverty	textiles	the States
drop out	the capital	a peasant

4 ▶ 38 Listen and see if your guesses were correct. Then discuss with your partner how each word in Exercise 3 is connected to the man's life.

5 ▶ **38** Listen again and complete the sentences with phrasal verbs.

1 The whole visit _____ far better than I'd dared to hope it would.

2 It _____ that his bark is much worse than his bite.

3 When he was thirteen, his dad _____.

4 He _____ selling ice creams ... and then _____ selling textiles door-to-door.

5 He decided that if he really wanted to _____, he'd have to move to the capital, and so he _____ to make his fortune.

6 He got there, somehow managed to _____ his own company ... and then just slowly _____ things _____.

7 His eyes _____ when I told him how much I got for that portrait I sold last year.

8 I didn't _____ that fact too much.

6 Work in pairs. Discuss the questions.

• What do you think are the pros and cons of coming from a very large family?

• In what ways might being from a first-generation immigrant family hold you back? And how might it benefit you?

• Do you know anyone you'd describe as a self-made man / woman? How did they make their fortune?

• How much responsibility do you think teenagers should be given? Why?

• Why do you think George likes the fact his girlfriend's father is still 'quite rough round the edges'? Do you see it as a positive quality yourself?

UNDERSTANDING VOCABULARY

Similes

A simile is a phrase that describes something by comparing it to something else. The comparison is introduced using *like* or *as*. Similes are often intended to be humorous or vivid and poetic.

*He still eats **like a peasant** and belches after dinner and stuff.*

Saying something is *as* + adjective + *as* something else is usually the same as saying *it's very* + adjective.

*She'd been out in the snow for ages and her hands were **as cold as ice**.* (= very cold)

7 Match 1–5 to a–e to make common similes.

1	I've got a memory	a	like the plague.
2	He smokes	b	like a fish out of water.
3	I felt	c	like a sieve.
4	I avoid him	d	like chalk and cheese.
5	They're	e	like a chimney.

Now match 6–10 to f–j.

6	He's as hard	f	as a dodo.
7	It's as dead	g	as the hills.
8	She went as white	h	as nails.
9	That joke is as old	i	as mud!
10	That's as clear	j	as a sheet.

8 Work in pairs. Answer the questions.

1 When might you feel like a fish out of water? What's the opposite?

2 Why might you avoid someone like the plague? How might it be done?

3 If two people are like chalk and cheese, does it mean they don't get on? What's the opposite?

4 Can you think of any athletes you'd say are as hard as nails? What other kinds of people might be described in this way?

5 When might someone go as white as a sheet?

6 What's the problem if something is as clear as mud? What's the opposite?

9 With your partner, discuss whether you have similar expressions to the ones in Exercise 7 in your language.

10 Complete the sentences with your own ideas. Be as funny, poetic or serious as you want.

1 Once he'd started up his business, he had to work like ...

2 She was the only teacher I ever had who treated us like ...

3 I come from a very argumentative family. Dinner at our house was usually like ...

4 Once I started university, I was as happy ...

5 He emerged from his childhood as tough ...

6 She's an amazing woman. She's got a voice as ... and she looks like ...

11 Work in groups. Compare your similes. Which is your favourite? Why?

CONVERSATION PRACTICE

12 Choose one of these tasks.

a Think of someone you know – or know of – that you feel has had an interesting life. Make notes on what you know about their personal history. Think about: where they were born, what kind of background they're from, some key moments in their life and why they were important, etc.

b Decide what have been the five key moments in your own life so far. Make notes on what happened and when, and why you feel these moments were so important.

13 Now work in groups. Tell each other about your people or your own lives. Your partners should ask questions to find out more. Are there any similarities between the different lives described?

▶ 27 To watch the video and do the activities, see the DVD ROM.

PRESENTING HISTORY

LISTENING

1 Work in groups. You are going to listen to a student presentation about an aspect of history. Before you listen, discuss the questions.

- In your country, are presentations a common part of learning and assessment at school / university? What do you think is good about doing them? What's bad?

- Have you ever given a presentation at school / university / work? What on? How did it go?

- Look at the tips for giving academic presentations. Discuss if each tip is *always* good advice. Choose and / or write five tips that you think are most essential.

2 ▶ 39 Listen to the introduction of the presentation. Decide:

1 what the presentation is about.

2 which of the presentation tips Courtney follows.

3 Work in pairs. Make a list of the impacts you think the Second World War had on society, women, welfare and state intervention.

4 ▶ 40 Listen to the rest of the presentation. Find out which – if any – of your ideas were mentioned.

TIPS FOR PRESENTATIONS

1 Write the whole presentation in advance and try to memorise as much of it as you can.

2 Introduce yourself to the audience.

3 Have a joke or interesting quote or statistic to begin.

4 Explain the structure of the talk.

5 Limit what you're going to talk about to one narrow area or argument.

6 Make your opinion clear near the beginning.

7 Engage the audience by asking and taking questions as you go along.

8 Make clear when one section has finished and another starts.

9 Give evidence and cite experts for the points you make.

10 Summarise what you have said at the end.

11 Add a final point before rounding off the presentation.

12 Talk slightly slower than you normally would in conversation.

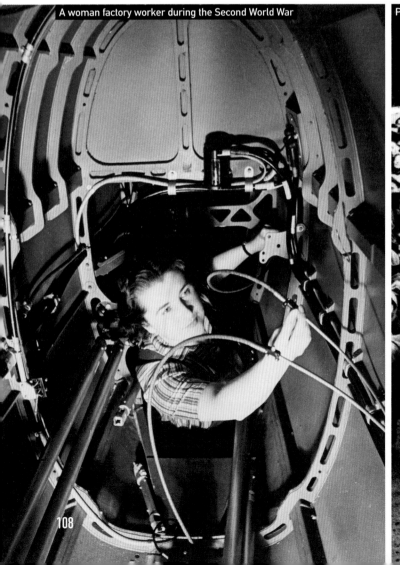

A woman factory worker during the Second World War

People waiting in line for fuel rations, 1940s

5 ▶ 40 With your partner, put the extracts below in the order you heard them. Discuss how each extract relates to the main argument. Then listen again and check your ideas.

a We somewhat take for granted the existence of state-run social support.

b It was simply untenable to continue their exclusion from politics.

c … cuts to public spending and changes to work regulations have affected women adversely.

d One of the other social shifts … was the number of women who were widowed.

e There now seems to be a deep fear of borrowing … and increasingly serious threats to break up the EU.

f It's difficult for us now to get our heads round the sheer scale of the devastation.

g … lots of companies and banks, even whole industries, were nationalised.

h The war sowed the first seeds of women's liberation that flowered in the 60s and 70s.

6 Work in groups. Discuss the questions.

- What mark out of ten would you give the presentation? Why?
- What advice would you give to improve it?
- Did you learn anything new? What?
- What do you think of Courtney's arguments?
- Do the points Courtney made apply to your country?

DEVELOPING CONVERSATIONS

Contextualised questions

When we ask a question after listening to a presentation, lecture or speech, we often need to contextualise the question to make clear which part of the presentation we are referring to. We may also summarise the part of an argument we wish to challenge or get more details on.

7 Look at the contextualised questions below. In each case, underline the phrases you could re-use about other presentations.

1 At one point you said something about the effect of inflation on the decline of the Roman Empire. Could you elaborate on that a bit?

2 I didn't quite understand the point you were making about the role of Christianity in the fall of the Romans. Could you go over that again?

3 You mentioned the rise in divorce after the war. Do you have any specific statistics on that?

4 In your introduction, you gave a quote from Churchill. Could you tell me what the source for that is?

5 You seem to be arguing that the reforms failed. Don't you think that that's a bit of an overstatement?

6 I think you cited a study by Brooks and Hart. Do you have the full reference for that?

7 You referred to something called the Doppler Effect. Could you just explain exactly what that is?

8 I think you claimed that doing grammar is a waste of time. What evidence do you have for that?

8 Write four questions to ask Courtney about her presentation using phrases from Exercise 7.

9 ▶ 41 Listen to the questions Courtney is asked. Were any of them the same as the questions you wrote? How well do you think they were answered?

10 Take turns to ask and answer the questions you thought of in Exercise 8. If you can't think of an answer, try to avoid giving one in some way.

VOCABULARY Historical events

11 Complete the sentences describing fictional historical events below with these pairs of words.

overthrow + established	election + marked
success + strengthened	introduction + saw
revelations + undermined	victory + pointed
massacre + restrict	declaration + fled
break-up + entered	reforms + sowed

1 The _____ of the new currency _____ inflation rise in many countries.

2 The _____ of the general strike _____ the power of the unions.

3 The _____ of the Hope Party government _____ a turning point in the country's history.

4 The _____ instigated by the Hope Party _____ the seeds of the economic growth we're experiencing.

5 After the _____ of the country, the region _____ a lengthy period of political instability.

6 The _____ in the town led to a period of soul-searching and calls to _____ gun ownership.

7 Following the _____ of independence, thousands _____ the country.

8 Following the _____ of the old regime, elections were held and a new parliament was _____.

9 The _____ of widespread corruption _____ people's faith in the political system.

10 The _____ of the liberation struggle was a source of inspiration for millions and _____ the way forward to a better future.

12 Work in pairs. Have any of the events in Exercise 11 happened in your country? What do you know about their causes and consequences?

SPEAKING

13 Work in groups. Choose one of these tasks.

a If you are from the same country, decide on the five most important events from the past that continue to have an impact today.

b If you are from different places, work on your own and choose one important event from the past that still has an impact today in your country.

Spend a few minutes preparing your ideas. Then work with your group and take turns to present your ideas to each other.

HISTORY MYSTERIES

SPEAKING

1 Work in groups. Look at the picture and discuss the questions.

- When and where do you think this picture dates from?
- What do you think is going on in this scene?
- Who do you think the different people shown are?
- How do you think each person is feeling? Why?

READING

2 Read this short article about an event similar to the one that inspired the picture. Find out:

1 what happened, where and when.

2 what contemporary theory was put forward to explain it.

3 in what way the attempt to tackle the problem was unorthodox.

4 how this particular event was brought to an end.

5 two reasons why this event is historically significant.

3 Work in pairs. Discuss what you think the words in bold in the article mean. Then use the words in bold to complete each group of phrases below.

1 trigger the ~ of war / a fatal ~ of food poisoning / fear another ~ of violence

2 a holy ~ / the museum is a ~ to modern art / a ~ to the dead

3 it's not a new ~ / an isolated ~ / one explanation of the ~ is ...

4 the ~ of troops / threaten the ~ of support / a sudden ~ of funding

5 she was ~ grief / he was ~ desire / I was ~ rage

6 the area was hit by a flu ~ / the ~ spread quickly / combat the global AIDS ~

7 experts ~ the theory / the president ~ the use of troops / investigators have ~ suicide

8 a new officer was ~ the case / be ~ the Madrid branch / we were ~ our groups

4 With your partner, discuss what theories you think may have been put forward to explain the dancing plague.

5 ▶ 42 Listen. What are the three main explanations for the plague? Which is put forward as the most likely? Why?

THE DANCING PLAGUE

Sometime in July 1518, a woman called Frau Troffea suddenly started dancing wildly in the streets of Strasbourg in North-East France. There was no music and she did not seem to be enjoying the act in any way. Rather, she simply seemed unable to prevent it from happening. She was still at it several days later, and within a week more than 30 other people had been **consumed by** a similar urge.

Unsure how best to respond to this peculiar **phenomenon**, concerned civic authorities sought the advice of medical experts, who **ruled out** supernatural or astrological causes. Instead, they decided, the dancing plague was a natural disorder caused by 'hot blood'. At the time, the usual treatment for such conditions would have involved the **withdrawal** of blood in order to restore what was seen as a correct balance. In this instance, however, the local authorities decided those affected would only recover if they were made to dance all day and all night. As such, they were **assigned to** special halls, where professional musicians were paid to entertain them and dancers paid to keep them moving. After a week or so, those with the weakest hearts started to drop dead, but still the craze continued.

By the end of the summer, over 400 people had experienced the madness. Only after dancers started being taken to a special healing **shrine** did the **epidemic** finally come to a halt. There had been many earlier instances of dancing mania, but this was by far the best documented, with local and religious records, doctors' notes and so on all surviving. Curiously, it was also the last major **outbreak** of its kind, with only a small handful of instances being reported since. To this day, researchers and historians continue to debate the cause of the dancing mania.

VOCABULARY
Discussing arguments and theories

6 Work in pairs. Decide if the words in italics have the same meaning in the context. If not, what's the difference?

1 One early theory *put forward* / *proposed* to explain the outbreaks of dancing mania was that they were carefully organised events staged by particular cults. However, it has since been *established* / *claimed* that many participants were psychologically disturbed.

2 Many psychologists *argue* / *contend* that extreme stress caused by harsh environmental conditions must have played a *significant* / *minor* role in the outbreaks.

3 Scholars have *asserted* / *demonstrated* that the decline of the Roman Empire *stemmed from* / *gave rise to* invasions.

4 The as yet unsolved murders were *allegedly* / *supposedly* carried out by a criminal organisation, although many have *questioned* / *cast doubt on* these claims.

5 By *highlighting* / *emphasising* the importance of ordinary people in national history, the paper *challenged* / *accepted* the conventional views of the time.

READING

7 Work in pairs. You are each going to read about something from history that is still hotly debated. Make notes on the main facts and the things still attracting debate.

Student A: read the article in File 28 on page 194.

Student B: read the article in File 29 on page 193.

8 Now tell your partner about your article. Discuss what you think the most likely interpretations are – and why. Use some of the vocabulary in italics from Exercise 6.

GRAMMAR

Dramatic inversion

We can add emphasis to sentences by inverting them. Inversion is more common in literary or journalistic writing than in spoken English.

At no time has it ever been *definitively established that both men acted alone.*

(= It has never been definitively established that both men acted alone.)

9 Work in pairs. Look at these inverted sentences from the three historical stories. Answer the questions below.

a *Only after dancers started being taken to a special healing shrine did the epidemic finally come to a halt.*

b *Never has it caused the strange behaviour most associated with dancing disease.*

c *Not until the 1950s was the theory disproved.*

d *Not only did he become the youngest man to hold office, but he is also the only Roman Catholic to have ever sat in the White House.*

e *No sooner had news of the killing started spreading around the world than the local police announced the arrest of Lee Harvey Oswald.*

1 How could each sentence be written in a less dramatic way?

2 What happens to the order of subject, auxiliary and verb in inverted sentences?

3 What happens when a sentence in the present or past simple is inverted?

4 What other changes can happen when sentences are inverted?

5 Can you underline all the negative adverbial phrases in the sentences?

 Check your ideas on page 179 and do Exercises 1 and 2.

10 Complete the sentences with your own ideas. Add sentences before / after if you need to. Then work in pairs and compare your ideas. Who came up with the most dramatic sentence?

1 Only when …

2 No sooner …

3 Nowhere else in the world …

4 Not only …, but …

5 Only once before …

6 Not until he was 21 …

 For further practice, see Exercise 3 on page 179.

SPEAKING

11 Work in groups. Discuss what you know about the historical figures below. Think in particular about the theories they put forward, the degree to which they have been accepted and what their greatest contribution to history has been. Use as much language from this lesson as you can to explain your ideas.

Karl Marx	Isaac Newton
Archimedes	Charles Darwin
Galileo Galilei	Sigmund Freud
Albert Einstein	Leonardo da Vinci
Nicolaus Copernicus	

VIDEO 6

THE SWORD EXCALIBUR

1 **Work in groups. Discuss the questions.**

• Do you know any of these people / things / events connected to the legend of King Arthur?

the sword in the stone	Guinevere
Mordred	the Lady of the Lake
Camelot	Merlin
the quest for the Holy Grail	Lancelot
Galahad	

• What do you think the picture says about King Arthur and his knights?

• Do you think myths and legends sometimes have a historical basis? If yes, in what way?

• If not, how and why do you think myths and legends are created?

2 📹 **28** Watch the video. Find out what myth is mentioned and what possible historical explanation for it is suggested.

3 📹 **28** Work in pairs. Discuss how the phrases below are connected to the story. Then watch again and check your ideas.

1 try in vain

2 step forward

3 the rightful and true king

4 the practices of the Ancients

5 cast some light on

6 a very expensive piece of technology

7 tin, copper and bronze

8 pour into a mould

9 a pretty magical process

10 transform raw material

4 **With your partner, discuss the questions.**

• How credible do you find the theory put forward to explain the legend of the sword in the stone?

• Can you think of any other explanations for this story?

• How useful or important do you think the kind of research discussed in the video is? Why?

• What do you think is the value of studying archaeology and history?

• What are the most important myths and legends in your country? What values do they teach?

• Do you know of any other myths or legends from around the world?

UNDERSTANDING FAST SPEECH

5 📹 **29** Listen to an extract from the video said at natural pace. Try to write down what you hear. Then compare your ideas with a partner.

6 📹 **30** Try again. This time you will hear a slower version of the extract.

7 Check your ideas in File 10 on page 189. Groups of words are marked with / and pauses are marked //. Stressed sounds are in CAPITALS. Practise saying the extract.

REVIEW 6

1 Complete the text with one word in each space.

Strictly [1]_____, I never planned to end up overseas. In fact, [2]_____ it not been for my friends, I might never have gone. Some of them went travelling after university and [3]_____ enthusiastic were they about their travels [4]_____ I started to get interested myself. You could say I gave in to peer [5]_____! When I arrived here, though, I felt [6]_____ a fish out of water. It's so different. On the one [7]_____ it's culturally quite alien and on the [8]_____, there's the language barrier. [9]_____ the fact I already spoke three languages, I struggled with it and it wasn't [10]_____ I'd been here five years that I started to feel comfortable.

2 Complete the second sentence so that it has a similar meaning to the first sentence using the word given. Do not change the word given. You must use between three and five words, including the word given.

1 I can't think of anywhere else where night markets are so much a part of the culture.
Nowhere _____ night markets so much a part of the culture. **WORLD**

2 The film was nowhere near as good as I'd hoped it would be.
To be honest, I found _____. **DEEPLY**

3 I could feel the blood draining from my face as I watched her open the letter.
As I watched her open the letter, I went _____. **SHEET**

4 He made it clear that he didn't want us mentioning the incident!
It was made clear to us that _____ to mention the incident! **CIRCUMSTANCES**

5 The store had to be evacuated due to a bomb scare.
The store was evacuated _____ ensure the safety of shoppers. **AS**

6 Don't worry, though. There is some good news.
Don't worry, though. It's _____. **GLOOM**

3 Choose the correct option.

1 They're a funny couple. They're *as cheese and chalk / like chalk and cheese / like cheese and chalk*.

2 No sooner *the new currency was introduced / had the new currency been introduced / was the new currency introduced* than inflation rose dramatically.

3 That joke is *as old as hills / old like the hills / like the old hills / as old as the hills*.

4 You need to have the courage of *convictions / your convictions / the convictions*.

5 Never before *the region had experienced / the region experienced / had the region experienced* a period of such dramatic growth.

6 He was suspended from school for a week *down to / on account of / in spite of* his poor attendance.

4 Decide which of these verbs are more usually connected to discussing theories and which are more usually connected to sport. Think of an example sentence for each verb.

assert	drop	fade	highlight
claim	emphasise	scrape through	sponsor
uphold	establish	put forward	contend

5 Match the verbs (1–10) with the collocates (a–j).

1 foster   a faith in the system / your confidence

2 feel   b a fight / a match

3 stimulate   c a decision / a verdict

4 flee   d a turning point / exam papers

5 modify   e the way forward / you in the right direction

6 fix   f stiff / a real sense of achievement

7 undermine   g your environment / your opinion

8 point   h family relationships / greater understanding

9 overturn   i the country / across the border

10 mark   j the imagination / the economy

6 Complete the sentences. Use the word in brackets to form a word that fits in the space.

1 It's one of those films that somehow seems to defy _____. (describe)

2 Following the _____ of independence, a new government was quickly established. (declare)

3 The collapse of the last government led to a period of political _____. (stable)

4 The country has changed beyond all recognition since the _____ struggle ended. (liberty)

5 He must've been furious to be _____ at half-time like that. (substitution)

6 The _____ of widespread _____ within the government have shocked the nation. (reveal, corrupt)

7 Complete the text with one word in each space. The first letters are given.

He had a remarkable life. He came from a deprived [1]ba_____, a fact he often [2]em_____ the importance of when explaining the origins of his drive. He was [3]or_____ at the age of three when his parents were killed in a car crash and was then brought up by his grandparents, who were both immigrants. As a child, he was [4]ex_____ to a wide range of cultural influences, which gave [5]r_____ to his global outlook. One of his cousins was [6]al_____ murdered after it became known he'd [7]co_____ with the occupying army, and this led to a period of [8]s_____-s_____ and increasing involvement in the [9]ra_____ politics of the time. Following the brutal [10]ma_____ of demonstrators in the capital, he [11]f_____ to a neighbouring country and then somehow won a [12]sc_____ to study at Harvard!

13

NEWS AND
THE MEDIA

IN THIS UNIT YOU LEARN HOW TO:

- understand news stories better
- comment on news stories
- recognise and use rhetorical questions
- discuss the issue of celebrity and the media
- report what people said

SPEAKING

1 **Work in pairs. Look at the photo and discuss the questions.**

- What do you think happened before the photo was taken? What happened afterwards?

- What might be the headline for this story on a news website?

- Is it the kind of story you would read? Why? / Why not? What kinds of stories do you read about? Are there any you avoid?

- Do you think we see sufficient good news stories? Why? / Why not?

A dramatic rescue operation

IN THE HEADLINES

VOCABULARY

Newspaper headlines

Newspaper headlines in English tend to use short and impactful words such as *blast* (= explosion) or *slash* (= cut heavily). Headlines also tend to use present tenses to make them sound more dramatic. Grammar words such as auxiliaries and articles are often missed out.

Girl stabbed at birthday party (= A girl's been stabbed at a birthday party.)

1 Replace the words in italics in the headlines with these words and phrases.

bars	cleared	hails
pulls out of	ups	clash
leak	rule out	toll
vows	seize	brink of

1 Bomb blast *number of dead* reaches 20

2 President *praises* breakthrough in peace process

3 Club *bans* fans in crackdown on hooliganism

4 Sanders *found not guilty* of bribery charges

5 Police *take* $10 million drugs in house raid

6 Win brings Boca to *the point at which they can win* league title

7 *A secret document that was given to the press* reveals plan to slash jobs

8 Kirov *increases* stake in Mac Industries in takeover bid

9 Police *battle* with protesters at union rally

10 Teachers *exclude the possibility of* strike action

11 Kohl *decides not to take part in* Open over sex scandal

12 Hector *promises* to continue despite outburst

2 Work in pairs. For each headline in Exercise 1, discuss:

  a what you think happened and who any people or organisations are.

  b what other information you would expect to hear / read about in the story.

  1 *A bomb exploded somewhere recently and so far they know 20 people have died.*

     In the article, you'd probably find out about: the police investigation; who may have done it; the state of other injured people in hospital; the response of the government.

3 Work in groups. Answer the questions.

  1 Can you give an example of a real blast? What caused it?

  2 Have there been any crackdowns in your country / city recently? On what?

  3 Can you give an example of a team / country / organisation / person on the brink of disaster or on the brink of success?

  4 Have you heard of any police raids? What happened? Did they seize anything?

  5 Why do people leak information? Can you give any real examples?

  6 Have you heard of any bids to break a record / win something / take over a company? Do you think they'll be successful?

  7 Have you heard of any clashes between political colleagues / work colleagues / a player and coach?

  8 Have you heard of someone pulling out of an event? Why? Why might an organisation pull out of a deal?

LISTENING

4 ▶ **43** Listen to five short conversations about the news. Answer the questions about each conversation.

  1 Which story from Exercise 1 are they talking about?

  2 Do the speakers agree or disagree?

5 ▶ **43** Complete the sentences from the conversations with the correct verb phrases. Think about the form and tense. Then listen again and check your answers.

  1 a It was so obvious he _____ his own pocket.

     b The case _____ on some kind of technicality.

  2 a There's an election _____ in just over a year.

     b Maybe the opposition _____ just _____ trouble.

  3 a They _____ such a fuss about nothing.

     b As if anyone _____.

  4 a I don't know. _____ in his shoes.

     b It's just a storm in a teacup. It _____ quickly enough.

  5 a It's about time, though why on earth _____ they _____?

     b I know. They're thugs. They _____.

DEVELOPING CONVERSATIONS

Rhetorical questions and common opinions

When people talk about news stories, they often put their point of view as a rhetorical question (questions that don't require an answer) or use expressions that show common opinions.

What did you expect? (= I'm not surprised.)

It's one rule for us and another for them.

6 Work in pairs. Look at audio script 43 on page 210. Look at the questions and underline the rhetorical ones. What opinion do the rhetorical questions show?

Look at it from their point of view. <u>Why would they</u>? = They have no good reasons to cut jobs.

7 Work in groups. Which of these common opinions could you imagine saying yourself? In what situation?

  1 It's one rule for the rich and another for the poor.

  2 They should lock them up and throw away the key.

  3 They're just in it for the money.

  4 Young people today! They have no respect.

  5 They haven't got a hope in hell.

  6 It's all about oil.

  7 It's about time they did something about it.

  8 If you live by the sword, you die by the sword.

CONVERSATION PRACTICE

8 Think of three different stories you have heard in the news recently, such as those in Exercise 1. Spend a few minutes preparing how to explain what happened and what you think of each story. Try to include a rhetorical question. Then write questions to begin the conversations using the patterns below.

  • Did you see / hear this thing in the news about ...?

  • Have you heard the news today? Apparently, ...

  • I can't believe they're talking about ... Did you hear X on the news this morning?

  • What do you think of this business with ...?

9 Have conversations with different students in the class. Start by asking your questions. Your partner should respond by either finding out more about the story or commenting on it. Continue for a short time before talking about a different story. Find out which stories in the class have been most talked about and what people think.

🎥◀ 31 To watch the video and do the activities, see the DVD ROM.

THE HUNT FOR NEWS

SPEAKING

1 Work in groups. Discuss the questions.

- What magazines or TV programmes do you know that focus on celebrity news? Do you ever look at them? How popular are they? Why?
- Which celebrities are in the news most at the moment? Why?
- Are there any famous people you would like to know more about? Who? What do you want to know?
- What different ways does the media use to gather celebrity news?
- What are the paparazzi? What image do you have of them?

READING

2 Read the article about a paparazzo. Decide which statements below you agree with.

1 The article made me think a bit differently about paparazzi.
2 I found some of the article amusing.
3 I found both the writer and the paparazzo annoying.
4 The analogy between photography and hunting is a good one.
5 The writer isn't critical enough of the paparazzo.
6 There's a bit in the article I didn't get.

3 Work in pairs. Compare your choices from Exercise 2 and explain your reasons.

4 Decide where each extract below should go in the article. There is one extract for each paragraph.

1 – the intrusions, the hassle, the lack of privacy
2 He shows me an almost identical shot from a week before.
3 – the dream shot, rumours of affairs, agencies squeezing prices –
4 He seems happy enough to be recognised (though I didn't know him!) and poses for us.
5 He also supplements his income teaching at an art college.
6 – you've literally blown your chance
7 The chase is on again.

5 Work in pairs. Discuss what you think the words and phrases in bold in the article mean.

6 In California, they have introduced laws to try to restrict paparazzi. Work on your own and think of reasons for and against this idea. Then work in groups and discuss your ideas.

UNDERSTANDING VOCABULARY

Common sayings

We often comment on situations using well-known sayings that express ideas most people feel are true.

If you live by the sword, you die by the sword.

(= If you use unpleasant means to get what you want, expect to be a victim of them at some point.)

In for a penny, in for a pound.

(= You intend to complete something you've started, whatever the consequences.)

However, we often don't say the whole saying. We generally just use the first part, as we saw in the article.

You know, we live by the sword and the celebs do too.

I'd rather go to bed, but in for a penny!

7 Work in pairs. Match 1–12 to a–l to make common sayings. Discuss what they mean. Do you have sayings in your language that express similar ideas?

1 When the going gets tough,   a on the other side.
2 People in glass houses   b catches the worm.
3 When in Rome,   c the tough get going.
4 If you can't beat them,   d has a silver lining.
5 It takes all sorts   e in the mouth.
6 The early bird   f shouldn't throw stones.
7 Never look a gift horse   g to make a world.
8 If it ain't broke,   h join them.
9 Too many cooks   i before they hatch.
10 Every cloud   j don't fix it.
11 The grass is always greener   k do as the Romans do.
12 Don't count your chickens   l spoil the broth.

8 With your partner, decide which saying from Exercise 7 you would use to respond to these comments.

1 Apparently, he loves being a paparazzo.
2 Maybe we could get a bigger place after you get the new job.
3 What? We have to eat with our hands?
4 Honestly, he gets away with murder. He didn't lift a finger to help.
5 Honestly, the organisation of the whole event was terrible.
6 I wish they hadn't interfered. We were doing fine without them.

9 ▶ 44 Listen to six short dialogues and check your ideas from Exercise 8.

10 With your partner, write four short dialogues based around other sayings from Exercise 7.

PAPS THEY'RE NOT SO BAD

Joan Archer spends a day with a paparazzo in New York looking for the full picture

It's getting on for one in the morning and it seems we have followed a false lead again. We are outside Catch, the exclusive New York restaurant where we've come in the hope of **landing our own big fish**. But the only A-list celebrity to be seen is on a torn page of a discarded magazine that lies in the gutter with the headline 'Jen Splashes Out'. A day ago I would've looked at the figure on the page jumping out of a cab on a damp street and pitied her for the life she has to lead. But now I look at it and wonder: how long was the photographer waiting in the pouring rain to get that shot? What did they finally earn for their trouble? Having spent the day with a real-life paparazzo, I look at this photo and rather than **revulsion** for their profession, I have, if not admiration, a certain amount of respect. Because I have been **on the go** for the last sixteen hours and I'm **dead on my feet**.

We started at 8.30 this morning when I watched a small crab-like group of photographers awkwardly **scuttle** down the street a few paces ahead of a star walking her kid to school. Miguel returned shaking his head. 'She's wearing the same outfit as always. She knows we won't be able to sell on the photos.'

We then cycle – yes, cycle – to a hotel in the Village where he's been tipped off that there may be some boy band action. When we arrive, we find an odd collection of smoking paparazzi and teenage girls with hearts painted on their faces. We spend the next three hours hanging around, the paps gossiping and moaning about the business and the teenage fans discussing the dream meeting with the lead singer, boy band habits and the cost of boy band paraphernalia. Eventually I have to go to the loo and when I return the crowd has gone. I feel a pang of disappointment, but it turns out nothing happened. The singer apparently **slipped out** via a side entrance, although I later find out he hadn't actually been there at all but in Singapore!

Miguel tells me there are possibilities over in Tribeca. We hop on our bikes again and the pattern of the day has been set: cycle, stand around, chat, hopes are dashed, move on. The best we get is a minor soap star, who Miguel spots **en route** eating a hot dog on a street corner. Miguel sends off the photo to his agency but is doubtful he'll see much money from it.

The demand for photos is rising with the spread of fashion magazines and so-called '**click bait**' Internet stories such as '18 stars who have grown old badly'. At the same time, of course, there is also increasing competition from amateur 'paps' exploiting opportunities with their smartphones, as well as from other professionals. As a result, apart from the very biggest exclusives, the money to be gained is not great. Still, Miguel sees it as steadier than the photojournalism he used to do.

> **You know, we live by the sword and the celebs do too. It's just a question of respect**

And despite the slow day, Miguel **remains upbeat**. 'Hey, this is how things can go. I sometimes go hunting with my father. You can spend time preparing a hide and sit for hours up a tree waiting for a deer to appear and then, when it does, you **screw up the shot** and it's gone. Other times you hit the target. Being a paparazzo is the same – it's just in the city and nothing gets killed!' I suggest that while no-one gets killed, people do get hurt. 'Yeah – and sometimes it's the paparazzo.' He knows several who have been punched by bodyguards and ended up in hospital, but he states this matter-of-factly and without complaint. 'You know, we live by the sword and the celebs do too. It's just a question of respect. It's like the hunting – you must respect the animal or it is not honest.'

There's a phone call. Apparently, Leo is at Up and Down. I'd rather go to bed, but in for a penny! This might be the one that finally makes the day worthwhile.

ON THE HOUR, EVERY HOUR

SPEAKING

1 Work in groups. Discuss the questions.

- Do you (or does anyone in your family) regularly read a printed newspaper or an online news site? If so, which one?
- Do you ever listen to news on the radio or watch the news on TV? If so, when?
- What are the main newspapers / news sites in your country? What do you think the main differences are between them?
- Which newspapers / news sites in your country do you think hold the most political influence?

2 Work in pairs. Check you understand the words and phrases in bold below. Then discuss to what degree you share each opinion – and why.

1 I find watching the news incredibly upsetting. It just leaves me **feeling helpless**.

2 Too much **power is concentrated in the hands of** too few **media barons**.

3 I'm quite **content** to just **keep up with** bits and pieces of news via social media.

4 I'm not interested in **foreign affairs**. What happens **overseas** has nothing to do with me.

5 Real news is what somebody somewhere wants to **suppress** – all the rest is advertising!

6 I wouldn't pay for any type of news. As a **citizen**, it's my right to know the news.

7 **Rolling 24-hour news** is incredibly addictive. People just **get totally hooked on** it.

8 There's too much **speculation** on the news and too few **hard facts**.

LISTENING

3 ▶ 45 Listen to the headlines at the start of a radio news bulletin. Take notes on what each of the six stories is about.

4 Work in pairs. Compare your notes. Then discuss which two nouns or noun phrases you think go with each story (1–6).

a thigh strain	bomb disposal
sham marriage	inflation
tear gas	health grounds
a private matter	the base rate
bravery	an appeal
petrol bomb	on good form

5 ▶ 46 Listen to the full bulletin. Find out:

1 which stories the words in Exercise 4 were connected to – and how.

2 what happened in each story.

6 ▶ 46 Work in groups. Discuss if each statement is definitely true, definitely false or still unclear – and why. Then listen again and read audio script 46 on page 210 to check your ideas.

1 Carol Dixon had argued over government policy.

2 She is suffering from heart problems.

3 The two men were killed in a blast.

4 The President has the support of most people.

5 Interest rates may rise again before the year's end.

6 Johnson was injured in training.

7 The team can afford to draw the match.

8 The couple said they wouldn't keep the compensation.

9 The payout may cause the newspaper to go bust.

10 Bodge works for the police.

7 With your group, discuss which of the six stories you'd be most / least interested to find out more about. Explain why.

GRAMMAR

Patterns after reporting verbs

When we report what someone said, we often summarise the content using a reporting verb. These verbs are followed by a number of different patterns. Here are the most common:

1 verb + (*that*) clause

*The government today **announced** that driverless cars will be allowed on the roads from May.*

2 verb + someone + (*that*) clause

*City officials **have warned** commuters that there will be severe delays over the weeks to come.*

3 verb + infinitive (with *to*)

*The President **has vowed** to take action against those responsible for the attack.*

4 verb + someone + infinitive (with *to*)

*Can I just **remind** you all to hand your reports in first thing tomorrow?*

5 verb + *-ing*

*In a recent survey, 52% of young adults **admitted** using a mobile phone while driving.*

6 verb + noun phrase

*The leader of the opposition **has criticised** the move.*

7 verb (+ object) + preposition

*Mr Burns today **apologised** for suggesting Ms Grice should resign.*

8 Work in pairs. Make similar sentences to those you heard in the news bulletin using the words below and the patterns in the box.

1 acknowledge / division / issue

2 deny / long-term opponent

3 refuse / comment / health reasons / departure

4 assure reporters / men died / car exploded

5 reject demands / government / change tack

6 urge / silent majority / make voices heard

7 accuse them / enter into / marriage purely for their mutual benefit

G Check your ideas on page 180 and do Exercise 1.

9 Decide how many options are correct in each sentence. Then correct the other verbs by changing the patterns that go with them.

1 I heard on the news that he'd *admitted / denied / been accused* stealing over £1,000,000.

2 In the end, she *convinced / suggested / persuaded* us all to go to the show.

3 When I saw her, she was *telling / grumbling / insisting* that she can't handle the weather here.

4 My aunt *urged / recommended / advised* me to go and get it looked at by a specialist.

5 He's *confirmed / discussed / vowed* never to marry again.

10 Work in groups. Can you think of someone you know or a famous person who has recently:

1 apologised for something? What? Who to?

2 forgiven someone? Who? For what?

3 acknowledged that they've made a mistake? What kind?

4 announced that they'll be doing something soon? What?

5 confessed that they've done something they shouldn't have? What?

6 grumbled that they have to do something unpleasant? What?

7 boasted that they've done something amazing? What?

8 promised to start – or stop – doing something? What?

9 warned you (not) to do something? What? Why?

10 been publicly criticised? For what? Was the criticism justified?

11 denied doing something they've been accused of?

12 threatened to do something bad? What? Who to?

G For further practice, see Exercises 2 and 3 on page 180.

14

Sotheby's
Lot Number: 122

USD ($)	560,000
EUR (€)	402,864
UK (£)	330,333
SWI (F)	490,582
JPN (¥)	56,956,295
HKD (HK$)	4,340,918

Sotheby's

Sotheby's, New York

IN THIS UNIT YOU LEARN HOW TO:

- discuss different aspects of running a company
- talk about how your business is doing
- network and make small talk
- discuss crime, banks and economics
- use some loanwords
- take minutes and take part in meetings

SPEAKING

1   Work in pairs. Discuss the questions.

- What do you think is happening in the photo?
- Have you ever been to an event like this? If yes, when? If not, would you like to?
- What do you think of the prices things like this are often sold for?
- Have you heard of any paintings or memorabilia being sold recently?
- If you could buy one painting or piece of memorabilia, what would it be? Why?

2   Work in groups. Discuss whether or not you would invest in each of the things below if you had the money – and why. Then think of two more good investments.

property in your town	a piece of art
a holiday flat abroad	gold or silver
a savings account	an oil company
a space travel company	a private pension
a start-up in a developing country	a language school

Sotheby's
Lot Number. 122

USD ($)	560,000
EUR (€)	402,864
UK (£)	330,333
SWI (F)	490,582
JPN (¥)	56,956,295
HKD (HK$)	4,340,918

BUSINESS AND ECONOMICS

BUSINESS MATTERS

SPEAKING

1 Work in groups. Discuss the questions.

- Do you know anyone who runs their own business? What kind? How big is it? Do you know how it's doing at the moment?

- Do you like the idea of running your own business? Why? / Why not?

- How good at business would you be? Give yourself a mark from 1 (= absolutely useless) to 10 (= exceptional) for each of the following and explain why.
  - raising start-up funds
  - developing and implementing a business plan
  - hiring and firing
  - providing leadership
  - building team morale
  - networking and developing new contacts
  - bookkeeping and managing your cash flow
  - assessing and taking risks
  - dealing with stress and long working hours

VOCABULARY How's business?

2 Work in pairs. Decide if the words in italics have the same meaning in the context. If not, what's the difference?

1 We've seen a definite *upturn* / *decline* in sales over recent months.

2 We're lucky in that we have *a solid client base* / *loyal customers*.

3 We've been *inundated* / *flooded* with orders.

4 We're actually going to be *relocating* / *moving* to a smaller town, where *rents* / *overheads* are cheaper.

5 We've had to *lay off* / *employ* about 30 people.

6 We're actually thinking of *floating* / *launching* the firm on the stock market.

7 If things don't *pick up* / *get better* soon, we're going to *end up going under* / *have to make serious cutbacks*.

8 Times are tough, but we're just about *hanging in* / *surviving*.

9 We're having to *diversify* / *consolidate* the range of services we provide.

10 We've had to *take on staff* / *make staff redundant* this year.

11 There's been a definite *downturn* / *drop* in sales this quarter.

12 We're in the middle of *terminating* / *pitching for* a big contract in Russia.

3 With your partner, discuss what you think each of the possible options in Exercise 2 is the result of.

A: *Maybe there's been an upturn in sales because they've cut prices.*

B: *Yeah, or it might be down to the fact that the economy is picking up and so people have a bit more money to spend.*

LISTENING

4 ▶ **47** Listen to two phone calls. Answer the questions about each conversation.

1 Why is the second speaker calling?

2 How's business?

3 What else do they talk about?

5 ▶ **47** Work in pairs. Try to remember the exact phrases or sentences the following were used in. Then listen again and check your ideas.

Conversation 1

1 panicking

2 this quarter

3 taken on

4 crawling

5 a bit of a pain

Conversation 2

6 the European Championships

7 chickens

8 overheads

9 half the staff

10 Thursday

DEVELOPING CONVERSATIONS

Small talk

In many business contexts, it is common to engage in small talk before or after more serious conversations. It is also a central part of networking.

6 Work in pairs. Discuss the questions.

- Do you like making small talk? Why? / Why not?
- What kind of things do you usually ask or talk about?
- Does it vary depending on who you're talking to? If yes, give examples.
- Do you think men and women make small talk about different kinds of things? If yes, give examples.
- Do you think small talk is important when doing business in your country?
- What would you recommend foreign business people make small talk about in your country?

7 With your partner, decide what questions produced these answers.

1 We can't complain. We're weathering the storm, which is more than many companies can say!

2 It was a lucky accident, to be honest. I graduated in something completely different – Art History – but then I got a summer job here and just really took to it.

3 Pretty dire, to be honest. It just seems to be sinking further and further into recession.

4 They're doing well. Johan's in his second year of secondary school now and Eva turned three last month.

5 I know. It's beautiful, isn't it? It was minus two and snowing when I left Malmö last night as well!

6 Oh, it's been really hectic. I'm glad it's the weekend tomorrow!

7 Don't ask! We're actually on the brink of relegation!

8 I'm having dinner with a client at seven, but after that I'm not sure, actually. Do you fancy maybe meeting up later on?

9 It was great. We stayed with friends down on the coast for ten days. It was much needed, I can tell you!

10 Oh, not too bad. There was a 45-minute delay in Frankfurt due to bad weather, but it could've been worse.

8 Ask each other your questions from Exercise 7 but give different answers.

CONVERSATION PRACTICE

9 Work in pairs. You are going to roleplay a similar conversation to the ones you heard in Exercise 4. Choose one of these reasons for making a phone call.

- chasing up an order that hasn't arrived yet
- arranging a convenient time and place for a meeting
- apologising for the delay in sending an order out
- checking whether or not a delivery has been received
- cancelling a meeting
- sounding out a colleague's feelings about a new product

Student A: you are the caller. Student B: you are going to take the call. Use your imagination to decide what kind of companies you work for and what your jobs are.

10 Now roleplay the phone call. Try to engage in plenty of small talk.

11 When you have finished, choose another reason from the list above and have another phone call. This time, Student B should be the caller.

32 To watch the video and do the activities, see the DVD ROM.

BANKING ON CHANGE

READING

1 Work in groups. You are going to read a blog post commenting on a court case. Think of as many types of crime as you can connected to banks and money. Which is the most serious? Why?

2 Read the blog post opposite. Then work in pairs and explain its headline.

3 With your partner, answer the questions by referring to the post.

　1 Were the executives taken to court for bankrupting the bank?

　2 Why do you think it took seven years for the executives to be jailed?

　3 What does the writer mean by *You do the maths*?

　4 What's *a period of austerity* and does the writer agree with it?

　5 According to the writer, what is it that made banks better in the past?

　6 Do you think overall the writer is optimistic or pessimistic about the future?

4 Read the comments on the post and decide how far you agree with them or think the suggestions are good ideas. Then write one more comment for yourself.

5 Work in groups. Discuss the comments on the post and the ones you wrote.

GRAMMAR

Relative clauses

Relative clauses relate back to a noun or noun phrase. Sometimes they are essential in order to define the noun; sometimes the relative clause adds extra (non-defining) information. The relative clause may start with a relative pronoun, adverb or phrase, such as *which*, *where* or *many of whom*.

6 Look at the relative clauses underlined in the post and comments. For each one, decide:

　1 if it is defining the noun or adding extra non-essential information.

　2 what noun or noun phrase it relates back to.

　3 if there is a relative pronoun, adverb or phrase – and why it is used.

　4 if there's no need for a relative pronoun.

G Check your ideas on page 181 and do Exercises 1 and 2.

7 Complete each sentence with a relative clause and your own ideas. Then work in pairs and compare your sentences.

　1 In our country, we are currently in a situation …

　2 I've heard of several cases …

　3 In my life, I'm getting to the point …

　4 I see absolutely no reason …

　5 I like the way …

　6 The success of our economy will depend on the extent …

G For further practice, see Exercises 3 and 4 on page 182.

UNDERSTANDING VOCABULARY

Loanwords

In the blog post, the writer used half of a French idiom – *Plus ça change (plus c'est la meme chose)*. It means: 'The more things change, the more things stay the same.' English has a number of French loanwords as well as from other languages. We may pronounce these words a bit like the original language but with an English accent!

8 Listen and check the pronunciation of these loanwords. Then work in pairs and discuss what they mean and if you use any of them in your language.

Plus ça change	déjà vu	chef	au fait
prima donna	zeitgeist	plaza	fiasco
fait accompli	en route	angst	kitsch
faux pas	guerrilla	macho	trek

9 With your partner, replace the words in italics with loanwords from Exercise 8. Then answer the questions.

　1 Can you think of something that is part of the *spirit of the age* now?

　2 Are there any nice *squares or open spaces* in your city?

　3 Do you know anywhere which has had *revolutionary fighters* conducting a war?

　4 How might you feel if someone presented you with a *choice which had actually already been decided for you*? Has it ever happened to you?

　5 Do you know any men who are *muscly and stereotypically very masculine*? Do you see it as a good thing?

　6 Do you know anyone who often suffers from *a strong feeling of worry about how to behave and what may happen*?

　7 Can you think of a time when someone made *an embarrassing social mistake*?

　8 Can you think of an example of something that is *produced to be popular but lacks taste or style*?

　9 Have you ever had a feeling of *dreaming about – or experiencing – the thing that's happening to you before it happened*?

Jailing of Icelandic bankers shows need to put people first

It's happened again. A bank has been involved in malpractice. *Plus ça change* you may think, but, finally, we may be seeing a difference. Instead of talking about banks as if they're some kind of organism [1]that has no free will and [2]whose only purpose is to grow, we're talking about people and the bad decisions [3]they make.

Four bankers, four *people*, have actually been prosecuted, found guilty and given jail sentences, [4]two of which were, even more amazingly, lengthened following the bankers' failed appeal. The four were executives of the Icelandic bank Kaupthing that collapsed in 2008, bringing the whole of Iceland to the brink of bankruptcy. The prosecution came about because just days before the collapse the four men had organised the sale of a 5% stake in the bank, [5]whereby they hoped to boost shareholder confidence. However, they failed to disclose to those shareholders that the money to buy the stake had been illegally loaned to the buyer by the bank itself.

It may have taken seven years to get to this stage, but Olaf Haukson, the prosecutor who was eventually chosen for the task, justifiably hailed the judgment as a breakthrough that demonstrated justice could be brought to bear on individuals. Well said indeed, though it's a message the rest of the world seems to be ignoring. Elsewhere, banks – the non-human entities – have been fined over £170 billion for a variety of offences, but, in the UK at least, not one of the people [6]who actually committed these offences has served time.

And of course the fines don't cover the perfectly legal mismanagement of their businesses or the creation of obscure financial products that produced such huge losses at the end of the noughties. This has resulted in a global debt crisis and a period of recession and austerity, [7]during which time the UK government alone has given up to £1.2 TRILLION to bail the banks out. You do the maths. This is also again a stark contrast to the Icelandic situation, [8]where the government let the creditors pick up the bill for their failing banks rather than the public and public services paying the greater price.

But there is a more important reason [9]why we should be focusing on people rather than institutions: institutions can't change themselves, only people can. We want people to make banks work for us rather than just see us as a source of profit. There was a time [10]when banking people had a real stake in ensuring businesses were supported, deposits protected and risks averted, because they were part of the *same community*. In some cases they were literally our friends. Is it so crazy to imagine we could go back to that situation? And is it any more crazy than our only punishment being to fine banks less than the money we've given them?!

Comments (16)

tootrue
Sunday at 10:38am

Well done Iceland! Great post. Couldn't agree more.

prettypolly
Sunday at 11:10am

It's easy for Iceland because it's such a tiny country. If banks had been left to fail in the UK or other big countries, it would've been a disaster.

changetheworld1
Sunday at 2:10pm

It's not just banks lacking personal responsibility – it's our whole corporate world. Definitely need to get back to small community-focused business.

inMTwetrust
Sunday at 2:14pm

changetheworld1 We live in a globalised world which has brought huge growth and wealth over the last 50 years. Crazy to talk about going back.

changetheworld1
Sunday at 2:19pm

inMTwetrust It's not crazy. There are banks which are more ethical and community-based – like the bank [11]I work for, Triodos.

inMTwetrust
Sunday at 2:28pm

changetheworld1 Don't get me wrong – there's a place for banks like Triodos and banking could be far more transparent. Just don't want to throw the baby out with the bathwater.

newhope
Sunday at 4:07pm

changetheworld1 I agree we can do things differently. Six years ago, we set up a community credit union where people could save and provide financial support to local people, [12]some of whom were really struggling. It's been a huge success. We've also managed to attract matching funding for a park project in our neighbourhood.

cityboy
Sunday at 4:19pm

We should stop bashing banks just because of a few bad apples. Banks are engines of growth and employment. I blame excessive government spending for the great recession.

 Share Add comment

Unit 14   Business and economics   127

ANY OTHER BUSINESS

VOCABULARY Business situations

1 Work in pairs. Think of two words or phrases that you associate with each of the business topics below.

business taxes	an industrial dispute	sales
cutting costs	a new product	a takeover

2 Match each group of phrases below to one of the topics in Exercise 1. Then with your partner, explain the connection between the phrases and the topic.

sales projections: Part of the research done when getting a new product to market is to ask markets for sales projections.

1 sales projections / launch a prototype / a gap in the market / conduct focus groups / positive feedback

2 ongoing negotiations / pay demands / reach an acceptable compromise / have a Plan B / threaten to call a strike

3 be a good fit / recommend it to shareholders / up their offer / a hostile bid / raise their stake

4 undertake restructuring / scale back / outsource / lay people off / negotiate new deals with suppliers

5 exceed targets / start from a low base / seal a major deal / increase fourfold / be dropped by a client

6 lobby / affect our bottom line / less competitive / fund government programmes / win concessions

3 Work in groups. Answer the questions.

1 Do you think big businesses are sufficiently taxed? Why? / Why not?

2 How much do you think companies influence politics? Is it a good or a bad thing? Why?

3 Are industrial disputes common where you live? If so, in what sectors?

4 Can you think of two different reasons why a firm may be dropped by a client?

5 Have you heard of any takeovers? Do you know if they were successful?

6 What do you think are the pros and cons of conducting focus groups?

7 Have you (or has a place you've worked in) ever had to cut costs? Why? How?

8 If you could 'outsource' something you do in your life, what would it be?

LISTENING

4 Work in pairs. Discuss the questions.

1 What is an **agenda**?

2 What does the **chair** of a meeting do?

3 What's the difference between **sales** and **marketing**?

4 What does a **minute taker** do?

5 What does **AOB** stand for? When is it usually discussed?

6 What meetings do you go to? What are they like? How are they run?

5 ▶ **49** You are going to hear part of a business meeting in a footwear company. First, listen to the six speakers below. Match the speakers (1–6) to their roles (a–f). The first one is done for you.

1	Katrin	a	head of product development
2	Peter	b	finance manager
3	Henry	c	operations manager
4	Rachel	d	marketing manager
5	Alex	e	sales manager
6	Marta	f	chair

When we take minutes:
- we summarise what people say in note form.
- we tend not to use full grammatical sentences.
- we often use reporting verbs such as *voice concerns, question*, etc.
- we don't record irrelevant things such as jokes, small talk, etc.

6 ▶ 50 Listen to the part of the business meeting where they discuss a financial loss and a new product. Take minutes of the meeting.

7 Work in groups. Compare the minutes you took. Then discuss the questions.
- What do you think of the Shoe Saver? Why?
- Do you think it'll make the company a lot of money? Why? / Why not?
- What do you think the company should do to improve its situation?

8 Using the minutes you took, discuss whether the sentences below are accurate. Make changes where necessary.

1 Henry stated the loss was down to state of the economy.
2 Rachel mentioned poor sales in Eastern Europe.
3 Katrin expressed doubts about ability to cut costs.
4 Henry denied there'd be redundancies.
5 Everyone v impressed by results of demonstration.
6 Alex said unit costs €35–45. Marta expects product will retail at €100–130.
7 Cost €35 if outsourced.
8 Proj. sales: Y4 250,000.
9 Henry questioned if proj. sales achievable.
10 Marta estimated shoes last 50% longer so would pay for machine. Main market rich homes. Said initial sales v good.
11 Katrin asked about patents.
12 Alex said technology not protected, but some parts of manufacturing process patented. Marta noted there are currently no other competitors.

9 Look at audio script 50 on page 212 and check your answers. Underline any phrases you could use when taking part in a meeting.

SPEAKING

10 Work in groups of four. You all work for a big electronics company. You are going to roleplay a meeting like the one you heard in the listening. The agenda is below.

Student A: you will chair the meeting. Look at File 30 on page 192.

Student B: you are the finance manager. Look at File 31 on page 189.

Student C: you are the head of product development. Look at File 32 on page 192.

Student D: you are the head of marketing. Look at File 33 on page 191.

Read the information and prepare your role.

> ### MEETING AGENDA
> 1. New products
> 2. Cost-cutting measures
> 3. Proposed takeover
> 4. Possible strike
> 5. AOB

11 Now have the meeting. Make sure you get your points across. Ask other participants for clarification or extra information where you feel things are still unclear. Above all, remember to be polite and to respect the chair.

VIDEO 7

COUNTERFEIT STRATEGY

1 **Work in groups. Discuss the questions.**

- Are counterfeit goods such as those in the photo available where you live? If yes, how do you feel about that?
- What other kinds of counterfeit items can you think of?
- Why do you think people buy counterfeit goods?
- Do you think you're good at spotting counterfeit products? How can you tell?
- In what ways are banknotes protected against counterfeiters?

2 **▶ 33** **Watch the first part of a video about counterfeit prevention in the United States (0.00–2.04). Find out:**

1 the three ways of combating counterfeiting that are mentioned.

2 two techniques sometimes used by counterfeiters.

3 **Work in pairs. Discuss how you think the words and phrases below might be connected to the processes by which counterfeit notes enter the system.**

1 in bulk
2 the victim
3 offload
4 at a discount
5 avoid detection
6 in a matter of seconds
7 a genuine bill
8 a special solution
9 revamp
10 large volumes

4 **▶ 33** **Watch the second part of the video (2.05–4.24) and check your ideas. Then work with your partner. Compare how much you can remember about what the speakers said using the words and phrases from Exercise 3.**

in bulk: Bad notes are passed in bulk through the black money scam.

5 **Choose one of the topics below to talk about. Spend a few minutes planning what you want to say. Then work in groups and discuss your topics. Your partners should ask questions to find out more.**

- a common scam you've heard of
- a successful counterfeit
- an organised crime gang and their activities
- a case of fraud or identity theft
- other ways the Secret Service protect security – and how you feel about it

UNDERSTANDING FAST SPEECH

6 **▶ 34** **Listen to an extract from the video said at natural pace. Try to write down what you hear. Then compare your ideas with a partner.**

7 **▶ 35** **Try again. This time you will hear a slower version of the extract.**

8 **Check your ideas in File 10 on page 189. Groups of words are marked with / and pauses are marked //. Stressed sounds are in CAPITALS. Practise saying the extract.**

REVIEW 7

GRAMMAR AND UNDERSTANDING
VOCABULARY

1 Complete the text with one word in each space.

I worked in Manchester for a couple of years, [1]_____ which time I got to know the city well. It was a time [2]_____ both Manchester clubs were doing well and I became quite au [3]_____ with football. I also made some good friends there, one of [4]_____ became my first husband! People [5]_____ me not to rush into things, but I didn't listen. Marriage just seemed like a fait [6]_____ from the moment we met. Soon, though, I found myself in a situation [7]_____ I'd lost my independence – and if I complained, he'd [8]_____ to leave me. In the end, I had to [9]_____ to myself I'd made a mistake. We finished last summer. Every cloud has a silver [10]_____ though, because now I'm engaged to my divorce lawyer!

2 Complete the second sentence so that it has a similar meaning to the first sentence using the word given. Do not change the word given. You must use between three and five words, including the word given.

1 It took me ages to get over the fact that he forgot our anniversary.
It was a long time before I was ready to _____ our anniversary. **FORGIVE**

2 Other people's situations often seem more attractive than our own.
_____ on the other side. **GRASS**

3 It's best not to expect too much. You may end up disappointed.
You know what they say – _____! **CHICKENS**

4 A takeover bid is a distinct possibility and may well be the best way out.
We've reached _____ a takeover may be the best solution to our current problems. **POINT**

5 It's my own fault. I should've noticed what was going on much earlier.
To be honest, I _____ what was going on earlier. **BLAME**

6 Ice was kept in caves and covered with wood. This ensured a supply for months to come.
People stored ice in caves and covered it with wood, _____ a steady supply. **MEANS**

3 Choose the correct option.

1 He's been accused *of / for / by* threatening to kill his ex-boss.

2 They raised over $1 million in start-up funds, *many of which / most of which / the extent to which* has been spent on day-to-day running costs.

3 We can grab a coffee *on / in / en* route to the airport.

4 I spoke to my boss and she suggested *to apply / me to apply / applying* for funding.

5 He insisted *to go / on going / going* back and apologising to everyone.

6 He's a person *for who / for whom / for which / whom* I have the greatest respect.

VOCABULARY

4 Match the verbs (1–10) with the collocates (a–j).

1 conduct   a a contract / a project
2 terminate   b jobs / production by 50%
3 rule out   c your target / your expectations
4 suppress   d your offer / your stake in the firm
5 seal   e the government / your MP
6 lobby   f focus groups / an experiment
7 up   g strike action / the use of troops
8 exceed   h serious cutbacks / staff redundant
9 make   i the news / your feelings
10 slash   j a major deal / an envelope

5 Complete the sentences with a preposition in each space.

1 Sales have doubled this year, but we did start _____ a very low base!

2 We've been inundated _____ orders since we launched the campaign.

3 I can't believe it! He's been cleared _____ all charges.

4 We've basically found a gap _____ the market – and we aim to fill it!

5 We've pulled out of the project _____ concerns for our workers' safety.

6 The club has barred over 100 fans _____ a major crackdown _____ hooliganism.

6 Complete the sentences. Use the word in brackets to form a word that fits in the space.

1 Sales have increased _____ this quarter, which is great news for all concerned. (four)

2 We need to _____ our range if we're going to survive. (diverse)

3 The board needs to decide whether or not to recommend the bid to the _____. (share)

4 They called off the strike after winning major _____ from their employers. (concede)

5 We're quite optimistic about the sales _____ for the coming year. (project)

6 I left when they decided to _____ to a small town in a desperate bid to cut costs. (location)

7 Complete the text with one word in each space. The first letters are given.

Last year was our best ever. We saw a significant [1]up_____ in sales and decided to [2]t_____ o_____ new people. Then when the recession started, we thought we'd be able to [3]w_____ the storm, but we've really had to [4]sc_____ b_____ since the start of the year. We may even need to start [5]l_____ people o_____ if things don't [6]p_____ u_____ soon. As things stand, though, we're just about [7]h_____ i_____, which is an achievement in itself when others have already [8]g_____ u_____. We're lucky in that we have a fairly [9]so_____ client base, which ensures a steady [10]ca_____ f_____. If we can just [11]co_____ our range of products and maybe think about [12]pi_____ for one or two new contracts, we'll be fine.

15

TRENDS

IN THIS UNIT YOU LEARN HOW TO:

- describe clothes and hairstyles
- repair misunderstandings
- give opinions on style
- discuss trends
- use some snowclones
- discuss the fashion industry and its impact
- define yourself in different ways

SPEAKING

1 Work in pairs. Look at the photo and discuss the questions.

- What decade do you think the photo is supposed to represent? Where do you think it was taken?
- What fashion and design in the photo do you like / dislike? Why?
- How similar do you think life was in your country during this time?
- What does the photo suggest about family relations? Do you think this has changed? In what way is it the same / different?

2 Work in groups. What do you know about the fashion, music and social trends in these decades? Which do you think was the best decade to live in? Why?

1920s   1940s   1960s   1980s   1990s   2000s

'The past is a foreign country. They do things differently there.' L.P. Hartley

IN STYLE

VOCABULARY Style and fashion

1 What are the current fashions in clothes and hairstyles? What do you think of them?

2 Work in pairs. Match the groups of words (1–9) to the descriptions (a–i) and decide which word in each group is the odd one out.

1 silk / denim / seam / linen / wool / polyester
2 scruffy / smart / conventional / skinny / formal / trendy
3 flowery / checked / zipped / tartan / paisley / stripy
4 stained / frayed / spotted / worn out / split / ripped
5 collar / pocket / lining / lapel / sleeve / laces
6 a strap / a ribbon / a bangle / beads / shades / a belt
7 a bob / a ponytail / bushy / gelled / highlighted / a wig
8 trainers / flats / high-heels / flares / wedges / sandals
9 summery / sturdy / revealing / loud / knee-length / wedding

a They all describe hairstyles except _____.
b They all describe dresses except _____.
c They're all materials except _____.
d They're all kinds of accessories except _____.
e They all describe damage to clothes except _____.
f They're all patterns except _____.
g They're all parts of a jacket except _____.
h They all describe kinds of shoes except _____.
i They all describe people's general clothes style except _____.

3 Which of the words in Exercise 2 can you see in the photos?

4 With your partner, answer the questions about the words in Exercise 2.

1 What's good / bad about the materials?
2 Can you give examples of people who are scruffy, smart, etc.?
3 Do you have any clothes with the different patterns?
4 How are the different kinds of damage caused?
5 Where do you wear the accessories?
6 How many of the different kinds of shoes are being worn in class today?
7 Which of the hairstyles and shoes do you associate with men, women or both?

LISTENING

5 ▶ **51** Listen to six short conversations about clothes and style. Match each conversation (1–6) to one of the sentences. There is one sentence you do not need.

Someone:

a had an accident.
b has had a haircut.
c is having an interview.
d is looking at an old photo.
e is inappropriately dressed for certain work.
f is thinking of changing their look.
g is commenting on a fashion magazine.

6 Look at audio script 51 on page 212. With a partner, discuss what the underlined expressions mean and how you would say them in your language.

7 Work in groups. Discuss the questions.

- Has your style changed much over time? If yes, in what way? If not, why not?
- Have you ever been taken aback by someone's appearance? Why? What happened?
- Why else might you stick out like a sore thumb? Has it ever happened to you?
- Can you think of a time something went wrong with your clothes? What happened?
- Do you know anywhere with a dress code – official or unspoken? What is it? Do you agree with it? Why? / Why not?

DEVELOPING CONVERSATIONS

Backtracking and correcting

When people misunderstand what we say or take it the wrong way, we often backtrack and correct the misunderstanding.

J: *Do you think I look scruffy?*

K: *No, that's not what I meant to say. What I'm trying to say is …*

8 Complete the second sentence with your own ideas to repair the misunderstanding.

1 A: You don't like my shirt?

   B: It's not that it's not nice. It's just …

2 A: Do you think I'd look silly if I dyed it blonde?

   B: No, I didn't say that. All I meant was …

3 A: What's wrong with the clothes I'm wearing?

   B: They do suit you. All I'm trying to say is …

4 A: So you don't like him?

   B: I do! What I meant to say was …

5 A: You don't think he's good enough for the job?

   B: No, that's not what I meant. What I'm trying to say is …

6 A: So you're saying doing the course is a waste of money?

   B: No, sorry. I'm not explaining myself very well. What I meant to say was …

9 Work in pairs. Take turns to say the first sentences in Exercise 8. Your partner should reply using their completed sentences.

10 Write three misunderstandings such as *Sorry, am I boring you?* or *You don't think …?* Then take turns to read your sentences. Your partner should repair the misunderstandings.

CONVERSATION PRACTICE

11 Work with a new partner. Choose one of these tasks.

a Look at the photos in this lesson and in File 34 on page 196, or find photos in a magazine or on the Internet. Discuss:
   - if you like the look or not – and why.
   - if the clothes / hair, etc. would suit you or your partner.
   - if the photos remind you of anyone or of clothes / things you have.
   - your general views on fashion.

b Choose one of the photos in File 34 on page 196 and one of the situations below. Student A, you are the person in the photo. Student B, start a conversation about what A is wearing.

   - Student A: employee; Student B: boss
   - Student A: son / daughter; Student B: parent
   - Students A & B: two friends who haven't seen each other for years and who meet in the street

▶ 36 To watch the video and do the activities, see the DVD ROM.

NOW TRENDING

SPEAKING

1 **Work in pairs. Discuss the questions.**

- Do you like the way the man in the photo opposite looks? Why? / Why not?
- Do you have – or have you had recently – a trend for beards and / or tattoos where you live?
- How do you think trends such as these begin?
- What explanations can you think of for why trends rise, peak and then fall?

READING

2 **Read the article about why trends rise, peak and fall. Find out:**

1 when some people believe the trend for beards began, why and how it spread.

2 how men with beards and fish with unusual colouring may be connected.

3 how Negative Frequency Dependence theory explains 'peak beard'.

4 what epidemics and social trends may have in common.

3 **Read the article again. Are the sentences true (T) or false (F)? How do you know?**

1 Professor Rob Brooks set out to invent a new phrase.

2 The writer claims that we're going to see less plastic surgery in the future.

3 Brooks believes there's nothing new about trends coming and going.

4 The paper he co-authored proved that NFD is the main cause of changing trends.

5 Fish with rare markings get eaten less and thus get to breed more.

6 According to Brooks's theory, far fewer women now find men with beards attractive.

7 The analogy with epidemics says nothing about how trends decline in popularity.

8 The writer is a fan of the grumpy cat memes.

4 **Find the nouns or noun phrases that go with these verbs in the article.**

pinpoint	emphasise	rate		enjoy	champion
trend	pick up	speculate		lose	urge

5 **Work in groups. Discuss the questions.**

- How far do you agree with the theories outlined in the article?
- Can you see any flaws with the theories – or think of any questions they don't answer?
- What other trends are happening where you live? Think about these areas:

consumer habits	technology
work and employment	youth / street culture
lifestyle	education
food and diets	travel and tourism

UNDERSTANDING VOCABULARY

Snowclones

Snowclones are groups of words often used together, with one or two parts that can be changed. They usually move into wider use via the media, advertising, pop culture and social media.

Have we reached peak *car / hipster / iPhone?*

Keep calm and *carry on / eat cupcakes / listen to Techno.*

You can search for variations of semi-fixed phrases using speech marks and stars. Try, for example, entering the following into a search engine: "Keep calm and *"

6 **Work in groups. Discuss what you think each phrase means. Then think of as many ways as you can to adapt the phrase by changing the words in italics.**

1 It was the mother of all *burgers*.

2 If you look up the word '*cute*' in the dictionary, you'll find a picture of *my son*!

3 It's *politics*, but not as we know it.

4 It's a fine line between *love* and *hate*.

5 Life's too short *for boring shoes*.

6 *Orange* is the new *black*.

7 The *neighbours* from hell!

8 *Trouble* is *my* middle name.

9 *What is this Internet* of *which* you speak?

10 You can take the *boy* out of *the city*, but you can't take *the city* out of the *boy*.

GRAMMAR

Prepositions

1 Many verbs are often followed by certain prepositions.

rely on, contribute to, specialise in

2 Certain adjectives also collocate with particular prepositions.

famous for, obsessed with, nervous about

3 Prepositions also often go with certain nouns in a particular context.

responsibility for, reaction to, increase in

4 There are also many short phrases that start with a preposition.

on average, in a few minutes, by and large

5 Prepositions can connect two parts of a sentence. When a verb follows a preposition, use the -*ing* form.

On finishing *college, she got a job with Dior.* (= when / after)

7 **Match the words and phrases in bold in the article to the patterns (1–5) in the box.**

 **G** Check your ideas on page 182 and do Exercise 1.

ALL THINGS MUST PASS

Ray Hutt wonders if we are reaching peak peaks

When the Australian researcher Rob Brooks declared in 2014 that we seemed to have reached the moment of 'peak beard', little could he have known that not only was he pinpointing a very specific tipping point in our culture, but also that his **choice of** phrase was set to become a trend in its own right. As the mainstream media jumped on his pronouncements, the question 'Have we reached peak X?' started to trend (an interesting word in itself and one that only started to verb following the success of social media site Twitter). We are now routinely informed by social commentators that everything from 'peak plastic surgery' to 'peak celebrity brand endorsement' is occurring.

The speed with which trends come and go can be slightly disorientating and, for fans of fads that are now on the wane, potentially even upsetting. So why does it happen? Some would argue it is just a social phenomenon or a conspiracy of the fashion community to make more money. For example, it has been suggested that the global growth in hairy hipsters had its roots in the 2008 crash, **with** some young men responding to the loss of financial power by choosing to emphasise another aspect of masculinity. This trend was then picked up by various celebrities to maintain their media profile and before long it had spread to the point where in certain parts of many cities beards had become the norm. However, in his co-authored article in the journal *Biology Letters*, Professor Brooks claims that the real cause that underlies the rise and fall of trends is actually at the heart of our very existence: evolution.

The research Brooks worked on showed that bearded men were rated as more attractive by women when seen among a group of predominantly clean-shaven peers, but that the same clean-shaven men then became more attractive when in a minority. In a bid to explain this, the paper speculates that a phenomenon called Negative Frequency Dependence (NFD) may be at play. In essence, NFD means that rare qualities enjoy an advantage. This simple idea has profound evolutionary implications. Imagine, for instance, that a certain male fish has an unusual combination of coloured spots. This will make it less likely to fall prey to predators as it's less instantly recognisable as an example of its breed. This, **in turn**, makes it a more attractive partner. Sadly, however, these 'individualist' fish become so popular that baby fish with their traits soon start appearing in large numbers. Before long, the fish with 'new' markings are so common that they become recognised by predators as the breed. The once-unusual fish are now targets again – and less appealing mates.

Brooks and his fellow researchers have suggested that rarity also operates in other realms and that, initially at least, women were more likely to **opt for** men with facial hair simply because they were unusual. As the fashion spread, however, it lost its edge and female preferences started shifting again. The science of memetics suggests this is remarkably similar to the way in which other trends suddenly attract a lot of attention: ideas, concepts or products are adopted by well-connected trendsetters, who champion them until they have been taken on board by a large enough minority to tip over into mass consumption. This process is often compared to the way epidemics build up slowly but then suddenly explode.

Viewed like this, of course, all manner of contagious cultural content will sooner or later pass into obscurity and be forgotten. I suspect I'm not **alone in** wanting to see the back of grumpy cats, extreme body piercing and postcards urging us to 'Keep calm and …' Unfortunately, however, there's no guarantee that what replaces them will be any more to our own liking. All we *can* be sure of is that whatever comes next, it won't be around forever!

8   **Decide how many options are correct in each sentence.**

1   Are there any contemporary fashions you really object *with* / *to* / *for*? Why?

2   Had you heard *about* / *from* / *of* hipsters before this lesson?

3   Do you know anyone who'd benefit *of* / *from* / *by* a style makeover?

4   Can you think of anything that you're pretty much alone *for* / *in* / *on* liking?

5   Have you ever bought any clothes or accessories you were very disappointed *with* / *by* / *in*?

6   Do you have a preference *to* / *for* / *of* any particular brands? If so, why?

7   Do you think things are better or worse where you live, compared *to* / *from* / *with* five years ago?

8   Do you know anyone who shows real dedication *for* / *to* / *in* keeping up with trends?

9   **Work in groups. Discuss the questions in Exercise 8.**

G   For further practice, see Exercises 2 and 3 on page 183.

MODEL BEHAVIOUR

SPEAKING

1 **Work in groups. Discuss the questions.**

- How important is the fashion industry in your country? In what ways?

- What are popular fashion magazines? How much attention do you give them?

- Does the fashion industry feature in the mainstream media? What programmes or news stories have you heard about?

- Who are the biggest fashion stars in your country at the moment?

- Do you think modelling is a good job? Why? / Why not?

- What three words / phrases would sum up the fashion industry for you?

LISTENING

2 ▶ **52** **Listen to the introduction to a radio programme called *Mixed Media*. Answer the questions.**

1 How many features will there be in the programme?

2 How do the features relate to each other?

3 What do you learn about Tess Holliday?

4 What do you learn about Dove and its advertising campaign?

5 What is the connection between Dove and Holliday?

3 **Work in pairs. Discuss the questions.**

- Why do you think Holliday describes herself as a 'body-positive activist'? What do you think being such an activist involves?

- What do you think of the Dove advert that's described? What do you think its message is?

- Have you seen any adverts for Dove? Could you explain them to your partner?

- Do you think these kinds of campaigns are needed or will make a difference?

4 **You are going to listen to the discussion in the programme. With your partner, discuss how these words and phrases could be connected to the topic.**

objectification	a maths test
selfies	shield
eating disorder	skin-lightening
manipulative	role model

5 ▶ **53** **Listen and check your ideas. Then discuss with your partner how each word and phrase in Exercise 4 is connected to the topic.**

6 ▶ **53** With your partner, decide which of the following points Margot van der Stegen either makes or agrees with in the discussion. Then listen again and check your answers.

1 Men have ultimately decided what the ideal of women's beauty should be through art and photography.

2 Self-objectification is a new phenomenon.

3 The theory of self-objectification explains an increased incidence of anorexia.

4 The research that Dove conducted wasn't valid.

5 Women should spend less time analysing the things they don't like and more time appreciating what they do.

6 Women often manipulate photos of themselves to 'look better'.

7 The ideal of beauty will change.

8 Both Dove's and Tess Holliday's campaigns have the wrong focus in terms of self-esteem.

7 Try to complete the sentences with three words in each space. Then look at audio script 53 on page 213 and check your answers.

1 We now live in an age of _____.

2 _____ fashion magazines can trigger self-criticism.

3 Researchers found the higher levels of anxiety had _____.

4 Certainly that _____ Dove's research.

5 There's certainly a contradiction _____ of Dove's campaign.

6 Most of their adverts are forcing women to define themselves _____ looks.

7 It doesn't play upon _____.

8 That brings us _____ our next item on role models and footballers.

8 Work in groups. Discuss the questions.

- How far do you agree with the points Margot van der Stegen makes?

- Do you think men can suffer from self-objectification? If yes, in what way?

- What other factors might be involved in eating disorders or anxiety?

- What's the best way to ensure children grow up with good self-esteem?

DEVELOPING CONVERSATIONS

Defining yourself

In the listening, Margot van der Stegen says of the pressure to be beautiful:

Both **as a mother and a researcher**, it's certainly something I worry about.

We often define ourselves in this way when talking about our opinions, beliefs, desires and concerns.

9 Write six sentences using the pattern below, defining yourself differently each time.

| As a | _____ , | I think
I believe
I try to
I want
I worry about
etc. | |

10 Work in pairs and compare what you wrote. Discuss how far you understand / agree with each other's point of view.

UNDERSTANDING VOCABULARY

Verb forms and word families

In the listening, the speakers talked about *self-objectification*, *a skin-lightening product* and *the dominant idealised look*. We can build up words like these in these ways.

Use -*en*, -*ify* or -*ise*/*ize* with an adjective or noun to make a verb. (American English prefers -*ize* to -*ise*.)

light	→	lighten	simple	→	simplify
ideal	→	idealise	strength	→	strengthen
object	→	objectify	authority	→	authorise

The verbs are sometimes then used as the basis for creating new adjectives or nouns.

lightening   justifiable   idealised
whitener   objectification   authorised

We may also add prefixes.
the theory of self-objectification
that may be a bit of an oversimplification

11 Complete the sentences using words based on the adjectives and nouns in brackets.

1 Men are increasingly being expected to live up to an _____ image too. (ideal)

2 It's ridiculous to avoid certain foods just because they are _____. (fat)

3 There is simply no _____ for girls under sixteen being used to model adult clothes. (just)

4 There is a _____ awareness of the issues of eating disorders these days, which is good. (height)

5 It's a bit of an _____ to say that the fashion industry only impacts on women negatively. (general)

6 The marketing of teeth _____ is part of an unhealthy obsession with perfection. (white)

7 The fashion industry is a symbol of the _____ gap between rich and poor. (wide)

8 There is increasing _____ taking place in all walks of life. (commercial)

9 I think the fashion industry needs to be _____ because people don't understand what really goes on. (mystery)

10 It's _____ that modelling is one of the very few jobs where women get paid more than men for the same task. (heart)

12 Work in pairs. Choose four of the sentences from Exercise 11 that you'd like to talk about. Then discuss what you think about each topic.

16

DANGER AND RISK

SPEAKING

1 **Which sentence best describes your feelings about the photo?**

1 He must be completely out of his mind. I'm terrified just looking at the photo!

2 I kind of get the appeal, but there's no way I could ever do anything like that!

3 I'm not much of a risk-taker, but I can imagine giving something like this a go.

4 I'd be totally up for something like this. Imagine the adrenaline rush!

2 **Work in groups. Compare your ideas and explain your choices. Then discuss the questions.**

- Why do you think some people feel compelled to take such extreme risks as this?
- What could the possible consequences of their actions be – both for themselves and for others?
- To what degree do you think young people should be encouraged to take risks?
- What risks do you think you take in your day-to-day life?
- Is total risk avoidance achievable – or desirable? Why? / Why not?

Yaroslav Segeda takes a selfie, Kiev, Ukraine

ACCIDENT-PRONE

VOCABULARY Accidents and injuries

1 Replace the words in italics with these synonyms.

banged	came to	heavily	ripped
break	cut	panicked	sliced
burnt	fainted	pouring	terrible pain

1 The machine almost *tore* one of my fingernails off!

2 When I *regained consciousness*, I realised I couldn't feel my hands.

3 It was horrible. Blood was *streaming* down my face.

4 I totally *freaked out* and started screaming.

5 I *whacked* my head on the ceiling and nearly knocked myself out.

6 I was bleeding quite *profusely* from the wound.

7 I *cut* my finger open when I was chopping onions.

8 I fell onto a nail and ended up with a huge *gash* on my arm.

9 I somehow managed to pour boiling water all over my hand and *scalded* myself really badly.

10 It was so crowded and hot and stuffy that I actually *passed out* on the train.

11 I heard the bone *snap*. It was horrible.

12 I was in *agony*. I was screaming my head off.

2 Work in pairs. Test each other.

Student A: say the words in italics in the sentences in Exercise 1.

Student B: close your books. Say the synonyms.

SPEAKING

3 Work in pairs. Discuss what kinds of accidents might happen in the places / situations below. Which is the most risky? Use vocabulary from Exercise 1 to explain your ideas.

a beach	doing DIY	an ice rink
a campsite	driving	jogging
cooking dinner	a football pitch	a nightclub
cycling	gardening	a mountain

LISTENING

4 ▶ **54** Listen to two conversations about accidents. Answer the questions about each conversation.

1 Who had the accident/s and what did they injure?

2 When and how did the accident/s happen?

3 Why do they start talking about the accident/s?

5 ▶ **54** Listen again. Are the sentences true (T) or false (F)? How do you know?

Conversation 1

1 Brian was shocked by what his brother did during dinner.

2 Anita is pleased Brian's brother feels relaxed around her.

3 The wall wasn't easy to climb.

4 Brian's brother wasn't really conscious of the pain caused by the broken teeth.

5 Anita realises that maybe she's judged Brian's brother too severely.

Conversation 2

6 The first accident happened during the holidays.

7 Doug's initial assessment of the injury was optimistic.

8 Doug had to have several stitches the following day.

9 He still holds the doctors responsible.

10 They both remember the news stories about the very strong winds.

When sharing stories with friends, it is common to use relatively informal expressions and more idiomatic language. It is also common to exaggerate and use irony.

---

6 Work in pairs. Discuss what you think the words and phrases in italics from each conversation mean in the context.

Conversation 1

1 What? The *business* with the teeth?

2 That really *freaked* me *out*.

3 Couldn't he have ... *sneaked off* to *the loo*, instead of *bashing* it back in right in front of us?

4 And *to top the whole thing off*, he didn't even really notice.

Conversation 2

5 I was *smart* enough to somehow walk straight into a head-height shelf.

6 I'd been out to a party with some friends one night, *stumbled* home and whacked myself.

7 It was unstitchable the following day! *Just my luck.*

8 My wisdom teeth *weren't too happy* either!

7 Work in groups. Discuss the questions.

• Which of the three accidents mentioned do you think sounds the most painful / serious? Why?

• Which accident do you think would've been easiest to avoid? Why?

• What's the first thing you would have done if you'd been present when each accident happened? Why?

• Have you ever heard of any other weather-related injuries or accidents? When? What happened?

DEVELOPING CONVERSATIONS

Interjections

Interjections are single words or noises made either to express emotions or to show you want people to do something.

A: *... and when I came to, I found my chin completely split open and my wisdom teeth weren't too happy either!*

B: *Woah!*

8 ▶ **55** Listen to twelve interjections. Make a note of each one.

9 Work in pairs. Discuss what you think each one means and in what kind of context it might be used.

10 ▶ **56** Listen to some short exchanges. See if you guessed the meanings and contexts correctly.

11 With your partner, discuss the questions.

• Are any of the interjections the same in your language? Which ones?

• Do you use any of them in English already?

• Do you think it's important to use interjections when speaking a foreign language? Why? / Why not?

• What interjections do you think someone studying your language should learn?

CONVERSATION PRACTICE

12 Choose one of these tasks.

a Think of any scars you have and how you got them.

b Think of an accident that someone you know had.

Spend a few minutes planning how to describe what happened. Try to use as much new language from this lesson as you can. Think about:

• when, why and how the accident happened.

• what the immediate result was and what the longer-term effects were.

• whether it could somehow have been avoided.

13 Now work in groups and share your stories.

🎥 37 To watch the video and do the activities, see the DVD ROM.

COMPENSATION CULTURE

SPEAKING

1 Work in groups. Look at the photos and discuss the questions.

- Would any of these scenes be common in your country? Why? / Why not?

- What aspects of risk – or risk aversion – does each photo illustrate? Which do you think are the most serious issues? Why?

- Which one do you think is a joke? What point is the joke making? Do you agree with it?

READING

2 Read this short news report about a case you will read more about later in the lesson. Decide:

1 which photo you think the story has most in common with – and why.

2 what you think of the case and the court decision.

3 if you think such a case could happen in your country.

4 what you think the words and phrases in bold mean.

WOMAN LOSES SEAGULL COMPENSATION CASE

A Scottish woman has lost her case against a property owner for the injuries she sustained as she fell trying to escape an attack by a seagull. Cathie Kelly was leaving the business centre where she works when the bird swooped down on her. As she turned on the steps to escape the attack, she stumbled. The fall resulted in injuries that required her to take two weeks' sick leave.

Lawyers for Kelly claimed the owners of the business centre Riverside Inverclyde had been **negligent** in not maintaining the property sufficiently to discourage the seagulls' presence and were seeking £30,000 in **damages**, of which Ms Kelly was set to receive £7,000. However, the case was **dismissed on the grounds** that there was insufficient evidence to prove that the gull had actually flown down from Riverside Inverclyde's building.

3 Work in pairs. Compare your answers and explain your ideas.

VOCABULARY Laws and regulations

4 Match these words to their definitions.

an appeal	a lawsuit	negligence
damages	legislation	non-compliance
liability	precedent	grounds

1 _____ is when you try to change a previous decision or verdict by the court.

2 _____ is a failure to do something or do it competently – often causing harm.

3 _____ is the responsibility you have for an accident or damage.

4 _____ is a collection of laws and rules.

5 _____ is a court case where you look for compensation.

6 _____ is a failure to follow regulations or law.

7 _____ is the money you get as compensation.

8 _____ are the reasons given for suing someone – or rejecting a case.

9 _____ is a decision or action that is an example for what people / courts should do now and in the future.

5 Complete the sentences with the correct form of these verbs.

admit	file	repeal	award	hold
sue	dismiss	overturn	set	

1 **The company** _____ **liable** for the accident and forced to pay damages.

2 The victim of the doctor's negligence, who can't be named for legal reasons, _____ two million dollars **in damages**.

3 The Republican Senator _____ **the paper for libel** after it published an article accusing her of lying.

4 His **conviction for** criminal negligence _____ **on appeal**.

5 Last year, a group of women prisoners _____ **a class-action lawsuit** against the local government because of conditions in their jail.

6 The doctor _____ **negligence** and agreed to **pay compensation**.

7 The decision by the court _____ **a precedent**, which means people now have the right to remove aspects of their online history.

8 A lot of people **oppose** the health and safety **legislation** and **want to see it** _____.

9 In the end, **the case** _____ **on the grounds of** insufficient evidence.

6 Work in pairs. How many of the phrases in bold in Exercise 5 can you think of real examples for? Explain what happened.

READING

7 Read the first part of the newspaper editorial related to the news report in Exercise 2. Answer the questions.

1 What is the paper's opinion of the case?

2 What six negative aspects of 'compensation culture' are identified?

3 What does the paper want to see happen?

4 What does the editorial show about the kind of paper it is and its politics?

8 Now read the List of Shame. Mark each example in the following way:

- a tick (✓) if you agree that they are mad
- a cross (✗) if you disagree
- a question mark (?) if you are not sure

9 Work in pairs. Compare and discuss your choices.

SPEAKING

10 Work in pairs.

Student A: read the short texts and related questions in File 35 on page 188.

Student B: read the short texts and related questions in File 36 on page 195.

Explain to your partner what you read and then discuss the questions.

Seagull attack compensation bid symptom of our scared victim culture

The failure of Cathie Kelly's claim in the now infamous seagull compensation case has to be welcomed, but we still wonder how it could ever have come to court in the first place. Ever since Stella Liebeck set an unfortunate precedent in absurd claims by winning $2.8 million dollars for spilling coffee on herself, it seems too many people go out looking for negligence where it does not exist rather than taking responsibility for their own actions.

Were the effects of these claims confined to some wasted court time, we may be less concerned, but the effects of compensation culture have infected all areas of our lives. As our List of Shame below shows, it has created a 'health and safety' culture that sees risk and danger in even the most normal activities as well as placing extra costs on businesses in the form of increased legal insurance to guard against such claims. It has wrapped businesses and institutions in red tape, it is causing inconvenience when we travel and it is smothering our children. So no doubt the Scottish court's decision is a step in the right direction, but this paper will continue to challenge these widespread attitudes of victimhood and campaign to see unnecessary regulations that reduce our freedoms repealed.

The List of Shame

▥ A survey of UK teachers found that almost half believed children were being held back by health and safety regulations.

▥ The same survey reported some pupils were required to wear goggles while using Blu-Tack and children had been barred from the playground because they had no hat or sunscreen.

▥ The UK has around 4,750 speed cameras compared to just 2,200 in France, taking millions of pounds in fines for minor violations.

▥ Airport safety regulations and security cost airlines £4.6 billion a year – and that's not counting the cost to passengers of all the wasted bottles of liquid and other unnecessarily confiscated items.

▥ Manufacturers have been required to print warning signs for sufferers of nut allergies – on packets of nuts!

▥ Kids' party clown, Barney Baloney, was forced to give up using his bubble-making machine because of the cost of public liability insurance – kids could slip over, apparently.

▥ Management at the city council in Oldham barred its staff from wearing flip-flops due to concerns about safety.

▥ Anglia Ruskin University banned the traditional throwing of students' mortarboards in the air on graduation for fears of the hats causing injury as they fell.

▥ A group of Idaho inmates filed a class-action lawsuit against eight breweries because they did not have warnings on their beer concerning the addictive nature of alcohol. They claimed it led to their alcoholism and subsequent imprisonment.

▥ A fire station in the south west of England has been built without the traditional 'fireman's pole' to slide down because of safety fears.

IGNORE AT YOUR PERIL

SPEAKING

1 Work in groups. Discuss what you understand by each of the terms below, why they are current issues and what you think about each one.

digital detox	digital footprint
the digital divide	digital hermits
digital disruption	digital literacy
the digital economy	digital natives

UNDERSTANDING VOCABULARY

Synonyms

As you saw in Exercise 1 on page 142, synonyms are often interchangeable in certain contexts. However, no two words are interchangeable all the time. Sometimes we choose one word over another to be more or less formal. With many words, though, the real difference between them is that they are used in different collocations and phrases.

2 The words *danger, peril, threat, hazard, menace* and *risk* all have similar meanings. Choose the correct option in each sentence.

1 If you're a parent, you ignore the websites your kids are visiting at your *danger / peril*.

2 The future of many small shops and businesses is under *danger / threat* because of ever-increasing online competition.

3 The ease with which prescription drugs can now be ordered online poses a real health *peril / hazard*.

4 They really should do more to combat the *menace / peril* of cyber bullying!

5 Cyber crime poses a grave *threat / peril* to national security.

6 People talk about hackers like they're some kind of *menace / peril* to society, but they're mostly pretty harmless.

7 If we impose too many controls on Internet use, we run the *danger / risk* of restricting civil liberties.

8 Internet dating is fraught with *threat / danger*.

9 Every time you shop online, you're putting yourself at *risk / danger*.

10 The Internet is in serious *danger / risk* of complete meltdown due to the enormous amount of online traffic.

3 Underline the whole phrase each correct word in italics forms part of. Which are new for you?

4 Work in pairs. Discuss how far you agree with the statements in Exercise 2. Explain why.

LISTENING

5 ▶ 57 Listen to a radio phone-in programme about the Internet. Take notes on the risks and problems mentioned.

6 Work in pairs. Compare your notes.

7 ▶ 57 Listen again and answer the questions.

1 What two recent news stories about the Internet does the presenter mention?

2 How does Joyce claim that access to the Internet has affected her students' study skills?

3 Why does Oliver mention digital natives?

4 What's his main concern?

5 What's Nigel's first suggestion?

6 What flaw with this idea does the presenter point out?

7 What alternative proposal does Nigel put forward?

8 What possible problem with this idea does the presenter see?

8 Work in groups. Discuss the questions.

• What do you think is the best treatment for kids who are addicted to the Internet?

• Do you agree that the Internet has had a negative effect on students' abilities to think? Why? / Why not?

• Do you think plagiarism is a problem in your country? If yes, how do you think it should be tackled?

• Do you agree that people sometimes share too much online? Why? / Why not?

• Do you think making an example of a few spammers or fraudsters would be a sufficient deterrent to others? Why? / Why not?

• Can you think of any other problems with the Internet that were not mentioned? Which do you think is the most serious? Why?

GRAMMAR

Talking about the future

There are lots of different ways of talking about the future in English. You have already studied the most common ones at earlier levels. However, we also use various verb and noun structures, some of which are used more frequently in journalism and the media.

9 Try to complete these sentences from the radio programme. Use the verbs in brackets.

1 This is a problem that _____ surely _____ worse. (get)

2 If the show _____, we need you to call up and tell us what's on your mind. (work)

3 I _____ work in the summer. (stop)

4 I honestly don't think things _____ any better in the foreseeable future. (get)

5 I just think that's _____ problems in the long run. (cause)

Now try to complete these sentences with the missing nouns.

6 I'm on the _____ of retiring.

7 And you're saying the _____ of people avoiding all this are pretty slim?

8 In all _____, most offenders are actually pretty harmless.

9 Hit them with the toughest sentences we can. Do that and the _____ are you'll put others off.

10 Do that and there's a distinct _____ you'll end up involved in a legal dispute.

10 ▶ 58 Work in pairs. Compare your ideas, then listen and check your answers. Discuss what you think each structure means.

G Check your ideas on page 184 and do Exercise 1.

11 Rewrite the sentences below using the words in brackets so they have a similar meaning.

1 In all probability, the situation will deteriorate. (bound)

2 There's a distinct possibility that our jobs will be at risk. (likely)

3 They're almost ready to finalise the deal. (verge)

4 Gamble online and the odds are you'll lose. (likelihood)

5 The work should be finished by May. (due)

6 Inflation will probably rise above 10% next month. (set)

G For further practice, see Exercises 2 and 3 on page 184.

SPEAKING

12 Work in groups of four or five. You are going to roleplay a radio phone-in programme. Choose one of the topics for discussion below.

- Today we'll be considering whether airport security is becoming too expensive to maintain.
- Are we doing enough to combat the threat of global warming?
- Today we'll be asking if the government is taking the risk of a global epidemic seriously enough.
- Today's question is: given the increasing risks of foreign travel, why not just holiday at home?

Choose one student to be the host. This student (Student A) should read the rolecard in File 37 on page 197. Each of the other students should think of at least two points they want to make about the chosen topic. Try to mention what you think may happen in the future and also plan to use other language from this lesson.

13 Now roleplay the phone-in programme.

Student A: manage the calls from the other students, summarise their main ideas and challenge them where appropriate in order to move the debate forward.

Students B–E: take turns to phone in and make your comments. You can call more than once. You can also comment on previous callers' opinions.

VIDEO 8

LONG NECK WOMEN

1 Work in pairs. Look at the photo and discuss the questions.

- Where do you think the photo was taken? What's the purpose of the painting in the photo?

- Do you know any other tribes that have a very distinctive appearance, way of dressing or jewellery? What do they look like? What do you know about them and their way of life?

- Do you think it is good to advertise people such as the woman in the photo to tourists? Why? / Why not?

2 📹 38 Watch the first part of the video (0.00–1.22) and answer the questions.

1 What different kinds of styles are mentioned?

2 Where is the woman in the photo from?

3 What risk is associated with the rings they wear?

3 Work in pairs. Write six questions about the long neck women that you would like answers to.

4 📹 38 Watch the second part of the video (1.23–4.50) and see if your questions are answered.

5 📹 38 Work in pairs. Discuss what the narrator said using the words and numbers below. Then watch the second part of the video again (1.23–4.50) and check your ideas.

1 matriarch

2 25 / 12

3 shackles

4 rods

5 a car tyre

6 clavicle / ribs

7 folklore

8 refit

6 Work in groups. Discuss the questions.

- In what ways do people in your culture alter their appearance or bodies? Why?

- Are there any risks associated with these alterations?

- Do you think this is any different to the Kayan women? If yes, in what way? If not, why not?

- Do you think groups like the Kayan will continue to exist in the future? Why? / Why not?

- Do you think that's a good or bad thing? Why?

- When abroad, can you spot someone from your country just by their appearance? How?

UNDERSTANDING FAST SPEECH

7 📹 39 Listen to an extract from the video said at natural pace. Try to write down what you hear. Then compare your ideas with a partner.

8 📹 40 Try again. This time you will hear a slower version of the extract.

9 Check your ideas in File 10 on page 189. Groups of words are marked with / and pauses are marked //. Stressed sounds are in CAPITALS. Practise saying the extract.

REVIEW 8

GRAMMAR AND UNDERSTANDING
VOCABULARY

1 Complete the text with one word in each space.

In all ¹_____, you'll be familiar with the idea of climate change. In fact, the ²_____ are you'll probably be sick and tired of hearing about it! However, the damage we're doing to our planet is something we ignore at our ³_____. Climate change poses a grave ⁴_____ to human health and we all share responsibility ⁵_____ the current situation – and, of course, we're all ⁶_____ of doing so much more! I realise the chances of this happening are pretty ⁷_____, but we need to overcome our addiction ⁸_____ oil. If we don't, we're ⁹_____ serious danger ¹⁰_____ making a bad situation far, far worse.

2 Complete the second sentence so that it has a similar meaning to the first sentence using the word given. Do not change the word given. You must use between four and five words, including the word given.

1 I heard you passed your exams, so I'm just calling to say well done.
I'm just phoning to _____ your exams. **CONGRATULATE**

2 To be honest, I didn't even know that law existed until very recently.
To be honest, I was totally _____ that law until very recently. **UNAWARE**

3 The whole business of predicting consumer trends is extremely risky.
The whole business of predicting consumer trends _____. **FRAUGHT**

4 Africa is set to become a major market for the company in the years to come.
Africa is _____ a major market for the company. **VERGE**

5 In many ways, being a genius is very similar to being mad!
There's _____ and madness. **FINE**

6 Sales are down this year but we expect things to improve over the next few years.
Sales have been poor this year, but things are bound to pick up _____. **TERM**

3 Choose the correct option.

1 I realise that I'm quite possibly alone *to think / for thinking / in thinking* this!

2 I don't think *it'll be likely / it's likely / it's unlikely* to make much difference, to be honest.

3 Her tireless dedication *for / to / with* the community has been remarkable.

4 I'm *due / bound / prior* to go to Marrakech on Wednesday for a week.

5 Doctors who fail to comply with the new guidelines run the *danger / risk / threat* of being sued by their patients.

6 What is this 'grammar' *of that / with which / of which* you speak?

VOCABULARY

4 Decide which of these words are connected to the top half of the body and which to things worn on the bottom half of the body.

bangles	flats	shades	trainers
bushy	lapel	sleeve	wedges
flares	wig	sturdy	sandals

5 Match the verbs (1–8) with the collocates (a–h).

1 file   a my head on the door / my knee
2 oppose   b the case / evidence
3 sue   c a precedent / a new world record
4 dismiss   d my finger open / some bread
5 whack   e a bone / at me
6 slice   f legislation / a plan
7 set   g a newspaper for libel / for damages
8 snap   h a lawsuit / a complaint

6 Complete the sentences with a preposition in each space.

1 It was awful. I was lying on the floor, screaming _____ agony!

2 She sued the company and won, winning over £2,000,000 _____ damages.

3 I was cooking and I somehow managed to pour boiling water all _____ myself.

4 He was just standing there, screaming his head _____ for no reason, as far as I could tell!

5 I can't believe you want to do that! You must be _____ of your mind!

7 Complete the sentences. Use the word in brackets to form a word that fits in the space.

1 The case was dismissed as a result of _____ evidence being presented. (suffice)

2 The whole situation has been made worse by widespread _____ with the law. (comply)

3 The guy who crashed into me accepted _____ and paid for all the repairs. (liable)

4 He was rushed to hospital and operated on but sadly never regained _____. (conscious)

5 The hospital admitted _____ and agreed to pay _____. (negligent, compensate)

8 Complete the text with one word in each space. The first letters are given.

I'm usually quite ¹sc_____, I suppose. I mean I'm most comfortable in old ²fr_____ jeans and trainers. Last month, though, I got invited to quite a ³fa_____ work do, so decided to try and dress as smartly as I could. I had my hair ⁴hi_____ blonde and then I wore a ⁵k_____-l_____ black dress and high ⁶h_____. I was surprised at quite how glamorous I looked! On making my grand entrance though, I stumbled and managed to ⁷k_____ myself o_____! When I ⁸c_____ t_____ a few minutes later, I realised I'd got a great big ⁹g_____ on my head and blood was ¹⁰p_____ down my face! To ¹¹t_____ the whole thing off, my dress was ¹²r_____ as well. It wasn't exactly the best way to announce my arrival!

Review 8 149

SPEAKING

1 Work in pairs. Look at the table and chart and discuss the questions.

- What are the main facts, predictions and trends that the table and chart show?
- What do you think is meant by 'developed' and 'developing' countries?
- Why do you think these trends are happening?
- Can you see similar trends in your country?
- How do you feel about these changes? What is good / bad about them?

World's biggest cities by population
(in millions)

2014			2030		
1	Tokyo (Japan)	37.8	1	Tokyo (Japan)	37.2
2	Delhi (India)	25.0	2	Delhi (India)	36.1
3	Shanghai (China)	23.0	3	Shanghai (China)	30.8
4	Mexico City (Mexico)	20.8	4	Mumbai (India)	27.8
5	São Paulo (Brazil)	20.8	5	Beijing (China)	27.7
6	Mumbai (India)	20.7	6	Dhaka (Bangladesh)	27.4
7	Osaka (Japan)	20.1	7	Karachi (Pakistan)	24.8
8	Beijing (China)	19.5	8	Cairo (Egypt)	24.5
9	New York (USA)	18.6	9	Lagos (Nigeria)	24.2
10	Cairo (Egypt)	18.4	10	Mexico City (Mexico)	23.9
11	Dhaka (Bangladesh)	17.0	11	São Paulo (Brazil)	23.4
12	Karachi (Pakistan)	16.1	12	Kinshasa (Democratic Republic of Congo)	20.0

city located on coast or major river

World rural and urban populations

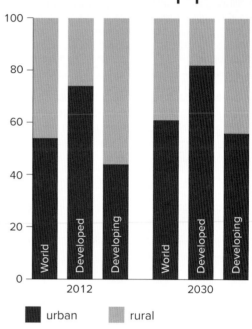

urban   rural

WRITING

2 Read the description of the data in the table and the chart. Find six factual mistakes.

The table shows the 12 largest cities in the world by area in 2014 and projected figures for 2030. As can be seen, with the exception of Tokyo, all of the five main cities are predicted to grow, which is unsurprising given the continued shift from urban to rural living illustrated in the chart. In the developed world, two out of every three people already live in cities, and between now and 2030, the global urban population is expected to rise by 25%, the bulk of which will occur in developing countries. This shift towards growth in developing regions is reflected in the table. It shows that the populations of cities such as Delhi, Shanghai and Mumbai will all increase quite substantially and by 2030, African cities (Lagos and Kinshasa) are forecast to have entered the top 12 for the first time. Perhaps most remarkably, the population of Dhaka in Bangladesh looks set to increase by almost 90%. It is interesting to note that a significant minority of the cities predicted to grow are located on the coast or on major rivers, reflecting the importance of trade in urban development.

3 Work in pairs and do the following:

1 Compare the mistakes you found and correct them.

2 Decide one other feature of the table and chart you would draw attention to.

VOCABULARY Describing percentages

4 Replace the words in italics with these words and phrases.

a tiny percentage	four out of five
the vast majority	almost a fifth
a significant minority	more than halved
slightly higher	fourfold

1 The chart shows there were around 20,000 immigrants, *93%* of whom came from other European countries.

2 The graph illustrates that urban sprawl increased by *19%* over this period.

3 As is illustrated in figure 1, violent crime *fell from 5% to 2%*, while burglary rates increased *from 1.5% to 6%*.

4 As can be seen in the pie chart, *80% of* customers were satisfied with the service, which was *6% more* than last year.

5 This is illustrated in figure 3, which shows that only *0.1%* of household income is spent on books.

6 The survey indicated that *43%* of respondents were concerned about the effects of the proposals.

GRAMMAR

5 Rewrite the sentences using the verbs in brackets.

1 By 2025, the population will have risen to 15 million. (project)

2 In the next 20 years, the rural population will start falling. (predict)

3 African cities will grow rapidly over the next few years. (expect)

4 China will become the world's largest economy in the next ten years. (forecast)

6 Work in pairs. Think of an example for each of the following. Discuss why they are happening / have happened and predict how they will develop in the future.

1 an upward trend

2 a downward trend

3 a general shift from one thing to another

KEY WORDS FOR WRITING

7 Rewrite each pair of sentences as one sentence using *of whom* or *of which*.

1 The government donates 0.6% of GDP as aid. The bulk of that money goes to countries in Africa.

2 There were 2,650 fatalities from car accidents last year. The vast majority of the accidents were caused by driver error.

3 The city has around 200,000 inhabitants. This figure includes 25,000 students.

4 There was a significant fall in crime in the last decade. A large part of the drop was attributed to rising living standards.

5 The survey interviewed 950 people altogether. The interviewees were mostly 18 to 25 years old.

PRACTICE

8 Work in pairs. Look at the visuals below and discuss the following:

- what the pie chart and graph generally show
- the main facts, trends and predictions
- key statistics that illustrate the trend
- any surprising aspects you would highlight

9 Write a description of the main trends illustrated in the chart and graph. Use between 150 and 200 words.

Fig.1 Website content languages

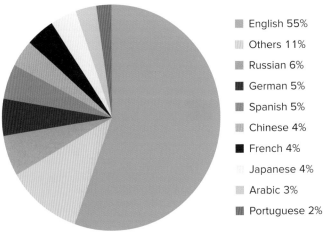

English 55%
Others 11%
Russian 6%
German 5%
Spanish 5%
Chinese 4%
French 4%
Japanese 4%
Arabic 3%
Portuguese 2%

Source: w3techs.com

Fig.2 Millions of adults learning English

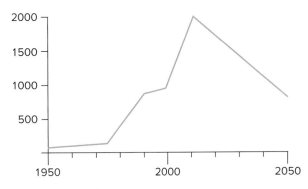

Source: The English Company

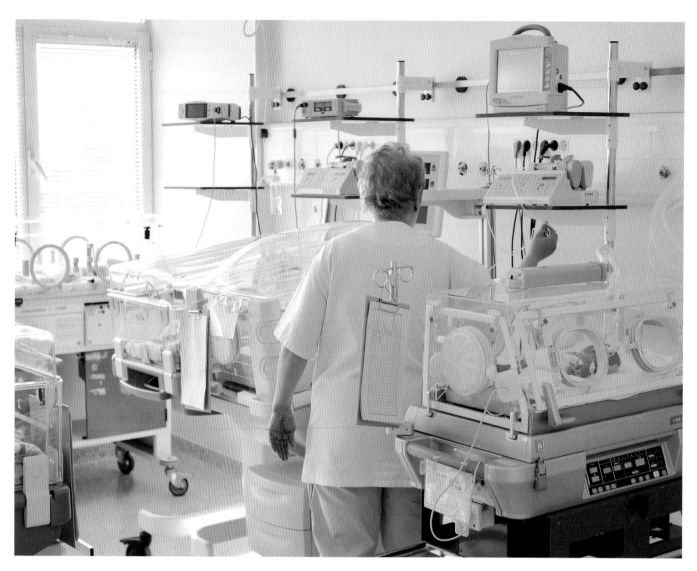

SPEAKING

1 **Work in groups. Discuss these questions.**

- Do you know anyone who works in health care? Who? What do they do? Do they enjoy it?

- How is health care funded in your country – through taxation, insurance or direct payments?

- What are the strengths and weaknesses of the health care system in your country?

- If you could change one thing about the system, what would it be? Why?

WRITING

2 **You are going to read an introduction to an essay with the title below. Before you read, work in pairs and discuss the questions.**

'The government should provide free health care for all.'

Discuss.

1 What makes the essay title relevant these days?

2 What are the main issues that need to be addressed in the essay?

3 What else might be included in the introduction?

3 **Read the introduction and see if it covers the same things you thought of in Exercise 2.**

'THE GOVERNMENT SHOULD PROVIDE FREE HEALTH CARE FOR ALL.' DISCUSS.

The health of a nation is clearly of paramount importance and measures of health and life expectancy are seen as key indicators of a country's success. Given this, some argue that health care provision is the government's responsibility and should be free for all. However, there are several points here that need addressing. Firstly, what do we mean by free? Secondly, *what* health care is to be 'free'? And, finally, what is the government's role? In this essay, I will argue that 'free for all' is an impossibility and that while a basic level of provision should be totally free to *a few*, the government's role in health care should be minimal.

4 **With your partner, answer the questions.**

1 What arguments do you think will be given to back up the writer's opinion?

2 How do you think the information in the essay will be organised?

5 **Read the rest of the essay opposite and check your ideas from Exercise 4.**

6 Complete the essay with these words.

| as such | furthermore | indeed | otherwise | such |
| firstly | however | in short | secondly | while |

The cost of health care is not 'free'. ¹_____, in many countries, costs are spiralling. Health care must be paid for either via taxation, through insurance premiums or by direct payments to doctors and ²_____ it is impossible for it to be free for *all*. The issue is, therefore, whether *some* people should be exempt from paying. I would argue that taxation should be limited to providing preventative health measures, such as vaccinations and hospital treatment in life-threatening emergencies, for those too poor to have health insurance. As well as maintaining social cohesion, ³_____ measures prevent the spread of diseases that threaten the whole of society and they also benefit everyone economically. However, some would claim there are economic and individual benefits to be gained from more health care intervention. They point to cancer treatments to extend life, operations that restore eyesight or therapy for depression. ⁴_____ this is largely true, in a 'free for all' system these individual claims compete for the limited funding that is available. Each individual sees their treatment as essential, but surely they are impossible to compare in terms of value to society. ⁵_____, would you trust the government to decide? Insurance-based systems, ⁶_____, do not have this problem. ⁷_____, insurance means money is spent by individuals on the treatment they personally need. ⁸_____, insurance companies provide an incentive to reduce risky behaviours such as smoking by charging higher premiums. In a 'free for all' system the effects of these antisocial behaviours are also *paid for* by all. ⁹_____ then, the government should provide free basic health care for a few through taxation, but ¹⁰_____ its role should be restricted to setting the legal framework for an insurance-based health system. This is better and fairer for all.

7 Work in pairs. Discuss the questions.

- How would you divide the text into paragraphs?
- Do you think the essay is otherwise clear and well organised? Why? / Why not?
- How does the writer indicate to the reader the arguments he / she finds weak?
- To what degree does the writer's opinion reflect your own? Where do you agree / disagree? Why?

KEY WORDS FOR WRITING

indeed

Indeed can be used:

1 to introduce a sentence that exemplifies or expands on a previously made point.
   *The cost of health care is not 'free'. **Indeed**, in many countries, costs are spiralling.*

2 for emphasis after *very* + adjective / adverb.
   *The cost of health care in the US is very high **indeed**.*

3 to emphasise that something there was some doubt about is actually true.
   *Despite the hospital's denial, statistics showed that the hospital was **indeed** underperforming.*

8 Add *indeed* in the correct place in the sentences. There are two examples of each of the uses in the box.

1 After much questioning, he was eventually forced to admit that there was something wrong.

2 There are those in society who do not pay sufficient attention to their own health. Many actively abuse it.

3 Following repeated accusations, it was later proven that the test results had been falsified.

4 The final results of the experiment were very strange.

5 Putting such a theory into practice would be hard. You might say almost impossible.

6 Cultural identities in any society vary so widely as to make the extraction of common features very difficult.

9 Write sentences to exemplify or expand on the sentences below.

1 The government simply cannot afford to expand health care any further. Indeed, …

2 Governments can always find money to fund things when it suits them. Indeed, …

3 Every election brings new pledges to increase spending on the health service. Indeed, …

4 In countries where free health care for all is the norm, the system does not always function as well as we might imagine. Indeed, …

10 Work in pairs and compare your ideas. Who wrote better follow-up sentences?

PRACTICE

11 Work in pairs. Discuss possible reasons why people might agree or disagree with each of the following statements and then discuss your own opinions.

1 'Nuclear energy is the most realistic long-term option we have.' Discuss.

2 'Rather than bringing countries closer together, globalisation has led to increased nationalism.' Discuss.

3 'There should be a maximum working week for all of 35 hours.' How far do you agree?

12 Write short introductions for each of the three essay titles, using the ideas and model in Exercises 2 and 3.

13 Compare your introductions with a partner. Can you see any ways in which your partner's work could be improved?

14 Write an essay of around 300 words in response to one of the titles in Exercise 11. You should aim for five paragraphs. Try to use *indeed* at least once.

3 WRITING Reviews

SPEAKING

1 Work in groups. Discuss the questions.

- How often do you do the things below? Are there any things you never do? Why not?
- Can you remember the last time you did each activity? What was it like?

see plays at the theatre	read novels
go to exhibitions	go to the ballet
go to small gigs	go to big concerts
see films at the cinema	go to the opera
see musicals	read poetry

VOCABULARY Reviews

2 Complete the sentences with these pairs of words.

abstract + sculptures	production + plot
album + encores	rhyme + collection
based + set	sets + choreography
orchestration + role	symphony + finale
prose + multi-layered	technique + partner

1 _____ on a true story and _____ in 1940s Texas, the new release by director Jackie Lee tackles issues of violence and sexism that remain highly relevant today.

2 Generally avoiding such conventions as _____ and punctuation, this _____ contains some wonderful, albeit challenging, pieces of poetry.

3 Opening with the fan favourite *Poverty Train*, the group then powered through the bulk of their latest _____ and ended up returning for two _____ packed with crowd-pleasers.

4 The _____ are amazing, the songs wonderful and the _____ is just out of this world.

5 Featuring both figurative and _____ work, this collection spans five decades of Morton's life and also features some of her rarely seen _____.

6 This is the fourth _____ of this classic that I've seen and it's undoubtedly the best. The cast are excellent and the _____ gripping from start to finish.

7 Dorothy Gilbert's powerful _____ allows her to both carve the most beautiful shapes and move gently through them, while newcomer Andrei Agapov is surely her ideal _____.

8 Despite the sparkling, imaginative _____, there were so many twists and turns that at times the _____ plot was nearly impossible to follow.

9 With its colourful, rich _____ and with tenor Richard Hamilton making his debut in the leading _____, this staging is one of the season's must-sees.

10 Whilst not my favourite _____, the orchestra's performance was nevertheless gripping and the grand _____ even brought tears to my eyes.

3 Match the sentences in Exercise 2 to the ten activities in Exercise 1.

4 Choose at least six words from Exercise 2 that describe things you've seen or read. Then work in pairs and tell your partner as much as you can about each thing.

WRITING

5 Read the review of a British musical. Then work in pairs and discuss the questions.

- How many stars out of five do you think the reviewer gave the musical? Why?
- Does *Billy Elliot* sound like the kind of thing you'd enjoy? Why? / Why not?
- What do you learn about the plot? Does it remind you of any other films / books, etc.?
- What's the function of each of the five paragraphs?

| ABOUT | REVIEWS | COMMENTS | NEWS | PHOTOS |

BILLY ELLIOT

Given that it has been adapted from the film of the same name, it is no surprise that the musical version of *Billy Elliot* is full of cinematic suspense. Set against the backdrop of the miners' strike in 1980s Britain, the plot revolves around a young boy who rejects his father's moves to push him into boxing in favour of ballet lessons, a decision which initially causes conflict in his family but which eventually leads him to fame and fortune.

The beautifully choreographed drama unfolds in a tense, gripping manner and the stage is exploited to the full. The scenes that alternate between Billy's ballet lessons and his father's battles against the police on the picket lines at the mine are particularly powerful. The sets are incredibly evocative and capture the mood of social unrest excellently, transporting the audience to another time and place.

When one stops to consider the extreme youth of its main star – Nat Sweeney, who plays Billy, is only twelve years old – the show becomes even more remarkable. Nat is dazzling and I found myself unable to take my eyes off him for the whole performance. He brings a vulnerability and tenderness to the role that left many in tears.

If I do have a criticism, then I suppose it would be the music, written by pop legend Sir Elton John. Whilst it is often uplifting and anthemic, it does start to feel somewhat formulaic after a time. Therein lies the other slight problem – at just over three hours, the show is perhaps 30 minutes too long. By the time the excellent cast had received three standing ovations, I'd been in my seat for almost 200 minutes!

Regardless of these minor flaws, this is nevertheless an outstanding spectacle and a must-see for anyone keen on contemporary musicals.

KEY WORDS FOR WRITING

given and nevertheless

Given means 'considering'. It shows you are taking account of a fact when you give an opinion.

Given *that it has been adapted from the film, it is no surprise that the musical version of* Billy Elliot *is full of cinematic suspense.*

Nevertheless is used with *despite, while, regardless*, etc. to emphasise that something is true despite what you first said. It is also used like *however* to refer back to a previous sentence.

Regardless of these minor flaws, this is **nevertheless** *an outstanding spectacle.*

The film lasts four hours. **Nevertheless,** *the time flies by.*

6 **Match the two parts of the sentences.**

1 The play received very poor reviews,
2 The play was a remarkable success,
3 Given that the concert was quite short and the band refused to give an encore,
4 Irrespective of the band's refusal to give an encore,
5 While Watson only plays a minor role in the film,
6 Given that Watson only plays a minor role,

a she nevertheless outshines everyone with her remarkable performance.
b but nevertheless went on to be hugely popular.
c it's remarkable that she won an Oscar.
d given how low expectations surrounding it were.
e it was nevertheless an amazing concert.
f it was unsurprising there were boos and complaints as the audience left the auditorium.

7 **Work in pairs. Think of three different ways to complete each of the sentences below.**

1 While her recent collection has been badly received by the press, I nevertheless found it …
2 Despite a huge budget, the film nevertheless …
3 Given the length of the novel, …
4 This is a very young orchestra. Nevertheless, …

PRACTICE

8 **Write a review of a concert, album, exhibition, ballet, musical or novel. Use between 250 and 300 words and try to use as much language from this lesson as you can.**

4 WRITING Describing processes

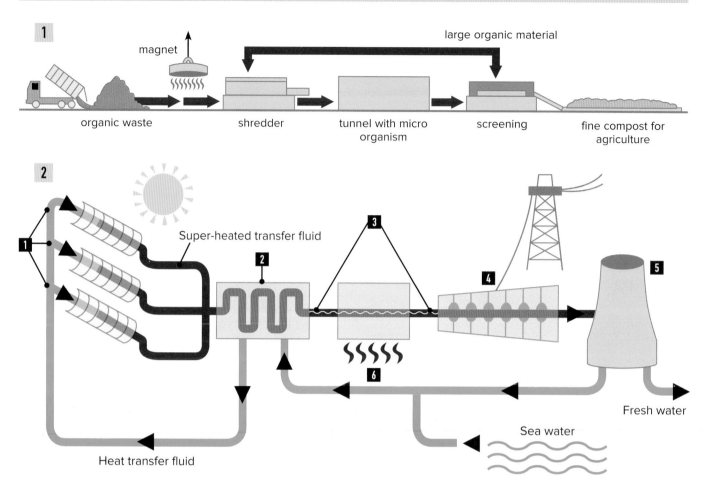

SPEAKING

1 Work in groups. Discuss the questions:

- What is involved in the following processes? Have you ever been involved in any of them?
  - a visa application
  - getting a non-emergency operation
  - buying and selling online
  - publishing a book or making a film
  - a criminal court case
  - getting compensation for something
  - getting rid of your rubbish
  - providing electricity or tap water

- Have you ever experienced a difficult bureaucratic / legal process? What happened?

- Do you think it's important to know about how we get consumer products and services? Why? / Why not? Are there any product or service processes you'd like to know more about?

WRITING

2 Work in pairs. Look at the two diagrams above. Discuss what processes you think they show and what you think might happen in each case.

3 Now read the text that describes Figure 2 and label 1–6 in the diagram.

4 Complete the description with these linkers.

meanwhile   whereby   thus   which   as

The diagram shows a process known as Concentrating Solar Power (CSP) [1]_____ solar energy is used to create steam to power electrical generators.

Large parabolic troughs are directed at the sun. The mirrored surfaces of the troughs reflect the sun's rays and concentrate them onto pipes carrying a fluid that is [2]_____ heated up to a very high temperature. This super-heated fluid passes through a heat exchanger, where it boils water and creates steam, before returning in a loop back to the parabolic trough. The steam [3]_____ is conveyed through pipes at high pressure to a generator, where it drives turbines to create electricity. [4]_____ the steam goes through the turbine it loses heat and is then further cooled in a tower, converting it back into water. The water then continues in a loop back to the heat exchanger, where it is again boiled to create steam. In the absence of sunshine, the steam is generated by supplementary gas-powered heaters.

CSP offers a number of benefits: it provides clean sustainable energy; it can make use of large tracts of unused desert land; and it can be adapted to make use of sea water, [5]_____ can be easily desalinated at the cooling-tower stage, thereby providing much-needed fresh water in arid zones.

5 What is the purpose of the three paragraphs? How does the writer avoid using personal pronouns (I, we, me, us, etc.) in the text? Would you avoid such pronouns in similar texts in your language?

SPEAKING

6 Work in pairs. Discuss the questions.

- Do you think the process you read about would be a good idea in your country? Why? / Why not?
- What benefits / problems are there with the following energy sources or energy-saving schemes? Do you have any of them in your country? Is there any opposition to them?
  - wind farms
  - fracking
  - solar farms
  - subsidies for renewable energies
  - oil / gas drilling
  - nuclear power plants
  - hydroelectric dams
  - subsidies for improving insulation

VOCABULARY Processes

7 Replace the words in italics with these words and rewrite each sentence in the passive.

insulate	categorise	assemble
screen	discard	ship
break down	box	power
remove	proofread	select

1 They *take out* plastic from the rubbish manually.
2 They *wrap* the pipes with foam to minimise heat loss.
3 They *check* the final product for impurities.
4 They *sort* the tea leaves into different grades according to size and quality.
5 They don't *throw away* anything during the process to maximise efficiency.
6 They *choose* potential jury members randomly from the electoral roll.
7 They *put together* the parts in a central plant.
8 They *check* the final manuscript for spelling mistakes and other errors.
9 They *package* the oranges and load them onto lorries.
10 They *drive* the turbines by forcing water through them.
11 They use microbes to *decompose* the oil into droplets.
12 They only take payment after they *send* the order from the warehouse.

8 Work in pairs. Discuss the questions.

- What processes do you think each of the sentences in Exercise 7 are part of?
- Why might different processes use these things?

a filter	a conveyor belt	a pump
a magnet	a furnace	an algorithm

KEY WORDS FOR WRITING

whereby, *thereby* and *thus*

Whereby explains the way something is done according to a method, agreement, rule, etc.

Thereby and *thus* both show the result of a particular process previously mentioned.

9 Complete the sentences with *whereby* or *thereby*.

1 Glassblowing is the process _____ glass is heated and then shaped.
2 The milk is heated to around 70%, _____ killing the vast majority of microbes.
3 We have to comply with strict regulations _____ our machines are inspected weekly, _____ ensuring total safety.
4 There's a trade-in scheme _____ any car over fifteen years old can be scrapped for $3,000 when buying a new car.

10 Work in groups. How many of these natural, industrial and legal rules and processes can you explain in one sentence with *whereby*? For how many can you add a possible result using *thus* or *thereby*?

desalination	Gaia
hydroelectric power	metamorphosis
a veto	photosynthesis
osmosis	auditing
distillation	landfill
an embargo	a high court appeal

PRACTICE

11 Choose either the diagram of the composting process (Figure 1) or draw a diagram to represent a process you discussed in Exercise 1 or 8.

12 Write a description of the process. Use between 150 and 200 words.

Archimede Solar Energy Power Plant, Perugia, Italy

5 WRITING Covering letters

SPEAKING

1 Work in pairs. Discuss the questions.

- What's the difference between a CV (Curriculum Vitae) and a covering letter? What kind of information might you typically include in each? Do you think they are both always needed? Why? / Why not?

- Do you have a CV? Are you happy with it?

- Have you ever had to write a covering letter or personal statement on an application form? In what language? Do you think it was effective?

2 Read the short text below and compare it with your ideas. Does it contain anything you didn't mention?

When applying for jobs where there is no standardised application form, we usually send:

- a CV (a résumé in American English)
- a short covering letter / email

The covering letter is meant to encourage the company you're applying to to take a closer look at your CV. It should clarify why you want to work for the firm and why you would be a good fit. Highlight key information from your CV, but don't just repeat what is listed. Match your skills, interests and experience to the specific job within the company and sell your qualities to the reader. The aim of a covering letter is to get you invited for an interview.

CONTENT

Your letter should be concise and relevant. It should:

- state why you are writing and what post you are applying for.
- explain where you learned about the job vacancy.
- say why you want the job.
- say why you would be a benefit to the company.
- request an interview.

Often online application forms will have an open section or personal statement where you can sell yourself as in a covering letter and explain why you want the job and how you would benefit the company.

3 Work in pairs. In light of the text in Exercise 2, discuss how you would sell yourself in your covering letter if you were applying for the job below.

CUSTOMER SERVICE AGENT

We are a leading online tourism agency looking for a full-time Customer Service Agent.

We require:

- ability to listen attentively and hear important information, and to provide clear information in excellent English
- proven ability to deal with customer enquiries
- previous customer service or call centre experience – desirable but not essential
- basic IT skills
- ability to work flexible (and sometimes long) hours

WRITING

4 Read the covering email sent by an applicant for the job and choose the correct option.

To whom it may concern,

I ¹*write / am writing* to apply for the post of Customer Service Agent, ²*as / which* advertised on www.jobseekers.com recently.

I feel I ³*would / will* be suitable for the post for several reasons. Firstly, I speak excellent English, ⁴*spending / having spent* the last year living and working in Canada. Secondly, I feel I possess the relevant customer service experience, having ⁵*worked / been working* in a range of service industry positions, many of ⁶*them / which* required me to represent businesses to the general public. My inter-personal skills and ability to communicate also benefited from having to deal with frequent customer complaints in my places of work. I am now keen to ⁷*implement / put* these skills into practice and to continue to develop myself and extend my range of abilities.

In addition to all this, I am a dedicated, motivated worker, able to act both independently and as part of a team. In my last job, I was responsible for setting up a new system for the collection and compilation of customer feedback, a process that exemplified my listening and communication skills as well as my competence with cloud-based surveys and social media for business. I enjoy new challenges and never give less than my ⁸*everything / all*. I trust you will agree that my track record so far, as detailed in my CV, shows this.

I am available for interview at any time and would be happy to provide references ⁹*should / when* you require them.

Please do not hesitate to contact me should you require any further information.

I look forward to ¹⁰*hear / hearing* from you soon,

Yours faithfully,

Karim Nourani

Siobhan Tebbs

5 Work in pairs. Discuss your opinion of the letter. Is it well written, too formal, too assertive, etc.? Would you interview this applicant for the post? Why? / Why not?

VOCABULARY

Achievements at work

It is common in covering letters to detail your previous achievements at work or in the field of education. After detailing achievements, we often go on to explain the skills these achievements demonstrated or developed.

I was responsible for setting up a new system for the collection and compilation of customer feedback, a process that exemplified my listening and communication skills as well as my competence with cloud-based surveys and social media for business.

6 Complete the sentences with these verbs.

achieved	conducted	implementing
advised	dealt with	negotiated
arranged	devised	promoting
budgeted	diagnosed	represented

1 I booked flights and _____ accommodation for colleagues who had to go away on business trips.

2 As events co-ordinator for a local charity, I was responsible for organising and _____ events to raise money.

3 In my HR role, I _____ staff on a wide range of legal and professional matters.

4 I _____ above-average grades in the majority of my end-of-school exams.

5 I _____ a survey among staff about proposed changes and presented the results to management.

6 I _____ some remarkably abusive customers during my time at the call centre.

7 I was in charge of _____ the new system for filing all the office paperwork and training staff.

8 I _____ the successes and failures of the business and thus helped determine the path we subsequently took.

9 I _____ a script for teleworkers, which was later implemented company-wide.

10 I _____ my money carefully during my time at university and was thus able to meet all my financial commitments.

11 I successfully _____ with my bank to reschedule my debt, saving me £80 a month.

12 I was elected as an official spokesperson and _____ my colleagues in meetings with the management.

7 Work in pairs. What skills or abilities do you think each sentence in Exercise 6 is evidence of?

KEY WORDS FOR WRITING

should

In formal writing, *should* is often used to mean *if*.

*I am available for interview and would be happy to provide further references **should** you require them.*

8 Put the words in the correct order to make common sentences using *should*.

1 further / please / contact / require / hesitate / any / do / you / should / not / information / me / to

2 available / request / references / should / them / on / are / you / require

3 please / the / possible / vacancies / become / any / opportunity / contact / at / should / earliest / available / me

4 test / after / days / you / should / retake / can / so / the / 60 / you / wish / to / do

5 wish / matter / phone / appointment / should / discuss / to / please / an / you / this / further / to / make

9 Work in pairs. Decide how the sentences in Exercise 8 might be worded in informal spoken English.

PRACTICE

10 Look at the three job adverts below and decide which one most appeals to you.

ART GALLERY ASSISTANT

Busy modern art gallery seeks full or part-time administrative assistant to work with gallery directors. Fluent English essential. You are a calm, intelligent, flexible, curious person who likes to get things done.

ASSISTANT SALES MANAGER

Large European hotel chain seeks assistant sales manager. You have a degree (or equivalent), sales experience and good communication and administrative skills. Must be driven, able to work under pressure and happy to travel 15–20 weeks per year.

OFFICIAL GUIDES WANTED

We are looking for guides with a keen interest in history or archaeology as well as excellent English skills to join our association. We organise high-quality cultural guided tours of historic sites.

11 Work in pairs and compare your choices. Discuss what experience or abilities applicants for each post need.

12 Write a covering letter to accompany an application for the post you chose in Exercise 10.

6 WRITING Magazine articles

SPEAKING

1 Put the inventions below in order: 1) of their usefulness to you personally, 2) of their impact on the world.

First vending machine (dispensing holy water) – invented by Hero of Alexandria (Egypt) in 50 AD

Pressure cooker – invented by Denis Papin (France) in 1679

Mercury thermometer – invented by Daniel Fahrenheit (Holland / Poland) in 1714

Lawnmower – invented by Edwin Beard Budding (UK) in 1827

Dynamite – invented by Alfred Nobel (Sweden) in 1866

Automatic teller machine (ATM) – invented by Luther Simjian (Armenia) in 1939

Soft contact lenses – invented by Otto Witcherle (Czechoslovakia) in 1961

CD-ROM – invented by Phillips / Sony (Holland / Japan) in 1985

2 Work in pairs. Compare your lists and explain your choices.

WRITING

3 A magazine has set a competition where people write an article to nominate an inventor and invention to be displayed in a new museum of design. Read the article below and then work in pairs and answer the questions.

1 Which photo shows the invention being described?

2 Where would you place the invention in your lists from Exercise 1? Why?

News | Articles | Comments | Search

His invention has saved thousands of lives, yet you probably take it for granted. It made its inventor millions of pounds, yet few know his name. I believe Percy Shaw is a great inventor and his cat's eye should be displayed in the Design Museum. Despite coming from a deprived background and leaving school at thirteen, Percy always showed inventiveness. He allegedly came up with the idea of the road reflector when he almost crashed into a wall. His headlights reflected in the eyes of a cat, which directed him back onto the road. Thinking how the cat's eye could be placed on the road itself, he devised a hard rubber casing for four small glass reflectors and set them in a metal shoe. When cars ran over the cat's eye, it pressed the rubber over the glass, wiping it clean with the aid of rainwater that collected in the metal shoe. It therefore needed little maintenance. Since its invention, the cat's eye has been fitted to roads throughout the world in order to make them safer. No doubt we can all think of things with apparently more impact – telephones, cars, computers, etc. - but how many of these were really invented by one man? Their inventors 'stood on the shoulders of giants', as Newton once said. Shaw's creation is different: it solved a real problem, it is unique and it is beautifully simple. Besides, few inventions can claim to have prevented so many deaths. Surely, therefore, Percy Shaw and his cat's eye deserve a prominent place in the new museum.

4 Work in pairs and do the following:

1 Think of a title for the article.

2 Divide the text into three paragraphs. What does the writer do in each one?

3 Find an example of these ways of creating interest and persuasion.
   a revealing the main topic of the paragraph in the last sentence of the paragraph
   b rhetorical questions
   c pairs of contrasting facts
   d quotations
   e 'tripling' – giving lists of three things or three related statements
   f using *surely*, *yet* or *besides*

4 Try and think of other famous quotations and other examples of tripling.

KEY WORDS FOR WRITING

surely, *yet* and *besides*

We use *surely* to mean 'without doubt' or to emphasise something is true, especially when you think people may disagree.

Surely, therefore, (they) deserve a prominent place ...

It is surely one of the greatest designs of the 20th century.

We use *yet* to emphasise that a fact is surprising given what you have just said.

His invention has saved thousands of lives, yet you probably take it for granted.

Besides gives an additional reason and often emphasises the final decisive argument.

... and it is beautifully simple. Besides, few inventions can claim to have prevented so many deaths.

Besides being cheap to produce, it needed little maintenance.

Notice where we use commas in the sentences above.

5 Rewrite the sentences below, replacing the words in italics with *surely*, *yet* or *besides*.

1 There was enormous interest in the new device. Actual sales were sluggish, *though*.

2 *Quite apart from the fact that it was* cheap to produce, it was beautiful to look at.

3 *There can be little doubt that* this is the greatest achievement of the 21st century so far.

4 Some may argue that many others were working on the problem, but *it seems clear to me that* his was the biggest and most decisive contribution.

5 The train was fast and comfortable and *what's more*, it was the cheapest option.

6 *Despite* making millions from his invention, he died in poverty.

GRAMMAR

Few, etc. as modifiers and pronouns

We use *few* / *many* with plural nouns and *little* / *much* with uncountable nouns. *A few* / *a little* mean 'some', but *few* / *little* (without the article) mean 'hardly any'.

These words are often used as pronouns and can be seen in contrasts and other rhetorical devices you looked at in Exercise 4.

It made its inventor millions of pounds, yet few know his name.

Many have done little to become famous. He did much of note but was hardly known.

6 Complete the sentences with (*a*) *few*, (*a*) *little*, *many* or *much*.

1 She received _____ education, yet she became a best-selling author.

2 _____ is known about its inventor, yet how _____ of modern life would be possible without it?

3 _____ reasons why you should choose this product: it costs _____, it looks great and it works fantastically well.

4 To quote Pythagoras: 'Don't say _____ in _____ words, say a great deal in _____.'

5 As Churchill once said: 'Never was so _____ owed by so _____ to so _____.'

7 Complete the sentences with your own ideas and (*a*) *little* / (*a*) *few*, etc.

1 It was a groundbreaking invention, and yet ...

2 The mobile phone is a fantastic invention: ...

3 ... has promised ..., yet ...

4 Many ... but ...

PRACTICE

8 You are going to write an article for the competition mentioned in Exercise 3. Work in pairs. Choose an invention that you think should go into the museum.

9 Working on your own, make a list of reasons why the invention is so good and some unusual or interesting facts about the inventor. Then work with your partner and compare your lists.

10 Write a three or four-paragraph article about the invention and inventor. Use as much of the language from this lesson as you can.

7 WRITING Applying for funding

SPEAKING

1 Look at the list of people seeking funding below. Think about who each project would benefit and how. Then rank the people from 1 (= most deserving of funding) to 8 (= least deserving).

a A single father is looking for funding to send his daughter to music school.

b An art student wants a grant to go and visit the galleries in Florence, Italy.

c An engineer wants her employers to pay for her to present at an overseas conference.

d A talented Psychology undergraduate student is seeking funding to do a Master's.

e The owner of a historic town centre house is seeking funding to pay for its renovation.

f A sales manager wants his boss to pay for him to do a part-time language course.

g A novelist is trying to crowdsource funding for a research trip to Iceland.

h A local community group wants money to pay for a public garden in a deprived area.

2 Work in pairs. Compare your lists and explain your choices.

VOCABULARY Stating outcomes

3 Complete the sentences with these pairs of words. You may need to change the order of the words.

attracts + communicate	facilitate + carry out
benefit + allow	raise + feed back
devote + forge	realise + give

1 **This would** _____ her **the opportunity to** study with excellent tutors and hopefully _____ her full potential.

2 The trip **would** _____ **me a deeper understanding of** the city's history and culture and **would** _____ **me greatly in terms of** my future studies.

3 **This would** _____ **the profile of** the firm and I would, of course, _____ on my experience on my return.

4 **The funding would enable me to** _____ myself to my postgraduate study and to then hopefully _____ a career in the field.

5 **A small grant would** _____ the repair of the property and **allow me to** _____ maintenance in years to come.

6 **I would then be able to** _____ our message to a far wider audience, which would, in turn, **ensure that** the firm _____ business in new markets.

4 Work in pairs. Imagine you are the people seeking funding in g) and h) in Exercise 1. Using the phrases in bold and words from the box in Exercise 3, write sentences stating the outcomes of funding in each case.

WRITING

5 You are going to read an email to an employer requesting funding for a course. Work in pairs. Decide in which order you would expect to find the information below.

a the applicant's previous study experiences and what they learned from them

b the content of the course

c how the course will benefit the company

d the length and cost of the course

e how the course will benefit the employee

f the employee's main reason for wanting to do the course

6 Read the email opposite. Then work with your partner and discuss the questions.

• Is the information structured in the way you expected it to be?

• What else not previously mentioned is also included in the email?

• Is there anything that you think could be added to make it more persuasive?

Dear Alex,

I am writing to request funding for a short course in online video strategy that I would like to enrol on. The three-day course runs four times a year at the University of the Arts and would require me to be present from 11:00 to 17:30 Monday through to Wednesday. The fees for the course presently stand at £625, and topics covered include building subscriber bases, as well as a range of approaches to announcing, distributing and promoting video content online.

As you will be aware, I have already studied social media marketing, and I trust that the skills I developed during that time are apparent in the work I have done building our social media strategy and enhancing online marketing campaigns. However, given the speed at which the field moves, it is a constant struggle to stay abreast of the latest trends and developments.

I feel the short course proposed would benefit me in several key ways. Primarily, it would help me to optimise our online channel videos with an evolving content strategy, whilst also enabling me to ensure consistency in our video production. In turn, obviously, this would result in an enhanced profile for the firm as a whole.

Whilst I realise my temporary absence would mean that cover would need to be provided, I feel confident of my ability to integrate the new skills learned into my daily work and I would, of course, also feed back on my experiences to my team.

Many thanks for considering this request. Please do not hesitate to contact me should you have any further related questions.

I look forward to hearing from you soon.

Sincerely,

Siobhan Tebbs

7 Find words or phrases in the email that could be replaced by the words and phrases below.

1 register for

2 am confident

3 improving

4 keep up with

5 increase the efficiency of

6 feel free to

KEY WORDS FOR WRITING

in turn

We use *in turn* to show that something is the result of a connected series of events.

*Primarily, it would help me to optimise our online channel videos. **In turn**, obviously, this would result in an enhanced profile for the firm as a whole.*

8 Match the two parts of the sentences.

1 This would facilitate the creation of a Chinese-language version of our website,

2 The space would provide a refuge for many living in difficult circumstances,

3 The course would greatly benefit me in terms of my own professional development,

4 The trip would grant me greater insight into the geography of the island,

5 This would contribute to the ongoing renovation of the old town centre,

a and this, in turn, would benefit the section as a whole.

b and this, in turn, would help to ensure the accuracy and clarity of my next work.

c which would, in turn, hopefully attract a considerable amount of new business.

d which would, in turn, boost tourism and bring in extra income.

e which, in turn, would help to reduce stress levels in the neighbourhood.

9 Work in pairs. Write two possible results of each situation below using *in turn*.

1 Funding for the health service is expected to be cut this year.

2 Free education for all goes some way towards ensuring equality, ...

3 Increased funding would encourage wider participation in the arts and ...

4 I received a grant that allowed me to make my first short film.

5 The firm was forced to increase the wages it paid.

PRACTICE

10 You are going to write an email requesting funding. Decide what you want funding for and who the email will be addressed to. Then think about the following:

• what the money would be spent on

• your main reasons for needing funding

• what the outcomes of the funding would be

11 Write an email of at least 200 words requesting funding. Use as much of the language from this lesson as you can.

8 WRITING Giving information

SPEAKING

1 **Work in groups. Discuss the questions.**

- Do you enjoy going to museums? Why? / Why not?
- What museums do you have in your town / city? Which would you recommend? Why?
- What social functions do you think museums serve?
- What ethical issues connected to museums may sometimes arise?
- What's the strangest museum you've ever heard of / been to?
- Which of the unusual museums below would you like to visit? Why?

THE CURRYWURST MUSEUM, BERLIN

This uniquely interactive museum is dedicated to the much-loved national sausage and allows you to see, hear, smell and take part in the currywurst experience!

PARASITE MUSEUM, TOKYO

This museum boasts over 300 different kinds of parasite, with the highlight being a 30-foot worm pulled out of an unsuspecting woman's stomach!

MUSEUM OF FUNERAL CARRIAGES, BARCELONA

Located in the strangely silent basement of the city's Municipal Funeral Services, the museum is home to many ornate carriages, some of which date back to the 18th century.

PARIS SEWER MUSEUM

Bored with the Louvre? Already seen the Eiffel Tower? Why not take a walking tour of the network of tunnels underneath the city? Not for those with sensitive noses!

WRITING

2 **You are going to read a web page giving information about a famous museum of art and design in London. Before you read, write five questions you would expect the web page to answer.**

3 **Read the web page. How many of your questions were answered?**

HOME | VISIT | COLLECTIONS | JOIN AND SUPPORT | LEARN | WHAT'S ON | SEARCH

1_____ a permanent collection of over four and a half million objects, the Victoria and Albert Museum is the world's largest museum of decorative arts and design. 2_____ in 1852, the museum now consists of 145 different galleries, and features among other things: pottery, glass, textiles, costumes, jewellery, sculpture and photographs. It is particularly celebrated for its East Asian and Islamic collections.

3_____ within walking distance of both underground and bus stops, the museum is easily accessible and lies at the heart of London's museum district, with the Science Museum and Natural History Museum both nearby. The nearest tube station is South Kensington, which is on the Piccadilly, Circle and District Lines.

4_____ the trend of other national UK museums, entrance to the museum has been free since 2001. Opening hours are 10am to 5.45pm daily, with a late opening on Fridays when the doors do not close until 10pm. The building does not open between Christmas Eve and Boxing Day.

The main entrance is on Cromwell Road and on 5_____ visitors will find cloakrooms and the main museum shop, which offers a huge range of books, stationery and gifts. 6_____ straight on, you come to the delightful John Madejski Garden with the café alongside it, which provides hot dishes, salads, sandwiches, pastries and cakes, as well as hot and cold drinks, wine and beer.

In addition to the permanent collection, there are frequent temporary exhibitions. Currently running is *Grace Kelly: Style Icon*, 7_____ the Hollywood star's spectacular wardrobe. Entrance £12. Concessions apply. Free for Members.

4 Complete the text with the correct form of these verbs.

enter	follow	house	walk
feature	found	situate	

GRAMMAR

Participle clauses with adverbial meaning

In more formal writing, we often use present (-*ing*) or past participles in clauses that function as adverbs. Present participles give an active meaning; past participles give a passive. Sometimes these clauses talk about reasons or results.

Situated within walking distance of both underground and bus stops, the museum is easily accessible. (= because it is situated near underground and bus stops)

Sometimes the clauses talk about conditions.

Walking straight on, you come to the delightful John Madejski Garden. (= if you walk straight on)

We can also use these clauses to talk about time.

Entering the museum, I was struck by how modern it was. (= as / when I entered the museum)

Note that we always use a comma to separate the clauses.

5 Rewrite the sentences in a more formal manner, using active or passive participle clauses.

1 As we walked into the museum, we were greeted by a vast dinosaur skeleton in the entrance hall!

2 During our walk round the museum, I started to realise just how amazing ancient Persia must've been.

3 The Elgin Marbles were removed from Greece at the start of the 19th century and have been controversial ever since.

4 The museum was fully refurbished following a fire and reopened in November 2013.

5 Because we didn't have long before closing time, we decided to just look round the Egyptian room.

6 Because I'm a regular visitor to the city, I'm quite familiar with all the museums there.

7 As it's about ten miles outside of town, the museum is quite difficult to get to.

8 A new law was introduced about ten years ago and the result was that all entrance fees were scrapped.

9 If you visit the museum during the morning, it's much less crowded.

10 The guide just pretended not to hear her questions and carried on with the tour!

KEY WORDS FOR WRITING

among and *within*

Among shows something is included in a larger group or list or is situated in the middle of a group.

Within shows something is inside a place, limit or range, or is situated close enough to walk, see, etc.

6 Match the sentence starters (1–7) to the pairs of possible endings (a–g).

1 The hostel is situated among
2 Smoking is not permitted within
3 The museum is among
4 The new wing of the museum is within
5 Visitors are free to handle the artwork within
6 The museum runs competitions among
7 The campsite lies within

a schools. / other ways of boosting participation.
b one month of completion. / sight of the river.
c the grounds. / 100 metres of the hospital.
d the pine trees. / several skyscrapers that dominate it.
e earshot of a motorway. / easy reach of the centre.
f reason. / the rules set down.
g several that open at night. / the largest in the world.

7 Complete the sentences with your own ideas. Then work in pairs and compare your ideas.

1 I live within …
2 Sometime within the next few years, …
3 Among the things I like about living here is …
4 … is among the best …

PRACTICE

8 You are going to write a web page giving information about a museum – or other cultural amenity – that you know. Find out and make notes about the following:

- its history
- what's special about the place
- its size and contents
- its location and how to get there
- opening times and entrance fee
- any noteworthy facilities
- any special exhibitions / current events

9 Write your web page. Use between 250 and 300 words.

GRAMMAR REFERENCE

1 CITIES

PERFECT FORMS

Present perfect simple

The present perfect simple shows that something happened or started before now. There is usually a present result.

*The Guggenheim Museum **has become** one of the most famous buildings in the world.* (= The change happened before now.)

*There **have been** some voices of opposition.*

Compare these present perfect and present simple forms:

*They **have invested** a lot of money in the area.* (= before now, we don't know if it's continuing)

*They **invest** a lot of money in the area.* (= generally)

I've had a car for six years. (= from six years ago to now)

*I **have** a car.* (= a present fact, time unknown)

Past perfect simple

The past perfect simple emphasises that something happened or started before another event or time in the past.

*The slum **had** effectively **created** a barrier between the affluent north and the more deprived south of the city.* (= before it was demolished)

*Up until the early 80s, Bilbao **had been dominated** by steel plants and shipbuilding.* (= before the 1980s)

Compare these past perfect and past simple forms:

*He had **gone** when I arrived.* (= He left before I arrived.)

*He **went** when I arrived.* (= First I arrived and at that moment he left.)

*He said **he'd been** a teacher.* (= When we spoke, he no longer taught.)

*He said he **was** a teacher.* (= When we spoke, he still taught.)

We also use the past perfect simple to refer to hypothetical events in the past (i.e. before now).

*If other mayors **hadn't secured** the city's finances before him, ...* (= The finances were secure.)

*I wish I **hadn't done** it, but I did.*

will have done (future perfect) and other modals

After a modal verb, we use infinitives without *to*. The perfect form is *will / may / should + have* + past participle.

*If we ever achieve a successful city for children, we **will have built** the perfect city for all citizens.* (= Before achieving it, you have to build it!)

*Other cities **may have failed** because they didn't take up the other strands of Bilbao's regeneration project.* (= before now; *may* shows possibility here)

*I **should have finished** work by six, but I'll call you if I haven't.*

Participle clauses

Sometimes we need an *-ing* form to form a participle clause.

***Having cleared** one space, Peñalosa's administration then expropriated the land of a private country club.* (= After they cleared / had cleared ...)

Compare these sentences:

*I was disappointed when I got there, **having read** so many good things about it.*

***Reading** about it now makes me want to go there.*

Exercise 1

Complete the pairs of sentences with the verbs in bold – one sentence with a perfect form, one not.

1 **not / call**
   a If I _____ by six, it means I'm not coming.
   b As a rule, I _____ anyone after nine at night.

2 **be done up**
   a It _____ a few years ago, but the place is already falling apart.
   b It used to be very run-down, but it _____.

3 **be struck**
   a It was the second time the city _____ by an earthquake.
   b Our house _____ by lightning last year.

4 **change**
   a I doubt anything _____ by this time next year.
   b I think things _____ if the Freedom Party wins power in the election.

5 **consult**
   a They should _____ the people who live here to find out what they want.
   b They should _____ more widely, but they just weren't interested in what others wanted and that's why the regeneration failed.

6 **be**
   a I wish he _____ here now.
   b It sounds like you had a great time. I wish I _____ there.

7 **spend**
   a _____ millions on the project, the city centre still looks awful!
   b _____ any amount of time there, you quickly start to feel stressed.

8 **undergo**
   a Following the disaster, the city _____ a huge transformation.
   b When the disaster struck, the city _____ a number of changes already.

Infinitive form

Sometimes we use an infinitive with *to* after certain verbs. Compare the perfect and simple forms:

*I **seem to have lost** my wallet.* (= before now)

*He **seems to lose** things all the time.* (= generally)

*He **is believed to have killed** several people.*

*He **is believed to be** dangerous.*

Exercise 2

Complete the second sentence so that it has a similar meaning to the first sentence using the word given. Do not change the word given. You must use between three and five words, including the word given.

1 I don't think my flight will get in in time to catch the last train home.
   LEFT
   The last train _____ the time my flight gets in.

2 The first time I saw anything like that was when I went to Mumbai.
   NEVER
   I _____ like that before I went to Mumbai.

3 I'm not sure I can give you any advice as it's so long since I've been there.
   RECENTLY
   Not _____, I don't think I can give you any advice.

4 When the current government came to power, they largely continued the previous government's policies.
   INITIATED
   The current government's policies _____ by the previous one.
5 People were moved out of the area before the storm hit so there were very few casualties.
   EVACUATED
   There would have been a lot more casualties if _____ before the storm.
6 As far as I can tell, things are much better than they were when I was there last.
   IMPROVED
   Things appear _____ since my last visit.

DID YOU KNOW?

We sometimes use *will / will have* to refer to the present to talk about what we believe.

*Many people **will have visited** the city just to see it and found a flourishing city with a vibrant nightlife. However, fewer **will be aware** of the profound change that the gallery symbolises.*

A: *Where are you from?*
B: *You **won't know** it. / You **won't have heard** of it. It's tiny.*

2 RELATIONSHIPS

WOULD

Conditionals

Would introduces the hypothetical result or consequence in a conditional sentence.

*I probably **would**'ve stayed with him if he'd apologised.*

*If they**'d** intervened, the situation would be a lot worse now.*

*If it hadn't been for my friend Andrew, I **would** never have got together with Ana.*

Would have + past participle refers back to a hypothetical past situation. Note that compared to *might, would* shows more certainty here.

Habits

We can use *would* instead of *used to* or the past simple to talk about habits in the past.

*When he was a toddler, I**'d** do the childcare most days.*

*Before the anger management classes, he**'d** often get into unnecessary confrontations.*

Note we also use *would* with *wish* to talk about present habits we (don't) want people to have.

*I wish he**'d** show a bit more commitment.*

*I wish they **wouldn't** interfere.*

Past of *will*

We use *would* as the past form of *will*. It tends to follow verbs such as *knew, said, thought, promised, threatened*, etc.

*I knew it **would** come to no good, but you can't really interfere, can you?*

*They said it **would** be miserable today, but it's actually turned out quite nice.*

*She promised she**'d** come, so I'm sure she'll be here soon.*

We often use *won't* to refuse to do something and so we use *would* to report it. Notice that this can also be applied to animals and machines!

*I remember once I asked him to change desks and he just **wouldn't** – just refused point blank.*

*For some reason, the car **wouldn't** start this morning so I'm waiting for the breakdown people.*

Advice

We use *I'd* to give advice. It sometimes goes with expressions such as *if I were you, if I were in your shoes*, etc., but it is more often used on its own.

*He should obviously be punished, but after that I**'d** still give him another chance.*

*I**'d** consider talking it over with a therapist.*

We sometimes use *would* in other advice expressions.

*I**'d** advise you to see a therapist.*

*I**'d** recommend taking a class.*

*You**'d** be best talking it over with someone.*

Being more cautious with opinions

We often use *I would / I wouldn't say* to introduce our opinions about people or a situation. Note we can also sometimes use *I would've said / I wouldn't have said* in the same way. These structures show more caution.

*I **would say** he has a stubborn streak and he's been prone to outbursts and answering back.*

*I **wouldn't say** it's a disaster – just a slight setback.*

*I **wouldn't have said** it's a big problem.*

Sometimes we use *would* to make a prediction or speculation sound more cautious. Compare the examples to the less cautious versions in brackets:

*Although he's a little frail now, I**'d expect** him to recover well. (I expect him to …)*

*I **don't imagine** there**'d be** a problem with that. (I don't think there'll be a problem …)*

*I**'d hope** to be back by six. (I hope to be back by six.)*

*I **would think** / I **would've thought** they**'d get married** at some point. (I think they will get married …)*

We also sometimes do this with requests because it can sound more polite.

***Would** it be OK to leave early? (Is it OK to leave early?)*

***Would** you **mind** helping me with this? (Do you mind helping me with this?)*

Exercise 1

Use *would*, the word in bold and up to four other words to complete the second sentence so it has the same meaning as the first sentence.

1 I'm completely with you on that.
   AGREE
   I _____ about that.
2 If you ask me, it wasn't his fault.
   SAY
   I _____ to blame.
3 We made several offers, but they rejected all of them.
   NOT
   They _____ our offers.
4 I think the best thing to do is walk away.
   INVOLVED
   I _____ if I were you.
5 He's always saying nasty things behind people's backs.
   BITCH
   I wish _____ behind their backs.
6 They shouldn't let him stay if he's going to behave like that.
   KICK
   If he behaved like that in my house, _____.
7 I'm unlikely to replace it.
   IMAGINE
   I _____ a new one.
8 It shouldn't take more than a week to arrive.
   EXPECT
   _____ get here before next Friday.

COMMON MISTAKES

We use *would* to talk about habits, but not about states like living, being, belonging, etc.

Before I moved to Birmingham, we ~~would live~~ **lived** *in Leeds.*

I sometimes wish I ~~would be~~ **was** *taller.*

When talking about habits or something we want to change in the future, we use *would* rather than past simple / *will*.

I wish he ~~stopped~~ **would** *stop talking sometimes.*

I wish it ~~will~~ **would** *snow soon.*

When reporting, we can use *will* if we think the action is still going to happen. Otherwise, we need to use *would*.

*He promised he***'ll** *give our assignments back tomorrow.* ✓

He promised he ~~will~~ **would** *be here on time today, but he was late again.*

We don't use *would* or *would have* in the *if*-clause of a conditional sentence to refer to unreal events or situations. But we do use it if we are talking about a real past habit.

If I'd had a bad day at school, my gran **would** *always comfort me.* ✓ *(= real past habit)*

If he ~~would've~~ **had confided in** *me, this wouldn't have happened.*

Exercise 2

Decide which five sentences are incorrect, then correct them.

1 I didn't think I would enjoy the course, but the teacher has been great.
2 I often got into trouble at school just because I would have really long hair.
3 I'd hope that it'd be all sorted out pretty quickly.
4 My parents wish we would live a bit closer to them.
5 I wouldn't be here if I wouldn't have had the surgery.
6 I wouldn't have said it was a big problem.
7 Seriously, I wish my brother shut up sometimes.
8 I tried to talk him out of it, but he wouldn't listen and carried on.
9 It doesn't surprise me. I knew he'll say that! He's so predictable!
10 I would've thought it'd be fine if you arrive a little bit late.

3 CULTURE AND IDENTITY

CLEFT SENTENCES

We can change the structure of the standard subject–verb–object sentence in order to add emphasis. We often do this when correcting what we or someone else has just said.

Fronting

We can place the highlighted part at the front of the sentence starting with *It* and then add a relative clause.

He seems to be struggling with **the people**. → **It's the people** *that he seems to be struggling with.*

I didn't see him on **Monday**. *I saw him on Tuesday.* → **It wasn't Monday** *I saw him; it was Tuesday.*

I blame **the government** *for the mess we're in.* → **It's the government** *who I blame for the mess we're in.*

the thing, what, all, etc.

We often emphasise aspects of the sentence starting with *the thing*, *what*, etc. and then add a relative clause. The table below shows some of the most common ways to start the first clause. Notice the patterns in the second half of the sentence after *be*.

	First clause	be	Noun or noun phrase / clause
Emphasising how we feel	**The thing that** annoys me	is	(the fact) that they did nothing.
	One thing (that) I find worrying	was	their stupidity.
	The main thing I like		being able to do what I want.
	What was great		people's outlook on life.
			how quickly they solved the problem.
Emphasising an action with *do*	**All** we **do**	is	(to) sit around all day.
	The only thing he **does**	was	(to) criticise.
	All I **did**		(to) question if he was right.
	What they **did** in the end		(to) pretend it hadn't happened.
Emphasising an action with *happen*	**All that happens**	is	(that) people shout a bit.
	The only thing that happened	was	(that) I felt a bit awkward.
	What happened in the end		(that) they fined me.
Emphasising a reason	**The reason why** they lost	is	(that) they didn't train enough.
	The main reason it happened	was	(that) no-one thought it could happen.
Emphasising a place	**The only place that's** worth visiting	is	the castle.
	The place (where) you're most likely to find it		Harrods.

Exercise 1

Complete the exchanges with one word in each space.

1 A: I bet it's difficult to work in the summer there. It must be so hot.
   B: It is, although _____'s not really the heat _____'s the problem for me; it's the humidity.

2 A: What I liked about them _____ their humour and the _____ they took the mickey out of each other.
   B: Really? It's exactly that _____ I found difficult to relate to. It's just not my kind of thing.

3 A: Apparently, they don't want to work with me. All I _____ was _____ some ideas to make things more efficient.
   B: I know, but _____ you have to realise _____ that losing face is a big thing in their culture.

4 A: The _____ that bothers _____ about life these days is _____ everything revolves around money and consumption.
   B: Yeah, it depresses me too.

5 A: Sorry we're late. The traffic was bad.
   B: Don't listen to him. The real _____ we're late is that _____ spent an hour getting ready.
   A: It wasn't like that! What _____ was I _____ almost ready and then I spilt some tea on my trousers and I had to get changed.

Emphasising how we feel

When we emphasise how something makes us feel, we often use a 'feelings' verb rather than an adjective:

frustrates me	upsets me	I love
disturbs me	amazes me	I can't stand
scares me	drives me mad	I find difficult
bothers me	I find weird	

We also use a number of different noun phrases to start the second clause:

the way ...
the fact that ...
the number of ...
the amount of ...

What scares me most about it is the amount of time I know it's going to end up taking.

What I love most about her is the way she's so enthusiastic about everything all the time.

What I'm finding weirdest about my new job is the fact that I'm actually enjoying it!

Exercise 2

Complete the sentences with these pairs of words and phrases.

frustrates + lack	concerns + number
disturbs + stance	upset + seeing
amazes + amount	angered + the fact
drives + way	worrying + level

1 The main thing that _____ most people is the total _____ of investment in basic health care and education.

2 What _____ me the most while I was there was _____ all the kids sleeping on the streets.

3 One thing that _____ me is the government's _____ on law and order – and their emphasis on punishment.

4 One thing that really _____ me crazy is the _____ people queue up – or rather don't queue up!

5 What _____ me is the _____ of kids leaving school unable to read and write properly.

6 The thing I find most _____ is the _____ of pollution in the city. There's just a constant cloud of smog.

7 It's done now, I know, but what _____ me most was _____ that he didn't think he should even apologise!

8 What _____ me is the sheer _____ of wealth those at the top of society possess.

Exercise 3

Rewrite the sentences so they emphasise how you feel.

1 The city is very cosmopolitan, which surprised me.
   One thing that _____.

2 He can be very nationalistic! It's very disturbing.
   What _____.

3 The growing wealth gap is a concern.
   The main thing that _____.

4 The whole society is ageing at an alarming rate. That's the really scary thing.
   What _____.

5 People assume that I must love football just because I'm Brazilian. I get really angry about it.
   One thing that _____.

4 POLITICS

CONDITIONALS 1

General truths

We can use conditionals to talk about things that are generally or always true. Both the *if*-clause and the result clause can use present tenses or *going to* + verb. The result clause can also use *will* / *should* / *might* and a number of other structures.

If they're earning that much, it encourages other people to ask for more.

If you keep lying to people, they're going to stop trusting you after a while.

If you're going to be late, you should phone me.

If you don't like them, don't vote for them.

If you really want to understand the situation there, you need to read more.

Likely future events

We can also use conditionals to talk about likely / possible events in the future. The *if*-clause uses present tenses. The result clause often uses *going to* + verb / *will* + verb, but a number of other structures are also possible.

Even if they do manage to introduce this new law, it's basically going to be unworkable.

As long as there's the official desire to make it work, then it'll work.

If we're lucky, we can host it without going into debt.

If they make further cuts, it's bound to lead to job losses.

If they win the election, I might have to leave the country.

If you have the time, I'd write to your MP about it.

Often the only way to work out whether a sentence is describing a general truth or a likely future event is by paying attention to vocabulary and context.

Imagined events now or in the future

We can use conditionals to talk about imagined / hypothetical events now or in the future. The *if*-clause uses past tenses. The result clause often uses *would* / *wouldn't* + verb, but *might* / *could* + verb are also possible.

And what would you include in pay? Supposing they were given a boat, or whatever, instead of money?

Imagine if we actually won it. It'd be a recipe for disaster.

If they raised taxes, there'd be a riot.

I'd quit my job tomorrow if I could.

If she weren't so busy, she could do more for local people.

Alternatives to *if*

As well as *if* there are other words used to introduce conditions.

Supposing (= what if / imagine if) they were given a boat, or whatever, instead of money?

Even if (= this condition does not change the result in any way) they do manage to introduce this new law, it's basically going to be unworkable.

Unless they (= if they don't) come up with some new policy ideas, they're going to lose the election.

They'd better come up with some new policies or (= because if they don't) they'll lose the election.

They'd better come up with some new policies. Otherwise, (= if they don't) they're going to lose the election.

It's going to happen whether you want it to or not! (= It doesn't make any difference even if you want it to.)

What changes do you think the deal will lead to, assuming (= if it's true – and I think it is) that it goes ahead?

As long as (= on condition that) there's the official desire to make it work, then it'll work.

So long as, *provided* and *providing* can all be used instead of *as long as*. They all mean the same thing.

Exercise 1

Complete the sentences with one word in each space. Contractions count as one word.

1 If it all goes wrong, _____ say I didn't warn you.

2 Supposing they do more to stop petty crime, it's _____ to have a knock-on effect on more serious crimes.

3 If you go there at night, I _____ take someone with you. It's a rough area.

4 If the softer approach is failing, maybe they _____ adopt a tougher position.

5 People here would _____ put up with a law like that. There _____ be riots!

6 People complain about public services, but then they moan if the government _____ up taxes.

7 If they _____ what they were doing, I'd have more faith, but they obviously _____.

8 You're very calm! I'd _____ furious if I _____ in your situation.

9 A: I see they're promising to cut taxes.
   B: I hope they do! To be honest, I don't think I _____ vote for them if they _____.

10 A: The papers are full of stories about his personal life.
   B: Maybe it's just me, but I honestly _____ care whether he _____ done any of those things or not.

11 A: I read somewhere that the prime minister is thinking of signing a new gas deal with them.
   B: I know. It's a terrible idea. If he _____, there _____ be huge protests against it.

12 A: I know it's never going to happen, but if you ask me, they should just ban junk food.
   B: Oh, come on! That's a bit extreme. Imagine what _____ happen if they _____!

Exercise 2

Complete the second sentence so that it has a similar meaning to the first sentence using the word given. Do not change the word given. You must use between three and five words, including the word given.

1 They won't achieve anything without popular support.
   UNLESS
   _____, they won't achieve anything.

2 I'm in favour of the idea so long as it's not too expensive.
   PROVIDED
   I basically support the idea, _____ too much money.

3 It doesn't matter if you don't like it. That doesn't stop it happening, does it!
   WHETHER
   It's always going to happen, _____ not!

4 The problem with nuclear power is that if an accident happens, it could totally devastate the area.
   SUPPOSING
   _____ at a nuclear power plant. Can you imagine the damage it could cause?

5 The economy's still doing badly so it's easy for the opposition to attract new supporters.
   LONG
   The opposition will continue to win new supporters _____ fails to improve.

6 There's no way the situation will improve without immediate action being taken.
   OR
   They need to do something pretty soon _____ worse and worse.

7 I know opinion polls aren't entirely reliable, but it doesn't look like they'll win an overall majority.
   ASSUMING
   _____ reliable, they're going to have to form a coalition with someone.

CONDITIONALS 2

General past truths

To talk about things that were generally true in the past, both the *if*-clause and the result clause can use past tenses. The result clause also often uses *would* + verb.

*It **helped** the programme's ratings if they **had** a kind of hate figure.* (= They had a hate figure and this boosted the show's popularity.)

*If there **was** a school council election, all these posters **would go up** all over the place.* (= Every time there was an election, this is what always happened.)

Imagined events in the past

To talk about imagined events in the past, the *if*-clause uses past perfect tenses. To talk about imagined past results, the result clause often uses *would / wouldn't* + *have* + past participle.

*If they**'d called** on another day, I **wouldn't have taken part**.* (= In reality, they called on a day I wasn't busy and so I took part.)

*I **might never have heard of** him if he **hadn't been taking part** in that radio show.* (= He was taking part in a radio show and that's when I first encountered him.)

Imagined events in both the past and the present

If the *if*-clause uses the past perfect, it is about an imagined past. If the *if*-clause uses the past simple / continuous, it is about an imagined present.

If the result clause uses *would / might / could* + *have* + past participle (or *would / might / could* + *have been* + *-ing*), it's about an imagined past result.

If the result clause uses *would / might / could* + verb (or *would / might / could* + *be* + *-ing*), it's about an imagined present result.

*I **might not have minded** so much if the calls **were** free, but they're making a fortune on them.* (= I minded / I was angry in the past because generally / still now the calls aren't free – they cost a lot!)

*If they **hadn't been** so reluctant to negotiate, we **would not be taking** this action now.* (= The reason we are taking action now is because in the past they were reluctant to negotiate.)

*It's unlikely we **would've abolished** uniforms if we **didn't have** a body like this.* (= It's because generally / still now we have a student council that we were able to abolish uniforms in the past.)

Exercise 1

Complete the sentences with the correct form of the verbs. In some cases, it may be possible to use more than one modal verb. Use the modal verb that makes most sense in the context.

1 They _____ (win) the election by a landslide if they _____ (change) their leader. As it was though, they won a very narrow victory.

2 In the end, I voted for the Liberals in the last election. I _____ (vote) Social Democrats, but I _____ (not / like) their stance on nuclear power. It just seemed very old-fashioned, to be honest.

3 He _____ (be) president now if he _____ (not / be mixed up) in that big scandal last year.

4 We _____ (not / be) as developed as we are today if she _____ (not / make) such radical changes when she was in power.

5 If the last government _____ (not / give) the banks so much power, we _____ (not / be) in this mess today! Honestly, I hold them responsible for all of it.

6 She really helped me a lot when I was at high school. If I _____ (need) someone to talk to, she _____ (be) there for me. If I _____ (have) problems, I _____ (go) and see her. She was amazing.

Exercise 2

Decide which options below are possible.

1 If I'd been told, ...
   a there wouldn't have been a problem.
   b we wouldn't be in this mess, would we?
   c I decided earlier.
   d I'd be doing something about it.
   e I had reported it to the police.

2 If we hadn't reported it when we did, ...
   a someone could've been seriously hurt.
   b we weren't sleeping afterwards.
   c the police hadn't known about it.
   d it'd be a health hazard.
   e we wouldn't have been able to forgive ourselves if and when something happened.

3 If we had a better system in place, ...
   a we wouldn't need to be having this inquiry.
   b none of this happened.
   c more incidents like this one could be stopped.
   d this had been stopped before it got so serious.
   e this might never have happened.

4 If there was an accident at the power plant, ...
   a I dread to think of the consequences.
   b there was going to be an official investigation into the causes.
   c I'd rather not be around!
   d you can expect a lot of casualties.
   e it'd show they hadn't been taking proper security measures.

5 GOING OUT, STAYING IN

NOUN PHRASES

We can add to basic nouns in the following ways.

Adding information before nouns

Names and the kinds of things they are

We often add the name of something to the kind of thing it is (or vice versa). No linker or relative clause is needed.

Visit the 18th-century stately home, Kenwood House, ...
We've chosen The Hackney Empire, a theatre ...

Compound nouns

Nouns can act like adjectives and define other nouns. The first noun isn't made plural.

cream teas   the boat race

Adjectives

Adjectives usually go before nouns (but see reduced relative clauses below). We don't tend to use more than three adjectives before a noun. As a general rule, we give opinions first, then facts.

classic English cream teas
cool young things
our best multicultural cheap eats

We sometimes make compound adjectives with number + noun. The noun is not plural.

a five-mile walk
a six-hour course

We also sometimes make compound adjectives instead of relative clauses (see below).

*... best known for it's **award-winning** Christmas pantomimes.*
(= pantomimes that have won awards)

Adding information after nouns

Prepositional phrases

You can add phrases beginning with a preposition after nouns. We can use them to show:
- where something is.

*a five-mile walk **up a steep hill***
- what it has or contains.

*Hampstead Heath **with its natural ponds***
*an 18th-century stately home **with a fine collection of art***

Some nouns collocate strongly with particular prepositions.
*increasing **interest in** politics*

You will learn more about prepositions in Unit 15.

Relative clauses

We can add a clause to the noun to explain what it is or to add extra information.

*the Geffrye Museum, **which contains living rooms from different periods***
*a theatre **that once hosted Charlie Chaplin***

You will learn more about relative clauses in Unit 14.

Reduced relative clauses

We often shorten relative clauses with present (*-ing*) participles or past participles. The present participle replaces active forms. The past participle replaces passives.

*four period gardens **which show** changing trends* →	*four period gardens **showing** changing trends*
*a classic 'chippie' **which is run** by second-generation Greek immigrants* →	*a classic 'chippie' **run** by second-generation Greek immigrants*
*its great Zoo Late evenings, **which are held** throughout the summer* →	*its great Zoo Late evenings, **held** throughout the summer*

Sometimes we reduce the relative clause to an adjectival phrase.

*one of the hippest places in town, **which is full** of trendy bars* →	*one of the hippest places in town, **full** of trendy bars*

Exercise 1

Underline the most basic subject, verb and object in the sentences.

1 The Oscar-winning director Joel Riley, whose latest documentary *Sick Life* is currently on release, gives a talk at the Barbican tonight, explaining his take on the current state of the film industry in the UK.

2 From its fourth-century origins in the deserts of the Middle East, through the many and varied forms of religious life it assumed during the Middle Ages, the tradition of a life of solitary retreat is explored in depth in this latest book by award-winning writer Denise Lawrenson.

3 The parents of two troubled teenagers who were caught at the scene of a robbery in Georgetown, supposedly after listening to subliminal messages in the music of their favourite band Death House, are seeking an as-yet-unspecified amount of damages in compensation from the thrash metal group concerned and their record label.

Exercise 2

Add the phrases in the box to the two nouns in the basic sentence below.

John Moffit stars in *The Dying*.

character actor	the three-hour
road movie	37-year-old
from Canada	award-winning
action-packed	by Tom Daley
based on the book	playing in his first lead role

Exercise 3

Shorten all the relative clauses as much as possible. You may need to use a present participle.

1 Visit the awe-inspiring cathedral which was designed by the architect Antonio Gaudi.

2 I read a fascinating article in the paper by the novelist whose name is Anne Tyler.

3 The exhibitions which are held in the centre are accompanied by workshops which are suitable for all ages.

4 There are a wealth of exhibits which are on show, which date back thousand of years.

Exercise 4

Rewrite the sentences using noun phrases in each space.

1 The course lasts six weeks and teaches a number of guidelines. If you follow them, you will be able to lose weight quickly and effectively.
_____ provides guidelines for _____.

2 When arms are supplied to other countries, the matter often causes controversy.
The _____ is a _____.

3 They want to create a new car tax, but a lot of people are opposed to the idea.
There's _____ to the _____.

4 The monument was built to celebrate the fact Jonson had been born a hundred years earlier.
The _____ celebrated the _____ anniversary _____.

6 CONFLICT AND RESOLUTION

WISH AND IF ONLY

We use *wish* and *if only* to talk about hypothetical situations – things we want but which are impossible. They are followed by *would*, the past perfect, the past simple or *could*. Often only the auxiliaries of these tenses and structures are used with *wish* / *if only*. *I wish* is more commonly used than *if only*.

if only / wish + would(n't)

This explains how you want people to behave differently.
If only *you'd put things away properly!*
*I **wish** you **wouldn't** shout.*
A: *It's a shame he doesn't cook more often.*
B: *I know – I **wish** he **would**. He's really good.*

if only / wish + past perfect

This explains how you would like the past to be different. Use *could've* + past participle to refer to an ability to do something. We often just use the auxiliary *had*.
*I **wish** you**'d said** something sooner.*
B: *I was going to take it to my room.*
A: *Well, I **wish** you **had** (taken it to your room).*
A: *I **wish** I **could've done** more to help.*
B: *You did more than enough. Thanks.*

if only / wish + past simple / could

This refers to things in the present that we want to be different. We may use the auxiliaries *was / were*, *did* or *could*.
A: *Can you give me a hand later?*
B: *I **wish** I **could**, but I'm working tonight.*
A: *Sorry, I have to go.*
B: ***If only*** *you **didn't**! I was planning on making us dinner.*
D: *What? You're joking?*
C: *I **wish** I **was** / **were**.*

Note that in spoken English *I wish I was* is more common than *I wish I were*. However, some people think *I wish + were* is more correct. In more formal situations, it may be better to use *I wish I / you / he / she were*.

wish and replies

When replying to *wish* / *if only* comments, we may want to talk about real situations – or continue to refer to the hypothetical situation. This affects the use of tenses.
C: *I **wish** you**'d said** something sooner.*
D: *I **would have** (said something, if I'd had the opportunity = a hypothetical situation), but you hardly come out of that office.*

A: *If only we **had** more money!*
B: *Yeah, well we **don't** (have more money = a real situation), so we **need** to find some other solution.*

A: *I wish you**'d tell** me if there's a problem.*
B: *I **would** (tell you = a hypothetical situation), but you**'ve been** so dismissive when I **have** (told you = a real situation) in the past!*

Exercise 1

Complete the exchanges with the correct auxiliary verbs. You may need a contraction such as *didn't* or *would've*.

1 A: I thought you were going to ask him to help?
B: I wish I _____. I just got distracted with other things.
A: It's a shame you _____ – we _____ been able to sort this out a lot quicker.

2 A: Are you going away during the holidays?
B: If only I _____, but I don't really have the money.
A: I wish I _____ lend you some, but I'm in the same boat.
B: Maybe we _____ win the lottery!

3 A: I seriously wish I _____ never even mentioned the issue. It's not really a problem.
B: Oh, don't worry. He _____ found something else to complain about anyway.
A: That's true. If only he _____ such a control freak.
B: I know. Work _____ be a lot easier.

4 A: You know I'm leaving tomorrow, don't you?
B: Yeah. I wish you _____. I _____ miss you.
A: Well, I wish I _____ stayed longer, but I have to get back.

5 A: I really wish you _____ invited him.
B: I _____ have, but the other day you said you felt sorry for him.
A: I do – kind of – I just wish he _____ stand there staring at people. It's a bit creepy.

Exercise 2

Complete the second sentence so that it has a similar meaning to the first sentence using the word given. Do not change the word given. You must use between three and six words, including the word given.

1 I really regret speaking to her like that.
ONLY
If _____ to her like that!

2 Not being able to go to university has been one of my big regrets in life.
COULD
I really _____ to university, but it just wasn't possible.

3 It annoys me that you get so upset over such a small thing.
WISH
I _____ over-sensitive about everything.

4 Basically, I'd like everyone to get along better.
FIGHT
I wish people _____ much.

5 It's a shame we have to work today.
NOT
I wish _____ work today.

6 It's no good you telling me that now!
IF
_____ that earlier!

7 SCIENCE AND RESEARCH

PASSIVES

Passives focus attention on who or what an action affects. We often use them when the subject of the sentence is not the doer or cause of the action. This is because the doer is either unimportant, obvious or unknown.

Different tenses

We're surrounded by statistics. (present simple)

Company B's actually being hugely outperformed. (present continuous)

It was published anonymously on the Web. (past simple)

The figures were obviously being twisted. (past continuous)

The article has been published in several well-respected journals. (present perfect simple)

Researchers had been pressured to come up with positive results. (past perfect simple)

Note that passive constructions aren't usually used in the present perfect continuous or the past perfect continuous.

Passives after modal verbs

We can form passives after modal verbs using *be* + past participle.

Statistics can be used to manipulate.

The data will be thoroughly analysed by a team of experts.

Similar results should have been seen, but for some reason weren't.

The research must have been funded by someone with a vested interest in the results.

get passives

With some verbs, *get* is often used instead of *be*. This is more common in informal spoken language than in academic writing or journalism. *Get* passives often show an action was unexpected or accidental.

Researchers may get pressured into finding positive results.

Thousands get hurt every year in avoidable accidents.

The laboratory got broken into and vandalised.

have something done

We often use a form of the verb *have* + past participle to talk about services we arrange and pay for.

A food company is having some research done.

The fish have cancerous cells inserted in their bodies.

My uncle had a kidney removed.

Note that we can also use *get* in this way. *Get* is more common with some verbs, *have* with others. There are no rules for this. It's best to just learn from examples you meet.

I got my legs waxed the other day.

I got my jacket caught in the closing door.

Reporting

In academic writing and journalism, we often use reporting verbs in the passive form where the source is unimportant or to suggest a degree of uncertainty.

So next, statistics – often thought to be the worst kind of lying there is!

The disease is believed to have a genetic component.

The government is said to be considering an enquiry.

It is argued that the research could provide a breakthrough.

He is alleged to have faked the experiments.

-ing forms

We use *-ing* passive forms after prepositions and some verbs.

They may worry about not being employed again.

It was accepted for publication after being reviewed by other experts.

I hate being interviewed.

Reduced relative clauses

If passives are used in relative clauses, the relative pronoun and the verb *be* are often left out.

Obviously, research in a respected journal, ~~which has been~~ reviewed by other experts, will be better than something ~~that is / has been~~ published anonymously online.

A paper ~~that was~~ published recently seems to prove a causal link.

The sample group consisted of people ~~who had been~~ chosen at random.

Avoiding passives

In more informal spoken English, we often use *you* or *they* to avoid passives.

You can buy tickets online. (= Tickets can be bought online.)

They've demolished the building. (= The building has been demolished.)

You could use statistics to manipulate people if you wanted to. (= Statistics could be used to manipulate ...)

Exercise 1

Complete the second sentence with a passive construction so it has the same meaning as the first sentence.

1 They've achieved a breakthrough in nanotechnology.
   A breakthrough in nanotechnology _____.
2 They gave me an injection before they stitched the cut up.
   I _____ and then they stitched the cut up.
3 Scientists believe this technique is the way forward.
   This technique _____ the way forward.
4 The dentist took one of my wisdom teeth out.
   I _____ out.
5 It's vital that thorough research supports policy.
   Policy should always _____ thorough research.
6 In the end, he got employment as a researcher with the FBI.
   He ended up _____ the FBI as a researcher.
7 Some think a mineral deficiency causes the disorder.
   The disorder _____ deficiency.
8 The government should fund our research.
   Our research needs _____ the government.

DID YOU KNOW

Need + -ing is a passive construction and can be used instead of *need / have to be done*.

The phenomenon needs investigating (OR needs to be investigated) further.

My house desperately needs repainting (OR needs to be repainted).

Exercise 2

Complete the sentences with the correct form (active or passive) of the verbs.

1 The research, which is due to be completed sometime next year, _____ by Tokyo University. (carry out)
2 The government says that since the outbreak started, those _____ have received full treatment, while all those in vulnerable groups _____. (affect, vaccinate)
3 Scientists _____ the research are confident it will lead to clean renewable energy that can _____ at a competitive price. (undertake, produce)
4 The results can't _____ by anything other than the people in the area _____ to radiation in the area for a number of years. (cause, expose)
5 After _____ from the organ, the sample tissue _____ for the disease and the results came out negative. (extract, test)
6 While the failure of the initial probe _____ the exploration of Mars, it _____ that the lessons learnt will _____ other problems further down the line. (set back, hope, prevent)

8 NATURE AND NUTURE

AUXILIARIES

Auxiliaries are words like *be*, *have*, *do*, *will*, *must*, etc. that we use to make negatives and questions. We also use them to avoid repetition and to add emphasis.

Questions

We use auxiliaries to form normal questions such as *Do you like it?* and *Have you been there?* We also use auxiliaries to form tag questions at the end of statements as well as short responses and rhetorical questions.

*After all, women are better communicators, **aren't they**?*

*Baron-Cohen's choice is simply based on the fact jobs in such fields have traditionally been occupied by women. And why **have they**?*

Tags

We often use tags to ask genuine questions to check things or to make polite requests. However, we also use tags when giving an opinion we expect people to agree with. Positive sentences normally have negative tags and negative statements use a positive tag.

*It was great, **wasn't it**?*

*You've never been there, **have you**?*

*You couldn't lend me your phone for a minute, **could you**?*

DID YOU KNOW?

We sometimes use a positive statement with a positive tag to express surprise or anger.

*Oh, you've got a son, **have you**? Why didn't I know that?*

*You want to borrow some money, **do you**? You haven't paid me back from last time yet!*

Short questions

We often use short auxiliary questions as responses to show interest and continue the conversation.

A: *I spent a month in Mongolia.*

B: ***Did you**?*

A: *Yeah, it was great. I went there as part of my degree.*

A: *I don't really like travelling.*

B: ***Don't you**? How come?*

Avoiding repetition

Auxiliaries help us to avoid repeating a verb or verb phrase we've already used.

*When talking to a boss, we won't butt in, but they **will** ~~butt in~~.*

Research in the journal Science *has shown both sexes talk equally as much, and in ~~talking equally as much~~ **doing** so use on average 16,000 words per day.*

*How people communicate has far more to do with social status and power than it ~~has to do~~ **does** with genetic make-up and 'nature'.*

Note that we sometimes need a different form of the auxiliary to the verb phrase we are replacing.

A: ***I'm not coming** tomorrow.*

B: ***Aren't** you (coming)? I thought you **were** (coming).*

A: *Yeah, I thought I **might** (come), but I've got to work.*

A: ***Did** you **speak** to him?*

B: *No, but I wish I **had** (spoken to him). It would've saved a lot of time.*

so and nor

When we avoid repetition with an auxiliary after *so* / *nor* / *neither*, the subject and auxiliary are reversed.

***We don't recycle** very much, but then **neither does anyone else** round here, apparently.*

A: ***We have foxes** living in our garden.*

B: *Really? **So do I**!*

Emphasising

Auxiliaries can add emphasis. We often add emphasis when we are contradicting what someone has said or written. In speech, we do this by stressing the auxiliary. If there's no auxiliary, we add *do* / *does* / *did*.

*Finally, if these supposed language differences **were** biological, we would expect ...*

*Some men **do** speak over others more, but this is not to do with gender.*

We also use auxiliaries in emphatic tags (see page 71).

*I'd love to go there, I really **would**.*

Exercise 1

Complete the exchanges with the correct auxiliaries. You will need to use negatives.

1 A: I'm not keen on zoos.
   B: Neither _____ I, but my kids _____, which is why we're going.

2 A: I'm a bit scared your dog will bite me.
   B: Don't worry. He _____. He's always pretty friendly.

3 A: That fish really _____ look very strange indeed!
   B: It _____, _____ it?!

4 A: He's always butting in!
   B: I know. I really wish he _____.

5 A: The car will be OK on the dirt roads, _____ it?
   B: Yeah, I would think so.

6 A: I hated the place, I really _____! I wouldn't go back there again.
   B: _____ you? What was so terrible about it?

7 A: My car's at the garage at the moment. If it _____, I'd come and get you from the airport, but I _____, I'm afraid.
   B: Don't worry about it. What's the problem with it, anyway?

8 A: Have you fed the dog?
   B: No I _____, but I _____ in a minute, OK?

9 A: Didn't you say at one point that you were going to Poland this summer?
   B: I _____, yeah – and I still _____. I just haven't sorted out all the details yet.

Exercise 2

Add an auxiliary verb in the correct place in each sentence (and make any other changes necessary) to emphasise the opinions.

1 He lives up to that stereotype of a macho man who hardly speaks.

2 Don't get me wrong. I liked the country to visit. It's just too dry and barren to really live there.

3 My son really enjoys playing with dolls, but I think that's fine.

4 The female of the species participates in the raising of the young, but it's predominantly a male job.

5 Tigers used to be quite common in the area, but they've been hunted to the verge of extinction.

6 He talks over you a bit, but his wife is worse!

Exercise 3

Write responses that contradict the statements.

1 A: You never told me you'd been to Venezuela.
   B: _____. You must have forgotten.

2 A: It looks a bit like a chicken.
   B: _____. It looks more like a swan, or something.

3 A: There's no way we'll get there on time.
   B: _____ – if you just start driving a bit faster!

4 A: It never really gets that cold there.
   B: _____. It actually snowed the year before last.

5 A: I don't think it's an endangered species.
   B: _____. I read there were only 400 left in the wild.

9 WORK

CONTINUOUS FORMS

Continuous forms use a combination of the verb *be* + *-ing*. Passives use a form of *be* + *being* + past participle. We usually only use passive forms with the present and past continuous.

*I'm not the only one who's **being taken** on now, then.*

*We **were being pressurised** to work late.*

Modals can be followed by both a present and perfect infinitive of *be*.

*I **wouldn't be investing** our money in it if I didn't think it would be a success.* (present)

*He **shouldn't have been driving** so fast.* (past)

Unfinished activities / events

We use continuous forms to show an activity or event is / was / will be unfinished at a particular moment in time or when another action took place.

*I **was** just **emailing** one of them to schedule a time for us all to meet when you arrived.*

*The car's **being repaired**.* (= So I have no car here now.)

*We've **been working** on a big infrastructure project, but it's been hit by financial problems.* (= before now)

*I **wouldn't be telling** you if I didn't think it was important!*

*He caught me surfing the Net when I **should've been working**.*

*Just imagine – this time next week we'll **be sunning ourselves** on the beach. I can't wait!*

Temporary activities / situations

Continuous forms emphasise that we see an activity or situation as temporary – rather than permanent or characteristic. (We may also assume it's unfinished.)

*I'm not the only one who's **being taken** on now, then.*

*She's probably **being** all kind and helpful now.*

*They've **been complaining** a lot for some reason.* (= before and including now)

*The economy's **improving**.*

*They **must be struggling** now they are both unemployed.*

Focus on the activity and duration

We sometimes use the continuous form about completed actions or characteristic habits to focus on the activity.

*I've actually **been hanging around** in the coffee bar over the road for the last hour.*

*I'd **been thinking** about moving out there for a while and I happened to get the house just before I got this job.*

*I **was working** all weekend. I could really do with a break.*

*They're constantly **letting** us **down**, but they're the only local supplier. We'd change them if we could.*

Arrangements and activities based on a previous decision

We tend to use the present continuous for future arrangements unless there is some uncertainty about it, in which case we often use *be supposed to be* + *-ing* or *might be* + *-ing*.

*Three or four more **are joining** in the next couple of weeks.*

*I'm not sure if I can make it. I'm **supposed to be attending** a conference that day, but maybe someone else could go.*

We often use *will* + *be* + *-ing* (the future continuous) to talk about an arrangement or activity based on a previous decision.

*I should've said – we'll **be working** alongside each other.*

*To be honest, you **won't be having** that much to do with them in your day-to-day dealings.*

These meanings may also apply to the 'future in the past'.

*I **was meeting** them the following week, so he gave me the documents to take with me.*

*When I joined, they said I'd **be travelling** a lot, but I didn't realise how much!*

Exercise 1

Complete the pairs of sentences with the verbs in bold – one sentence with a continuous form, the other with a simple form.

1 **draw up**
   a I _____ the contract. You just need to sign it.
   b I _____ the guidelines for the new project and I've got a couple of issues I need your input on.

2 **lose**
   a They had to make huge cuts because they _____ so much money.
   b It was strange but when I _____ my job, it actually gave me a new lease of life.

3 **deal with**
   a On this new project Molly _____ finance, so any queries about that – go to her.
   b I _____ Martin if you want. I know how awkward he can be.

4 **have**
   a We _____ so many problems with him that in the end we decided to let him go.
   b I was really upset to lose that watch because I _____ it since I was a kid.

5 **process**
   a Over 200,000 orders _____ in this plant every week.
   b My visa application _____ as we speak, so hopefully I'll receive it sometime in the next week or so.

6 **not / sit**
   a If it hadn't been for that chance meeting, I _____ here now.
   b I _____ there if I were you. That's the CEO's chair!

7 **interview**
   a It was mildly embarrassing because I got a bout of hiccups while I _____. I had to ask for some water.
   b Before I _____, I did some meditation to calm myself down.

8 **show**
   a You're supposed to _____ your ID card when you come in, but half the time the security guard doesn't look.
   b Can you cover the phone for me after lunch? I'm supposed to _____ a client round the factory – if they actually turn up, that is.

Trends

When describing trends, you can use either the present continuous or the present perfect continuous.

*Jobs **are becoming** more insecure.*

*Jobs **have been becoming** more insecure.*

However, certain time phrases go with one form but not the other.

present continuous	present perfect continuous
at the moment currently these days nowadays	over the past / last for since

Non-continuous verbs

Some verbs are not used in the continuous form, eg *agree, believe, belong, doubt, matter, own, seem,* etc. Some don't use the continuous with certain meanings.

She **has** *several duties within the company.* (= show you must do certain work)

*I'm **having** a baby in January.* (= give birth)

*I **see** you've finished everything already.* (= look / understand)

*We've **been seeing** each other for a while now.* (= go out)

*I **don't mind** working late tonight.* (= it's OK for me)

*I'm **minding** the store while my brother's away.* (= looking after)

Exercise 2

Decide which seven sentences are incorrect, then correct them.

1   I wouldn't be asking you if I knew the answer!
2   He must've done at least 80km/h when he crashed.
3   The company took over a chain of shops last year so they're owning over 1,000 stores now.
4   We can't meet in the office at the moment because it's doing up.
5   We're actually supposed taking on some new people soon, but I don't know when.
6   Apparently, he sees the boss's daughter for the last year, but the boss still doesn't know.
7   She's come up with several solutions to the problems we're having at the moment.
8   Over the last year, the company has been recruiting a lot of new staff.
9   I'll sort out those files later so if you finish early, come and give me a hand.
10   I don't know why he's such a pain, he's not normally like that.

10 HEALTH AND ILLNESS

MODAL AUXILIARIES

will / shall

Will shows certainty in your predictions and opinions. *Will* can refer to the past and present as well as the future. *Shall* can also have this meaning, although it's much less common.

*I just know they'**ll have been searching** the Internet for hours.* (= I'm sure this is what has happened, based on my experience and knowledge.)

*Don't call him now. He'**ll be eating**.* (= I'm sure this is what he's doing.)

*We **won't lose**.* (= I'm sure of this.)

*I **shall qualify** next year.* (= I'm sure of this.)

Will can show certainty in decisions and willingness (not) to do something, which we often describe as offers, promises, threats, refusals, etc.

*They **won't admit** to not knowing what the problem is.* (= They refuse to admit …)

Will can refer to typical habits or characteristics that we see as true now.

*Nowadays, most TV dramas **will have** more flawed characters.*

*He'**ll sit** and **watch** repeats of* House *for hours.*

*The anaesthetic **will** usually **be administered** about half an hour or so before the operation.*

Shall is most commonly used with *I* and *we* to make offers and elicit suggestions.

***Shall** I **get** you a glass of water?*

*What **shall** we **do**?*

can / could

We use *can* and *could* to talk about what's (not) possible because of (a lack of) ability, permission or logical explanation.

*They **can't have searched** the Internet.* (= It's not possible that they searched the Internet.)

*It **can't** / **couldn't cost** that much.* (= It's not possible for it to be that expensive, from what I know.)

*They **can** / **could issue** a sick note.* (= It's possible for them to issue a sick note.)

*If we come across a disease we don't immediately recognise, we **can feel** lost.* (= It's possible for us to feel lost – sometimes but not always.)

*The date **can** always **be rearranged**, if needs be.* (= It's possible for someone to do this.)

We don't use *can* to talk about the possibility of a specific future event.

*I ~~can~~ **could** / **might be** late this evening. It depends on work.*

Could is sometimes used as the past form of *can. Could* may also show hypotheticality.

*I **couldn't swim** till I was sixteen.* (= It wasn't possible for me to swim because I hadn't learnt.)

*He **could've** easily **helped** me.* (= It was possible for him to help, but he didn't.)

*You're lucky. You **could've been hurt**.* (= but you weren't)

must

We use *must* to show we are certain about the thought or conclusion. We think there's no other explanation.

*Imagine what that patient **must've gone through**.*

*He **must have suffered** a lot of abuse.* (= I'm sure he suffered, based on what I know.)

*It **must hurt** having an injection like that.* (= I'm sure it hurts, even though I've not experienced it.)

*He **must be feeling awful**.* (= I'm sure he's feeling bad.)

We also use it to express a strong obligation where we feel there's no other choice.

*They give poor treatment because they **mustn't admit** to not knowing what the problem is.*

might / may

We use *might* or *may* to show we are less certain about our opinions and predictions and that it's possible that there are other outcomes or explanations.

*Imagine what that patient **might be going through**.* (= what he is possibly going through)

*We use it as a springboard for a discussion on the processes that **may take place**.*

*It **might have been** my fault.* (= It's possible it was my fault.)

DID YOU KNOW?

May used to be used specifically to ask for and give permission and to make offers, but these days this use has been largely replaced by *can / could.*

***May** / **Can** / **Could** I go home now?*

***May** / **Can** / **Could** I help you?*

should

We use *should* to show we think something is (not) the right thing or a good thing to do. It sometimes also shows hypotheticality.

*Nowadays, they **should have** more flawed characters.* (= The right thing is to have …)

*You **shouldn't be walking** around yet.* (= It's not right that you're walking around – but you are.)

*We use it as a springboard for a discussion on the processes that **should've taken place**.* (= The processes were the right thing to do but didn't happen!)

*You **shouldn't have been drinking** if you were on antibiotics.*

Should can also describe something that is probable in the future, based on what's normally true.

I **should qualify** next year. (= It's probable that I will qualify next year as most people pass.)

We **should have** the result back by next week.

It **shouldn't be** a problem.

would

For information on *would*, see Unit 2.

Exercise 1

Complete 1–6 by using each modal auxiliary in bold once and the correct form of the verbs in brackets. You may need to form a negative.

1 **could, must, should**
   That _____ (be) very painful. It looks really bad. Maybe you _____ (go) and get it X-rayed. It's probably just badly bruised, but it _____ (be) broken.

2 **should, might**
   I know it's too late to worry about now, but you _____ (talk) to a few different doctors. They _____ (see) something your doctor didn't.

3 **can, will, may**
   They think he _____ (murder), but they _____ (know) for certain until they've carried out an autopsy. In the meantime, I guess they _____ (stop) the press speculating.

4 **shall, should, could, can**
   What are you thinking? You _____ (play) in the road there! You _____ (kill) if that car had been driving any faster. _____ I _____ (take) you down to the park so you _____ (play) there instead?

5 **could, must, can**
   All that medication _____ (be) good for you. It _____ (have) something to do with how you're feeling. My sister's a doctor – she _____ probably _____ (tell) you more about the side effects.

6 **should, will, could**
   I know him. He _____ (say) anything to anyone else about what he's going through, but I think he _____ (tell) people. He _____ (get) more help and support if people knew.

Exercise 2

Rewrite the sentences using modal verbs in place of the words in italics.

1 *I bet that was* painful.
   _____

2 *It was a bad thing that he didn't stop* smoking earlier.
   _____

3 *It's not possible for it to be* hard to do.
   _____

4 Given their resources, *it was impossible for them to do* any more to help.
   _____

5 *It's not possible that it was* cheap.
   _____

6 *It wasn't the right thing that he was* taking those pills.
   _____

7 *It's possible that you'll need* three or four operations.
   _____

8 *There's no other explanation other than he was* lying!
   _____

9 *It's possible that she picked up* the cold from my son.
   _____

10 Don't worry. *If she responds as people normally do it's probable that she'll make* a complete recovery after the operation.
   _____

11 PLAY

LINKING WORDS AND PHRASES

There are so many different words and phrases used to join parts of sentences together and to link ideas across sentences that it is impossible to go into detail. Even linkers with very similar meanings and functions often have different grammatical patterns connected to them and may appear in different positions within sentences. To get used to how items are usually used, the best thing to do is read widely and to find examples in a good learner's dictionary.

The Key words for Writing sections throughout the *Outcomes* series also give information on these linking words.

Contrast

1 These start a new sentence and refer back to the previous one:

*Point taken about gaming addiction and its effect on student attentiveness. **That notwithstanding,** / **Nevertheless,** / **Nonetheless,** / **All the same though,** you're wrong about gamification.*

*Girls tend to read more. Boys, **on the other hand,** spend more time online.*

*They're spending a huge amount of time online. **However,** it's not helping them develop very much.*

Note that *on the other hand* and *however* can go after the main subject of a sentence (and any auxiliary verbs) as well as at the start of the sentence.

2 These contrast two clauses within one sentence:

Whilst / **While** / **Despite the fact that** / **In spite of the fact that** *I absolutely loved it, I realised what a major time suck getting into computer games can be.*

Even though *they're spending all that time online, they're not getting any smarter.*

*Gaming can have a positive effect on social development, **although** only if done in moderation.*

*Girls tend to read a lot more, **whereas** / **while** / **whilst** boys spend more time online.*

DID YOU KNOW?

Even though shows something that makes the main fact in the sentence very surprising. Note that *although* can also be used in this way, but *even though* is more common.

*I beat him **even though** / **although** I'd never played before.*

Although is also used in the same way as *but* – to show a contrast or contradiction between two things.

*You can find cheats on the Internet for computer games, **although** I don't use them.*

3 These link a noun phrase and a clause:

Despite / **In spite of** *the friendships they may be cementing during these late-night sessions, during the day they're letting themselves down.*

In spite of / **Despite** *all that time online, they're not ending up any more informed about the world around them.*

Condition

1 These can start a new sentence and refer back to the previous one with the condition:

*We really have to start getting boys more involved in learning. **Otherwise,** / **If we don't,** we'll lose a whole generation.*

2 These are alternatives to *if (not)*:

*I'm going to end up dead in this game **unless I** / **if I don't** form a new coalition.*

*That's all fine, **so long as** / **provided** / **providing** / **as long as** it's done in moderation.*

3 We can add emphasis like this:

Whether or not / **Even if** *they start out with the intention of studying, before too long their evenings are lost to the virtual realm.*

4 *In case* links something we do to prevent another thing happening:

I've set up parental controls **in case** *my son tries to play games that aren't age-appropriate.*

Time / order

1 These need *and* in order to join two clauses in a sentence. Otherwise, they start a new sentence.

Time flies by and they game till they drop – **and then** / **subsequently** / **after that** / **afterwards** *(they) drag themselves into class.*

Time flies by and they game till they drop. **Subsequently** / **Then** / **After that** / **Afterwards** *they drag themselves into class half-asleep at best.*

Girls spend more time doing homework. **Meanwhile,** / **At the same time**, *boys are busy playing games.*

2 *During* links a noun phrase to a clause:

Despite the friendships they may be cementing **during** *these late-night sessions,* **during** *the day they're letting themselves down.*

3 These link two clauses:

He often sits up gaming **until** *he falls asleep at the computer.*

Some of them fall asleep **once** / **when** / **as soon as** / **the minute** / **the second** *they get to class!*

Purpose / result

1 Notice the different patterns after the linkers:

Girls work harder **so as to** / **in order to** *achieve more at school.*

Girls work harder **so that** *they can achieve more at school.*

2 Grammatically, these are like *subsequently*, etc. above. They start a new sentence or within one sentence they are preceded by *and*.

Nights of good intentions went bad: 'I'll just get to the next level and then I'll turn off' turned into early hours sessions and **consequently** / **thus** / **as such** / **so** / **as a result** / **therefore** *I began to understand why many of my school students arrived at school bleary-eyed.*

Addition

1 These add two ideas within the same sentence:

They're less attentive than I'd like them to be, **not to mention** / **as well as** *less verbal.*

Addiction can not only have a terrible impact on gamers' education, **but also** *on health.*

2 These start a new sentence and add an idea to the sentence or paragraph that went before:

Moreover, / **On top of that,** / **Furthermore,** / **In addition,** / **Additionally,** *in spite of all that time online, they're not ending up any more informed about the world around them.*

Addiction can have a terrible impact on a gamer's education. **Similarly,** / **Likewise**, *health can also be affected.*

Cause

1 These link the cause (a noun phrase) to the result clause – or vice versa.

Partly this is **down to** / **a result of** / **due to** *the fact that girls read more.*

Linguistic and social skills develop **on account of** / **as a result of** *the hours spent online.*

Thanks to / **As a result of** / **Due to** / **Because of** / **Owing to** *the introduction of basic coding classes in schools, we're seeing some of the most exciting developments in education for decades.*

The gaming market is failing to develop **owing to** / **because of** / **as a result of** / **on account of** *government regulations.*

Exercise 1

Decide how many options are correct in each sentence.

1 They need to encourage more men to become teachers. *Otherwise* / *In case* / *Consequently,* boys won't have sufficient male role models.

2 Lots of schools go digital *so as not to* / *in order to not* / *so that* be seen as old-fashioned.

3 Obviously, there are good educational games out there. *Nonetheless* / *Although* / *That notwithstanding,* most kids I know would still rather play first-person shooters!

4 Increasingly, fathers are having to work longer hours and *so* / *thus* / *similarly* spend less time with their sons. *On top of that* / *Subsequently* / *Additionally,* the education system has become more feminised over recent years.

5 She's threatening to leave him *if* / *unless* / *provided* he gets help for his gaming addiction.

6 It's become a bit of a problem. I mean, I find myself checking Facebook *the second* / *as soon as* / *so long as* I wake up!

7 My school ended up completely banning phones *on account of* / *owing to* / *a result of* all the secret texting and stuff that students were doing in class.

8 I learned most of my French *thanks to* / *due to* / *down to* this amazing app I use.

9 *Whereas* / *On the one hand* / *Whilst* some people see technology as a problem, I see it as an incredibly powerful tool for learning.

10 Many games these days are incredibly involving *as well as* / *at the same time* / *not to mention* beautifully designed.

11 *Even though* / *Despite* / *Although* my brother's better than me, I still beat him sometimes *so long as* / *whether* / *providing* I play at the top of my game.

Exercise 2

Complete the second sentence so that it has a similar meaning to the first sentence using the word given. Do not change the word given. You must use between three and six words, including the word given.

1 He always upgrades his software in order to be able to play all the latest games.
   SO THAT
   He always upgrades his software _____ play all the latest games.

2 Don't worry if you missed the show. It's bound to be online somewhere.
   IN CASE
   The show is bound to be online somewhere _____ it.

3 You seem to believe it's all genetically predetermined, whereas I think it's nurture.
   HAND
   You seem to believe it's all genetically predetermined. _____ think it's nurture.

4 I think you're wrong, although obviously I respect your right to say what you're saying.
   DESPITE
   I respect what you're saying, _____ think you're wrong.

5 Research has shown that gaming not only improves visual skills, but may also improve learning ability for those skills.
   TOP
   Research has shown that gaming improves visual skills _____ it may also improve learning ability for those skills.

6 The game's success is basically thanks to product adaptation.
   ACCOUNT
   It's basically _____ that the game has been such a success.

12 HISTORY

DRAMATIC INVERSION

We use inversion to add emphasis. It is far more common in academic, literary or journalistic writing, though it is sometimes used in more formal speech or to make stories more dramatic.

Dramatic inversion involves changing the normal order of a sentence. We often do this by putting a negative adverbial phrase and the auxiliary before the subject and the main verb. If there is no auxiliary, we add *do / does / did*.

Only after dancers *started* being taken to a special healing shrine *did* the epidemic finally *come* to a halt. (= The epidemic only came to a halt after dancers started being taken to a special healing shrine.)

Never has it *caused* the strange behaviour most associated with dancing disease. (= It has never caused the strange behaviour most associated with dancing disease.)

Not until the 1950s *was* the theory *disproved*. (= The theory wasn't disproved until the 1950s.)

Not only did he *become* the youngest man to hold office, *but* he *is also* the only Roman Catholic to have ever sat in the White House. (= He became the youngest man ever to hold office and he is also the only Roman Catholic to have ever sat in the White House.)

No sooner had news of the killing *started* spreading around the world *than* the local police *announced* the arrest of Lee Harvey Oswald. (= As soon as news of the killing started spreading around the world, the local police announced the arrest of Lee Harvey Oswald.)

Here are some more examples:

Not only was he saved, *but so were* thousands of others.

No sooner was the castle finished *than* it was attacked.

At no time has it ever been definitively established that both men acted alone.

At no time in history have our kids been more overweight.

Only after an enquiry had been held *were we able to* grasp the horror of what had occurred.

Never before had one nation controlled so much of the world.

Nowhere else in the country *will you* get a better impression of what it was like in the old days.

Not until 2002 was independence finally gained, after more than 30 years of waiting.

Only when the national bank went bust *did* the size of the financial crisis we were facing become apparent.

In no way did the Occupation lead to the end of the resistance movement. If anything, it strengthened it.

Diplomats made it clear to him that *on no account was he to* use such language again.

Exercise 1

Complete the sentences with these words.

at no time	not only	nowhere else
never before	not until	only

1 They were exciting times. _____ was the country globally recognised again, but it felt as if we'd reached a new maturity as a nation.

2 I surprised even myself because _____ whatsoever did I panic. I remained remarkably calm throughout.

3 It was a time of tense industrial relations. _____ had the unions been quite so militant or well organised.

4 _____ it was too late did people begin to realise what was really going on.

5 People headed west to make their fortunes. _____ in the world could one acquire wealth so rapidly. _____ in America were millions made – and lost – overnight.

Exercise 2

Rewrite the sentences in a more dramatic style. The first words are given.

1 It was the first time we'd witnessed an international relief operation on such a scale.
Never before _____.

2 The first women's team didn't come into existence until 1996.
Not until 1996 _____.

3 Nobody tried to prevent the tragedy at any point.
At no time _____ prevent the tragedy.

4 We've only had one honest leader in the whole of our recent history.
Only once in our recent history _____.

5 It's the best place in the world to combine business and pleasure.
Nowhere else in the world _____ quite so well.

6 The soldiers were ordered to never surrender or take their own lives.
It was made very clear that under no circumstances _____ or take their own lives.

7 After America rebelled against the high import taxes imposed on tea in 1773, coffee become more popular.
Only after _____.

8 He was a poet as well as being a military leader.
Not only _____.

9 The government put taxes up as soon as they took office.
No sooner _____.

10 He only admitted his involvement in the scandal when it became obvious it could no longer be contained.
Only when it _____.

DID YOU KNOW?

There are several other ways of inverting sentences:

Such is the romance of this theory *that* even today people who identify as Druids still gather at Stonehenge for the summer solstice. (= This theory is so romantic that even today ...)

So mysterious is the prehistoric monument of Stonehenge *that* over a million people a year make the journey to Wiltshire to marvel at it. (= The prehistoric monument of Stonehenge is so mysterious that over a million people ...)

Had it not been for the bombing raids undertaken by the air force, the greatest tank battle of all time might've ended differently. (= If it hadn't been for the bombing raids ... the greatest tank battle ...)

Were he not so ignorant of history, he might've made slightly better decisions. (= He might have made better decisions if he wasn't so ignorant of history.)

Exercise 3

Correct the mistake(s) in each sentence.

1 Never before so few people did so much for so many.

2 Not only she campaigned against injustice of all kinds, but she was also the first female minister.

3 Only when a society refuses to acknowledge its past failings it starts to lose its moral authority.

4 No sooner the truce had been called than peace talks began in earnest.

5 Only after tighter checks were introduced corruption finally was tackled.

6 A law was passed saying that on no account foreigners would be allowed into the city centre.

7 Had the missiles reached their intended target, the result would be disastrous.

8 Such severe was the damage after the attack that the whole area needed to be rebuilt.

9 So sure of victory he was that he spent the afternoon sleeping in his tent.

10 If were the management to agree to our terms, the strike would end tomorrow.

13 NEWS AND THE MEDIA

PATTERNS AFTER REPORTING VERBS

Verb + (*that*) clause

acknowledge	announce	argue	boast
claim	confess	confide	confirm
declare	deny	grumble	guarantee
insist	reiterate	state	vow

She **acknowledged (that)** there had been division on the issue.

She categorically **denied that** her retirement was connected to recent criticism.

Demonstrators **claim (that)** the victims were crushed.

Verbs in the 'that clause' use past forms unless the facts / actions are still true now – or are yet to take place.

He **reiterated** that he **had never seen** the victim before.

He **confirmed** he **was** / **is going to compete** in the Olympics.

Verb + someone + (*that*) clause

assure	convince	notify	persuade
promise	remind	tell	warn

A police spokesman **assured reporters that** the men died when a car exploded.

DID YOU KNOW?

The verbs *admit*, *announce*, *confide*, *confess*, *point out* and *report* use *to* before the object with this pattern.

He **admitted to police (that)** he'd been drinking.

He **announced to waiting reporters that** the mayor had been removed from his post.

Note: He **(dis)agreed with** me that it had been a mistake.

Verb + infinitive (with *to*)

demand	guarantee	promise	refuse	threaten	vow

She **refused to comment** further on the health reasons for her departure.

The National Bank **refused to rule out** further increases this year.

The couple ... **promised to donate** the money to charity.

Verb + someone + infinitive (with *to*)

advise	beg	encourage	instruct	invite
order	persuade	remind	urge	warn

He **urged what he termed a silent majority to make** their voices heard.

Note that the verb *plead* uses *with* before the object with this pattern:

He **pleaded with them to help**.

Verb + -*ing*

admit	advise	consider	defend
deny	discuss	recommend	suggest

I've never **denied being** a long-term opponent.

Verb + noun phrase

cite	confirm	criticise	declare
express	praise	reject	voice

The President ... **rejected demands for the government to change tack**.

Carol Dixon **has confirmed rumours that she is to retire on health grounds**.

Manager François Houllier **expressed confidence in Johnson's replacement, Paul Harrison**.

Corporal Hassan Cleaver ... **praised the work of the whole unit**.

Verb (+ object) + preposition

accuse of	apologise for	blame on / for	criticise for / over
forgive for	insist on	threaten with	

The President **blamed the rioting on subversive groups** trying to destabilise the country.

When one verb has a preposition connected to it, the verb that follows will use the -*ing* form.

The Enquirer **had accused them of entering** into the marriage purely for their mutual benefit.

Note also that many of the verbs above can be followed by more than one pattern.

Exercise 1
Choose the correct option.

1 The President *cited / stated* his father as a source of inspiration.
2 The party leaders *urged / reiterated* everyone who could to go out and vote.
3 The two parties have *rejected / refused* to cooperate.
4 The government *criticised / blamed* the stalemate on the opposition.
5 Our landlord suddenly *announced / notified* that he was putting up the rent.
6 He's *instructed / demanded* his lawyers to evict us if we don't pay.
7 My son *begged / pleaded* with us to buy him a car and in the end we gave in.
8 I heard him *boasting / praising* that his parents were rich.
9 Manager François Houllier said he had *threatened / considered* resigning several times.
10 Members of his own party had *criticised / warned* him that the law would prove unpopular.

Exercise 2
Complete the second sentence so that it has a similar meaning to the first sentence using the word given. Do not change the word given. You must use between three and six words, including the word given.

1 'I can't believe they have decided to put up taxes.'
   ANGER
   He voiced _____ rises.
2 'I haven't told anyone before, but I was terrified.'
   ME
   She confessed _____ been terrified.
3 'I'll definitely have it ready by Friday.'
   DONE
   He guaranteed _____ by Friday.
4 'You two should really visit sometime.'
   URGED
   He _____ sometime.
5 'We have worries regarding a possible deterioration in the situation.'
   CONCERN
   They _____ might deteriorate.
6 'If you don't do as I say, I could get you sacked.'
   TO
   He _____ if I refused.
7 'The plan was flawed. I never denied that.'
   ACKNOWLEDGED
   The minister _____ flawed.

DID YOU KNOW?

We sometimes use the noun forms of reporting verbs.

He was a great coach – always there to shout **encouragement** *to the team.*

The document provides the first official **acknowledgement** *that prisoners were mistreated.*

Exercise 3

Complete the sentences using noun forms of the verbs in italics and the other words given.

1 The management has sought _____. *assure* / the problem is being dealt with

2 The president has come in for fierce _____. *criticise* / her decision

3 We turned down an _____. *invite* / work with them on the project

4 They made an _____. *announce* / they / getting married

5 After hours of questioning, he finally made a full _____. *confess* / the police

6 The report made several _____. *recommend* / protecting children on the Internet

7 We're considering all options, including a _____. *refuse* / pay the fine

8 The school gives _____. *encourage* / students / apply for university

14 BUSINESS AND ECONOMICS

RELATIVE CLAUSES

Defining relative clauses

Sometimes relative clauses, are needed to complete a sentence in order to make sense of a noun or noun phrase. With defining relative clauses, we don't add a comma after the noun that the relative clause relates to.

As of yet, not one of the people. (= wrong / incomplete)

As of yet, not one of the people **who / that actually committed these offences has served time.**

Non-defining relative clauses

Sometimes the relative clause is non-defining. It adds extra information which is relevant but not essential to the understanding of the sentence and so the relative clause is separated from the rest of the sentence by commas.

Four people were given jail sentences.

Four people were given jail sentences, **two of which were lengthened following the bankers' failed appeal.**

We don't use *that* in non-defining relative clauses.

There are times when it is unclear how essential the information is and you may choose to use a comma or not.

Relative pronouns and adverbs

Relative clauses may start with a relative pronoun (*that, who, which, whose*) or a relative adverb (*where, why, when, whereby*). The nouns / noun phrases they relate to are underlined below. Notice that in the first example we can join two relative clauses with *and*.

Instead of talking about banks as if they're some kind of organism **that** *has no free will and* **whose** *only purpose is to grow …*

There was a time **when** *banking people had a real stake in ensuring businesses were supported.*

The four men had organised the sale of a 5% stake in the bank, **whereby / by which means** *they hoped to boost shareholder confidence.*

There is a more important reason **why** *we should be focusing on people rather than institutions.*

This is also again a stark contrast to the Icelandic situation, **where** *the government let the creditors pick up the bill for their failing banks.*

We also sometimes use a phrase with *which* or *whom* (*two of which, many of whom, by which time, some of which, the year in which, from which, beyond which*, etc.).

This has resulted in a period of recession and austerity, **during which time** *the UK government alone has given up to £1.2 TRILLION to bail the banks out.*

They should've spent some of those trillions on people in debt, **many of whom** *have ended up being evicted from their houses instead.*

See also *of whom / of which* in Writing 1 page 151 and *whereby* in Writing 4 page 157.

Some abstract nouns commonly go with particular relative pronouns or adverbs:

a situation where	in cases where
a reason why	a time when / that
a period in / during which	ways in which
the extent to which	the point at which
a process whereby	

No relative pronoun

We often don't use a relative pronoun / adverb in defining relative clauses when the noun they relate to is the object of the clause.

We're talking about people and the bad decisions **they make**. (= They make bad decisions.)

We've fined banks less than the money **we've given them**. (= We've given them the money.)

Compare that with this example, where the relative pronoun is needed:

It is a kind of organism **which has no free will**. (= The organism has no free will.)

Prepositions

Prepositions connected to a verb can go at the end or beginning of a relative clause, but having the preposition at the beginning sounds very formal.

Normal	Very formal
the bank I work **for**	*the bank* **for which** *I work*
the place that we stayed **in**	*the place* **in which** *we stayed*
the people they lent money **to**	*the people* **to whom** *they lent money*

When you use *where* as a relative adverb no preposition is needed:

I really liked the place where we stayed ~~in.~~

The bank where the executives worked ~~for~~ *went bankrupt.*

Exercise 1

Decide if the sentences in the following pairs are both correct. Correct any mistakes.

1 a Banks, which generate huge profits, should be taxed more.
   b Banks which generate huge profits should be taxed more.

2 a The company he invested all his savings in went bust.
   b The company which he invested all his savings went bust.

3 a I think that's the bank who's manager was arrested last year.
   b I think that's the bank whose manager was arrested last year.

4 a The police are interviewing two men that were arrested last night.
   b Two men, that are not thought to be suspects, are being interviewed by police.

5 a The people paying for the banks' losses are taxpayers, many of whom have debts themselves.
   b Taxpayers, many of whom have debts themselves are paying for the banks' losses.

Exercise 2

Rewrite each pair of sentences as one sentence. Start each sentence with the underlined words. You will need to leave some words out.

1 Improvements can be made in some areas. <u>We have to identify</u> these areas.

_____

2 <u>My boss</u> heard everything. Her office is next to mine!

_____

3 We borrowed €10,000 <u>in January</u>. Most of it has already been spent.

_____

4 We chose 2004 <u>for the starting point of our study</u>. Our president submitted his first budget that year.

_____

5 To some extent, large corporations influence the economic health of nations. <u>I wanted to explore</u> this.

_____

6 <u>We have over 9,000 employees</u>. The vast majority are based in China.

_____

7 <u>We've reached a crucial point</u>. We can't cut costs any further without having to lay people off.

_____

8 <u>The S and L bank</u> has finally returned to profit. The bank was bailed out by the government. The bank's executives were imprisoned for fraud.

_____

Exercise 3

Join the sentence halves using _which_ or _whom_ after a suitable preposition.

1 _Our founder was Mr Johnson, after whom the company is named._

1 Our founder was Mr Johnson,
2 We're lucky enough to have an incredible team,
3 After much research, we've come up with a prototype
4 We're conducting research into the Kazakh market,
5 I'd like to say thanks in particular to my boss,
6 Naturally, we are all influenced by the things

a we currently know very little.
b I've learned a huge amount.
c we are all very satisfied.
d we surround ourselves.
e we would never have survived this difficult year.
f the company is named.

Exercise 4

Rewrite the six sentences above in a less formal way by putting the prepositions at the end of the relative clauses.

1 _Our founder was Mr Johnson, who the company is named after._

15 TRENDS

PREPOSITIONS

Verb + preposition

Many verbs are often followed by certain prepositions.

Women were more likely to **opt for** men with facial hair simply because they were unusual.

Here are some more common examples:

account for	bother about	enquire about	participate in
appeal to	compete with	insist on	pray for
approve of	elaborate on	listen to	stem from
benefit from	engage in	object to	succeed in

Sometimes more than one preposition can be used with a verb with no real change in meaning.

I **heard of** / **about** this place from a friend of mine.

Little **is known about** / **of** Coco Chanel's early life.

However, different prepositions are often used depending on the context.

I**'ve been thinking about** fashion and gender roles quite a lot recently. (= concentrating my mind on)

I**'ve been thinking of** quitting and going back to college. (= considering a possible future plan)

DID YOU KNOW?

Some verbs are often followed by an object and then a preposition.

I love your dress. It **reminds me of** this thing I used to wear when I was young.

They **accused me of** trying to steal the shoes. I couldn't believe it!

I'm just writing to **congratulate you on** passing your exams.

Adjective + preposition

Certain adjectives also collocate with particular prepositions.

I suspect I'm not **alone in** want**ing** to see the back of grumpy cats.

This process is often **compared to** the way epidemics build up slowly but then suddenly explode.

Here are some more common examples:

absorbed in	envious of	immune to	short of
addicted to	fed up with	keen on	suspicious of
capable of	fond of	lacking in	suitable for
conscious of	grateful to	prior to	unaware of

Sometimes more than one preposition can be used with an adjective with no real change in meaning.

I was quite **disappointed with** / **by** the service.

I lost my temper and got really **angry at** / **with** him.

However, different prepositions are often used depending on the context.

You should eat more of it. It's really **good for** you. (= keeps you healthy)

She's always been **good with** her hands. (= able to use something well)

I've never been any **good at** things like this. (= able to do something well)

Noun + preposition

Prepositions also often go with certain nouns in a particular context.

Little could he have known that ... his **choice of** phrase was set to become a trend in its own right.

Here are some more common examples:

addiction to	ban on	fondness for
investigation into	admiration for	belief in
habit of	knowledge of	advantage of
decline in	insurance against	preference for
awareness of	dedication to	resistance to

Sometimes more than one preposition can be used with a noun with no real change in meaning.

*They eventually managed to come to an **agreement on** / **about** funding.*

However, different prepositions are often used depending on the context.

*There's been a sharp **rise in** the number of young people suffering from eating disorders.*

*The papers have been going on about the **rise of** male cooks at home.*

Prepositional phrases

There are also hundreds of short fixed phrases that start with a preposition. They are often followed by a noun. The best way to learn these phrases is to note them down – in context – every time you meet them.

*This, **in turn**, makes it a more attractive partner.*

*... fads that are now **on the wane** ...*

*... baby fish with their traits soon start appearing **in large numbers** ...*

Here are some more common prepositional phrases:

at random	in danger	in moderation	off the pace
at risk of	in debt	in the long term	on trial
by far	in decline	on purpose	out of control
by law	in effect	off balance	under oath

Linking sentences

Prepositions can link two parts of a sentence.

*The global growth in hairy hipsters had its roots in the 2008 crash, **with** some young men responding ... by choosing to emphasise another aspect of masculinity.* (= used when considering one fact in relation to another)

Look at the meanings prepositions used in this way can sometimes have:

***On** finishing college, he got a job at Dior.* (= when / after)

***By** improving the design, SPM have leapt ahead of their competitors.* (= this was the method used)

***Besides** having a nine to five job, I write novels.* (= as well as)

***With** the heatwave, sales of swimsuits took off.* (= because)

Exercise 1

Complete the second sentence so that it has a similar meaning to the first sentence using the word given. Do not change the word given. You must use between three and six words, including the word given.

1 They deliberately lost the game to win a bet.
   PURPOSE
   They lost _____ win a bet.

2 The company was in a terrible state before he arrived.
   HIS
   Prior _____, the company was failing.

3 We've made it more accessible as a result of the reduction in costs.
   ENABLED
   By _____ more people to buy it.

4 It's fine for the time being, but it won't last forever.
   TERM
   It's fine now, but _____ it'll need replacing.

5 23% of our exports are connected to fashion.
   ACCOUNTS
   The fashion industry _____ a quarter of all our exports.

6 The researchers didn't use any particular method when they were selecting people.
   RANDOM
   Participants _____.

7 The proposal met with stiff opposition.
   RESISTANCE
   _____ the proposal.

8 I was amazed that they managed to bring together all sides of the dispute for talks.
   SUCCEEDED
   Amazingly, they _____ all sides of the dispute together for talks.

9 Every day I have to check the stock.
   BASIS
   I have to check the stock _____.

10 I think it's good in terms of the overall design.
   REGARD
   I think that _____ it's fine.

Exercise 2

Add a preposition in the correct place in each sentence.

1 A number of factors have contributed the trend towards small families.

2 The news that girls are more risk of online negative experiences comes as no surprise.

3 We'd simply never thought it'd be necessary to take out insurance natural disasters.

4 Reactions the new trend have been very mixed so far, it must be said.

5 The magazine prides itself being cutting edge.

6 She just seems to be famous being famous.

7 The arrival of the miniskirt in the early 1960s symbolised a rejection conservative values.

8 Gaining power, Napoleon introduced new dress codes in court.

DID YOU KNOW?

Look at these commonly confused prepositions.

as / like

As shows the job, use or duty something actually has. We use *like* to make comparisons. It's followed by a noun.

from / of

From shows the origin or the condition before it changes. Of often shows who or what a thing belongs or relates to.

into / to

Into shows what someone or something becomes – or a movement entering or hitting something. *To* shows the direction someone or something is moving.

up to / until

Up to shows the maximum amount possible (how much). *Until* shows when something stops.

for / during / throughout

For shows how long. *During / throughout* go with dates, events, etc. and show when. *Throughout* shows that the action didn't stop; with *during*, it may have happened just once.

Exercise 3

Decide which six sentences are incorrect, then correct them.

1 As an actor he was amazing, but as a parent he was awful.

2 Hats were essential clothing during centuries, but during the 20th century they fell out of fashion.

3 They have grown to one of the biggest companies in the country.

4 It's a translation of Arabic.

5 We sometimes have to work until seven hours without a break.

6 He was sacked from the design firm he used to work for.

7 I somehow managed to crash to the car in front of me.

8 We were very close. She was as a mother to me.

9 The temperature can reach up to 45 degrees in the summer.

10 The fashion was widespread throughout the Middle Ages.

16 DANGER AND RISK

TALKING ABOUT THE FUTURE

Verb structures

Be set to is often used in journalism when something is likely to happen. We also use *be set for* and *looks set to*.

*This is a problem that's surely **set to get** worse.* (= It'll almost certainly / It's bound to get worse.)

*Campaigners **are set to challenge** the decision in court.* (= They're going to / ready to ...)

*The banking sector **is set for explosive growth** this year.* (= It's going to / about to experience explosive growth.)

*The strike **looks set to intensify** after talks broke down.* (= It's almost certainly going to intensify.)

Be to basically means the same as *be going to*. It's often used in *if*-clauses to show that one thing needs to happen before something else can. It's also sometimes used in journalism to talk about actions that have been officially arranged or scheduled.

*If the show**'s to work**, we need you to call up and tell us what's on your mind.* (= You need to call because if you don't, the show won't work!)

*The Queen **is to meet** the President in private tomorrow.* (= She's meeting / going to meet ...)

Be due to is used to show something is planned to happen at a particular time.

*I**'m due to stop** work in the summer.* (= I'm going to stop ...)

*The next train **is due to arrive** on Platform 3 in six minutes.* (= It's going to arrive ...)

We can also use other prepositions with *be due*.

*All three films **are due for** release this month.* (= They're supposed to / They should be released then.)

*The baby **is due in** December.* (= That's when the doctors say it'll arrive.)

*I**'m due at** a meeting in a minute or two.* (= I'm supposed to / I should be there.)

Be likely to shows we think something is highly probable. It is often used for making predictions.

*I honestly don't think things **are likely to get** any better in the foreseeable future.* (= I don't think they will get any better.)

*The offer **is highly likely to be rejected** by shareholders.* (= It'll almost certainly be rejected.)

*Critics claim the legislation **is not likely to** / **is unlikely to stop** the problem.* (= It probably won't stop the problem. / It's doubtful that it will stop the problem.)

Be bound to shows you're 99% sure something will happen – usually because of past experience.

*That**'s bound to cause** problems in the long run.* (= It'll inevitably / I'm certain it will cause problems.)

*He**'s bound to hear** about it sooner or later.* (= He's certain / sure to hear ...)

Noun phrases

There are several nouns and noun phrases used to talk about future events – and to show how sure we are of things happening.

*I**'m on the verge of** retiring.* (= I'm about to retire. / I'm due to retire very soon. / I'm on the brink of retiring.)

*The **chances of people** avoiding all this **are pretty slim** / **small** / **slight**.* (= It probably won't help.)

*The **chances of it** happening are pretty good / high.* (= It'll probably happen.)

*There**'s no** / **a slim** / **a good chance of** it working.*

In all likelihood, most offenders are actually pretty harmless. (= In all probability, they're harmless. / They're most likely harmless.)

*The **probability** / **likelihood is that it'll** require surgery.* (= It'll probably / most likely need surgery.)

*The odds are you'll** put them off.* (= It's highly likely / probable that you'll put them off.)

*The **odds** / **chances of it** happening are pretty high / low.*

*There's **a distinct possibility you'll end up** involved in a legal dispute.* (= It's highly likely / probable you will ... / The odds are that you will ...)

Exercise 1

Decide if both options are possible in each sentence.

1 There's a *distinct / probable* possibility that you'll experience side effects from the medication.
2 He's *about to be / on the verge of being* kicked out of school for good.
3 We are *due to / just about to* hold meetings on the matter in a few months' time.
4 There's a *slim / slight* chance we might be late.
5 It seems *probable / likely* that the election will be held in June.
6 In all *chances / likelihood*, we'll be done by tomorrow.
7 They're *set to announce / on the brink of announcing* record profits.
8 The odds of things going wrong are pretty *high / likely*.
9 They're *bound / set* to find out about it sooner or later.
10 If the company *is to / will* survive, it'll need to make some serious cutbacks.

Exercise 2

Complete the sentences with the correct prepositions.

1 The likelihood _____ them listening is pretty low.
2 He's due _____ court tomorrow.
3 The stage is set _____ a thrilling race.
4 I'm _____ the brink of quitting, to be honest.
5 Apparently, I'm due _____ a tax refund.
6 The odds _____ getting hurt are too high to make it worth the risk.
7 _____ all probability, it'll be a struggle to maintain the principles of Internet openness.

Exercise 3

Complete the second sentence so that it has a similar meaning to the first sentence using the word given. Do not change the word given. Use between three and five words, including the word given.

1 Arrangements have been made for a team of international inspectors to oversee the work.
   IS
   The work _____ a team of international inspectors.
2 In all probability, the news will damage his reputation.
   SURE
   The news _____ his reputation.
3 Police believe they're close to finding the killer.
   BRINK
   Police believe they're _____ the killer.
4 We're on the verge of being evicted.
   ABOUT
   We _____ evicted.
5 Where there is passion, it is inevitable that success will follow.
   BOUND
   Where there is passion, _____ follow.
6 Prices will almost certainly rise this year.
   HIGHLY
   Prices _____ this year.

INFORMATION FILES

FILE 1

Unit 1 page 10   READING

Group A

BOGOTA

The ex-mayor of Bogota, Enrique Peñalosa, has argued that if we ever achieve a successful city for children, we will have built the perfect city for all citizens. In Bogota, the capital of Colombia, they have tried to fulfil this ideal by transforming what was once a chaotic city – badly affected by congestion and gripped by fear of crime – into one far better for children. Peñalosa is largely credited with this transformation through the **large-scale reforms** he initiated at the turn of the century. However, if other mayors hadn't secured the city's finances before him and developed his reforms afterwards, the changes wouldn't have been so successful.

One of the first steps he took was to **clear a large slum** that dominated the centre of Bogota and replace it with a large public space. The slum had been a no-go zone for police and had effectively **created a barrier** between the affluent north and the more deprived south of the city. By demolishing it, the city was immediately brought closer together. Having cleared one space, Peñalosa's administration then **expropriated the land** of a private country club in the north of the city. Its golf course and polo fields were converted into a free park with sports facilities for all.

They then started to **tackle congestion** and the lack of facilities for pedestrians and cyclists. Wide pavements were built and cars were prevented from parking on them – a move that led to huge **protests**. The government built

miles and miles of cycle lanes and set up a huge network of buses, again using separate lanes. They also **imposed restrictions** on car use and increased taxes on petrol, the proceeds from which went back into the new transport system.

Finally, they **poured money into** education – building new schools and a network of libraries, several in the most deprived neighbourhoods. The schools were also given thousands of computers connected to both the Internet and the libraries. The programme resulted in a huge **increase in enrolment** and school attendance.

During his time in office, Peñalosa did not **escape criticism** and after his three-year term in office, he failed to be re-elected in subsequent attempts. Some critics hate aspects of the road laws; others complain new housing is far from their original home in the city centre.

FILE 6

Unit 1 page 13   SPEAKING

Student B

A friend of a friend of mine heard this story from a guy he met in Ireland.

Apparently, there was a student who was trying to get home from a party one night. He'd missed the last bus and so decided to hitchhike. It was pouring with rain and he'd been waiting for ages so when he saw a car coming slowly towards him, he just jumped in.

He soon realised, though, that there was nobody behind the wheel and the engine wasn't running. The car carried on moving slowly and as they neared a curve in the road, a hand appeared through the window and turned the wheel. By this point, the student was terrified so when he saw the lights of a café come into view, he leapt out and ran to safety. He rushed inside and started telling everybody about the horrible experience he had just had.

Then the door opened again and two more men walked in from the dark and stormy night. Looking around and seeing the shaking student, one said to the other, 'Look, James ... there's that idiot that got in the car while we were pushing it!'

FILE 8

Unit 2 page 21   SPEAKING

Student B

1   Your neighbours seem to be going through a very rough patch and are constantly shouting. You've just heard several things being smashed and a woman screaming 'Stop it! Stop it!' at the top of her voice.

2   You've had a few problems with a project at work through no fault of your own, but you think a colleague has been going behind your back in order to undermine you and get your job.

3   The doctor wants to discharge a member of your family from hospital, but you aren't convinced they are ready to come home and you're not sure if you'll cope.

MANCHESTER

On 15th June 1996, a huge bomb in Manchester, in the north-west of England, **devastated the city centre**, causing nearly a billion pounds' worth of damage. The bomb, which had been planted by a terrorist group called the IRA, injured over 200 people but remarkably killed no-one as police had **evacuated the area** following a warning from the IRA.

Manchester had already **undergone some changes** as it recovered from the recession of the early 1990s that had destroyed much of its industry and created large-scale unemployment. It had won the right to **host the Commonwealth Games** (a large sporting event) and redeveloped some deprived areas through the building of the National Velodrome, an exhibition centre and an award-winning concert hall. However, at the time of the bombing, the city centre was still **badly neglected** – dominated by the hideous Arndale Shopping Centre (once described as looking like an enormous public toilet) and squares that were run-down and affected by drug addiction. So, dreadful though the bombing was, it actually provided an opportunity to start again that might not have happened otherwise.

Within weeks of the explosion, the government had set up a public-private company to manage the recovery and **launched an international competition** to design the redevelopment. The winning plan involved restoring the historic buildings that had been damaged, demolishing and rebuilding some of the ugly buildings, creating new public spaces and improving life for pedestrians. Alongside this, the council reduced traffic in the centre by **diverting main roads** and developed an integrated public transport system, making access to the centre easier. Since these improvements, the city has attempted to **boost tourism** by using some of the city's historical sites for major public events and by creating the Urbis building, which now houses the National Museum of Football. In turn, these changes have been **key in attracting** new investors, such as the Qatari royal family who own Manchester City Football Club.

Since 1996, the Manchester economy has grown in all areas. However, there are some concerns that **inequality has also increased**. Nor are all the new spaces appreciated. One new garden square designed by an international architect was rated as the worst attraction in the city. Others argue that in swapping market stalls and industry for luxury consumption and sparkling glass buildings, the city has **lost some of its soul**.

Oldbury is a town of 250,000. It is to receive £500 million of funding to halt the decline that has been taking place over a number of years. There's a chemical works on the outskirts of the town which produces nasty fumes. The city has a number of deprived areas and high unemployment. The small historical centre, which is very run-down, dates back 300 years.

Ideas for improving Oldbury

- set up a recycling centre
- provide grants for people starting up new businesses
- restore the historical centre and build a tourist centre
- provide low-interest loans to improve homes
- shut down the chemical works and relocate it on the coast
- set up youth centres to give young unemployed people something to do and to keep them off the street
- recruit more officers to police the poorer parts of the city
- plant trees in every street and increase the amount of green space available for public use

---

Student B

Someone you know was diagnosed with kidney disease last year. The doctor said it was because of high blood pressure.

Decide what you think caused the high blood pressure, how long they'd had the problem, and how long it took to get the problem diagnosed.

They were placed on a waiting list.

Decide how long they had to wait, what the process was for finding a donor, and how / when a donor was finally found.

They had the transplant.

Decide how they coped with the operation.

They took part in a rehabilitation programme.

Decide how often they had to do this, how long for, what kind of thing you think it involved, and how they are now.

FILE 5

Student A

A friend of one of my cousins told me this story.

Outside the zoo in his city there's this big car park. It must hold something like 150 cars and maybe ten or fifteen coaches. They charge cars £2 to park and coaches £5. Anyway, there was this really nice parking attendant working there who used to make jokes and smile and everyone loved him. This guy must have been there for something like 25 years all in all. And then one day he just didn't turn up for work. It was like he'd vanished.

The zoo called the local council to let them know and to request a new parking attendant, but you can imagine their surprise when they were told that the parking area was *their* responsibility. They queried this and said surely the council employed the attendant. 'No,' came the answer, 'we'd always assumed you did!'

Somewhere, in a far-off distant land, there must be a retired man who'd been taking around £400 a day, seven days a week, for the last two decades. He must have taken well over two million pounds!

And no-one even knows his name!

FILE 11

Student A

A poor desperate man is *looking* into a bin desperately searching for something to sell to buy some food. Then a man *goes* past him on the street and *looks* at the poor man as if he's awful and worthless. The man is obviously wealthy – he's *holding* an expensive leather briefcase; he's *talking* on a top smartphone, and the poor man also spots he's wearing a Rolex watch. The poor man's absolutely desperate and angry at the way the wealthy man *looked* at him, so he *goes* up behind him, *holds* his neck and *says*, 'Give me all your money!' The wealthy man *says*, 'You can't do this to me, I'm a Member of Parliament.' To which the poor man replies, 'Well in that case, just give me back MY money!'

FILE 15

Student A

Article 1

Two male penguins are rearing a chick together after they were given an egg to look after. The male pair had previously been seen imitating heterosexual behaviour and zookeepers wanted to see how they would react to real fatherhood. The pair immediately sheltered the egg and saw it hatch. They have since continued to look after it and behave as a normal mother and father. Zoologists say that homosexual-type behaviour is quite common in animals of all kinds.

FILE 7

Student A

1 Two good friends of yours have fallen out badly. You're having a few friends over for your birthday and would like them both to come, but you don't want a scene or bad atmosphere between them to spoil the evening.

2 Your father is looking after your mother, who is very frail and unsteady on her feet, but he himself has become very forgetful and is struggling to cope.

3 Your son takes a very laid-back attitude to his studies and although he's taken things in his stride so far, you're worried he might fall behind and fail.

FILE 13

Student A

Conversation 1
You share a house with Student B and three other people. For some time now, you've felt that Student B doesn't really fit in, but you don't want to find someone else at this point. He / She always complains about the noise and about everyone else's inability to stick to the rota of household chores, yet doesn't seem to realise his / her own failings. He / She has a short temper and frequently ends up screaming and shouting or slamming doors after rows. Start the conversation by saying 'Good morning' to Student B and asking, 'How are you?' Try to work through the issues with your partner and find a solution to the dispute.

Conversation 2
You work for an import-export company. You really like the company and want to stay but have had problems with Student B, who is your line manager. He / She has asked to have a word with you. You've felt for some time that Student B sometimes picks on you and a few months ago you reported what you felt had been bullying behaviour to the regional manager. You fear Student B is still angry about this. However, you're also worried it could be about a company event you attended recently where you ended up talking to a colleague and mentioned some new plans for the company. You now realise you shouldn't have talked about the plans. Your partner will start the conversation. Try to clear the air while making clear how you feel.

Article 2

A Californian company, My DNA Fragrance, is producing scents based on the DNA of famous dead people such as Marilyn Monroe, Elvis Presley, Einstein and Michael Jackson. The DNA has been extracted from pieces of hair that have been acquired by John Reznikoff, who has the world's largest collection of hair from famous people dating back to the sixteenth century. The company says that the resulting fragrance is the 'essence' of the star rather than being their actual smell but that the process is entirely scientific. The perfume varies in price but on average costs around $90.

FILE 12

Unit 4 page 36   UNDERSTANDING VOCABULARY

Student B

A politician goes and visits one of his counterparts in another country and they're *going* round the garden of his colleague's house. The place is beautiful! The garden has a heated swimming pool, a tennis court and a lovely lawn; the house has three storeys, six bedrooms – it's fantastic! The visiting politician *says*, 'Wow, they must pay MPs a lot more here than in my country.' His host laughs and *says*, 'Not really ... but you look at that motorway over there.' The visiting politician *looks* into the distance and *spots* a brand-new six-lane motorway with a few cars speeding along it. He turns back to his colleague who simply *laughs*, winks and pats his pocket. And then the light bulb goes on in the head of the overseas guest, who *says*, 'Say no more!'

Anyway, a few months later, the politician's counterpart returns the visit and comes to see him at his home. He's amazed when he sees the house. He's speechless! He just *looks* at the four-storey mansion, the ten bedrooms, the lovely grounds around it with a huge swimming pool, a sauna, a Jacuzzi, two tennis courts. Then there's a Rolls Royce and a Ferrari parked outside. Eventually, he *says*, 'But ... but I thought you said that MPs were badly paid here.' And the politician *laughs* and says, 'Well, you know, have a look at that new motorway over there.' And his foreign counterpart *looks* into the distance and scans the horizon, 'But there's nothing there.' And the politician just *laughs*, winks and pats his pocket.

FILE 14

Unit 6 page 53   CONVERSATION PRACTICE

Student B

Conversation 1

You share a house with Student A and three other people. You like the house – it's in a great location and is good value. However, you have issues with some of your housemates. It's Tuesday morning and you haven't slept very well because someone was playing music and chatting loudly until 2am. You have exams next week and feel your housemates are being inconsiderate. You are also generally fed up with how messy everyone else is and are really reaching your limit! You've come down to the kitchen to make some coffee. Student A will start a conversation with you. Try to persuade them to establish some rules.

Conversation 2

You have recently been appointed departmental manager for an import-export company. You get on badly with Student A, who works under you in the company. You have reason to believe he / she has revealed information about a forthcoming deal because a friend in a different department heard it mentioned at a recent social event. You're worried it could be a much bigger problem if the plans become more widely known. You also feel he / she often undermines you and have not forgotten that a few months ago you had words. Student A went over your head and complained about you to the regional manager. Start the conversation by raising your worries. You want to establish a better working relationship.

FILE 35

Unit 16 page 145   SPEAKING

Student A

**Read the three short texts and the related questions below.
Be ready to explain to your partner what you read and to discuss the questions.**

The documentary *Hot Coffee* revisited the Stella Liebeck case. It argued that the case had been widely misrepresented in order to undermine consumers' rights and reduce possible compensation claims. It was widely reported that Mrs Liebeck had been driving when she spilt the coffee, but as the film showed she had in fact been in a parked car and had spilt the coffee while trying to remove the lid. The coffee had been super-heated under instructions from McDonald's training manual, a practice that had continued despite persistent complaints from customers and frequent reports of accidents. The scalding had left Mrs Liebeck with severe injuries that required skin grafts and left her with substantial hospital bills. The often-quoted figure of $2.8 million, which had been awarded by the jury to punish the company's wilful failure to deal with previous incidents, was actually greatly reduced on appeal.

The banning of liquids in airports came about following a plot in the UK to blow up several aeroplanes by mixing liquid explosives once on the plane. The plot was foiled and six men were eventually convicted on a variety of charges. A machine to scan liquids in bottles is currently under trial. If successful, this may allow the relaxing of the restrictions. Each machine costs around £40,000.

The International Labour Organisation estimates that over two million people die in work-related accidents worldwide. The figure was 143 last year in the UK.

- Do the extra pieces of information affect the way you think about the editorial you read and the List of Shame? If yes, in what way? If not, why not?

- What else might it be useful to know if you wanted to assess the validity of each of the prevention strategies mentioned in the List of Shame?

- Do you ever check facts you read by looking at other sources? Why? / Why not?

- How trustworthy are the following sources of information for you? If it depends, what on?

a web page	a school textbook	a newspaper
Wikipedia	an academic article	a friend
TV news	government stats	

FILE 9

Unit 2 page 21   SPEAKING

Student C

1 You have been assigned to collaborate with a new classmate on an assessed project, but you find her quite hard work. She doesn't contribute much to discussions and you feel she's not pulling her weight in other ways.

2 Your best friend has started going out with someone who from the first moment got on your nerves. It's difficult to put your finger on why you just don't like him / her, but recently you've had the feeling that maybe he / she fancies you!

3 You think your husband / wife is too soft with your children and far too indulgent. You often refuse to buy the children things and you set clear rules, but then they go to your husband / wife and he / she gives in immediately and undermines you.

FILE 31

Unit 14 page 129   SPEAKING

Student B

As the finance manager, your main role is to provide advice and support to colleagues to enable them to make sound business decisions. You are keen to prevent any risky ventures and to keep costs at a sensible level. You have the following concerns about the items on the agenda:

1 New products

You want to know production and retail costs.

You want to know if every effort has been made to keep costs down.

You want sales projections and to know more about any market research that's been done.

2 Cost-cutting measures

Despite the fact marketing prides itself on saying all products are locally made, you want to suggest outsourcing production of some items to a lower-cost environment. You feel that if outsourcing does not happen, there will either need to be major pay freezes over the coming years or redundancies.

3 Proposed takeover

You realise the bid that has been received is hostile but feel obliged to note it's a good offer. If it could be slightly increased, you'd recommend it to shareholders.

4 Possible strike

The unions are demanding a 5% pay rise. Negotiations are ongoing. Management is offering 1% and is prepared to go to 2%. There's not yet any kind of Plan B in place.

5 AOB

You want to compile a report for shareholders explaining the benefits of the takeover.

FILE 10

UNDERSTANDING FAST SPEECH

Groups of words are marked with / and pauses are marked //. Stressed sounds are in CAPITALS.

Video 1 page 22

I need a LONG DIStance / to MAKE a TURN NOW / like I CAN'T / there's NO WAY I could MAKE ONE of these TURNS down these STREETS / I'm going to have to GO DOWN // and cut Over THREE LANES / to MAKE a LEFT-HAND TURN DOWN THERE

Video 2 page 40

when euroPEans / first CAME to ausTRAlia / what they SAW // in THEIR EYES // were JUST these SAVages / LIving on the LAND / and NOT DOing ANYthing WITH it // and in FACT / they MISSED OUT / ON / one of the GREAtest / SUbtle phiLOsophies / of ANY / CULture / on the PLAnet

Video 3 page 58

the Images proVIded by the HUbble SPACE TElescope / conTInue to aSTOnish / AND aMAZE // AND proVIDE a WINdow / on the WONders of SPACE / no MAtter HOW / you SEE them

Video 4 page 76

i would've been surPRISED // NOT to get that FINding // er beCAUSE it's ACtually / VEry conSIStent with what we KNOW from // FINdings in a LOT of er / NON-human SPEcies.

Video 5 page 94

I HAD to GIVE her mediCAtion / Every TWO HOURS / for aBOUT SEventy-TWO HOURS // i THINK I SLEPT aBOUT / MAYbe THREE or FOUR HOURS / those FIRST COUple of NIGHTS // i would GO through ANY LENGTHS / to SAVE maXINE

Video 6 page 112

that MIGHT be // and i HAVE to GIVE it / SOME WEIGHT // that MIGHT be the Origin / of / the STOry of the SWORD / in the STONE

Video 7 page 130

GENuine US CUrrency / is a COtton and LInen combiNAtion // THAT / ACtually HAS a VEry disTINCT FEEL / and / THERE ARE / RED and BLUE seCUrity / FIbres / THAT ARE / MIXED IN / WITH the CUrrency PAper / AS it's BEing MADE

Video 8 page 148

To the OUTside WORLD / they are the LONG NECKS // WEARers of SHIning RINGS of BRASS / that disFIgure / and deFORM the BODies of THOSE who WEAR them.

FILE 16

Student B

Article 1

Japanese scientists have made see-through frogs commercially available. The frogs, which are sold for around $100 each, were bred for educational purposes. Rather than getting killed and cut open in class, the transparent frogs now allow students to see internal organs in action.

Researchers in Boston had previously created transparent fish to aid them in their study of the development of cancer. The fish, which are genetically similar to humans, have cancerous cells inserted in their bodies so researchers can watch them grow. Studies on normal animals only show cancer development via medical examinations carried out after death. It is hoped a greater understanding of cancer growth will pave the way for new treatments.

Article 2

A nuclear physicist who had had funding requests for research into time reversal rejected has raised $40,000 from the public to carry out his experiment. Professor John Cramer, a leading scientist in quantum mechanics, is attempting to tackle a famous mystery in quantum theory. Sub-atomic particles that have been split in half can travel faster than the speed of light and 'communicate' directly with each other. It may sound like science fiction, but one theory for this is what has been dubbed 'retrocausality' – in other words, the idea that the future can affect the present or past. Professor Cramer's experiments are seen as a first step towards a full exploration of the theory. If successful, he hopes to attract further funding from government.

FILE 19

Group B

ONE OF A KIND

The Aye-Aye **resembles a cross between** a small monkey and a rat because of its rodent-like front teeth. It lives in **the canopy of trees** in the Madagascan rainforest, usually nesting in a fork of the tree. As well as fruit and vegetation, it also eats small worms and insects living in the trees, which it finds in a similar way to a woodpecker. It **taps on the trunk** until it detects a hollow sound, then gnaws away at the bark with its teeth to make a hole before inserting its elongated middle finger in through the hole to pull the grubs out. There is only one other animal that uses this technique: the striped possum.

When **foraging for food**, Aye-Ayes may cover over four kilometres a night as they leap from treetop to treetop. Aye-Ayes are generally **solitary creatures** that only socialise in order to mate, with the female of the species being dominant. The males will often aggressively compete for a female's attention.

The Aye-Aye is endangered because of a number of factors. Firstly, its habitat is being destroyed, increasingly forcing it to **raid villages** for food. It is quite fearless in approaching humans, but unfortunately humans are not always friendly towards it. Villagers not only kill Aye-Ayes because they are a nuisance and eat farm crops, but also because they are believed to be evil – capable of **creeping into homes** and puncturing a person's heart while they sleep.

Although laws exist against killing them and several **reserves in the jungle** have been set up, their numbers continue to decline. Captive breeding programmes are also working to preserve them.

FILE 26

Student A

go wild (crowd / shout / score)

abuse (the referee / scream / shout)

on the edge of your seat (film / excited)

be substituted (manager / replace / change)

sponsor (money / charity)

cramp (muscle / pain)

struggle (difficult / lose / fail)

foster (help)

modify (change / better)

swell up (big / hurt)

a lump (find / cancer)

drift (mind / wander)

stroke (pet / cat / dog / hand)

a break-in (steal / house)

oversee (control / manage)

deadline (hand in / finish)

make redundant (lose / job)

slavery (pay / money / work)

underdog (favourite / win / lose)

grumpy (bad mood / shout)

FILE 21

Unit 10 page 89   CONVERSATION PRACTICE

Student A

Someone you know broke his arm quite badly last year.

Decide how.

It was incredibly painful.

Decide what they did to ease the pain.

They were taken to the Accident and Emergency department of the nearest hospital.

Decide how long they had to wait and what it was like.

They X-rayed the arm and found it was broken. The arm was put in plaster for at least four weeks.

Decide how long the cast stayed on in total and how this affected their life.

They then had to have extensive physiotherapy for a few weeks.

Decide what this involved – and how everything is now.

FILE 33

Unit 14 page 129   SPEAKING

Student D

As head of marketing, your main role is to promote the company's brand and its products. You are very involved in identifying markets and planning promotional campaigns. You have the following concerns about the items on the agenda:

1 New products

Two new products are being put forward by product development: an electronic toothbrush that connects to an app which analyses your brushing routine, and a mini drone – a tiny, remotely controlled, computerised flying machine. You think the latter has far more potential than the former, even though it's much more expensive to produce.

Invent sales projections for each product. Also decide on target markets for each item.

2 Cost-cutting measures

In terms of brand identity and advertising message, it's vital that production stays within your country. If you move production, you fear it will affect profits and make the product seem less reliable. You feel that if savings really need to made, the toothbrush could be sacrificed.

3 Proposed takeover

Use the mention of the takeover to remind everyone that if production goes overseas, share prices will drop. To retain the value of the firm, production needs to stay local.

4 Possible strike

Work on the product must continue. If it's delayed, the drone won't get to market in time for the promotional season. Even if this means offering the workers more money, it's money well spent.

5 AOB

Given the potentially huge market for the drone, you would like an increased marketing budget to allow you to carry out a massive promo campaign.

FILE 24

Unit 11 page 99   CONVERSATION PRACTICE

Student A

You are going to have a conversation with Student B about a sponsored run you have done recently. Look at the notes below and prepare for the conversation. You are going to talk about your topic first.

A few months ago, you took up running again after a long break.

Decide how your general training has been going – including one problem.

Then talk about a run you recently did for charity.

Decide the following:

- *how long it was and where you ran*
- *what time you managed and / or what position you came*
- *how you felt*
- *what you were raising money for*

Student B went to see a sports event last weekend. Think of some questions to ask. Then start the conversation with, 'So what did you get up to at the weekend?'

FILE 20

Unit 9 page 85   SPEAKING

A 63-year-old man was made redundant as part of a round of redundancies and his job was given to a junior colleague who had previously offered his resignation, apparently with a view to developing his career elsewhere. The older man claimed age discrimination and unfair dismissal because his colleague had not had to compete for the job through the redundancy procedure.

During the tribunal it was revealed colleagues sometimes referred to the 63-year-old as Yoda, the wise old Jedi Knight from the film *Star Wars*.

A man is claiming unfair dismissal after he was fired from the branch of the supermarket chain he had worked in for nine years for using his staff discount card in another branch. The store card had been given to all workers as a perk in previous years, but the company had recently restricted its use. The man claims he had been off work sick and was unaware of these changes. Shortly after breaking the news of his sacking to his family, his wife suffered a stroke and died. The company insists the man was guilty of deliberate abuse of staff privileges and all staff had been informed.

A 54-year-old nurse claims her employers have discriminated against her on grounds of her faith after she was taken off front-line duties for refusing to remove the cross she wears around her neck. The woman feels her bosses tried to prevent her from expressing her religious beliefs. The hospital, however, says its actions were motivated by health and safety concerns and that its dress code prohibits staff wearing any type of necklace.

FILE 25

Unit 11 page 99   CONVERSATION PRACTICE

Student B

You are going to have a conversation with Student A about a sports event you saw last weekend. Look at the notes below and prepare for the conversation.

You went to a sports event last weekend.

Decide the following:

- *what the event was*
- *why you went*
- *what the result / score was*
- *two or three key things that happened*

Student A took up running a few months ago after a long break. They recently ran a race for charity. Think of some questions to ask. Student A is going to talk about their topic first. You start the conversation with, 'So how's the running going?'

FILE 30

Unit 14 page 129   SPEAKING

Student A

As Chair, your job is basically to run and control the meeting – and to stop things going too far off track. You will need to:

- introduce and explain the background and purpose of agenda items.
- ensure all items on the agenda are covered.
- mediate if disagreements emerge.
- ensure all sides are heard and that polite interaction is maintained.
- lead debate on each point to some kind of conclusion, summarising where needed.

Try to use some of the phrases below.

- So shall we get started / get down to business, then?
- We seem to be losing sight of the main point here.
- We seem to be getting a bit sidetracked here.
- Could I just bring the discussion back to ..., if I may?
- Can we leave this for now and maybe come back to it later?
- (Name), would you care to add anything to that?
- We haven't heard your thoughts on this yet, (Name).
- So, just to summarise, what you're saying is ...
- So let's move on to the next point on the agenda, shall we?
- Does anyone have any other business they would like to raise?
- Well, I think that covers everything for today.
- The meeting's now officially closed.

FILE 32

Unit 14 page 129   SPEAKING

Student C

As head of product development, your main role is to come up with new ideas for products, conduct market research, oversee the manufacturing and testing, and then launch the product. You are very keen for at least one of your new products to get to market soon. You have the following concerns about the items on the agenda:

1 New products

You have two new products in development: your favourite is an electronic toothbrush that connects to an app which analyses your brushing routine. There's also a mini drone – a tiny, remotely controlled, computerised flying machine.

Invent details of market research that has been carried out, gaps in the market and possible production costs per item.

2 Cost-cutting measures

You believe the most important thing is getting high quality work done – not finding the cheapest provider. You prefer to use companies you know. If work is done overseas, you're worried about shipping times and costs, language barriers and quality controls. You would rather cuts were made to middle management than production, even if this means job losses there.

3 Proposed takeover

You don't have strong feelings about the takeover but want guarantees put in place to ensure your products will continue to get backing if it goes ahead.

4 Possible strike

The strike would delay production. You want to suggest finding other local workers who could do the work if it goes ahead.

5 AOB

Given the amount of work you are involved in, you would like to take on a new member of staff to assist you. They would need to be relatively experienced.

Student B

THE ASSASSINATION OF JOHN F KENNEDY

THE FACTS

When John Fitzgerald Kennedy was elected President of the United States in January 1961, not only did he become the youngest man to hold office, but he is also the only Roman Catholic to have ever sat in the White House. The following two years were eventful, to say the least: the Soviet Union sent the first man into space starting the space race in earnest; the construction of the Berlin Wall began; US-USSR tensions came to a dangerous head with the Cuban missile crisis, and the civil rights movement at home gathered momentum. Kennedy also suffered serious health problems and was engaged in numerous extramarital affairs.

Shortly after midday on 22nd November 1963, he was assassinated as he was being driven in an open-topped car through Dallas, Texas. No sooner had news of the killing started spreading around the world than the local police announced the arrest of Lee Harvey Oswald, an employee at the Texas School Book Depository, from which the shots were believed to have been fired. Oswald denied the charges and claimed he was being framed. To add spice to the story, he was a former US marine who had defected to the Soviet Union three years earlier and had only returned six months before the killing.

Two days later, Oswald was in transit to the local county jail when, in front of millions of Americans watching live on TV, he was fatally shot by a man named as Jack Ruby, a local nightclub owner. Ruby was then arrested and charged with murder but died of cancer in police custody in 1967.

An initial inquiry concluded both killers had acted alone. Later inquiries, though, challenged these findings and suggested there may well have been two gunmen involved in the President's assassination.

THE DEBATE

Despite most academic research supporting the 'lone wolf' theories, at no time has it ever been definitively established that both men acted alone. Indeed, over 60% of Americans still believe one of the numerous conspiracy theories that have been put forward, with the most popular being:

1 The Soviets / KGB did it

At the time of JFK's death, relations with the USSR were at a low and many contend that the then Soviet Premier Nikita Khrushchev ordered the killing after the embarrassment of having to withdraw nuclear missiles from Cuba.

2 The Mafia did it

The Mafia had invested heavily in Cuban casinos and were badly affected by the failed US attempt to invade the nation. As such, some suggest they vented their anger by ordering the hit.

3 The Cubans did it

As it is known that JFK tried unsuccessfully to have Cuban President Fidel Castro assassinated on several occasions, it seems logical to believe the reverse may also have been attempted. Indeed, Lyndon Johnson, the man who succeeded Kennedy as President, made the claim on ABC News in 1978.

4 Lyndon Johnson did it

Who stood to gain the most from Kennedy's death? The man who would follow him into the White House. One theory is that the killing was organised by Johnson, motivated by greed and ambition and assisted by members of the CIA.

Student B

chant (sing / repeat)

fade (tired / race)

doping (drugs / ban)

scrape through (tournament / exam)

fix (repair / bribe)

overturn (change / referee / judge)

trigger (start)

defy (refuse / impossible)

collaborate (help / work together)

let off steam (angry / relax)

a pun (same / funny)

a filling (tooth / hole)

mortality (death)

shrug (move / don't care)

glare (angry / stare)

a falling-out (friend / speak)

input (put in / computer)

strategy (tactics / plan)

childcare (nursery / child / son)

subsidise (money / cheaper)

STONEHENGE

THE FACTS

So mysterious is the prehistoric monument of Stonehenge that over a million people a year make the journey to Wiltshire in the west of England to marvel at it. Consisting of over 150 massive upright stones placed in a circular layout, the site is owned by the Crown and maintained by a charity called English Heritage.

The larger stones used in its construction are believed to have been sourced locally. They reach up to nine metres and weigh over 20 tons. The smaller stones come from the Preseli Hills in Wales over 150 miles away, though the method by which they were transported remains unknown.

It is generally accepted that the stones were erected over a period of hundreds of years and experts estimate that the work must have required at least 30 million man-hours. To put this in perspective, that's four times more man-hours than were needed to construct the Empire State Building! The builders of Stonehenge must have used advanced mathematical and structural techniques, though who put up the stones, how they managed it and why all remain hotly disputed.

THE DEBATE

Who built Stonehenge?

In the seventeenth century, an archaeologist called John Aubrey claimed the site was the work of Celtic high priests known as Druids. The subsequent discovery of linked burial sites boosted support for this notion. Not until the 1950s, when carbon dating indicated it originated at least 1,000 years before the arrival of the Celts, was the theory disproved. Nevertheless, such is the romance of this theory that even today people who identify as modern Druids still gather at Stonehenge for the summer solstice.

It is now generally believed that three separate tribes were involved in the lengthy construction process, each undertaking a different phase. The degree to which information was transmitted from one group to another is still not known.

How was it built?

We know that different sections of the monument were built at different times, but the greatest mystery is how stones weighing about four tons were brought from Wales. Numerous theories have been put forward: many have argued they were rolled on tree trunks or tiny rocks; others have claimed that icy glaciers could have carried them near to the site. And, of course, there will always be those who believe aliens were somehow involved – or magic!

What was Stonehenge for?

One popular theory is that ancient astronomers used the site as a form of solar calendar and that it helped them track the movements of the sun and moon. This idea stems from the fact that the entrance faces the rising sun on the longest day of the year, 21st June. A connected notion is that it may have been built on a supposedly sacred site already used for solar worship.

Recent excavations have cast doubt on these theories, however, as hundreds of human bones have been uncovered. The bones date across a thousand years, giving rise to the idea that Stonehenge served as an ancient burial ground for high-ranking individuals.

In the end, only one thing is sure. In the absence of any documentary evidence, speculation will continue for years to come.

FILE 17

Student C

Article 1

Researchers have discovered that autism sufferers who inhale the hormone oxytocin are better at noticing facial signals and maintaining eye contact. The so-called 'love' hormone is found in high levels in breast milk and is thought to be responsible for the development of the special, close relationship between mother and child. Previous studies have also shown those with autistic conditions may have an oxytocin deficiency.

The experiment focused on sufferers who did not have particularly impaired language skills but who struggled with face-to-face contact. Currently, other drugs are prescribed to deal with more visible symptoms such as anxiety, but researchers believe this could be a breakthrough in dealing with the underlying causes of autism.

Article 2

A study by vets in Britain has revealed that, on average, cat owners are more intelligent than dog owners as cat owners typically have a higher level of education. The researchers suggest that this is unlikely to be a result of exposure to the famously independent and cunning pets but rather is due to the fact that cats tend to require less attention and are thus a better fit with busy lifestyles. As highly educated people are likely to work longer hours in more high-powered jobs, they tend not to have the time to look after a dog. This is just one finding of a census undertaken by the Department of Clinical Veterinary Science at the University of Bristol.

FILE 36

Student B

Read the four short texts and the related questions below.
Be ready to explain to your partner what you read and to discuss the questions.

The UK Health and Safety Executive, which monitors compliance with health and safety regulations and sets guidelines, investigated several hundred examples of 'health and safety gone mad' stories and suggested that at least 200 were unfounded. Some stories were simply invented, some were misunderstandings of actual events, while others utilised the idea of excessive health and safety regulations in order to deflect attention from other unpopular decisions. For example, a story about making children wear goggles to play a playground game called 'conkers' was actually just based on a joke the head teacher had made. The fire station that was built without the traditional pole was not the result of excessive regulations but rather of a lack of space. Finally, while many accidents are caused by having improper footwear, the HSE suggested there were not actually any health and safety issues with regard to flip-flops in offices.

Statistics have found that road traffic accidents in the UK almost halved from 4,229 in 1992, the year when speed cameras were first introduced, to 1,754 twenty years later. A similar effect happened in France, where fatalities fell from 7,655 to 3,963 in the ten years post introduction. France currently makes €1.5 billion from speeding fines, while the system itself only requires €200 million for maintenance and improvements.

The Centre for Disease Control and Prevention in the US estimated that the cost to society of excessive alcohol consumption was well over $200 billion.

The survey of teachers quoted in the List of Shame was conducted with 600 teachers by a TV channel called Teachers' TV.

- Do the extra pieces of information affect the way you think about the editorial you read and the List of Shame? If yes, in what way? If not, why not?
- What else might it be useful to know if you wanted to assess the validity of each of the prevention strategies mentioned in the List of Shame?
- Do you ever check facts you read by looking at other sources? Why? / Why not?
- How trustworthy are the following sources of information for you? If it depends, what on?
  a web page　　　　　Wikipedia　　　　　TV news
  a school textbook　　an academic article　government stats
  a newspaper　　　　a friend

FILE 18

Unit 8 page 71   CONVERSATION PRACTICE

FILE 34

Unit 15 page 135   CONVERSATION PRACTICE

Group C

BILBAO

Since its completion in 1997, the Guggenheim Museum in Bilbao, the capital of the Basque region of northern Spain, has become one of the most famous buildings in the world. Many people will have visited the city just to see it and found a flourishing city with a vibrant nightlife. However, fewer will be aware of the profound change that **the gallery symbolises**. Up until the early 80s, Bilbao had been **dominated by steel plants** and shipbuilding, which brought wealth but which also created heavy smog that choked the city. However, during the latter part of that decade, the city was hit by an economic downturn that saw many factories close down and **unemployment soar**. The city was also affected by threats and acts of terrorism by the Basque Separatist group, ETA. Apart from causing problems for local people, all of this also **discouraged inward investment** and tourism to the city. Over the years, many factories closed down and thousands of people **abandoned the city**, leaving contaminated land and large numbers of condemned buildings.

To halt the decline, the city **embarked on a strategy** to reinvent itself as a centre for culture, tourism and new technologies. Obviously, constructing a series of major buildings designed by famous international architects was a key part of this process. However, it's important to recognise it was only *one* part of the strategy. Other cities trying to replicate the so-called 'Guggenheim effect' may have failed because they didn't take up the other strands of Bilbao's regeneration project. These included **ongoing heavy investment** in training and education with a

particular focus on computing and technology. The city improved transport links and created two metro lines, and also developed service industries such as **hosting events** and conferences. It also modernised what remained of its more traditional industries and attracted new companies to the technology park on the outskirts of the city.

There have been some **voices of opposition** that suggest the process did not benefit many of the working-class people most affected by the original crisis. Nevertheless, it's difficult to deny it's been a success which has seen the city return to its previous population levels and **survive the major recession** that began in 2008.

Student C

Someone you know got badly burned a few months back.

Decide how.

They were rushed to hospital and put on a drip.

Decide who went with them, what the hospital staff were like and how everyone felt.

They had to have a skin graft.

Decide where and add any extra details about the procedure that you want.

An infection developed under the graft.

Decide how and what was done about it.

The scarring took a while to heal.

Decide what impact it had on your friend's life – and how they are now.

Student A

You are the host of the programme. Think about how you are going to introduce the show and summarise today's talking point. You may want to mention recent incidents that you feel are connected to the topic. Also, think of two or three more related questions you might put to callers.

AUDIO SCRIPTS

UNIT 1

▶ TRACK 1

1

A: How was your trip?

B: Great. Really amazing. Have you ever been there?

A: No. What's it like?

B: It's really wild. It took me by surprise, actually.

A: Yeah?

B: Yeah. I don't know what I expected, really. I just thought it'd be quieter, but the nightlife is totally insane.

A: Really?

B: Honestly. We went out with these people and ended up in a place at about four in the morning and it was absolutely packed.

A: Yeah?

B: Seriously. You literally couldn't move. In fact, the whole city was still buzzing. You can still get stuck in traffic at that time of night.

A: Wow!

B: Actually, that was a bit of a pain, the congestion.

A: Really? Is it bad?

B: Unbelievable! You just spend hours and hours in the taxi crawling along with everyone sounding their horns. You'd be quicker walking, really.

A: So did you?

B: No, it's unbearably humid, so at least the car has air con. Honestly, you walk out of your hotel and it's like hitting this thick wall of heat. You just die walking in that heat for any length of time.

A: There must be a fair amount of pollution, then.

B: That as well. The smog is incredible. I mean, our hotel was supposed to have this amazing view – and I guess it would be on a clear day – but half the time you can hardly see a thing. And you nearly choke on the fumes when you're outside.

A: Sounds pretty awful. Are you sure it's so great?

B: Well, you know, it does have its drawbacks but, as I say, it just has a real buzz – especially downtown with the skyscrapers and the neon lights flashing and the people and the noise. It's just a really, really vibrant place.

2

C: What's your home town like? It's supposed to be nice, isn't it?

D: It is, if you like that sort of place.

C: What do you mean?

D: It's just very conservative. You know, it's very affluent – you see loads and loads of people in fur coats and posh cars, and the streets are spotless, but it's also just incredibly dull. There's not much going on.

C: Right.

D: I know it's a bit more run-down here, but at least it's more lively. There's more of a music scene, you know.

C: Yeah, I know what you mean. So you wouldn't consider going back to live there?

D: Maybe. I mean, don't get me wrong, it is a good place to live if you're bringing up kids – everything works very smoothly and, as I say, there's not a trace of litter on the streets. So if I were to settle down, I might move back. It's just not what I want right now.

C: Fair enough.

▶ TRACK 2

1

A really terrible thing happened to a woman I used to work with. One day, she woke up and found her car had been stolen from outside her house. So she called the police and reported it, but when she got back home from the office that night, the car had been returned. It was in the driveway. It had been completely cleaned and there was a note on the driver's seat apologising for taking it. Whoever had written the note said that his mum had been taken ill and he'd had to drive her to hospital. Next to the note there were a couple of tickets for a concert the following day. The woman was really thrilled, you know, so happy – her car back, two free tickets, fantastic! So she called a friend and they both went to the concert and had a really fantastic time. Once she got home though, ...

2

Someone told me a story about a guy from Tokyo who'd gone on a golfing holiday. On the third or fourth day, he suddenly collapsed and had to be rushed to hospital for treatment. Eventually, they diagnosed him as having been poisoned and they reported the incident to the police. The detective in charge of the case questioned the man, but he couldn't think of any reason why anybody would want to poison him. It was something really silly in the end. They worked out ...

3

This mad thing happened to a guy that a friend of my brother knows. Apparently, one day he went to a supermarket to buy a few bits and pieces and as he was walking up and down the aisles looking for the bread, he noticed this elderly woman just staring at him with these desperately sad eyes. He turned away, grabbed a loaf and went off in search of some milk. Once he'd found the milk, he turned round only to see the same woman there again – still just staring like mad at him. Anyway, he was getting a bit freaked out by this, as you would, so he rushed off to pay, but then he remembered that he'd run out of toilet paper and so he went back to get some. When he got back to the cashier, there was the old woman again – in front of him in the queue and her trolley was almost full to the brim. This time she turns to him and she says, 'I'm really sorry for staring, but the thing is, you're the spitting image of my son who died last year.' She's wiping her eyes, getting all tearful, and she says, 'You've got the same eyes, the same hair. It's incredible.' As she was packing all her stuff away, she whispered to the guy and said, 'Could you do me a tiny little favour? Could you just say "Goodbye, Mum" when I leave? It'd mean the world to me.' Well,

what was he going to do? This little old lady and her tragic story, trying to hold back the tears. So, as she's leaving the store, struggling with all her shopping, he shouts out, 'Goodbye Mum.' He felt like he'd done his good deed for the day, but then ...

▶ TRACK 3

1

Once she got home though, she discovered she'd been burgled and all her valuables had been stolen. Then, to top that, about a week later, the police called her and told her that her car had been used as the vehicle to get away from a major bank robbery on the day that it had gone missing. That is so unlucky, no?

2

It was something really silly in the end. They worked out that the man had actually poisoned himself by accident. Apparently, when he was playing golf he used to hold the tee – that plastic thing you put the golf ball on – between his teeth as he was walking round between the holes, but the golf course had been sprayed with pesticide, so he was basically just sucking in toxic pesticide.

3

He felt like he'd done his good deed for the day, but then the cashier told him his bill was like £300. He said there must've been a mistake as he'd only bought a few things, but then the cashier explained. She said, 'Yes, I know, but your mother said you'd pay for all her shopping as well!'

UNIT 2

▶ TRACK 4

1

A: So how's it all going? Any better?

B: I'd say things are worse if anything, to be honest. He doesn't seem to have a clue how the department should work or what's expected of him and he's dragging the whole team down with him. I've tried to talk to him about it, but he always just gets really defensive and puts up this great big barrier and basically just tells me to get on with my work. What really drives me mad, though, is the man's arrogance. He's so full of himself! He's one of those people who'll just never accept they've made the wrong decision. He just blames it all on everyone else – mainly those below him.

A: Sounds like an idiot to me! Maybe you need to go over his head and talk to his line manager about it.

B: Oh, it's not worth it. He isn't exactly the most approachable person and from what I've heard he wouldn't take any notice, anyway. They seem oblivious to criticism, these people. All they're interested in is sucking up to whoever is above them in order to get ahead.

2

C: I can't stand him.

D: Really? I've always thought he comes across as a really decent guy.

C: You're joking, aren't you? He's so fake!

D: D'you think so? In what way?

C: All that rubbish about saving the world and helping the starving millions that he's always going on about.

D: What's wrong with that? I quite admire the fact that he's prepared to stand up for what he believes in. There are plenty of people in the public eye who just aren't bothered about those things. It'd be easier for him to just keep his mouth shut.

C: I wouldn't say that. I'd say it's all just self-promotion. It's just to sell more of his music. If he was really bothered, he'd give his millions away and really help people. He just likes to be seen to be doing good.

D: I just think you've got him wrong. He's done a lot to raise awareness of various different causes and he works really hard to make a difference. You're just a cynic.

C: And you're just naïve!

3

E: So what're the people on your corridor like? Are you getting on OK with them all?

F: Yeah, more or less. I haven't really seen much of the guy next door. I think he studies Medicine so he's either at lectures or studying. He certainly keeps himself to himself, anyway.

E: OK.

F: But the girl opposite is great. She's really nice and very bright and chatty. We hit it off straight away.

E: That's good, then.

F: Yeah, she's from the States and came over to do a Master's in International Law.

E: Really? So she's a bit older than you, then.

F: Yeah, but she certainly doesn't make a thing of it. She's a great laugh. The only problem is she kind of takes over the bathroom every morning. She's in there for hours doing her hair and her make-up. It's really annoying because we've only got the one bathroom.

E: Oh no! Really? That'd drive me mad, that would!

F: And the guy on the other side of me seems pleasant enough, but he strikes me as a bit of a slacker. I mean, I see him throwing a frisbee around with people outside the hall or sitting around smoking, but I've never seen him go to any lectures or anything, and he just seems ... well ... extremely laid-back about it.

E: To the point of horizontal, then, eh?

▶ TRACK 5

1 The new restrictions? Oh, they brought them in last year.

2 He's not just messing up his own career. He's dragging us down as well.

3 We realised as soon as we embarked on it that it was a good strategy.

4 He made millions, but then gave it all away.

5 Life brings many changes – and I've gone through them all!

6 The buildings aren't fit to live in anymore so they've decided to knock them down.

7 It's quite an ambitious plan, so make sure you set it out clearly.

8 There's a big recycling centre there. They set it up a few years ago.

9 If those are your principles, you've got to stick to them.

10 I can never get in the bathroom in the morning. She totally takes it over.

▶ TRACK 6

1

When he was a toddler, I'd do the childcare most days and he was always a bit of a handful. I did try and instil a bit of discipline into him, but I'm not sure it really happened at home. My son would shout and tell him off, but then he'd burst into tears and his mother would comfort him, so totally mixed messages. I knew it would come to no good, but you can't really interfere, can you? Not that he's all bad. He's helped me out sometimes since I've been unsteady on me feet. But really, if it's true, I hope they treat him severely. It's what he needs to get back on the straight and narrow.

2

The frustrating thing is he's a bright lad, but I would say he has a stubborn streak and he's been prone to outbursts and answering back. I remember once I asked him to change desks to sit next to this girl and he just wouldn't – just refused point blank – and then we got into this ridiculous confrontation with neither of us willing to back down. I had to call the Head in the end. So yeah, I guess it doesn't entirely surprise me he's ended up in this kind of trouble. What should happen now? Well, he should obviously be punished, but after that I'd still give him another chance rather than exclude him permanently. I'm sure he'll learn.

3

Oh yeah, hugely talented and I would've thought he could go all the way and turn professional, so this has come as a big shock. Maybe there's more to it than appears to be the case. He certainly conducted himself well here. You know, I push them hard, but he's just taken that in his stride and done everything I've asked of him. He's had the odd dispute on the pitch, but I always took that to be part of the game rather than something particular to him. He confided that his parents were going through a rough patch and I was aware that he had a few issues at school, but I think training and matches were always an escape from that and I made sure he was always focused. Hopefully, this is just a setback rather than the end of his career prospects.

4

I've been treating him since he came in here. He suffered some quite severe blows, but the operation went very well. It helped he was in remarkably good health for someone of his age and although he's a little frail now, I'd expect him to make a complete recovery. We're going to monitor him for a few more days, but we'll probably discharge him next week. From what I understand, he's still a bit confused about what happened, but he seems to think the young man who was arrested had actually come to his aid.

5

He's in my class and we kinda went out for a while. He can turn on the charm and that, but he was just too unreliable. When it came down to it, the only thing he was committed to was his football. We'd arrange something, but then he'd be like, 'Oh, the coach wants to put us through our paces', or 'Coach says we're getting complacent, gotta stay on', 'Early night. Coach says I've gotta conserve my energy for the game.' Tch! I said, 'You might as well go out with Coach cos you've let me down too often!' I probably would've stayed with him if he'd apologised, but he's too proud, inne. Just walked away. It was cold. It's been awkward in

class. I actually saw him the night it happened at this friend's party. I don't know what was up with him. He was acting strangely – staring at the people I was with – and there was, like, a bit of a scene, but I still doubt he'd do something like that.

UNIT 3

▶ TRACK 7

1

C = Chrissy, Z = Zoe

C: Zoe! I'm over here.

Z: Chrissy. How are you? You're looking great!

C: Thanks, so are you. I like that top.

Z: Yeah, it's nice, isn't it? Mehdi got it for me.

C: Very good taste. How is he?

Z: Oh ... he's OK. A bit down.

C: Really? Fed up with the miserable winter?

Z: No, no, not really. It's the people that he seems to be struggling with.

C: Oh?

Z: Yeah, apparently he's sick of our British hypocrisy!

C: Oof, that's a bit harsh, isn't it? It's not as though everyone's like that.

Z: Mmm, I have pointed that out ...

C: Oh, so what's brought that on? Doesn't sound like him.

Z: It's not and I try not to take it personally. It's really more about his work.

C: Oh? Not paying him enough?

Z: Well, that too probably. No, what he hates is all the bitchy comments and gossip.

C: Really? He's not just misinterpreting it? You know, people sometimes just take the mickey and don't mean things to be taken seriously.

Z: Yeah, I know it can be like that sometimes here, and they are more formal where he's from – at least in the work setting.

C: Mmm.

Z: Then again, it might not be the usual jokes.

C: Right.

Z: And I guess the bottom line is that he's just not like that and it makes it difficult to fit in.

C: Tch, oh, that's not good.

Z: No. I mean, people are polite to him, but he just feels it's a bit superficial and that he's always going to be an outsider.

C: Aww, that's such a shame. He's such a lovely bloke.

2

A: How did it go?

B: Oh man, the bureaucracy here! It just drives me insane. We're in the 21st century! You should be able to do everything online rather than doing it in person.

A: I know. Mind you, the thing that really frustrates me is the fact that they only ever seem to have one person serving you.

B: Yeah, yeah. When I went this morning ... it wasn't that they were short-staffed. There were plenty of others in the rest of the office, but all they did was stare at their computer screens or file papers.

A: I know! And when I went to get a parking permit, there was a queue of about 100 people even before the place opened, but they only had two people actually dealing with them all.

B: Oh, tell me about it!

A: Still, people were very funny about it, in that dry, understated way they have here, you know, which I guess is the best outlook to have.

B: Yeah, but then again, how will anything ever change?

3

C: So, how did you find it?

D: Really, really amazing.

C: Yeah, the people there are so welcoming – and the hospitality!

D: I know! I was invited into people's homes or offered tea or dinner so many times.

C: Absolutely. And the other thing I loved about it was the fact that they've managed to maintain their culture and traditions.

D: I guess.

C: You don't think?

D: Yeah, but the flip side is it must be difficult if you don't conform.

C: Mmm, I suppose so.

D: And women are still looked down on and have fewer rights.

C: I'm not sure about that. Just because most take on that traditional home-building role, it doesn't mean they're looked down on, does it?

D: No, of course not, but what I heard from people there is that with the economy developing, more women are starting to study and even work now, and it's the women who are pushing the government to do more to break down barriers. So, you know, there's still a fair way to go.

C: Oh, right, OK. I hadn't grasped all that.

▶ TRACK 8

1   Savannah

I grew up in London, which is incredibly multicultural, so my feelings about British culture have obviously been influenced by that. Half my friends were mixed race like me and we all grew up going to the Notting Hill Carnival, eating curry and kebabs, listening to Jamaican music, American music. You know, a real mixed bag of stuff. Now, though, I live in Lincolnshire, which is much more what you might call traditionally English. It's much whiter, for a start! I'm enjoying it, though, I have to say. I love the countryside up here and the big, empty skies, and I love all the local car boot sales as well. I've picked up some mad stuff there. I've started gardening too and getting into baking, which is a whole new thing for me. My London friends would die laughing if they could see me now!

2   Callum

One thing that bugs me is people talking about 'British' culture when what they really mean, whether they're aware of it or not, is English! Scotland's a separate country with its own distinct cultural heritage. Politically, we're more left wing, but that's not reflected in the British government, which is still dominated by these southern English public school boys.

We're more in control of what goes on up here than we used to be, but personally I'd like even more autonomy – and maybe one day independence! Also, I don't understand why we still cling on to the Royal Family. The only 'God Save the Queen' I'll sing along to is an old anti-royalist punk song! In some ways, I'd like to be seen as a republican and a citizen of the world first, then European and Scottish, or even British – but never English!

3   Amir

Some people might not expect someone like me to be running a fish and chip shop, but for most of me customers it's just not an issue. I was born here as were my parents and I'm as British as anyone else. I just happen to be Muslim as well, that's all. It's no big thing. I mean, it's not exactly unusual nowadays, is it? I do get the occasional comment about it, but I don't let it bother me.

The only time I ever feel vaguely conflicted about my identity is when England play Pakistan at cricket. I can't help it, but I always want Pakistan to do well. There's generally a bit of friendly joking about that with the local lads, but, as I always say, I'm sure most English blokes who end up moving to Spain still want their kids to support the English football team. It's human nature, isn't it?

▶ TRACK 9

1   It's really no big thing.

2   It's just not the done thing.

3   chance would be a fine thing

4   It's the furthest thing from my mind.

5   first thing in the morning

6   It's the sort of thing that makes you glad to be alive.

7   what with one thing and another

8   One thing just led to another.

▶ TRACK 10

As you're no doubt all aware, we live in troubled times, and one reaction to global uncertainty has always been to cling onto this idea of a unified national culture, a culture that everyone living in a particular land shares and participates in. It's an idea that many find very comforting. Sadly, though, I'm afraid it's also something of a myth.

The reality is that identity is a very personal thing, and the individual cultural identities of people living in pretty much any society that you care to name vary so much that it's basically impossible to define common features. And of course, our identities aren't fixed or static. They change over time as a result of our interactions. And in an increasingly globalised world, a world that's driven by commerce, our interactions are becoming more and more complex and multi-layered.

We can easily find ourselves eating a breakfast that's been manufactured by a Swiss company while watching a French TV show we recorded last night on our Korean-made TV. We might then put on a Chinese-produced T-shirt, some American-made jeans and some Italian shoes before getting into a German-made car to drive to work. I should know – that's exactly what I did this morning!

If our habits as consumers complicate our ideas about what it means to belong to a national culture, then so too do our relationships with others. As we get older, we often grow into the many distinct roles we play in life. These different roles often exist independently of each other and when playing a particular role, we sometimes end up only interacting with those directly affected by whatever the role is. This is why it's quite possible for one person to be, for instance, a mother, a wife, a ballet lover, Welsh, British, Jamaican, black, and a marketing manager – without any contradiction.

At the same time, though, we also need to realise that for some people these different roles can cause terrible tensions and can result in individuals abandoning certain roles as they feel they're no longer compatible with the main ways in which they have come to see themselves. I'm sure you can all think of examples of this kind of thing from your own experience of the world.

So where does all of this leave national identity? The historian Eric Hobsbawm has argued that many of the ideas about national cultures that are spread through the education system, through the media, and through public ceremonies and monuments are basically a form of myth-making – and it's the ruling elite who encourage these stories and, of course, who benefit.

UNIT 4

▶ TRACK 11

1

A: I don't know about you, but personally I'm in favour of limiting the salaries of people like bankers and executives.

B: Yeah? Really? How would you do that, though?

A: I don't know. I'm sure it's not without problems, but something's got to be done. Honestly, I just think some of these salaries are obscene – especially when there are people in the same company who you know are earning peanuts.

B: Mmm, yeah. I do know what you mean.

A: And it just distorts everything else because if they're earning that much, it encourages other people to ask for more, and it all just pushes up prices.

B: Mmm, restricting salaries may be OK in principle, but in practice? I mean, even if they do manage to introduce this new law, it's basically going to be unworkable, isn't it?

A: I don't see why. We have a minimum wage so why not a maximum one? The bottom line is that as long as there's the official desire to make it work, then it'll work.

B: Maybe, I guess. So how would this maximum amount be decided? And what would you include in pay? Supposing they were given a boat, or whatever, instead of money?

A: Well, they'd just declare it as part of their income in the normal way, no? And it could be, say, ten times the lowest wage.

B: Only ten? I'm sure they'd be able to find ways round it. And you don't think it'd discourage people from doing those jobs?

A: Some, maybe, but I don't see that as a bad thing. I mean, maybe they'd think about doing other jobs that are more useful. Anyway, I thought you said it was a good idea in theory.

B: I did. I'm just playing devil's advocate. But, as I said, I do have major doubts about how it'd work.

A: Well, personally, I think the benefits far outweigh the difficulties.

2

C: Did you hear about this proposal to bid to hold the Olympics here?

D: Yeah. You don't sound too happy about it.

C: No, absolutely not! I'm totally opposed to it. It's a complete waste of money. Aren't you against it?

D: I'm not really sure where I stand on it, to be honest. Won't the Games make a lot of money if we get them?

C: No! They always talk about them leaving a good legacy and boosting the economy, but it's all rubbish.

D: Really? I can't pass judgement. I don't know enough about it.

C: Doh! Have a look on the Internet. I mean, take Montreal, for example. The Olympics were held there way back in 1976 and the city then took another 30 years to clear off the debt the whole thing created!

D: Seriously?

C: I'm telling you! It's lucky we don't have a hope in hell, so they'll only waste the money on the bid. Imagine if we actually won it, though! It'd be a recipe for disaster. It'd probably bankrupt us!

▶ TRACK 12

A politician has died and has arrived at the gates of heaven **clutching** his bags. The gatekeeper stops him and says, 'Don't make up your mind just yet. Try out hell and heaven first and see what you think.' The politician **hops** in the lift down to hell and when he gets out he finds he's in an incredible seven-star hotel. Many of his old friends are lounging round the huge pool, sipping expensive drinks and **chattering** to each other. When they see him, they all **cheer** 'Hello!' and welcome him over. Later in the day, he **strolls** round the fantastic golf course with his best friend and scores his lowest score ever. Later in the evening, there's a huge party and he dances the night away.

The following day, he goes back to heaven with the music and laughter ringing in his ears. He **steps** into heaven and into a lovely restaurant overlooking a beautiful beach. There is soft classical music and the murmur of gentle conversation. After his meal, he **strolls** along the beach and **gazes** at the beautiful sunset. He returns to his hotel and settles into his super-comfy bed and falls fast asleep.

In the morning, he goes to the gatekeeper who asks him, 'So, what d'you think? Have you decided?' And the politician says, 'You know, don't get me wrong, heaven was great – all very relaxing and lovely – but, I have to say, I would never have imagined that hell could be so much fun.' So, he waves goodbye and happily **skips** into the lift to take him down to hell.

When the doors open, though, he is faced with a scene of devastation. It's like there's been an earthquake, or something. He **peers** into the distance and **spots** some people on the horizon. As he walks towards them, he sees that they are his friends **trudging** along under the weight of heavy rocks while the devil **yells**, 'Work harder!' Some are **crawling** on the floor in exhaustion and hunger. The politician goes up to the devil and **gasps**, 'But what are you doing? What's happened? Where's the hotel? The golf? The party?' The devil **chuckles** and shakes his head. 'Oh dear, you should know. That was the election campaign and now you've voted!

▶ TRACK 13

1

I used to like watching *Star Quality*, but since this scandal has erupted I've lost interest in it. This story leaked out that they were encouraging people to phone in even though they'd already decided the result. They were manipulating things so that one guy didn't get voted off because it helped the programme's ratings if they had a kind of hate figure. I might not have minded so much if the calls were free, but they're making a fortune on them.

2

We only called a vote because negotiations were going absolutely nowhere and, despite the massive support we've received from our members, the management is persisting with a ridiculous offer that will basically result in a drop in the value of wages next year. If they hadn't been so reluctant to negotiate, we would not be taking this action now. We understand the public's anger and frustration – we share it – but the blame for this dispute lies firmly with the train company, not with us.

3

I'm totally in favour of a vote on the issue. The way the current system works, some parties get a seat with only 100,000 votes, while others who poll more than twice that don't get any. In the run-up to the election, the New Party had promised to hold one if they got into power, but in the event all that talk has faded away. I guess if they hadn't won a landslide victory, they'd be keener to bring about electoral reform, but I truly believe the vast majority of the electorate still wants to see a change and would vote yes, whatever their reservations.

4

To be honest, I suspect that if they'd called on another day, I wouldn't have taken part, but I was at a bit of a loose end when the researcher called and so had some time to spare. It took about half an hour, and I have to admit I quite enjoyed it – moaning about the government! Mind you, when the results were published in the paper, I was a bit taken aback. It seems I'm in a small minority. People must be mad!

5

It's easy to be cynical and to say that it changes nothing – that it's all just done to create the illusion of fairness and inclusivity – but I can assure you that simply isn't the case here. Given that relatively few people vote these days, we feel it's essential for young people to learn that democracy can contribute to positive change. Apart from deciding things like the end-of-term trips, pupil reps can also decide on policy. It's unlikely we would've abolished uniforms if we didn't have a body like this. It isn't compulsory to vote, but nearly everyone does.

UNIT 5

▶ TRACK 14

1

A: Hey, Maddy. You're in late today. Are you OK? You look tired.

B: I am. I'm exhausted. I didn't crawl home till almost three.

A: Yeah? How come?

B: Oh, this friend of mine … it was her 25th and we'd organised a surprise party.

A: Oh, that's nice. I bet she was pleased.

B: Yeah, she was, although she actually burst into tears when she first came in.

A: Oh no!

B: Yeah. She's been through a lot recently, which is partly why we'd planned the do.

A: Cheer her up?

B: Yeah, exactly. Anyway, she was clearly a bit overwhelmed by it all at first, but she soon got over it.

A: Oh, well, that's good. Where was it?

B: In this bar in town. We hired a room and managed to book this band who were friends of hers.

A: Oh really? Were they any good?

B: Yeah, brilliant. They do this kind of old school rock and roll stuff and they went down really, really well. Honestly, everyone was up dancing.

A: Was Marco there?

B: But of course! Giving it his all on the dance floor as usual.

A: Ah, he's so full of himself, that guy. He thinks he's God's gift to women!

B: Oh, that's a bit harsh. He seems pretty harmless to me. He just loves a good dance.

A: Yeah? Well, it could just be me, I suppose. Glad he behaved himself, anyway.

B: Yeah. Hey, talking of dancing, are you still going to those tango classes?

A: Yeah, on and off.

B: You must be getting quite good, then.

A: I wouldn't go that far. I'm still a bit prone to treading on toes.

2

C: Oh, Almir. Hi. I'm glad I caught you. I just wanted to check whether you've managed to sort everything out for the big meeting yet.

D: Yup. It's all in hand – and I've also booked a table at St John's for the evening.

C: That sounds perfect. I didn't mean to hassle you. I'm just stressing about it.

D: That's all right. I'm sure it'll all be fine.

C: Yeah, of course it will. It's just that I could do without it at the moment. I've got far too much on.

D: I can imagine. Anyway, as I said, it's all under control.

C: That's great. Thanks for being so on top of things.

D: No problem at all.

C: Oh, by the way, how was your meal the other night?

D: It was great, thanks. We went to this new place, Porchetta?

C: Oh yeah. How was the food?

D: Amazing, but there was so much of it! They do something like six or seven courses. I lost count after a while.

C: That must've been quite filling.

D: It was. I was ready to burst by the end of it all! It was a bit too much, to be honest.

C: Mmm.

D Actually, I almost forgot … there was a bit of a scene while we were there.

C: Oh?

D: Yeah. This guy at a table in the corner just suddenly burst out screaming at one of the waiters.

C: Really? How come?

D: I'm not sure, actually. I didn't catch it all, but it was about something daft – like a dirty fork, or something.

C: Strange!

D: I know. There was a kind of awkward silence in the room while it was all going on.

C: I bet. That can't have been much fun.

D: Mmm.

C: So what happened in the end, then?

D: Oh, they managed to get him to leave. But otherwise, yeah, it was good.

▶ **TRACK 15**

1 A: That must've been pretty dull.

   B: Awful! I couldn't stop yawning.

2 A: You can't be feeling your best at the moment.

   B: Actually, I feel surprisingly fresh.

3 A: He can't have been very pleased when he found out.

   B: You can say that again! He went totally mental!

4 A: You must be glad you didn't go now.

   B: Absolutely! It obviously didn't live up to the hype.

5 A: That can't have been cheap.

   B: You'd be surprised, actually. It wasn't as pricey as you'd think.

6 A: She must've been feeling quite unwell.

   B: Yeah, I guess so. I mean, she's usually the last person to leave, isn't she?

7 A: Judging from his accent, he can't be from here.

   B: No, I know. He sounds Australian or something, I thought.

8 A: You must be joking!

   B: No, honestly! I'm deadly serious.

▶ **TRACK 16**

P = Presenter, B = Bryan Sewer

P: For several years now, Mark Zuckerberg, the billionaire co-founder of Facebook, has been making very public – and often quite eccentric – New Year's resolutions. There was the year he promised to only eat meat that he'd killed himself and the time he vowed to learn Mandarin Chinese; then there was the year when he tried to meet a different new person who wasn't an employee every single day. And then in 2015, he announced he'd be switching his media diet towards reading more books. He planned to get through one every fortnight. To aid him in this pursuit, he set up a page called *A Year of Books* on his own social networking site, where recommendations could be dissected and discussed. Its impact was both dramatic and immediate.

With its focus on learning about different cultures, beliefs, histories and technologies, the page soon had half a million followers, and was making a huge difference to sales of selected titles. Purchases of *The End Of Power* by Venezuelan journalist Moisés Naím rocketed after it was chosen as the first title for consideration, with the book jumping to the top of Amazon's economics chart overnight!

The degree to which Zuckerberg will continue to influence popular purchases remains to be seen, but the venture is very much in keeping with broader cultural trends. Social media has had a marked influence on reading choices over recent years, with, for instance, tens of thousands sharing current enthusiasms on Twitter, using hashtags like 'amreading' or 'fridayreads'. We are also seeing what UNESCO has dubbed 'a mobile reading revolution' across the developing world, where in the past paper-based products were hard to come by. Now though, according to one recent survey, 62% read more as they can freely access books on their phones. This has resulted in initiatives such as the Africa-wide cell phone book club, started by a Zimbabwean librarian. Of course, all this online activity is an extension of the face-to-face reading groups which have thrived since the start of the century. If you'd googled the phrase 'book club' back in 2003, it would've returned around 400,000 hits; try it today and you're guaranteed more than 30 million! In Britain alone, there are now an estimated 40,000 reading groups, with people meeting to discuss their latest literary loves in private homes or cafés, in libraries and in bookstores. This phenomenon has resulted in specialist gatherings, such as a Vegan Book Club and a Socialist Feminist group, as well as meetings specifically targeted at lovers of crime novels and even comics! Now, let's say each club has around ten members, and picks perhaps six books a year, then that's 60 books per club and almost two and a half million sales per year. And that's before you even factor in the power of Facebook! Not everyone, though, sees these trends in such a positive light. Here's literary critic Bryan Sewer:

S: Let's face it, most reading groups are little more than gossiping circles, or else simply a literary guise for dating clubs! I know from my own observations that when members do finally get round to discussing books, the discourse is generally basic and displays limited insight or intelligence. I also suspect that these groups consume far too much sentimental autobiographical writing. One can only assume it must be easier for a mass audience to digest.

P: Such opinions, though, seem to have had little impact and certainly haven't halted the spread of communal reading. Indeed, one book club favourite, *Reading Lolita in Tehran* by Azar Nafisi, details the impact that the experience of reading and discussing frequently banned Western books in the Iranian capital in the 1990s had on the lives of eight young women. The appeal, it would seem, is universal.

UNIT 6

▶ **TRACK 17**

1

A: Argh!

B: What've you broken? Oh my word! What a mess!

A: Don't!

B: OK! Calm down! It's not the end of the world!

A: Don't tell me to calm down. If only you'd put things away properly!

B: I'm sorry?

A: That is your bag, isn't it?

B: Oh … yeah, I was going to take it to my room …

A: Well, I wish you had. I almost broke my neck!

B: OK. Sorry. It's not as though I did it deliberately.

A: That's not the point. You're constantly leaving your stuff lying around. You know, I'm not your mother to clear up after you.

B: Right, of course – Mr Perfect!

A: Come on! That's not what I'm saying!

B: Well, that's what it sounds like. It's not as if you're the only one who does stuff round the house.

A: Yeah. OK. Whatever. Listen, forget it. I wish I hadn't said anything.

B: No, if that's how you really feel …

A: No, it came out wrong. I'm sorry. It's just that it's been a long day and this was the last straw.

B: OK. Well, I am sorry. I will make an effort, although in this particular case I went to answer a phone call and then I forgot about it.

A: Whatever. It's done. Can we just move on?

B: OK. Can I give you a hand?

A: Yeah. Can you grab the dustpan and brush?

2

C: Miriam, could I have a word?

D: Erm, could we not talk later? I'm actually in a bit of a hurry, as it happens.

C: I'd rather not leave it.

D: Oh, OK. What's wrong?

C: Listen. I just had a phone call from that group who were coming in July and they're cancelling.

D: What? You're joking?

C: I wish I was. Apparently, they were unhappy with the service they were getting.

D: What? They haven't even been in touch recently. I assumed everything was fine.

C: They said they'd asked about discounts, but you hadn't got back to them.

D: Er … yes, but I passed that on to you.

C: When?

D: A couple of weeks ago! I assumed you'd dealt with it.

C: Why? Didn't you even reply to them?

D: No.

C: Or think to bring it to my attention?

D: Well, you were the one who said you wanted to take control of everything.

C: What? When?

D: Last month – in the departmental meeting.

C: What? That's not what I said at all.

D: You said, 'We've got to get a grip of costs' and that everything had to go through you.

C: That was different.

D: Really? You kind of left us feeling as if we were doing it all wrong and it was as though we'd been wasting money left, right and centre.

C: Really? That certainly wasn't my intention. I wish you'd said something sooner.

D: I would have, but you hardly come out of that office.

C: Well, it's just that I have a tremendous amount on.

D: We actually understand that, but try to see it from our point of view. We want to help, but how can we if you don't communicate more with us?

C: I send out a weekly update.

D: OK, no offence, but that's not exactly the most human thing. I'm not saying it's not helpful – it's just that we'd all appreciate a bit more face-to-face contact.

C: OK, I hear you. And I can see we've got our wires crossed.

D: That's OK, I should've followed up the email. I was probably being a bit petulant, for which I apologise.

C: OK. Well, it's done now. I'm glad we've cleared the air.

D: Is it worth getting back to them?

C: No, I've spoken to them already. Let's just move on. There's no point crying over spilt milk.

▶ TRACK 18

1

A manager of the soft drinks company Jazz Drinks is standing trial today accused of spying for its biggest rival, Pit-Pots. Dan Craddock, a high-level manager at Jazz, is said to have sold crucial strategic information to Pit-Pots for over two million dollars. Over recent years, the two companies have been engaged in a fierce battle to capture market share, pouring money into ever more extravagant advertising campaigns. Last year was Jazz Drinks' best ever and as Pit-Pots was losing ground, it is claimed they secretly recruited Mr Craddock, a sales director at Jazz, to pass on information on marketing and pricing strategy for the coming year. Mr Craddock denies the charges. The case continues.

2

The TV presenter Jonas Bakeman is fighting to save his career after stories appeared of his affair with a researcher on his programme, *Justice Fight*. As reporters laid siege outside his home, he released a statement expressing regret over the affair, but defended himself against allegations that he'd initiated it after aggressively pursuing the woman, Petra Campbell. He claimed the affair had been brief and he had simply surrendered to a foolish moment of weakness at a production party. However, Ms Campbell has made available evidence that she had been bombarded with emails and text messages of a personal nature, and that the affair had been far from 'brief'. Bosses of the TV company are to meet tomorrow to consider Mr Bakeman's future.

3

Campaigners have claimed victory in their battle against full-body scanners in airports following a court decision supporting a woman who refused to accept a scan. A number of civil liberties groups had joined forces to back the woman in an attempt to defeat the government's proposals that everyone travelling by plane should have to pass through the machines. The campaigners say it is a gross invasion of privacy as the scanners can see through clothing. The government has said that it will not retreat in its policy and believes the scanners play a crucial role in protecting the public from terrorism. It plans to appeal against the decision.

4

And finally, peace has now broken out in the village of Paulston. A dispute had been raging over a statue of St John of Bidshire, the multi-prize-winning pig of local farmer Tim Langford. The three-metre pink sculpture, which had been standing at the entrance of the village for over a year, had split the village, with half saying it was hideous, while supporters of Mr Langford said it stood as a proud symbol of the local produce for which Paulston is famous. Protesters had marched onto Mr Langford's land and sprayed the statue with paint. There were then revenge attacks against the vandals. Now the local council has stepped in as peacemaker to solve the dispute. Mr Langford has agreed to the statue being relocated to a nearby sculpture gallery, but it will be moved back to the village during the three-day summer festival.

▶ TRACK 19

1 The two companies have been engaged in a fierce battle to capture market share.

2 ... to pass on information on marketing and pricing strategy for the coming year.

3 He released a statement expressing regret over the affair.

4 She had been bombarded with emails and text messages of a personal nature.

5 Campaigners have claimed victory in their battle against full-body scanners in airports.

6 The scanners play a crucial role in protecting the public from terrorism.

7 ... a statue of St John of Bidshire, the multi-prize-winning pig of local farmer Tim Langford.

8 It stood as a proud symbol of the local produce for which Paulston is famous.

UNIT 7

▶ TRACK 20

1

A: Did you read that thing about transplanting the noses of mosquitoes?

B: What? Are you serious? I didn't think mosquitoes even had noses!

A: Yeah, well, it's obviously not a nose in the sense of our noses, but apparently it's like the smelling receptors on the antennae on their heads. And what they do is they somehow get these receptors to grow inside frog's eggs so that they can do tests on them.

B: How on earth do they do that?

A: To be perfectly honest, I'm not really sure. They extract the DNA from the receptors, or something, and then insert it into the eggs. It's a bit beyond me, really. I just thought it was amazing.

B: It sounds a bit peculiar, if you ask me. I mean, what's the point?

A: Well, apparently, they use them to see what smells trigger the receptors.

B: And?

A: Well, it's to stop the spread of malaria. Obviously, mosquitoes are strongly attracted to the smell of human sweat, but if they can find smells which create a bigger stimulus or which produce no trigger, then they could use those smells to manufacture traps to tempt the mosquitoes away from humans, or spray-on repellents that mask human smells.

B: OK. I suppose that makes sense. I have to say, though, I still find all that gene manipulation a bit worrying.

A: What d'you mean?

B: Well, it's a slippery slope, isn't it? One moment it's mosquito noses, the next they'll be engineering babies.

A: Come off it! It's hardly the same thing!

2

C: Did you read that thing about building a sun shield in space to prevent global warming?

D: No. It sounds a bit unlikely, though. I mean, how big would it have to be?

C: Well, apparently, about 60,000 miles long!

D: 60,000! That's ridiculous! I mean, how on earth are they going to build something that big, let alone get it up there? They struggle to build a stadium here on time and on budget.

C: Well, that's it – the idea with this is it's not like one big structure; it's millions of little reflectors which form a massive 'cloud'.

D: But how many would you need?

C: Trillions. They reckon if they launched a pile of these things every five minutes or so, it'd take ten years to make.

D: Hardly an instant solution, then!

C: No.

D: And what about the cost?

C: I've no idea, to be honest, but they claim it's all quite possible. Anyway, this guy got a grant to look into it further.

D: You're joking! What a waste of money! Are you sure it isn't just a scam or some made-up story?

C: It was on a fairly reliable website. They wouldn't have just made it up.

D: Pah! Mind you, I sometimes wonder whether the whole climate change thing isn't all just a scam. I mean, there are a lot of rich and powerful people out there who stand to benefit from us being scared into believing it's all true.

C: You're not serious, are you?

D: Yeah, why not?

C: Because the evidence is pretty conclusive.

D: Says who?

▶ TRACK 21

1 What on earth for?

2 Why on earth would they want to do that?

3 What on earth's that?

4 Who on earth would buy something like that?

5 Where on earth are they going to get the money for that?

6 What on earth is he going on about?

▶ TRACK 22

P = Presenter, T = Tom Hunter

P: So next, statistics – often thought to be the worst kind of lying there is! A recent survey found that 60% of Britons believe the probability of tossing a coin twice and getting two heads is 50%, rather than the correct answer of 25%. Our guest today, Tom Hunter, thinks this is a worry and says we need to get to grips with stats. Tom, welcome.

T: Hi.

P: So, what's the problem? We don't really make use of stats and probabilities in our daily lives, do we?

T: Oh my! Well, that's a common belief, but gosh! I mean, we're surrounded by statistics: opinion polls, crime figures, product claims in advertising ...

P: Exactly! I mean, it's just used to sell stuff and so we ignore it!

T: Well, of course, statistics can be used to manipulate, but they also inform policy development, scientific progress and many individual decisions. The heart of the matter is that there are good statistics and bad ones. And knowing the difference is empowering.

P: OK. So, how can we tell the good from the bad?

T: Well, we need to recognise that different approaches to data collection have different degrees of validity. And we need to look for underlying problems with any research we encounter.

P: For example?

T: Well, say a food company is having some research done to see if its product has health benefits, right? It has a vested interest in the process, so researchers may get pressured into finding positive results. They may worry about not being employed again, which may affect their conclusions. Similarly, asking 50 people on social media will be less valid than a survey of 5,000 people chosen at random. That's not just because the sample size is too small, but also because social media will tend to attract people of similar views, so this grouping affect may exaggerate the results further.

P: Shouldn't publishers filter out this poor research?

T: Mmm, you'd hope so. Obviously, research in a respected journal, reviewed by other experts, will be better than something published anonymously online, but even peer reviews can underestimate aspects like sample size. And interpretations can also be wrong. So, we always need to be on our guard.

P: Yeah, you mean the wrong conclusions may be drawn, whatever the data?

T: Absolutely. Take the issue of relative and absolute figures.

P: Relative and absolute?

T: Yeah. Say Company A produced 10,000 units last year and increased it to 12,000 this year. That'd be a 20% rise relative to its previous performance and an absolute increase of 2,000 units. Company B, on the other hand, produced 1,000 units last year and 1,400 this year – a rise of 40%. So, by comparing the relative changes, Company B could say it performed twice as well as its rival, but in absolute terms its rival produced an extra 1,600 units compared to Company B.

P: I see.

T: But what's more, Company B may have employed more people to get its increase, while Company A may have achieved theirs whilst cutting staff. So, far from doing 100% better than a rival, Company B's actually being hugely outperformed. And, of course, one year doesn't make a trend. It could just be an anomaly.

P: Maybe they had one client who ordered a huge amount and won't repeat it.

T: Exactly. So you can see it's the focus on either a relative or absolute figure and choosing the start and end point for the figures that can be used to twist data to suit your own ends.

P: Sure. So, what about the probabilities we started with?

T: Well, the initial problem is basic maths. However, people also misunderstand how probability works as a prediction tool. They don't understand variables and the degree to which they're dependent.

P: OK ...

T: If you had just thrown a head, or indeed six heads or ten, the probability of the next throw being a head is still 50%, not 25% or smaller. That's because these are random events out of your control. However, the probability of having a heart attack, say, is dependent on whether you've had one before. If you have, the risk of another is greatly increased.

P: Time to cut down on salt!

T: Well, maybe, but claims about direct correlations also need to be treated sceptically. As an extreme comparison, the fact that TV sales may increase in line with crime does not prove that one affects the other!

P: Well, you're beginning to convince me, but can you give some other examples ...

▶ TRACK 23

Story 1

The main issue here is that it's difficult to interpret this story without knowing the number of accidents per journey or mile travelled. If there were twice as many journeys in fair weather, then the snowstorm has indeed led to an increase in the accident rate. Really, you'd need more evidence over a period of time to fully establish a correlation between accidents and weather. It could be that bad weather really does reduce incidents due to people driving more carefully.

Story 2

The statistics themselves in this study were accurately collected and described. However, the lobby group who commissioned the study were so-called 'stay-at-home mums', and in the interpretation and the narrow time frame of the study, there was a strong element of twisting the data to fit a conclusion they'd set out to find.

The truth, which was ignored in the analysis, is that aggression is a normal developmental stage in which children test boundaries. Not only is aggression normal, it doesn't usually last. The study failed to measure the stay-at-home toddlers' behaviour when they were mixed in groups, where the same levels of aggression can be observed. Indeed, a follow-up study by different researchers discovered that those kids who had been kept at home exhibited more aggression later at school than those who'd been in nursery, i.e. it simply appeared at a later stage.

Story 3

This statistic seems counterintuitive, but only if you ignore other evidence. The study fails to mention that the number of fatalities dropped dramatically. As more people survive accidents, more are treated for injury. Of course, the statistic as it stands also tells us nothing about the severity of the injuries.

Story 4

The group was self-selecting so we might imagine those strongly against animal testing would be more likely to take part, and there's already probably a bias in terms of the readership of the magazine. Furthermore, the poll was actually conducted following a news report on cruelty and mistreatment in one laboratory.

Story 5

The base numbers are all true. However, the starting point that was chosen was the year when there had been a terrorist bombing in the city, which obviously inflated the figures. In previous years, the figures had actually been 94 and 98. Of course, whether any fall in murders can be attributed to government policy is another thing. There could be a number of underlying causes.

UNIT 8

▶ TRACK 24

1

A: Is that you there?

B: Yeah.

A: Where is that? It looks pretty high up.

B: It was in the Dolomites. It's a range in northern Italy. That peak was about 3,000 metres, I think.

A: Wow! The view from up there must've been pretty breathtaking!

B: Yeah, it was stunning, it really was.

A: So, was there a cable car, or something?

B: Cable car! What? You don't think I'm fit enough to climb up?

A: No, no, it's not that. It's just that it looks pretty terrifying. I mean, that's a proper rocky ridge.

B: Yeah, it looks a bit worse than it actually was, to be honest, and there are these fixed metal ropes that you can clip yourself onto. I mean, it's a bit of a scramble, but you don't need any great technical expertise. You can more or less just pull yourself up the worst bits.

A: Really? I'm not sure I'd trust some rusty old cables.

B: No, they're fairly secure. I mean, you need a head for heights, but it's fine. It's not like these guys we saw base jumping.

A: What?

B: You know what it is, yeah? Where they just throw themselves off a cliff and parachute down?

A: Yeah, yeah. It's nuts.

B: I know! We saw people doing it. I mean, all round that area there are these peaks and deep gorges with these incredible sheer cliffs and we watched some guys jump off one in these kind of flying suits.

A: They must have a death wish, those people, they really must.

B: There are videos of them all on YouTube – just search Dolomites and base jumping.

A: Wugh! It gives me the fear just thinking about it!

2

C: Who's that, then?

D: Oh, that's my uncle and cousins ... and that's me.

C: Uh? Oh yeah! How old are you there?

D: I must've been seven or eight, I guess.

C: So where is that?

D: Mauritius. My dad's from there originally and there was a family reunion.

C: Really? So where is Mauritius?

D: It's basically a tropical island in the Indian Ocean.

C: Wow! I was gonna say – you look like you're in a jungle.

D: Yeah, I think it's a national park. There are some more photos if you flick through.

C: Wow! Look at that! Is that a waterfall there?

D: Yeah. That's where we went. I think it might be an old volcanic crater. I'm not sure, I might be making that up.

C: What? And you walked through that?

D: Yeah. They've already hacked trails through it so it's not that hard. I mean, anywhere else and it's really thick dense jungle. You really have to stick to the tracks.

C: Aww. Look at him there in this one, looking all upset.

D: Alright, alright. There's no need to take the mickey. You would've been a bit freaked-out if you'd just been attacked by some creepy-crawly.

C: Aww! Shame. You poor thing.

D: Yeah, yeah. Actually, my mum said I moaned pretty much incessantly on that trip.

C: Oh gosh! Yeah! You look miserable there too, you really do. How can you not be happy there? Look at that. White sand, crystal clear water, palm trees. What's wrong with you? It's like paradise. It's amazing.

D: I was a little English boy, wasn't I? It was too hot. And there's scorpions and snakes and jellyfish and stuff. I was missing home!

C: Man, I'd love to go there, I really would.

D: Yeah, well, I'd probably appreciate it more now.

C: You haven't been there since?

D: Nah, can't afford it. Dad said he spent years in debt from that trip! Hopefully, one day, though.

▶ TRACK 25

1 I wouldn't drive it if I were you, I really wouldn't.

2 The views were just stunning, they really were.

3 The scenery takes your breath away, it really does.

4 I just love it there, I really do.

5 It made no difference whatsoever, it really didn't.

6 He'll never change, he really won't.

7 I've never been anywhere like it, I really haven't.

8 That sounds amazing, it really does.

▶ TRACK 26

It's common knowledge that men and women do things differently, isn't it? The male of the species, we're told, goes quiet and retreats into a cave to brood at the slightest sign of stress, whilst the female reaches out and shares her feelings. After all, women are better communicators, aren't they? That's certainly what writers like John Gray would have us believe, but on what basis do they make this argument? And does it matter?

It's easy to assume these books must be based on valid scientific research, but in reality very few are. Indeed, even a cursory inspection of the literature of linguistics and gender reveals that men and women communicate in remarkably similar ways. Take the notion that women talk more. A book in 2007 reported that women used 20,000 words a day and men just 7,000, but when the claim was challenged, the author, Louann Brizendine, couldn't provide a source and promised to withdraw it from later editions. In fact, research in the journal *Science* has

shown both sexes talk equally as much, and in doing so use on average 16,000 words per day. There's obviously huge variety – from 500 to 45,000 words a day – but significantly, the three chattiest people in the study were all men!

Then there's the belief that men interrupt more because they are biologically more aggressive and programmed to use language more competitively. Evidence from Janet Hyde actually suggests that in neutral situations, where people speak on equal terms, women and men interrupt equally. The neutrality of the situation is important. Some men do speak over others more, but this is not to do with gender but rather the power relationship between the speakers. When talking to a boss we won't butt in, but they will. In fact, when Chambers reviewed a number of linguistic studies investigating gender difference in this and other areas such as empathising, aggression and wordplay, he found an overlap of 99.75% in the way the sexes communicate. In short, no difference whatsoever!

Finally, if these supposed language differences were biological, we would expect them to be universal to all cultures. However, to take just one example, a study in the village of Gapun, Papua New Guinea, found the men pride themselves on their ability to speak indirectly and never say what they mean, while the women frequently give voice to their anger by launching into lengthy swearing sessions – behaviour which is a reversal of the Mars and Venus stereotypes of aggression and indirectness.

So, why do these myths of biological difference and communication persist? Well, sweeping generalisations such as 'Women are more in touch with their feelings' appeal because they match longstanding stereotypes. We look for and cite evidence to back up a traditional view, but ignore or fail to search for contradictory evidence! Take the psychologist Simon Baron-Cohen, who argues in his book *The Essential Difference* that male brains are analytical and goal-orientated, which makes them wonderful scientists and lawyers; while the female's empathetic brain is best for jobs like teaching and counselling.

However, as Deborah Cameron notes, a career in education or as a therapist just requires a mix of verbal, people and analytical skills, and Baron-Cohen's choice is simply based on the fact jobs in such fields have traditionally been occupied by women. And why have they? Because they're less well paid, less varied, and have less power in a society that has been dominated by men for centuries. Furthermore, all of this is often reinforced by our biased use of language, where we'll still often specify a *male* nurse or a *female* doctor.

Ultimately then, when and how people communicate has far more to do with social status and power than it does with genetic make-up and nature. It's vital to challenge these myths because, in many cases, stereotypes around gender and communication serve to hide the structural problems in societies that maintain male power and hold back women.

▶ TRACK 27

1

Unusually for this species, it can swim underwater as well as tunnel underground, which is handy as it inhabits low wetland areas. Its long claws are adapted for tunnelling through the earth and its water-resistant fur allows it to remain underwater. The long thick tail is thought to store extra fat to draw upon during the mating season. The mole is functionally blind, which is why it has developed the distinctive star-shaped set of feelers that give it its name. These feelers allow it to sense nearby movement.

Uniquely, the mole can also smell underwater. It does this by blowing out tiny bubbles through its nose in order to capture scents that are sucked back in. These adaptations are highly efficient and the star-nosed mole is apparently the fastest eater in the animal kingdom, being able to identify, snatch and consume its prey all in a matter of milliseconds.

2

While the sparrow hawk is more commonly found in woodland, its short broad wings and long tail allow it to manoeuvre quickly through the trees, while the light striped markings on its breast and its darker upper parts help it to blend into the background, as it tends to lie in wait for its prey before shooting out. It has relatively long legs that enable it to kill in mid-flight. The long slender central toe is adapted to grasp, while a small projection on the underside of the claw enables it to grip and hold onto its prey whilst flying. Its small hooked beak is used for plucking and tearing flesh rather than killing. It also sometimes hunts on foot through vegetation. In recent years, it has appeared more and more in cities, where it has no predators and where it is often seen as a pest, damaging garden bird populations.

UNIT 9

▶ TRACK 28

H = Harry, T = Tasneem, B = Bianca

H: Hi, I'm looking for Tasneem.

T: That's me. You must be Harry.

H: That's right.

T: Nice to meet you. Did you find us OK?

H: Yeah, yeah. Well, I came here before for my interview.

T: Right. So, where do you live? Does it take you long to get here?

H: I've just moved to Redditch, but it was quicker than I expected. I've actually been hanging around in the coffee bar over the road for the last hour.

T: Really? You were eager to get here, then.

H: Well, I didn't want to be late and, you know, first-day nerves and all that.

T: Sure. Anyway, I'm sure you'll settle in quickly. We're a pretty good bunch. Nobody bites. Well, almost nobody!

H: Right.

T: So, raring to go, then?

H: Absolutely.

T: OK. Well, just dump your stuff down here for the moment and I'll show you the ropes.

H: OK.

T: I should've said – we'll be working alongside each other on this new project. I liaise with our external service providers. I was just emailing one of them to schedule a time for us all to meet when you arrived. Anyway, as you can see, the office is mainly open-plan. We'll sort you out with a spot later.

H: Right.

T: It's a bit chaotic at the moment with all the changes. We've been rushed off our feet, so it'll be good to have more people.

H: I'm not the only one who's being taken on now, then.

T: No. Three or four more are joining in the next couple of weeks.

H: That's good. There'll be some others in the same boat.

T: Yeah. This is Bianca. She's our main admin assistant. She'll sort out any travel or bookings and other stuff. Bianca, this is Harry.

B: Hiya. Nice to meet you. Hope Taz is treating you well. She's a real slave driver, you know.

H: Really?

B: Oh yeah, she's probably being all kind and helpful now, but wait till you get started.

H: That sounds ominous.

T: Take no notice. She's just pulling your leg. You need to watch her!

B: I don't know what you mean! Actually, Harry, can I just take a quick photo while you're here? I'm just sorting out your entry card and setting up your email.

H: Sure.

B: OK. Say cheese … Lovely, very handsome. That's it. Anything you need or you're not sure about, don't hesitate to ask.

H: Thanks. I'll get the card later, then, yeah?

B: If that's OK.

T: OK, let's move on. That lot over the far side are the sales team. We won't disturb them now – I can introduce you later. To be honest, you won't be having that much to do with them in your day-to-day dealings.

H: OK. What about these rooms? Are they offices?

T: Um, the last two are the boardrooms for meetings. The near one is Mary's office. She's the managing director.

H: OK. What's she like?

T: She's OK. She comes across as being quite down-to-earth … the few times we've talked.

H: She's not in the office that much, then.

T: No, she's here most days, but, as I said, I guess we've all been so busy that everybody just sticks to their own tasks. Anyway, just going back to the rooms … that one with the door open is the photocopier room. I'd better show you how it works. It's a bit temperamental. It has a tendency to jam if you don't treat it with tender loving care.

H: OK.

T: So, how come you moved to Redditch? It's not that close to here.

H: No, but I'd been thinking about moving out there for a while and I happened to get the house just before I got this job.

▶ TRACK 29

You were eager to get here, then.

I'm not the only one who's being taken on now, then.

She's not in the office that much, then.

▶ TRACK 30

Is David Bolchover's experience a freak occurrence? Well, maybe, but only in the sense that he was allowed to stay at home to not work. Bolchover argues that much of the workforce in many big companies is badly under-employed at work and backs up his arguments with a barrage of statistics. One in three of all mid-week visitors to a UK theme park had phoned in sick. In one year, there were nine million questionable requests for sick notes from the doctor. That's about a third of the working population! Two-thirds of young professionals have called in sick because of a hangover, and on it goes.

Once at work, things don't improve. On average, employees spend 8.3 hours a week accessing non-work-related websites and 14.6% of all so-called 'working' Americans say they surf the Net constantly at work. 18.7% send up to 20 personal emails a day and 24% said they had fallen asleep at their desk, in a toilet or at a meeting.

Bolchover argues that there's a conspiracy of silence over this workplace slacking. Workers have no vested interest in saying they do nothing, while businesses want to maintain their image of being highly efficient.

Under-employment happens, he suggests, because workers feel a disconnection with big companies. Unlike with small companies, employees don't see how their small contributions fit into the whole picture. Furthermore, managers typically fail to develop or motivate workers because, he claims, in large corporations people progress not by looking down but by looking up. Instead of managing effectively and getting the most out of those under you, the way to get ahead is by advertising yourself and networking with those above you. People below you don't give promotions.

With smaller companies, slacking happens less because workers see how failure to pull your weight can directly impact on colleagues and the company. Bolchover suggests the solution, therefore, is to break up large companies into smaller competitive units. From a worker's view, doing nothing might seem fun at first, but in the end it's soul-destroying and a waste of talent.

▶ TRACK 31

1

A 27-year-old call centre worker has been fined and has lost his job after eating a colleague's biscuits. While working a night shift, Michael Campbell decided to dip into what remained of a biscuit tin that had been left in the office. The following day, however, a co-worker returned to find her £7 biscuit selection gone and decided to search CCTV footage so as to find the culprit. Campbell was charged with stealing and brought before a magistrate, who ordered him to repay the cost of the biscuits as well as a £150 fine. He was also dismissed from his job as a result of the incident and is currently retraining as a bar manager.

2

Firefighters are holding a one-day strike today as part of a long-running dispute over pensions. With swingeing cuts taking place throughout the public sector, the government wants to raise the retirement age for firefighters from 55 to 60 and say it'll mean they can avoid making redundancies in the service. The firefighter's union, however, has concerns about the ability of staff to fulfil all their duties beyond 55 given the nature of the work. It claims the government had previously promised to guarantee the pensions of firefighters who fail the compulsory medical at 55, but now it was going back on that promise. The government denies this and condemns the strike, and is assuring the public that emergency calls will be dealt with. The action has also prompted some MPs to call for legislation preventing employees in essential services from striking.

3

A postman who was sacked after taking a week off work to mourn the death of a pet has been awarded £10,000 compensation. The employment tribunal was told David Portman had a history of sick leave due to a number of accidents and injuries, and had been absent for a total of 137 days in just five years. In his defence, Mr Portman claimed the majority of his injuries were incurred during the course of his duties at work. However, when he took further leave following the death of his dog, he was sacked. The tribunal concluded this was a step too far as his previous leave had been legitimate and managers had failed to inform Mr Portman that he could have applied for compassionate leave.

4

A report commissioned by the ECA, which represents European pilots, has raised concerns about aviation safety. The report found 17% of pilots were on insecure contracts and not employed directly by the airline, with young pilots being particularly badly affected. Many of them have no guarantees of work and not only have to pay for initial training, uniforms and overnight stays, but in some cases even subsidise the airline through pay-to-fly schemes, whereby young pilots can gain flying experience. The ECA is concerned about this casualisation of contracts because the report found pilots in this group were more reluctant to disobey the airline's instructions even if they had safety or health concerns. It also claims the pilots may miss out on important training. The pilot union is therefore calling for new rules to crack down on these atypical contracts.

5

A woman has failed in her discrimination claim against the company which employed her, which refused to pay her wages in full when she went on maternity leave. What makes the case unusual is that the company, Kapp's Kitchen Tiles, is a family business run by her own father. Mandy Platt claimed the decision was the final straw in a series of incidents where her father had expressed displeasure at the pregnancy. Her father, Andy Kapp, was relieved at the verdict, saying he'd fulfilled the statutory requirements with regards to his daughter, and was simply ensuring his business remained secure to pass on to all his children.

UNIT 10

▶ TRACK 32

1

A: You look really different without your glasses on. I almost didn't recognise you there.

B: Hey, the glasses have gone! They're a thing of the past.

A: Yeah?

B: Yeah. After months and months of toying with the idea, I finally got round to having my eyes done the other day.

A: Cor! Really? Did you get them lasered?

B: Yeah.

A: Woah! That's brave of you. Did it hurt? I've always imagined it must be really painful.

B: No, not really. It's actually pretty quick and easy these days. Well, at least if you're shortsighted like I am ... was!

A: OK.

B: It is a bit scary though, because what they do is they numb your eyes and then they sort of clamp them open so they can slice this tiny little flap in the front of the eye – and you kind of have to watch as the whole thing happens.

A: Oh! It sounds horrendous, it really does! How did they give you the anaesthetic? Was it an injection or something?

B: No, they just poured in a load of these eye drops and they did the job. Oh, and they dosed me up with a couple of Xanax as well, just to calm me down.

A: So how long does the whole thing take?

B: It's over in a matter of minutes. After they cut the eye open, you have to stare at this laser for a few seconds and that reshapes the inside of your eye – and then you're done.

A: And how long does it take to recover from?

B: To be honest, the next day I woke up and I pretty much had perfect vision. They're still a bit sore and I have to go back a few times for the aftercare and everything, but it's all very quick. I should've got it done years ago, honestly!

A: Right. Wow! I still think I'll stick with contact lenses for the time being, though, personally.

2

C: So, where did you rush off to the other day, then?

D: Oh sorry. Didn't I tell you? I had to get to the dentist's.

C: Oh no! How come?

D: Well, about a week ago or so, I got this excruciating pain in my upper jaw so I went along to get it looked at, and he told me that one of my teeth had died somehow and that I'd need a root canal.

C: Died? How did that happen?

D: Don't really know, to be honest. He said I must've taken some kind of knock. I'm not sure, but I think it might've been my daughter actually, thrashing her arms and legs around while I was changing her nappy one day, you know.

C: Kids, eh! All that work and that's the kind of thanks you get!

D: Tell me about it! And then today I went in and he drilled a hole in the back, cleaned everything up and then he stuck some kind of temporary filling in to prevent bacteria or anything getting in.

C: That can't have been much fun. Did it hurt at all?

D: No, not really. I mean, I was conscious of what he was doing, but I couldn't feel anything.

C: Do you have to go back again sometime?

D: Yeah, next week. They'll remove the temporary filling and put a more permanent thing in, but then I'm done.

C: How much is all that gonna set you back, then? It must be quite expensive.

D: It's not that bad, but it's not cheap either. I mean, I won't see much change from £500.

▶ TRACK 33

1

Medical dramas on TV here have changed a fair bit over the years. Before, the doctor was just a saint that could do no wrong, but nowadays they'll have more flawed characters and the hospitals are more like my own. My favourite remains *House*, even though it finished a while back. It's basically about this highly unconventional doctor and the team he leads. He's a brilliant clinician, but he's also cynical and downright rude to colleagues and patients alike. He's also ridiculously unethical in his approach. In one episode, he gets a junior colleague to break into a patient's apartment to solve the mystery of their condition. In another, he totally breaches patient confidentiality just to prove a point. Of course, this is where the show parts with reality, but I've found it a really useful springboard for my students to discuss ethics, the processes that should've taken place, and how to improve bedside manner.

2

When I see the mass of printouts in their hand, my heart just sinks. I just know they'll have been searching the Internet for every possible diagnosis or quack cure you can think of! It's like that joke: a man goes to his doctor and tells him he's suffering from a long list of illnesses. 'The trouble with you,' says the doctor, 'is that you're a hypochondriac.' 'Oh no,' says the man, 'don't tell me I've got that as well!' Seriously though, these people are often timewasters and to my mind they're also kind of undermining my professionalism – 20 years of study dismissed in favour of Google! My main aim is to get them out of the surgery as quickly as possible.

3

There's a cliché that doctors make the worst patients because we don't take the advice we would give to others. That's definitely true. I read a survey that found 80% of Norwegian doctors had reported into work with illnesses that they would have issued a sick note to others for. Underlying this is a bigger problem of how we see our role. Our purpose is not to suffer but to see symptoms, diagnose a disease, treat it and cure it.

As a result, we sometimes feel lost if we come across a disease or condition that we don't immediately recognise or know how to treat. We're good at dealing with definites, not the unknown. The truth is, when we're faced with uncertainty, many of us don't deal with it very well and that can lead to communication breakdowns.

As a sufferer of a major chronic condition myself, I've been on the receiving end of this. It can start from the first encounter, where the doctor starts the examination without even introducing themselves; to a wrong diagnosis or poor treatment because they won't admit to not knowing what the problem is; to secrecy and silence when there's a relapse and the news is bad. Being a patient actually taught me the most valuable lesson: see the person first, not the condition.

4

I started my studies back home in Sierra Leone, but I had to stop because of the Ebola outbreak. I volunteered to work with the response teams going from house to house informing people of the dangers and uncovering suspect cases. It made me realise the importance of communication and education in health. I had wanted to be a surgeon, but now I'd like to get into community health. I later won a scholarship to come and study here in France and I should qualify next year.

5

I've worked and carried out research in a number of countries and perhaps the biggest thing I've learnt is how you need to be aware of not just the disease but also the person and culture it occurs in. I remember seeing a guy who suffered from a rare hormonal condition called Addison's disease. What happens is that two small organs – the adrenal glands – don't produce sufficient amounts of the hormone cortisol, which in turn leads to increased pigmentation in the skin. Essentially, their skin turns black. That perhaps wouldn't be so much of a problem these days, but this was 40 years ago in South Africa when the country imposed strict racial segregation. Imagine what that patient must've gone through?

UNIT 11

▶ TRACK 34

1

A: How was the tennis?

B: Good.

A: Who won?

B: Mena, but it was pretty close.

A: Really?

B: Don't sound so surprised.

A: No, sorry. I just thought you said she was really good.

B: She is. I mean, she's not exactly Steffi Graf, but, you know ...

A: Steffi who?

B: She was ... Oh dear. Am I showing my age?

A: Don't worry, I won't tell. So, what was the score?

B: Er, 6-4, 6-1, I think.

A: Oh, right. Very close!

B: No, honestly, it was ... kind of! We actually had some pretty long rallies. I even had a couple of shots down the line.

A: Look at you!

B: Seriously, I was very proud. Shame my serving was utterly rubbish towards the end.

A: The coaching sessions are paying off, then.

B: No, they definitely are! Let's just say there's still room for improvement. And Mena's just a bit fitter and stronger than me.

A: Well, that's because you're so ancient and she's so young.

B: Ah, yes, well, there is that! Good job I don't look it.

A: Well, that's true.

2

C: Hiya. How's it going?

D: Yeah, alright. Is there enough water in the kettle for me too?

C: Yeah, should be.

D: So, how are you? I haven't seen you for a while? Have you been away?

C: I was back in Spain.

D: Oh, cool. Was that seeing family?

C: Mmm, kind of, but actually the main reason I went was for this big swim. Didn't you sponsor me?

D: Did I? Remind me again.

C: It was a 6K swim from the coast to this island.

D: Oh yeah, yeah, yeah! Sorry – a memory like a sieve. So, how did it go?

C: Well, I just about made it.

D: Sounds bad.

C: Mmm, it was tough! And I got cramp.

D: You're joking! I've had that playing football and I was just clutching my leg in agony.

C: Yeah, it was horrible.

D: But how does that work when you're in the water?

C: There were some support boats that brought me water and I just kind of floated on my back.

D: Still.

C: Yeah, horrible, but I managed to get over it.

D: Well done.

C: I shouldn't have set off so fast because we got diverted because – how do you say – a swarm of jellyfish?

D: You are kidding!

C: No, no. We maybe did an extra kilometre.

D: Wow!

C: It was about 30 degrees too! I was fading so badly by the end.

D: Hey, I wouldn't have even managed to get off the beach!

C: Ha!

D: So, how much do I owe you?

C: £20.

D: Twenty! That's a bit much! You only did 7K in 30-degree heat round swarms of jellyfish.

C: Ha ha! You forgot the swim back.

D: What? You ...?

C: No!

3

E: Did you catch the game last night? I had to work.

F: Yeah. It was incredible. For a neutral, anyway. I'm not sure how you'd have felt.

E: 2-2 away. It sounds crazy.

F: Hey, Arsenal were lucky to draw. Honestly, it could've been about 5-0 after the first 20 minutes. The Arsenal keeper made some great saves and Manu managed to kick the ball over the bar from about a metre out. Honestly, my granny could've scored it.

E: Ah, Manu ... he's so overrated. There's no way he's worth 60 million, or however much he cost us. He's rubbish.

F: You're right. He is totally useless ... which is why he scored two fantastic goals after that!

E: OK, OK. He is good, just not that good!

F: No, I do know what you mean, and actually for his first goal the Arsenal keeper messed up badly.

E: Right. So, how did they manage to get back in the game, then?

F: Well, they made some substitutions and brought on Wallace, who made a huge difference.

E: Really?

F: Yeah, really. He scored a great goal, which got the whole team going. Then he won them a very dubious penalty and got a Bayern defender sent off.

E: It wasn't a penalty, then.

F: Well, let's put it this way. If he touched him at all, it certainly wasn't enough to send him crashing to the ground like he'd been shot. Anyway, it was an amazing game. Ridiculously open, even after Bayern went down to ten men.

E: Yeah. We'll thrash them in the home game!

F: Probably. But two of your defenders are suspended and you have a couple of other people injured. And Arsenal will be the underdogs, so they won't have any pressure on them. You never know – you could still get knocked out.

E: By Arsenal? Not a chance.

▶ TRACK 35

C = Christine Wright, A = Antoine Smith, K = Karen Lu

C: Hello, I'm Christine Wright and welcome to *The Wright Word*. Following our recent podcast on dying languages, one listener sent me a link to a fascinating article about a version of Scrabble developed for the Carrier Language in Canada. Now, there are only around 1,000 Carrier speakers left in that region, and this project is part of a campaign to try to encourage the Carrier tribes to maintain their distinct language. As an avid Scrabble and Words with Friends player myself, I was obviously attracted to the idea, but I have been wondering how far this project could work and what word games and, more broadly, wordplay can do for language learners. So here to discuss this with me today I'm joined by multilingual friends Antoine Smith and Karen Lu, both of whom speak ... I think it's five languages?

A: Yep.

K: Yeah, that's right.

C: So, Antoine, what do you think of the idea of Scrabble for a minority language?

▶ TRACK 36

C = Christine Wright, A = Antoine Smith, K = Karen Lu

A: Well, it's interesting, but I'm not sure how far it'll take the language. I mean, a lot of words you use playing Scrabble in English are pretty random. You know, things like *zho*, which are a hybrid cattle, or *mu*, which is a Greek letter. Not exactly the kind of thing you'd drop into casual conversation! I imagine that a Carrier version of Scrabble would be similar – you'd end up having lots of obscure words just because they get a high score.

C: Yeah, but ...

A: And in fact, it's more about maths and strategy. Apparently, one world champion didn't even speak English – he'd just learned the dictionary by heart.

C: But they won't be really playing to win, will they? That's not the point here.

A: What? Not playing to win?

C: Yeah, OK, that's your over-competitiveness! But playing with language is universal, isn't it, Karen?

K: Absolutely, but not all cultures play in the same way. I mean, I'm guessing the Carrier language has an oral tradition ...

A: Exactly ...

K: So maybe Scrabble isn't the best game for this language.

A: You took the words out of my mouth.

K: I mean, in Chinese we don't do crosswords because the language is based on characters.

C: Of course! Yeah.

K: Well, there are *some* kinds of crosswords but with idioms and sayings.

C: Because each character in Chinese is like a word?

K: Yeah, exactly, and the two sayings will share the character where they cross. And sometimes one character has two meanings.

C: Yeah, yeah. Actually, I heard that puns are a big thing in Chinese.

K: Oh yeah, definitely. Like when someone gets married, we sometimes give the couple dates and peanuts because the characters for the words 'dates' and 'peanuts' are pretty much the same as the saying 'May you soon give birth to a boy.'

C: Not a girl.

K: No, I know. It's a bit sexist, but that's the tradition.

C: OK. Well, let's not get into that now! Are there any other word games which might be good for practising language?

K: We have another one with idioms. So, I give a saying and then you have to say another one starting with the last word or sound in my one.

A: Doesn't sound so easy.

K: No, maybe not. We also play something like Taboo – you know that, right?

C: Yeah. Where you explain a word – say, 'library' – for others to guess, without using words like 'book' or 'borrow'.

K: Exactly. That's good. We also do tongue twisters.

A: Oh yeah, I like them. I learnt one in Spanish: *El perro de San Roca no tiene rabo porque* ... Oh man, it's slipped my mind now ... er ...

C: And what does it mean?

A: Oh, the dog of San Roca doesn't have a tail because ... I think it was a mouse stole it?

C: Ha ha! Not the kind of thing you'd drop into casual conversation.

A: Er, no, that's true.

C: Mind you, we did a podcast recently on how you get a lot of this kind of alliteration or rhyming just in our normal choice of words. You know, like 'everything's ship-shape' or 'here and there' – maybe because it makes it more memorable.

A: Although apparently it hasn't helped me!

C: Well, there's always an exception that proves the rule.

A: Ha ha, whatever! It wasn't just about learning. Doing that tongue twister was fun – like a competition with my classmates – and then it spun off into a general discussion on what we found difficult in Spanish.

C: Well, that's the point I was trying to make before with Scrabble. The words themselves might not be so useful, but it's all the chat that goes on around the game.

A: Yeah, no, you're right. I actually heard that some people on Words With Friends have got married through the app's chat feature.

C: Well, I wouldn't go that far, but I think it does prove my point, which is always a good place to call it a day!

K: Absolutely.

A: Who's competitive now!

C: I'd never deny it. Anyway, thanks to you both and thanks to everyone who's listened.

▶ TRACK 37

1 Three free throws.
2 A really weird rear wheel.
3 She sells seashells on the seashore.
4 Peter Piper picked a pickled pepper.
5 How can a clam cram in a clean cream can?
6 How much ground would a groundhog hog if a groundhog could hog ground?

UNIT 12

▶ TRACK 38

A: So, how did it go with Kim's parents, George?

B: Oh, it was surprisingly good, actually. The whole visit passed off far better than I'd dared to hope it would.

A: Yeah? Even with her father?

B: Yeah. It turns out that his bark is much worse than his bite. We had a long talk over dinner on Saturday and got on really, really well. He's a pretty amazing guy, actually.

A: Yeah? In what way?

B: Well, he's just had an incredible life. I mean, he's from a first-generation Chinese immigrant family, and he grew up in this very strict, very close-knit community, not really speaking Indonesian or any of the local languages in Borneo, where he was living, and basically just living in total poverty.

A: Wow! You'd never know any of this from just meeting Kim, would you? I mean, not a clue!

B: No, I know, but it sounds like a properly deprived kind of background, you know. And then to make matters worse, when he was thirteen, his dad passed away and as the oldest son he found himself having to support the family.

A: Seriously? Is it a big family?

B: Yeah, enormous! Twelve brothers and sisters. So he had to drop out of school and start working.

A: That's very young to be working. What was he doing?

B: He started off selling ice creams on the streets of Pontianak and then moved on to selling textiles door-to-door, and by the time he was about seventeen he was going off all round the island selling and making deals.

A: That's amazing. I was still living at home stressing about my end-of-school exams at that age.

B: Yeah, exactly. Then, when he was about 21, he decided that if he really wanted to get ahead, he'd have to move to the capital, and so he set off to make his fortune. He got there, somehow managed to start up his own company selling outboard motors for boats, and then just slowly built things up until he got to where he is today, where he can afford to have all his kids educated in the States and go off on holiday whenever he feels like it.

A: So he really is a proper self-made man, then.

B: Yeah, completely. I mean, he created his whole empire from scratch, you know. But what's great about him is that he's still quite rough round the edges. Like, for instance, he still eats like a peasant and belches after dinner and stuff, which – me being me – I kind of found quite endearing.

A: And what did he make of you and the idea of his daughter dating an artist, then?

B: Well, he's still coming to terms with that obviously, trying to get his head round it all, but his eyes lit up when I told him how much I got for that portrait I sold last year. Basically, I think he just wants to see that she'll be provided for.

A: Despite the fact she's earning twice as much as you are already!

B: Yeah, well. I didn't dwell on that fact too much.

▶ TRACK 39

Hi. Thanks for coming. As you know, I'm, er, Courtney and I'm doing History and Politics. So this is my presentation on the impact of the Second World War both in Europe and the wider world.

So, yeah, I guess many of you may have seen commemorations of the First and Second World Wars in recent years and maybe you think, 'So what? Old people, old times. It's nothing to do with me and today's world.' But what I want to suggest is that nothing could be further from the truth. The consequences have been massive – whether you look at geography, politics, culture or society. I mean, huge numbers of countries we know today gained independence thanks in part to the fact that the old colonial powers were so crippled by debts they incurred during the war that they could no longer maintain their colonies. The UN, NATO and a number of other international institutions were all established then and are still powerful today. In addition, our views on human rights date back to this event, as does society's embrace of science and technology. Even the modernist architecture that dominates many cities today can be traced back to those years. Obviously, I've only got a very short time today, so what I'm going to do is focus on two main areas: the impact of the war on society and particularly on women, and then I'll tackle welfare and state intervention. I'll conclude with a few comments on how this all contrasts with responses to financial catastrophes more recently. If you have any questions from the presentation, I'll be happy to answer them at the end.

▶ TRACK 40

So, first of all, society. I think life would be quite different for women now but for the war. For example, women in countries such as France, Italy and Japan achieved the right to vote following the war. In France, for example, many women had been central to the resistance movement that had fought against the German occupation, and it was simply untenable to continue their exclusion from politics. Everywhere, women had entered the workforce in large numbers, often for the first time, to support the war effort while the men were fighting. Alongside this was an increase in independence for women, a greater mixing of women and men from different backgrounds, and there was also more widespread sexual freedom during the war years. So, even though the 1950s were very conservative for a while, I would argue that the war sowed the first seeds of women's liberation that flowered in the 60s and 70s and that has brought us to where we are today.

Which brings me to welfare. One of the other social shifts caused by the war was the number of women who were widowed, the thousands of children who were orphaned and the millions of men who were left disabled after serving in the army. In many European countries, welfare systems simply hadn't existed before the war or were fragmented, so there was a real need to establish more comprehensive and joined-up systems. We somewhat take for granted the existence of state-run social support for those from broken homes or the unemployed, the disabled and sick, but it may never have developed to what we now have but for the war.

Yeah, um, state intervention also extended to the huge process of rebuilding and re-establishing businesses and kick-starting the economy. I think it's difficult for us now to get our heads round the sheer scale of the devastation that took place. Keith Lowe's book, *Savage Continent*, gives a very vivid account of this. But anyway, in many countries, to enable the recovery to take place, lots of companies and banks, even whole industries, were nationalised and they were supported through the Marshall Plan, where the US provided a huge amount of money to do it. Part of the deal for this support was that the US demanded Europe work more closely together, and that eventually led to the formation of what was then called the EEC and went on to become the European Union.

What I think is interesting about this response is it's kind of almost the opposite of what's happened in response to the financial devastation many countries experienced at the start of this century. Certainly in the UK, but maybe elsewhere as well, there's a lot of evidence to suggest that cuts to public spending and changes to work regulations have affected women adversely. Where the rebuilding of economies was once funded on the back of debt, there now seems to be a deep fear of borrowing. This has been coupled with an effort to reduce state intervention and welfare spending and increasingly serious threats to break up the EU. So, I guess that begs the question of whether we are doing the right thing and perhaps whether we could learn lessons from our history. Um ... and that's it. Thank you. Er ... any questions?

▶ TRACK 41

C = Courtney, S = Students

S1: You seem to be suggesting women's liberation wouldn't have happened without the war. Don't you think it was already happening before then?

C: Er, yes, um, that's an interesting point. Yeah, I mean, that is kind of true to some extent. I mean, obviously in some countries, women already had the vote, but ... but I think, you know, the points I made are still very valid. I guess, you know, it was more a catalyst. Maybe it would've happened anyway, but it was the spark. It kind of made sure these things happened for sure.

S2: You referred to something called the Marshall Plan. Could you just explain exactly what that is?

C: Um, yes. It was basically just a big fund to support European reconstruction. It's named after the US Secretary of State at the time, George Marshall ... I think. I'm not absolutely sure.

S3: You mentioned the scale of the devastation. Do you have any specific statistics on that?

C: Um, yeah. I think across Europe something like 20% of all property was either destroyed or damaged, but that was a lot higher in some cities. I mean, in Warsaw it was, I think, over 90%. I don't know if you've been there, but, like, the centre looks medieval. It was totally reconstructed after the war though. It's amazing. And in, like, other countries, I mean, Japan, it was really high too. But ... but yeah, I think Lowe's book has more details if you want.

S3: OK, thanks. Do you have the reference for that?

C: Oh, right. No. Yeah, I should've ... yeah, I can get that for you. I don't have it in my notes here, but you can find it on the Internet. It's Lowe, L-O-W-E and it's called *Savage Continent*. I think he's got another one coming out soon about the impact of the Second World War.

S4: You said something about cuts affecting women. Could you elaborate on that a little?

C: Oh, er, yeah. Thanks for asking. Er, yeah, there's quite a bit of evidence about that, but I'm afraid I've run out of time now. If you catch me after the other presentations, I can tell you more about it then, though. OK. Thanks.

▶ TRACK 42

While numerous theories for the cause of the dancing mania have been proposed, it still remains unclear whether it was an actual illness or whether it was more a result of some kind of social process.

Some assert that the Strasbourg situation was a result of dancers having eaten poisoned wheat, which is known to result in hallucinations and physical aches and pains. Never has it caused the strange behaviour most associated with dancing disease, though.

Others have put forward the theory that the dancers were members of some kind of cult, pushing their bodies to extremes in pursuit of religious ecstasy. However, contemporary reports highlighted the fact that dancers were unhappy and begged onlookers to help them stop.

The most plausible explanation is that as the whole area was severely affected by disease and famine, these factors played a significant role in the explosion of some kind of mass hysteria. This would also explain the trance-like states and loss of self-control that dancers claim to have experienced.

UNIT 13

▶ TRACK 43

1

A: Have you seen the news today?

B: Yeah. Did you see that MP got off?

A: Well, what did you expect? It's one rule for us and another for them, innit?

B: It makes me sick. It was so obvious he's been lining his own pocket. I don't know how he's got away with it.

A: Apparently, the case was dismissed on some kind of technicality.

B: Typical. As you say, if it'd been someone lower down, they'd have been convicted.

2

C: What do you think of this story about the government's proposals for public sector cuts?

D: I'll believe it when it happens.

C: You don't think it will?

D: No. I mean, look at it from their point of view. Why would they? What do they have to gain? There's an election coming up in just over a year. It'd be a disaster for them.

C: That's true. Maybe the opposition is just stirring up trouble.

D: More likely. I don't think they've said the source of the story, have they?

3

E: I can't believe they're still going on about this guy and his affair. They're making such a fuss about nothing.

F: I don't think she'd see it like that!

E: No, I know. It's obviously a big deal for her, but I don't see how having it all over the papers will help. What's it got to do with us? And what's it got to do with playing tennis?

F: Nothing. It's all to do with money and sponsorship, innit?

E: Exactly. As if anyone cares. It's such nonsense.

4

G: Did you see that thing about the Secretary of State and what he said?

H: Yeah. I can't believe he's refusing to resign!

G: I don't know. Put yourself in his shoes. Can you imagine the pressure politicians are under when there's so much news coverage? It amazes me they don't make more slips.

H: I know, but it's not the first time and I think it undermines our standing in the world. What are other countries going to think?

G: Oh, it's just a storm in a teacup. It'll blow over quickly enough.

H: You think so?

5

I: Did you see that business with the Hampton supporters?

J: Yeah, it was a disgrace. They're just animals. They should do something about them.

I: Didn't you hear? They have! A whole load of them have had their season tickets confiscated.

J: Well, it's about time, though why on earth aren't they being prosecuted? The amount of damage they caused! Not to mention the intimidation.

I: I know. They're thugs. They should be locked up.

▶ TRACK 44

1 A: Apparently, he loves being a paparazzo.

B: Really? Takes all sorts, I suppose.

A: I know. I can't think of anything worse.

2 A: Maybe we could get a bigger place after you get the new job.

B: Hey, let's not count our chickens. I haven't even had the interview yet.

A: I know, but I have confidence in you!

3 A: What? We have to eat with our hands?

B: Hey, when in Rome ...

A: I'd rather not, though. Do you know the word for 'spoon'?

4 A: Honestly, he gets away with murder. He didn't lift a finger to help.

B: Yeah, well, glass houses and all that. We didn't exactly do a lot either.

A: We did! Well, more than him anyway.

5 A: Honestly, the organisation of the whole event was terrible.

B: I know. I think it was a case of too many cooks.

A: Probably. There did seem to be quite a lot of contradictory information flying around.

6 A: I wish they hadn't interfered. We were doing fine without them.

B: Absolutely. I mean, if it ain't broke ...

A: Exactly.

▶ TRACK 45

A = Announcer, N = Natalie Davis,
C = Carol Dixon

A: And now on SBC, the six o'clock news with Natalie Davis.

N: Good evening and welcome. The headlines this evening: Finance Minister Carol Dixon has today announced her retirement and has swiftly moved to counter rumours she's being forced out of her post.

C: At this stage, I'm not willing to comment further other than to say this has been my decision and mine alone, and the reasons for it are personal, not political.

N: And also tonight: two people have died as rioting continues in Manova; interest rates are set to rise; Jermaine Johnson is out of the final World Cup qualifier; the celebrity couple Simon Crouch and Jennifer Ponting have won their libel case against the *News Enquirer*; and there's a medal for a very special sniffer dog.

▶ TRACK 46

N = Natalie Davis, C = Carol Dixon,
P = Paul King, M = Malaika Hussain,
F = François Houllier, A = Anita Karaji,
L = Lawyer, H = Hassan Cleaver

N: Finance Minister Carol Dixon has confirmed rumours that she is to retire on health grounds. She categorically denied that her retirement was connected to recent criticism of the government's decision to build two new nuclear power stations, although she acknowledged there had been division on the issue.

C: There was a dispute over nuclear energy. I've never hidden that and I've never denied being a long-term opponent, but I lost that argument. And on broad policy, I remain totally behind this government.

N: However, she refused to comment further on the health reasons for her departure, stating only that it was a private matter. Elsewhere, rioting over government reforms has continued in Manova, with two men being killed. Crowds throwing missiles confronted armed police in the main square and conducted running battles in the surrounding streets throughout the day. Paul King reports.

P: There are conflicting reports about the deaths. A police spokesman assured reporters that the men died when a car exploded after being set alight by a petrol bomb thrown by rioters. Meanwhile, demonstrators claim the victims were crushed when police fired tear gas to disperse the crowd in the square, forcing people down narrow side streets. As the news of the deaths spread, protesters rampaged through the surrounding area. The rioting lasted most of the day until an uneasy calm fell upon the city this evening. Addressing the country on television, the President blamed the rioting on subversive groups trying to destabilise the country and rejected demands for the government to change tack. He urged what he termed the silent majority to make their voices heard. However, there are no signs that that call will be heeded. Paul King, Manova.

N: Interest rates look set to rise by half a point, taking the base rate to a ten-year high of 4%. The National Bank refused to rule out further increases this year as it bids to control inflation. Malaika Hussain reports.

M: Thanks Natalie. Yes, today's announcement had been widely expected after recent warnings by the head of the National Bank that caution was needed in the battle against inflation. Now, of course, there will surely be concerns that the rise could trigger an economic slowdown, but it seems those fears are outweighed by real concern about rising food and fuel costs and, as you said, it wouldn't be a surprise if there were further hikes later on in the year.

N: And now sport, and the national football team have been dealt a further blow in the run-up to their crucial World Cup qualifying match against Russia. Goalkeeper and team captain Jermaine Johnson has been ruled out with a thigh strain. The team have struggled and must win if they are to go through to the finals next year. Manager François Houllier expressed confidence in Johnson's replacement, Paul Harrison.

F: Obviously it is not ideal, but, er, Paul is a great keeper and has been on good form, so I am not so worried.

N: The Hollywood couple Simon Crouch and Jennifer Ponting have won their libel action against the paper *News Enquirer*, following allegations that theirs was a sham marriage. Anita Karaji reports.

A: During the compelling three-day hearing, the court heard claim and counterclaim about the state of Crouch and Ponting's marriage, which, yes, the *Enquirer* had accused them of entering into purely for their mutual benefit. In the end though,

the judge found in their favour, awarding $560,000 damages. In a statement read by their lawyer, the couple thanked supporters and promised to donate the money to charity.

L: Simon and Jen would like to thank all those fans who never doubted the outcome of this case. They would also like to make clear that all the proceeds from this decision will be given to good causes because this case was never about personal gain, only personal truth.

A: *News Enquirer* said it disagreed with the decision and was considering an appeal.

N: And finally tonight: a sniffer dog has received a medal for bravery for his work in a bomb disposal unit. Bodge has worked in several war zones over the last six years and has helped find over 200 bombs and mines to be deactivated. His handler, Corporal Hassan Cleaver, said it was a proud day and praised the work of the whole unit.

HC: It's just fantastic. He deserves it, as do lots of the dogs we work with. What they do is unbelievably important. They're fantastic.

N: And that's the news from SBC. Good evening.

UNIT 14

▶ TRACK 47

1

K = Katherine, S = Susie

K: Hello, InTech Corporation. Katherine speaking. How can I help you?

S: Oh, hello there, Katherine. It's me, Susie.

K: Oh, hi. How're you?

S: Not too bad, thanks. Listen, I'm just calling to check whether the delivery we sent out on Monday has reached you yet.

K: It has, yeah. It came in this morning, I believe.

S: Oh, that's good. I was just panicking over nothing, then.

K: Well, better safe than sorry, isn't it?

S: Exactly. Anyway, how're you? How're things your end?

K: Oh, you know. We're hanging in there. Sales have actually picked up a bit this quarter, so that's good, and we've actually taken on a couple of new people, so can't complain, you know. How's life with you? How's the little one?

S: Oh, she's good. She's just coming up to one now and she's crawling around everywhere and babbling away to herself all the time.

K: Aww!

S: Yeah. I'll send you pictures if you want.

K: That'd be lovely, yeah. And how's Mark?

S: He's OK. He's been away a lot with work recently, actually, which has been a bit of a pain, but hopefully that'll ease off a bit soon.

K: Mmm, yeah, that can't be easy. Hey, how was your holiday? Didn't you go away somewhere recently?

S: Yeah, that's right, we did. Two weeks in Crete. Oh, it was lovely. Over far too quickly, of course, but much needed.

K: Oh, that's good, though.

S: Yeah.

2

M = Matt, D = Dietmar

M: Hello. CNC.

D: Hi, is that Matt?

M: Yeah, Dietmar. Hi. I was just thinking of you, actually. I saw the draw for the European Championships.

D: Oh yeah. I'm sorry, but England have to lose to someone.

M: Don't count your chickens yet! Let's wait and see.

D: I admire your optimism.

M: Well, you have to look on the bright side, don't you? Especially in our line of work.

D: Tell me about it! How're things, anyway?

M: Oh, not too bad, all things considered.

D: And what's happening with the relocation?

M: Well, it's still on the cards, apparently. We've told them it's a bad idea, but they just won't listen!

D: Well, just think of all the savings you'll make on your overheads.

M: And on wages if half the staff who're threatening to leave actually do!

D: A lot of that's just talk, I'd imagine. They'll soon come round.

M: I hope you're right. Anyway, what can I do for you today?

D: Well, I was just wondering if we could maybe sort out a time for a meeting during the trade fair next week. It'd be good to talk through Mexico with you.

M: Yeah, of course. Is Thursday any use to you?

D: Yeah, maybe. What time?

M: Um ... well, I could squeeze you in in the morning, if you want. Say 10? 10.15?

D: Yeah, 10.15 should be fine. I'll pencil it in.

M: Great. See you then, then.

▶ TRACK 48

Plus ça change	chef
prima donna	plaza
fait accompli	angst
faux pas	macho
déjà vu	au fait
zeitgeist	fiasco
en route	kitsch
guerrilla	trek

▶ TRACK 49

Katrin

I've also been approached by the unions, but perhaps that can wait till AOB at the end of the meeting.

Peter

OK, so let's move on to the next item on the agenda.

Henry

OK. Well, I've handed out the spreadsheet of current figures and, as you can see, we're set to make a substantial loss this year.

Rachel

We've exceeded our sales targets in Eastern Europe.

Alex

So, this is a prototype of what we're calling the Shoe Saver.

Marta

We'd be looking for it to retail at between €100 and €120.

K = Katrin, P = Peter, H = Henry,
R = Rachel, A = Alex, M = Marta

K: I've also been approached by the unions, but perhaps that can wait till AOB at the end of the meeting.

P: OK. Thanks Katrin. I've got that noted. We'll come back to that later on, then. OK, so let's move on to the next item on the agenda. We've already touched on the background to this, but perhaps, Henry, if you could just restate the situation?

H: OK. Well, I've handed out the spreadsheet of current figures and, as you can see, we're set to make a substantial loss this year. Obviously, it's been a volatile year for everyone in the industry, but we can't simply blame economic problems. We've also underperformed.

R: Well, not entirely! We've exceeded our sales targets in Eastern Europe.

H: Yes, that offers some hope, Rachel, but that was starting from quite a low base. I know there are high hopes for this new product, but I really feel the way forward is to cut back on costs.

K: Cutting costs? I would've thought we were at the limit, to be honest. People are already overstretched.

H: It doesn't have to mean more work. We could renegotiate deals with suppliers and then scale back operations.

K: You mean layoffs?

H: Well, some redundancies, maybe, but hopefully they'll be voluntary.

K: Really? I ...

P: OK. Katrin, I think we're getting ahead of ourselves here. Henry, why don't you put together some costed proposals for cutbacks to present at the meeting next week? Then we can see what the possible implications might be. Is that OK with everyone?

P: Now, moving on to our next item. Marta, I believe you and Alex have something exciting to show us.

M: We certainly do. And, as Henry suggested, we do have high hopes for it. If we can tap into the right market for this, it may even help to ease some of the financial problems that have just been highlighted. I'll let Alex talk you through things. Alex.

A: Yeah, thanks Marta. So, this is a prototype of what we're calling the Shoe Saver. As you can see, it's basically a compact box. This is a basic design, but we're planning others. Essentially, you pop your shoes inside and give it a blast to remove all the smells. I've brought along a pair of my son's trainers to demonstrate.

R: Oh, they smell dreadful!

A: Yeah. They've been left damp in a bag to show you just how effective the box is. So, I put them in ... and switch it on. It takes a minute. Yes, Rachel?

R: How does it work? I mean, what's the science here?

A: Yeah, right. So what it does is it uses tiny particles of silver, which have antibacterial properties once ionised, and they essentially kill the microbes that cause the odours.

R: Right, OK. I'm not sure what 'ionised' means, but isn't the silver expensive?

A: Yeah, but we're talking tiny amounts. OK ... there. Done. Have a sniff.

R: Wow! That's amazing.

P: Yeah, great.

K: Very impressive.

H: Very. So what margins are we looking at with this?

A: Well, unit costs are between €35 and €45.

M: And we'd be looking for it to retail at between €100 and €120.

R: Which would certainly improve our bottom line.

H: Why such uncertainty about production costs? That's quite a big range you've given.

A: Well, we're looking at a deal to outsource production, which could bring significant savings. The higher figure would be if we used our own factories and that's also very much erring on the side of caution.

H: Sure. And what kind of sales projections do you have? Rachel?

R: We've estimated something in the region of 10,000 units in the first year, followed by 30,000 in year two, 100,000 in year three and a quarter of a million by year four.

K: Gosh.

M: I know that sounds ambitious, but we're all really excited about this product. Henry, you don't look convinced.

H: Yeah, I don't want to be the bad guy, but have you really thought this through? You know, there's already a range of products that can solve this problem. Will people really want to pay €120 for this?

M: No, it's a fair question. I think the first point is that this is far more effective than the sprays and insoles currently on the market. We estimate it could extend a shoe's life by up to 50%, so it'd pay for itself. Secondly, our initial market is not actually homes but health clubs and gyms. Longer term, growth would come from high-end consumers and we've already had some positive feedback from focus groups.

P: I think Katrin wants to come in.

M: Sure.

K: Er, yes, erm. What about patents? Is this original technology?

A: I'll take this one, if I may.

M: Sure.

A: Well, the technology's been around for a while, so that's not something we control, but we have patented a couple of the manufacturing processes that we think will give us an edge over any competitors.

M: Plus, of course, we'll have a head start in establishing the brand.

UNIT 15

1

A: Oh my word, you were a bit of a rock god.

B: That's kind.

A: I had no idea. Look at those skinny jeans! Good grief! Did you spray those on?

B: Yeah, it was a bit of a struggle getting them on even in those days.

A: And all that bushy hair!

B: Mmm ...

A: Where did it all go wrong?

B: Well, I like to think I've made up for the loss in other areas.

2

C: So, how was it?

D: Well, I thought it was going to be a very formal do so I even borrowed an outfit from a friend and these ridiculous high-heels. And then when I got there I'd obviously got my wires crossed somewhere because no-one else seemed to be that dressed up and I stuck out like a sore thumb.

C: Oh well. Still, I'm sure you looked gorgeous.

D: Yeah, well, not after my dress split down the seam when I was dancing.

C: Oh no!

D: Yeah, it ended up being a bit more revealing than I wanted it to be!

3

E: Jason, could I have a word?

F: Sure.

E: Do you mind taking the shades off?

F: Oh, right, yeah, sure. Have I done something wrong?

E: No, no, not at all. We see you as a great asset. In fact, we'd like you to take on a bit more responsibility.

F: Cool.

E: It's just that ... well ... you might want to smarten up a bit.

F: Do you think I look scruffy?

E: No, that's not what I meant to say. I know the ripped jeans and paisley shirts are your thing, but what I'm trying to say is if you're interacting with clients a bit more ... well, they expect something a bit more conventional.

F: Right, OK. No, that's fine. Sure.

E: Good. You might want to go a bit more easy on the gel, too.

4

G: Oh, my gosh, Fi! Look at her outfit.

H: You don't like it?

G: A flowery dress with a checked shirt? And the ribbon in her hair? And then those army boots!

H: Hey, it wouldn't work for me, but I think she pulls it off. It's quite a funky look. I might lose the ribbon, but those kind of clashing patterns are really in at the moment.

G: Well, it's not a trend I like. And the boots?

H: Well, they kind of show off her legs in a funny way.

G: I think they make them look like sticks. They look as if they'd snap them in two. She'd be better off in some heels or wedges.

5

I: Are you going in that?

J: You don't think it's suitable?

I: No, it's not that. But you've got a stain on the lapel.

J: What, that? You can hardly see it.

I: Let me see if I can rub it off.

J: Don't fuss. It'll be fine. Anyway, they're not interested in my dress sense. I'll be in a lab all day if I get it.

I: Well, at least tie up your laces properly – don't want you tripping over when you walk in the room!

6

K: Gosh! That's a bit radical, isn't it?

L: You don't like it?

K: No, no, you look fantastic. It just took me aback when I first saw you. So, what brought this on?

L: Oh, I just fancied a change and I've taken up running again and, well, I mean, you can have it in a ponytail or tie it up, but ... I don't know ... I was a bit sick of it.

K: No, I know what you mean. I wish I could get away with having it like that – it'd be so much easier.

L: You don't think you could?

K: No – my face is too round. I'd look like a lollipop!

L: That's a bit of an exaggeration! You could have it in a bob. That'd work.

K: Mmm, I'm not convinced.

▶ TRACK 52

A = Announcer, S = Sheila Tinkelman,
M = Margot van der Stegen

A: And next on Radio Talk we have *Mixed Media* with Sheila Tinkelman.

S: Hello! Role models, Twitter storms and sweet soul music – today we'll be looking at how the media can impact on our mental states. Are footballers really role models and to whom? Or is it an excuse by the media to justify click bait? Jon Ronson's book on the very real and devastating impact of committing a faux pas in the virtual world, and the researcher discovering the power of music in calming Alzheimer's patients.

But first, images of beauty and the fashion industry. The model Tess Holliday has attracted a certain amount of press attention with her growing Instagram following and social media campaigns against what she calls 'beauty standards'. Holliday is a size 26 and supposedly the largest woman to be signed by a mainstream modelling agency. She styles herself as a body-positive activist and has been held up as a force for change in the fashion industry. But haven't we been here before? It's over ten years now since the toiletries brand, Dove, launched its Campaign for Real Beauty, with its first iconic adverts of women of various shapes and sizes, and since then a number of its commercials have gone viral. A recent video featured large public buildings round the world where a pair of entrances had been labelled either 'Beautiful' or 'Average'. Women were secretly filmed hesitating as they chose which door to go through and some were then interviewed about their choice. Holliday's social media campaign may be somewhat more grassroots and in-your-face than Dove's, but both essentially aim to broaden the images of beauty beyond those presented by the fashion industry and to see beauty as a personal choice. The question is whether campaigns like these are needed at all. And if they are, do they make any real difference? So, here to discuss these and other issues with me is the academic Margot van der Stegen. Margot, thank you for joining us.

M: My pleasure.

▶ TRACK 53

S = Sheila Tinkelman,
M = Margot van der Stegen

S: So Margot, your research is in the area of self-objectification, which I think would argue that the kinds of fashion images we are bombarded with these days have a consistent impact on women's mental states.

M: Absolutely. Basically with all of these images, women are essentially objects of the male gaze. The argument is that for women this objectification has become internalised and part of their way of being. In other words, we look at ourselves as outsiders and monitor our appearance – generally in critical ways and in comparison to the dominant idealised look.

S: Beautiful, white, young, tall and skinny.

M: Exactly. Of course, this process has existed for centuries, er, particularly through Western art, but we now live in an age of unprecedented visual saturation, which affects all corners of the world and all classes of society.

S: And it's affecting our mental health and giving rise to eating disorders such as anorexia?

M: Well, yes. I mean, that's a bit of an oversimplification, er, there's obviously a number of factors involved in eating disorders. But what experimental studies have shown is how simply flicking through fashion magazines can trigger self-criticism. There's also one seminal study that found women who were asked to try on a swimsuit suffered more anxiety than those who tried on a sweater. What's more, the researchers found the higher levels of anxiety had a knock-on effect in that the women who had tried on the swimsuit got lower marks in a maths test they were given afterwards! None of these things were true of men in the study. So it seems reasonable to believe that self-objectification may at least contribute to mental health issues for women.

S: Certainly that also chimes with Dove's research that found that while over 70% of girls between the ages of ten and seventeen felt pressure to be beautiful, only 4% of women worldwide would describe themselves as such.

M: Yes, that pressure is very real and, both as a mother and a researcher, it's certainly something I worry about.

S: So, do you think campaigns such as Dove's or Tess Holliday's make a difference?

M: Well, I think there's certainly a contradiction at the heart of Dove's campaign in that it's essentially a brand selling shampoo and body wash, and I don't see that as having much to do with self-esteem. Indeed, in some parts of the world, its parent company sells cosmetics such as skin-lightening products that don't exactly support the idea that we are all equally beautiful.

S: Sure, but you don't think women should be encouraged to 'spend less time analysing the things they don't like and more time appreciating what they do' – as one of the participants in a Dove ads puts it.

M: Of course that's a good message for anyone but actually I'd say most of their adverts are forcing women to define themselves in terms of looks. I mean, why not choose between doors marked 'Average' and 'Intelligent' instead, or, I don't know, 'Caring' and 'Selfish'? And then a previous advert actually encouraged teenagers to take selfies and analyse them! OK, Dove would say it's done in a positive way, but it's pure self-objectification. And do they know how many women Photoshop their selfies?

S: Well, perhaps as the actress Cameron Diaz once said, we all actually want to be objectified. Maybe we just need to change the terms. Isn't that what Tess Holliday is saying too?

M: Yeah, I mean personally, I find her campaign less emotionally manipulative in that it doesn't play upon women's existing insecurities, and simply says I am beautiful, you are too. But ultimately, yes, she's a model and it's about beauty.

S: So, not fully empowering?

M: No. I mean, within the fashion industry it is good to have people like her, but, for me, real change has to come from the home. I think generally parents should shield their kids from the whole fashion industry. They should strengthen their children's self-esteem by basing it on being a good person rather than appearance. Fathers can be role models by not objectifying women. Mothers can be role models in not openly self-objectifying – difficult though that might be.

S: Well, that brings us rather neatly to our next item on role models and footballers, so I'll stop you there. Margot van der Stegen, thank you.

M: Thank you for inviting me.

UNIT 16

▶ TRACK 54

1

A = Anita, B = Brian

A: Well, Brian, I have to say, I certainly wasn't expecting your brother to do that!

B: What? The business with the teeth?

A: Yeah. I mean ... yuck! Seriously! In the middle of a meal as well. That really freaked me out.

B: I guess it was a bit odd. I'm sort of used to it now, though.

A: It was gross. I mean, couldn't he have kept it hidden, and just sneaked off to the loo, instead of bashing it back in right in front of us? Incredible! Honestly! Just ... wow!

B: Ha ha. I'd take it as a compliment. It means he's comfortable in your presence now!

A: Lucky me!

B: Have I ever told you how that happened?

A: No, but I'm not sure I want to know, to be honest.

B: Oh, it's not that bad. It was back when we were kids. We'd just moved to this place out in the country and we were exploring, you know, having a wander around, and there was this big old wall at the end of the garden. We were trying to haul ourselves up it, but then when he got near the top, the whole thing collapsed and he came crashing down and landed face first, knocking those two front teeth out.

A: Fff! Ouch! Nasty.

B: Yeah, there was blood everywhere, you know, pouring down his face ...

A: Oh, stop it! You're just saying it to make me feel worse now.

B: And to top the whole thing off, he didn't even really notice because he somehow snapped his wrist in the fall as well.

A: Aww, poor guy.

B: Yeah, he was in agony.

A: I guess perhaps I should cut him some slack, then.

2

C = Chloe, D = Doug

C: How did you get that scar, if you don't mind me asking?

D: Which one? The one on my chin?

C: No, I meant the one on your forehead. It's pretty nasty.

D: Oh, that. Yeah, well, I was smart enough to somehow walk straight into a head-height shelf when I was eighteen. I was working at this summer camp in the States and I'd been out to a party with some friends one night, stumbled home and whacked myself when I got back to my cabin. I decided that, while it hurt a bit, it'd probably be OK and that what I really needed was my bed. I woke up in the morning to find there was blood everywhere – all over the bed, the floor – and, most shockingly, when I looked in the mirror, I realised my face was covered in dried blood, which I really hadn't been expecting! The doctor said he could've stitched it if I'd seen him right away, but that it was unstitchable the following day. Just my luck!

C: Oh, that's awful.

D: Yeah, well, it's my own stupid fault, really.

C: And, um, I'm scared to ask now, really, but what about that other one?

D: You won't believe me when I tell you. Honestly.

C: Oh, OK. Is it gruesome?

D: Not really. Just odd. I don't know if you remember, but a couple of years ago, there were all these reports of people getting blown off their feet by high winds and even someone getting killed by being blown head first into a door.

C: No! That must just have completely passed me by somehow.

D: Yeah? Well, it was pretty crazy. What happened with me was that one night I just got totally blown down the drive at the side of my house – completely out of control! I somehow managed to go head first between two parked cars, whacking my head on both of them and landing on my chin in the middle of the road.

C: Ouch!

D: Yeah, and when I came to, I found my chin completely split open – and my wisdom teeth weren't too happy either!

C: Woah! You're fairly accident-prone, really, aren't you?

D: I've got another one, actually, if you want to hear about it ...

▶ TRACK 55

1 Wow!
2 Fff! Ouch!
3 Yuck!
4 Gosh!
5 Phew!
6 Mmm!
7 Ahem!
8 Mmm
9 Um
10 Oi!
11 Shhh!
12 Oops!

▶ TRACK 56

1 A: She speaks six different languages.
    B: Wow! That's impressive.

2 A: I was running and I heard something in my knee just snap!
    B: Fff! Ouch! Painful!

3 A: His false teeth fell out onto the floor and he just picked them up and put them straight back into his mouth again.
    B: Yuck! That's disgusting!

4 A: I've still got a scar. Look.
    B: Gosh! That's awfully big!

5 A: The doctor I went to for a second opinion said I'd been given the wrong diagnosis and it wasn't as serious as they'd thought.
    B: Phew! That's a relief, then.

6 A: Mmm! This is delicious! What's yours like?
    B: Yeah, not bad.

7 A: Ahem!
    B: What? ... Oh, sorry.

8 A: And then she said, like, you know, that she thought it was a bit too big, you know, not really the right fit, but I wasn't sure so ... Are you listening to me?
    B: Mmm. Yeah. Course.

9 A: So, how come you decided to do that, then?
    B: Um, that's a good question, actually. I'd have to think about that.

10 A: Oi! What do you think you're doing?
    B: Quick! Run!

11 Shhh! The baby's sleeping.

12 A: And then I realised I'd copied my boss in on the email by mistake!
    B: Oops! That wasn't very clever.

▶ TRACK 57

M = Michael (presenter), J = Joyce,
O = Oliver, N = Nigel

M: Now I'm guessing that many of you – like me – may have raised an eyebrow this week when you heard that kids as young as eight are receiving treatment for Internet addiction. And this is a problem that's surely set to get worse, of course, given that it's just been announced that over 40% of the world's population – a whopping three billion people – is now online. Three billion! Can you believe it? And that's why today we're turning our attention yet again to the World Wide Web, and asking whether the Internet is becoming more of a curse than a blessing. As ever, if the show's to work, we need you to call up and tell us what's on your mind. And I think we have our first caller on line one. It's Joyce in Crawley. Joyce, hello.

J: Oh, hello, Michael. Thank you. Yes, erm, well, I've been a university lecturer for some 40 years now and I'm on the verge of retiring. I'm due to stop work in the summer and I must say I'm awfully glad about it.

M: Why's that, then, Joyce?

J: Well, to be frank, I think the Internet has created a generation of idiots and I honestly don't think things are likely to get any better in the foreseeable future.

M: Well, that's a fairly bleak appraisal. What is it about the Web that particularly concerns you, Joyce?

J: Well, the main thing is simply the ease of access it provides. I'm obviously not opposed to people being able to access useful information, but most students nowadays have lost the ability to construct their own essays or think their own way through a question. They simply cut and paste and hand things in, which appals me.

M: So, plagiarism, in short?

J: Exactly. But you try telling them that!

M: Well, luckily, I don't have to, Joyce, and on the plus side, you won't have to either for that much longer. Next up, I think it's Oliver phoning in from Barnstable. Are you there, Oliver?

O: Yes, Michael. Can you hear me?

M: Loud and clear, Oliver. What's on your mind?

O: Well, what worries me, Michael, is the fact there's no delete button on the Web.

M: OK. You're going to have to expand on that a bit, Oliver. I'm not quite sure I know what you mean.

O: Well, look. People like me, what you might call digital natives, right. We've grown up with the Internet and sharing online is a normal part of how we live. Most young people don't think twice about what they share when – and I just think that's bound to cause problems in the long run.

M: You think there's some over-sharing going on then, Oliver?

O: I do, yeah, and I think people are pretty naïve too. You know, they'll post up crazy photos from parties and fire off comments in the heat of the moment and just assume that they can delete it all later.

M: Well, there are firms that can tidy up your online profile these days, aren't there?

O: Yeah, sure, to a degree ... but you can never really know if someone's copied what you've posted, can you? And things can easily come back to haunt you later on.

M: And you're saying the chances of people avoiding all this are pretty slim?

O: To put it mildly, yes. People need to wake up – and wise up, really.

M: Sound advice, I'd say. Next up is Nigel, in Manchester. Hello.

N: Hello there, Michael. Nice to be with you. Long-time listener here. What I wanted to say was, it's time we got tough and cracked down more on the Web.

M: And how do you propose we do that, then?

N: Well, if it were up to me, I'd arrest anyone caught looking at banned websites. I mean, they must know who these people are, mustn't they, the government?

M: That's a huge online policing presence you're suggesting there, Nigel. And in all likelihood, most offenders are actually pretty harmless when it comes down to it.

N: Yeah, OK, but maybe we should make an example out of one or two people, then, you know. Hit them with the toughest sentences we can. Like all the spammers and online fraudsters, and so on. Do that and the odds are you'll put others off.

M: Or do that and there's a distinct possibility you'll end up involved in a legal dispute about appropriate punishments, I would've thought, to be honest.

▶ TRACK 58

1 This is a problem that's surely set to get worse.

2 If the show's to work, we need you to call up and tell us what's on your mind.

3 I'm due to stop work in the summer.

4 I honestly don't think things are likely to get any better in the foreseeable future.

5 I just think that's bound to cause problems in the long run.

6 I'm on the verge of retiring.

7 And you're saying the chances of people avoiding all this are pretty slim?

8 In all likelihood, most offenders are actually pretty harmless.

9 Hit them with the toughest sentences we can. Do that and the odds are you'll put others off.

10 Do that and there's a distinct possibility you'll end up involved in a legal dispute.

**NATIONAL
GEOGRAPHIC**
L E A R N I N G

**Outcomes Advanced
Student's Book**
Hugh Dellar and Andrew Walkley

Publisher: Gavin McLean

Publishing Consultant: Karen Spiller

Development Editor: Katy Wright

Editorial Manager: Scott Newport

Head of Strategic Marketing ELT: Charlotte Ellis

Senior Content Project Manager: Nick Ventullo

Senior Production Controller: Eyvett Davis

Cover design: emc design

Text design: Alex Dull

Compositor: emc design

National Geographic Liaison: Leila Hishmeh

Audio: Tom Dick & Debbie Productions Ltd

DVD: Tom Dick & Debbie Productions Ltd

For product information and technology assistance, contact us at
Cengage Learning Customer & Sales Support, cengage.com/contact

For permission to use material from this text or product, submit all requests online at **cengage.com/permissions**
Further permissions questions can be emailed to
permissionrequest@cengage.com

Student Book ISBN: 978-1-305-09342-3
Student Book w/o Access Code ISBN: 978-1-305-65192-0

National Geographic Learning
Cheriton House, North Way, Andover, Hampshire, SP10 5BE
United Kingdom

National Geographic Learning, a Cengage Learning Company, has a mission to bring the world to the classroom and the classroom to life. With our English language programs, students learn about their world by experiencing it. Through our partnerships with National Geographic and TED Talks, they develop the language and skills they need to be successful global citizens and leaders.

Locate your local office at **international.cengage.com/region**

Visit National Geographic Learning online at **NGL.Cengage.com/ELT**
Visit our corporate website at **www.cengage.com**

CREDITS
Although every effort has been made to contact copyright holders before publication, this has not always been possible. If contacted, the publisher will undertake to rectify any errors or omissions at the earliest opportunity.

Photos
6–7 © Paul Nicklen/National Geographic Creative; 8 © R. Hackenberg/Corbis; 10 (l) © nito/Shutterstock.com; 10 (r) © Raymond Patrick/National Geographic Creative; 11 © Mark Lovatt/Getty Images; 12 © Chris Bickford/National Geographic Creative; 14–15 © ZUMA Press, Inc/Alamy Stock Photo; 16 (tl) © Paul Bradbury/Getty Images; 16 (tm) © Alan Powdrill/Getty Images; 16 (tr) © Don Mason/Getty Images; 16 (bl) © Roger Wright/Getty Images; 16 (bm) © Adam Berry/Stringer/Getty Images; 16 (br) © UniversalImagesGroup/Getty Images; 17 (t) © Emmanuel Faure/Getty Images; 17 (b) © ullstein bild/Getty Images; 18–19 © Fritz Hoffmann/National G eographic C reative; 20 © Randy Belice/Getty Images; 22 © Alex Treadway/National Geographic Creative; 24–25 © Sean Gallup/Getty Images; 26 © Cory Richards/National Geographic Creative; 29 © Tomaz Levstek/Getty Images; 30 (tl) © Peter Evans/Alamy Stock Photo; 30 (tr) © Jim Richardson/National Geographic Creative; 30 (bl) © Jack Sullivan/Alamy Stock Photo; 30 (br) © Mark Runnacles/Stringer/Getty Images; 31 (t) © Cate Gillon/Getty Images; 31 (b) © Matthew Taylor/Alamy Stock Photo; 32–33 © Lou Avers/dpa/Corbis; 34 © Daniel Roland/AFP/Getty Images; 37 © EMPPL PA Wire/Associated Press/AP Images; 38–39 © Arnd Wiegmann/Reuters/Corbis; 40 © Frans Lanting/National Geographic Creative; 42–43 © Oso Media/Alamy Stock Photo; 44 © MASSIVE/Getty Images; 45 © Yadid Levy/Alamy Stock Photo; 47 (t) © Richard Newstead/Getty Images; 47 (bl) © Miles Willis/Stringer/Getty Images; 47 (br) © Oliver Knight/Alamy Stock Photo; 48 © Victoria Pearson/Getty Images; 49 The Hunger Games. Text copyright © Suzanne Collins, 2008. Reproduced by permission of Scholastic Ltd. All rights reserved.; 50–51 © Joel Sartore/National Geographic Creative; 52 © Bill Whitehead/Cartoonstock; 53 © Bill Whitehead/Cartoonstock; 54 © Ed Darack/Getty Images; 55 © Chris Hopkins/Stringer/Getty Images; 56 © Phil Walter/Getty Images; 58 © Yury Dmitrienko/Shutterstock.com;

Printed in Greece by BAKIS sa
Print Number: 03   Print Year: 2018

60–61 © Mark Thiessen/National Geographic Creative; 62 © Rick & Nora Bowers/Alamy Stock Photo; 65 © Photos 12 / Alamy Stock Photo; 66 © Fran/Cartoonstock; 67 © Glenn and Gary McCoy/Cartoonstock; 68–69 © Michael Nichols/National Geographic Creative; 71 (t) © Bill Hatcher/National Geographic Creative; 71 (b) © Bruno Kolberg/EyeEm/Getty Images; 73 © David Burch/Getty Images; 74 (tl) © MVPhoto/Shutterstock.com; 74 (tml) © Thomas Marent/Visuals Unlimited/Corbis; 74 (tmr) © Colin Monteath/ Hedgehog House/Getty Images; 74 (tr) © Mark Medcalf/Shutterstock.com; 74 (bl) © Roderick Paul Walker/Alamy Stock Photo; 74 (bml) © Ken Catania/Visuals Unlimited/Corbis; 74 (bmr) © dexterous simpson/Shutterstock.com; 74 (br) © Kevin Schafer/Alamy Stock Photo; 76 © STR/Reuters/Corbis; 78–79 © Lynn Johnson/National Geographic Creative; 80 © LinaandTom.com/emc design ltd; 83 © olaser/Getty Images; 84 © Paul Fell/Cartoonstock; 85 © Joel Sartore/National Geographic Creative; 86–87 © David Evans/ National Geographic Creative; 88 © Joel Sartore/National Geographic Creative; 91 © Dave and Les Jacobs/Lloyd Dobbie/Blend Images/Corbis; 92 © AF archive/Alamy Stock Photo; 94 © Islandstock/Alamy Stock Photo; 96–97 © Ian Kington/Stringer/Getty Images; 98–99 © Robert Michael/Corbis; 100 © Erik Tham/Alamy Stock Photo; 102 © jvphoto/Alamy Stock Photo; 103 © Stockbyte/ Getty Images; 104–105 © Priit Vesilind/National Geographic Creative; 106 © Solent News/REX/Associated Press/AP Images; 108 (l) © Mary Evans/Robert Hunt Collection; 108 (r) © INTERFOTO/Alamy Stock Photo; 110 © North Wind Picture Archives/Alamy Stock Photo; 114–115 © Rodrigo Arangua/AFP/Getty Images; 116 © Jason Edwards/National Geographic Creative; 119 © dpa picture alliance archive/Alamy Stock Photo; 121 © Suzanne Plunkett/Reuters/Corbis; 122–123 © Philip Scalia/Alamy Stock Photo; 124 © Image Source/Alamy Stock Photo; 127 © Matt Mawson/Getty Images; 128–129 © Will Ireland/Computer Arts Magazine/Getty Images; 129 © Nick Kim/Cartoonstock; 130 © Pascal Deloche/Getty Images; 132–133 © sturti/Getty Images; 134 (l) © 4FR/Getty Images; 134 (m) © Edward James/WireImage/Getty Images; 134 (r) © Nick Dolding/Getty Images; 135 (l) © Blend Images/Trinette Reed/Getty Images; 135 (m) © Olivier Morin/AFP/Getty Images; 135 (r) © Thomas Concordia/FilmMagic/Getty Images; 137 © Eugenio Marongiu/ Corbis; 138 © Joel Sartore/National Geographic Creative; 140–141 © Solent News/REX Shutterstock/Associated Press/AP Images; 142 © Ben McLeod/Getty Images; 144 (t) © ZUMA Press, Inc./Alamy Stock Photo; 144 (mt) © Justin Kase zsixz/Alamy Stock Photo; 144 (mb) © Philippe Lopez/AFP/Getty Images; 144 (b) © Natalia Bratslavsky/Shutterstock.com; 146–147 © C.J. Burton/Corbis; 148 © Tino Soriano/National Geographic Creative; 152 © Stoyan Yotov/Shutterstock.com; 155 © Paul Brown/Demotix/Corbis; 157 © Franco Origlia/Getty Images; 160 (tl) © SteveWoods/Shutterstock.com; 160 (tr) © nulinukas/Shutterstock.com; 160 (m) © kim7/ Shutterstock.com; 160 (bl) © sirnength88/Shutterstock.com; 160 (br) © FooTToo/Getty Images; 162 © Blend Images/Shutterstock. com; 164 © IR Stone/Shutterstock.com; 185 © Raymond Patrick/National Geographic Creative; 186 © Mark Lovatt/Getty Images; 190 © javarman/Shutterstock.com; 193 © Pictorial Press Ltd/Alamy Stock Photo; 194 © jaroslava V/Shutterstock.com; 196 (tl) © Worldpics/Shutterstock.com; 196 (tr) © Anton Ivanov/Shutterstock.com; 196 (mtl) © Ammit Jack/Shutterstock.com; 196 (mtm) © Alexandra Lande/Shutterstock.com; 196 (mtr) © pavel dudek/Shutterstock.com; 196 (mbl) © S. Kuelcue/Shutterstock.com; 196 (mbm) © Goodluz/Shutterstock.com; 196 (mbr) © Imfoto/Shutterstock.com; 196 (bl) © Mila May/Shutterstock.com; 196 (bm) © Stefano Tinti/Shutterstock.com; 196 (br) © taniavolobueva/Shutterstock.com; 197 © nito/Shutterstock.com.

Cover

Cover photograph © Henry Sudarman/500px.

Illustrations

70 Martin Sanders/Beehive Illustration; 112 JuanBJuan Oliver/Beehive Illustration; 156 KJA Artists.

Text

The publisher would like to thank the following sources for permission to reproduce their copyright protected texts: page 83: from *The Living Dead* by David Bolchover, copyright © Capstone, Wiley-Blackwell.

Acknowledgements

The publishers and authors would like to thank the following teachers who provided the feedback and user insights on the first edition of *Outcomes* that have helped us develop this new edition: Rosetta d'Agostino, New English Teaching, Milan, Italy; Victor Manuel Alarcón, EOI Badalona, Badalona, Spain; Isidro Almendarez, Universidad Complutense, Madrid, Spain; Ana Bueno Amaro, EOI Roquetas de Mar, Almería, Spain; Isabel Andrés, EOI Valdemoro, Madrid, Spain; Brian Brennan, International House Company Training, Barcelona, Spain; Nara Carlini, Università Cattolica, Milan, Italy; Karen Corne, UK; Jordi Dalmau, EOI Reus, Reus, Spain; Matthew Ellman, British Council, Malaysia; Clara Espelt, EOI Maresme, Barcelona, Spain; Abigail Fulbrook, Chiba, Japan; Dylan Gates, Granada, Spain; Blanca Gozalo, EOI Fuenlabrada, Madrid, Spain; James Grant, Japan; Joanna Faith Habershon, St Giles Schools of Languages London Central, UK; Jeanine Hack; English Language Coach.com, London, UK; Claire Hart, Germany; David Hicks, Languages4Life, Barcelona, Spain; Hilary Irving, Central School of English, London, UK; Jessica Jacobs, Università Commerciale Luigi Bocconi, Milan, Italy; Lucia Luciani, Centro di Formaziones Casati, Milan, Italy; Izabela Michalak, ELC, Łódz´, Poland; Josep Millanes Moya, FIAC Escola d'Idiomes, Terrassa, Catalonia; Rodrigo Alonso Páramo, EOI Viladecans, Barcelona, Spain; Jonathan Parish, Uxbridge College, London, UK; Mercè Falcó Pegueroles, EOI Tortosa, Tortosa, Spain; Hugh Podmore, St Giles Schools of Languages London Central, UK; James Rock, Università Cattolica, Milan, Italy; Virginia Ron, EOI Rivas, Madrid, Spain; Coletto Russo, British Institutes, Milan, Italy; Ana Salvador, EOI Fuenlabrada, Madrid, Spain; Adam Scott, St Giles College, Brighton, UK; Olga Smolenskaya, Russia; Carla Stroulger, American Language Academy, Madrid, Spain; Simon Thomas, St Giles, UK; Simon Thorley, British Council, Madrid, Spain; Helen Tooke, Università Commerciale Luigi Bocconi, Milan, Italy; Chloe Turner, St Giles Schools of Languages London Central, UK; Sheila Vine, University of Paderborn, Germany; Richard Willmsen, British Study Centres, London, UK; Various teachers at English Studio Academic management, UK.

Authors' acknowledgements

Thanks to Karen Spiller and Katy Wright, and to Dennis Hogan, John McHugh and Gavin McLean for their continued support and enthusiasm.
Thanks also to all the students we've taught over the years for providing more inspiration and insight than they ever realised.
And to the colleagues we've taught alongside for their friendship, thoughts and assistance.

205834